Employment Tribunal Procedure

A users' guide to tribunals and appeals

JEREMY McMULLEN, QC, MA, MSc is a member of the English and Northern Irish Bars and a part-time chairman of industrial tribunals in England and Wales. He is a specialist in employment law and author of *Rights at Work* (Pluto Press, 2nd edn 1983).

JENNIFER EADY, BA(OXON), DIP LAW is a member of the English and Northern Irish Bars, a member of the panel of junior Treasury counsel and standing junior counsel to the NUM and NUJ.

Employment Tribunal Procedure
A users' guide to tribunals and appeals

JEREMY McMULLEN, QC
and
JENNIFER EADY, *barrister*

 Legal Action Group
1996

This edition published in Great Britain 1996
by LAG Education and Service Trust Limited
242 Pentonville Road, London N1 9UN

British Library Cataloguing in Publication Data
A CIP catalogue record for this book is available from the British Library

ISBN 0 905099 47 8

Phototypeset by Datix International Limited, Bungay, Suffolk
Printed in Great Britain by Bell & Bain Ltd, Glasgow

Foreword

By LORD ARCHER OF SANDWELL QC
Chairman, Council on Tribunals

Industrial tribunals are the offspring of two historical processes. First was the stormy relationship between organised working people and the law. Where the common law had been left to develop according to the predilections of judges, employees in general, and trade unions in particular, found no greater understanding of their needs and aspirations among the judiciary than among their own employers. It is scarcely surprising, then, that employees felt greater confidence in a forum labelled 'tribunal' than they would have felt in a court.

Secondly, the rule of law had traditionally been declared to reside in the historic courts which dealt with disputes between individuals or between the individual and the executive. It was not until the Franks Report, in 1957, that specialist tribunals were accepted not as an exception to the rule of law, but as a constitutional part of it.

These two processes, then, converged in the mid-1960s, when newly-recognised rights to security in employment were enshrined in a succession of statutes. Since then successive governments have sought to reconcile the trade union movement to a system of adjudication without the unhappy associations of the courts, and in the last 30 years the jurisdiction of industrial tribunals has expanded to meet new forms of dispute and new needs. Unusually among tribunals, they deal largely, although by no means exclusively, with disputes not between citizen and government, but between citizen and citizen.

One consequence is that the jurisdiction is exercised in a relatively informal atmosphere, with a lawyer in the chair, and two colleagues whose contribution is not legal expertise, but some knowledge of the context in which industrial disputes arise. Yet the law administered in industrial tribunals is far from simple, and if it is to meet the varied situations found in a complicated world, it is likely to defy attempts at simplification. Even more confusing are the jurisdictional and procedural rules which are necessary to ensure that proceedings are heard in an orderly way, that everyone concerned understands the issues in the case, and that no-one is taken by surprise.

At the heart of such dispute resolution must be access to justice. Those who litigate in industrial tribunals are likely to need a guide through this labyrinth. *Employment Tribunal Procedure* will ensure that applicants throughout the country do not enter the process blind to the perils ahead. Those unfamiliar with this forum will benefit from its lucid guidance. The appendices are of particular value and the chronological approach of the text will help clarify and demystify tribunal procedure.

Few employees, and only a moderate proportion of smaller employers, are in a position to pay the fees of solicitors and counsel. If neither party has had access to advice, the tribunal is confronted with the dismaying task of extracting the essential issue from the evidence, while if one party enjoys competent representation and the other is denied it, we know from the research of Professor Hazel Genn and others that no tribunal, however competent and conscientious, can ensure a level playing field. If an issue is raised, or evidence is produced, at the hearing without previous warning, the tribunal is confronted with the options of excluding the new material, or of adjourning the hearing, with additional costs and delay to the parties, and the wasting of such time could have been allocated to other cases.

Everyone, then, has an interest in ensuring that litigants understand the jurisdiction which they are invoking, and take the proper procedural steps at the proper time. As yet, legal aid is not available for proceedings before industrial tribunals. Sometimes, competent help is obtainable from a trade union, a CAB, a law centre or the Free Representation Unit, but for many reasons, it is not always to hand at the necessary place and time. In this situation, there is an urgent need for a book setting out clearly in non-technical language the provisions which form the jurisdiction and procedure of industrial tribunals. This is such a book. It presents all the provisions clearly and accurately, and in a form which takes the reader quickly to the relevant information. While it comes to the aid of the puzzled litigant, it will also prove a blessing to trade union officials, personnel officers and others who help to prepare and present cases. For lawyers, too, it should provide a *vade mecum* which will spare much time-consuming research.

I venture to hope that it may inspire similar procedural guides to other systems of tribunals.

Preface

This book is written mainly to help advisers of people facing a tribunal hearing. We also hope it will be accessible to people bringing their own claims without the help of lawyers or specialist advisers. We have tried to show how working people can enforce their rights through the tribunal procedure; we take this commitment as being consistent with the legislation, which is about employment *rights* and anti-discrimination. What we say will be equally useful to employers and their advisers responding to claims.

It may seem odd, but we advocate using the tribunal procedures in the way we describe *only as a last resort*. Legal steps are no substitute for handling workplace problems at the workplace in accordance with agreed procedures. All parties will be better off if a dispute can be settled by negotiation without resort to a tribunal.

We are grateful to many legal, trade union and tribunal colleagues and clients who have given us ideas for this book and in particular Tony Pullen, Isabel Manley, Vereena Jones, Emma Smith, Alice Leonard and Colette Chesters for detailed comments on the text. What appears is not their fault. We also thank Adam Brett for his assistance and our clerks for their support.

Throughout this book we have used 'chairman' to describe those who preside over industrial tribunals. This is in accordance with the language of the legislation but, of course, it refers to both male and female holders of this office. References to tribunals are to industrial tribunals or, as they are likely to be renamed, employment tribunals and to the Employment Appeal Tribunal.

We state the law as we see it on 1 June 1996, but anticipating the coming into force of the Amendment Regulations, the two consolidating Acts, the Employment Rights Act 1996 and the Industrial Tribunals Act 1996 in August 1996 and the Disability Discrimination Act 1995 on 2 December 1996.

Note on the law in Scotland and Northern Ireland

The procedure in tribunals in Scotland and Northern Ireland is similar to that in England and Wales, although each has its own set of rules. The substantive law of contracts of employment differs slightly in Scotland, and the terminology is quite different.

References in this book are to the regulations and rules for England and Wales, and wherever there is a Scottish or Northern Irish variation, we say so.

J McM
J E

Contents

Table of cases   xv
Table of statutes   xxvi
Table of statutory instruments   xxx
Proposals for change   xxxvii
Abbreviations   xxxix

1   Constitution   1
General   1
Position of industrial tribunals in the legal system   2
Location and administration   3
Composition   4
Tribunal consultative groups   8

2   Types of claim   10
Jurisdiction: general   10
Territorial jurisdiction   11
Table of industrial tribunal jurisdiction and time limits   12

3   Stages before the originating application   17
The correct respondent   17
Insolvent employers   19
Letter before action   20
Questionnaires   21
Financing a case and costs implications   21
Checklist   23

4   Time limits   24
General principles   24

When does time start running?   29
The rules on counting time   33
Commencement of proceedings   34
Extending the deadline   35

5   The originating application   45
Introduction   45
Minimum requirements and Form IT1   45
Originating application distinguished from pleadings   47
Presentation of the originating application   48
Action on receipt of the originating application   48
The contents of the originating application   50

6   Notice of appearance   55
Minimum requirements and Form IT3   55
Time limits   57
Action on receipt of a notice of appearance   58
Contents of the notice of appearance   59
Applicant's notice of appearance   66

7   Amendment   67
Amendment of the originating application   67
Amendment of the notice of appearance   69
Amendment and striking out   69

8   Defining the issues: questionnaires, further particulars,
      written answers   70
Questionnaires   70
Further particulars   74
Written answers   77

9   Discovery   80
Introduction   80
General principles   80
Power to order discovery   82
Discovery and inspection: general principles   84
Privilege   85
Documents from third parties   93
Oppressive requests   94
Equal pay and discrimination cases   95
Checklist   97

10 Interim relief 99
Dismissal for union or health and safety reasons 99
Procedural steps 100
The hearing 101
Remedies 101

11 Interlocutory stages 103
Joinder 103
Combined proceedings 105
Test cases 107
Witness orders 108
Striking out 110
Directions hearings 113
Checklist 114

12 Pre-hearing review 115
Procedure 115
Order to pay a deposit 116

13 Preliminary hearings 118
Preliminary hearings on jurisdiction 118
Preliminary point of law 120
Reference to the European Court 120

14 Adjournment and postponement 122
The positionof the party making the application 123
Factors relevant to a decision 123
Costs on adjournment 126

15 Settlement and conciliation 128
General considerations 128
Compromising statutory rights 130
ACAS 132
Compromise agreements and contracts 135
Decisions by consent 137
Checklist 140

16 Preparing for the hearing 142
Notice of the hearing 142
Listing 142
Preliminary points of law 143

Chairman alone? 143
Hearing in public 143
Written representations 143
Skeleton arguments 143
Agreed facts 144
Witness statements 144
Documents 145
Authorities to be referred to 145
Warning witnesses to attend 145

17 The hearing 147
Administration 147
Procedure 149
Chairman and members 149
Hearing in public 151
Representation at the tribunal 153
The issue to be determined 154
Late amendment, new allegations, late disclosure 156
Who goes first? 156
Conduct of the hearing 159

18 The decision 172

19 Costs 176
When costs can be awarded 177
Relevant considerations for a costs order 180
How to make the application 182
Amounts to be awarded 183

20 Equal pay claims 185
European law 185
Procedures under the Equal Pay Act 186
Equal value claims 190
Tactical advice to applicants 199

21 Review 201
Scope 201
Clerical mistakes 202
The power to review 202
Review and appeal 211
Checklist 213

22 Enforcement 215
Non-monetary awards 215
Monetary awards 215
Interest 216
Rights after death 217
Insolvent employers 217

23 Appeals 218
Constitution 218
Questions of law 220
Academic appeals 222
Time limits 222
Preliminary matters 223
The hearing 225
New points of law 226
New evidence 227
Judgment 227
Costs 228
The order 228
Review and appeal 229

APPENDICES
1 Tribunal forms 233
1. Originating application (IT1) 234
2. Acknowledgement of originating application (IT5) 240
3. Notice of orginating application sent to respondent (IT2) 241
4. Notice of appearance (IT3) 242
5. Suggested dates for hearing (IT4D2) 244
6. Notice of hearing (IT4) 245
7. Notice of hearing: entitlement to bring or contest proceedings 247
8. Notice of an industrial tribunal preliminary hearing 248
9. Notice of pre-hearing review 249
10. Notice of pre-hearing review (respondent's contentions) 250
11. Respondent employer's claim in contract (IT1(c)) 251
12. Acknowledgement of employer's claim (IT5(c)) 252
13. Notice of employer's claim in contract sent to applicant (IT2(c)) 253

14. Notice of appearance by applicant to employer's claim in contract (IT3(c)) 254
15. Notes on tribunial decisions (IT9) 255
16. Questionnaire: sex and race discrimination 259

2 Precedents 265
A. Originating applications and notices of appearance 265
B. Interlocutory requests and responses 278
C. Settlement and conciliation 282
D. Post-decision: reviews and appeals 285

3 Statutes, Regulations and Practice Directions 289
1. Industrial Tribunals Act 1996 289
2. Industrial Tribunals Extension of Jurisdiction Order 1994 322
3. Industrial Tribunals Extension of Jurisdiction (Scotland) Order 1994 325
4. Industrial Tribunals (Constitution and Rules of Procedure) Regulations 1993 327
5. Industrial Tribunal Rules 1993 (Schs 1 and 2) 333
6. Industrial Tribunals (Scotland) Regulations 1993 361
7. Industrial Tribunals Regulations (Northern Ireland) 1996 361
8. Employment Appeal Tribunal Rules 1993 362
9. Industrial Tribunals Practice Direction 1994 376
10. Employment Appeal Tribunal Practice Direction: Procedure (1996) 383

4 Addresses 394

Index 399

Table of cases

Aberdeen Steak Houses v Ibrahim [1988] ICR 550;
   [1988] IRLR 420, EAT   160, 162, 165
Acrow (Engineers) Ltd v Hathaway [1981] ICR 510,
   EAT   112, 138, 208
Ainsworth v Glass Tubes and Components Ltd [1977]
   ICR 347; [1977] IRLR 74, EAT   187
Aldridge v British Telecommunications plc [1989] ICR
   790; [1990] IRLR 10, EAT   189, 191
Alfred Crompton Amusement Machines Ltd v Customs
   and Excise Commissioners (No 2) [1974] QC 405,
   HL; [1973] 2 All ER 1169, HL   86
Allen v Gulf Oil Refining Ltd [1981] AC 1001, HL   119
Arthur Guinness Son & Co (Great Britain) Ltd v Green
   [1989] ICR 241; [1989] IRLR 288, EAT   175
Ashmore v British Coal Corporation [1990] ICR 485;
   [1990] IRLR 283, CA   107, 108, 110, 111
Automatic Switching Ltd v Brunet [1986] ICR 542,
   EAT   125
Avon County Council v Foxhall and Others
   (unreported) EAT/113/89   190
Avon County Council v Haywood-Hicks [1978] ICR
   646; IRLR 118, EAT   38
BRB v Natarajan [1979] ICR 326; [1979] IRLR 45, EAT   86
Bagga v Heavy Electricals (India) Ltd [1972] ICR 118,
   NIRC   204, 227
Balfour v Foreign and Commonwealth Office [1994]
   ICR 277   88
Barber v Guardian Royal Exchange Assurance Group
   [1990] ICR 616; [1990] IRLR 240   27
Barclays Bank plc v Kapur [1991] ICR 208; [1991]
   IRLR 136, HL   32, 118
Barnes v BPC (Business Forms) Ltd [1975] ICR 390   160
Bastick v James Lane (Turf Accountants) Ltd [1979]
   ICR 778, EAT   125, 221

Beacard Property Management and Construction Co
  Ltd v Day [1984] ICR 837, EAT   77, 79
Bengey v North Devon District Council [1977] ICR 15,
  EAT   48
Biggs v Somerset County Council [1996] IRLR 203, CA   25, 26, 27, 28
Bilka-Kaufhaus v Weber von Hartz [1987] ICR 110;
  [1986] IRLR317, ECJ   190
Birds Eye Walls Ltd v Harrison [1985] ICR 278, [1985]
  IRLR 47, EAT   81
Birkett v James [1978] AC 297   112
Blackpool Furniture Ltd v Sullivan [1978] ICR 558,
  EAT   212
Blue Star Ship Management Ltd v Williams [1978] ICR
  770; [1979] IRLR 16, EAT   60, 69
Bodha v Hampshire Area Health Authority [1982] ICR
  200   41
Boorman v Allmakes Ltd [1995] IRLR 553, CA   131
Borden (UK) Ltd v Potter [1986] ICR 647, EAT   205
Bowater plc v Charlwood [1991] ICR 798; [1991] IRLR
  340, EAT& CA   122, 125
Bradley v Edward Ryde & Sons [1979] ICR 488, EAT   100
Bradley Egg Farm v Clifford [1943] 2 All ER 378   19
British Aerospace plc v Green and Others [1995] IRLR
  433, CA   95
British Coal Corporation v McGinty [1988] IRLR 7,
  EAT   102
British Coal Corporation v Smith [1993] ICR 529; [1993]
  IRLR308; [1994] ICR 810; [1994] IRLR 342, CA;
  (1996) Times 23 May, HL   119, 186, 191
British Gas plc v Sharma [1991] ICR 19; [1991] IRLR
  101, EAT   174
British Midland Airways v Lewis [1978] ICR 782, EAT   10, 207
British Newspaper Printing Corporation (North) Ltd v
  Kelly [1989] IRLR 222   68
British Publishing Co Ltd v Fraser [1987] ICR 517,
  EAT   229
British Railways Board v Paul [1988] IRLR 20, EAT   30
British Telecommunications plc v Sheridan [1990] IRLR
  27, CA   220, 221
British Waterways Board v Norman (1994) 26 HLR
  233, DC   181
Bromley v H & J Quick Ltd [1988] ICR 623; [1988]
  IRLR 249, CA   158, 188, 189, 190, 193,
                                                         195
Brooks v British Telecommunications plc [1991] ICR
  286; 1991IRLR 4, EAT aff'd [1992] ICR 414; [1992]
  IRLR 66, CA   86, 113
Burmah Oil Co Ltd v Bank of England [1980] AC 1090,
  HL   87

Burns International Security Services (UK) Ltd v Butt
  [1983]ICR 547; [1983] IRLR 438   46
Byrne v Financial Times Ltd [1991] IRLR 417, EAT   75, 77
Campagnie Financiere du Pacifique v Peruvian Guano
  Co [1882]11 QBD 55, CA   84
Capital Foods (Retail) Ltd v Corrigan [1993] IRLR 430,
  EAT   37, 40, 48
Carr v Allen-Bradley Electronics Ltd [1980] ICR 603;
  [1980] IRLR 263, EAT   180
Carr v British International Helicopters Ltd (in
  administration) [1994] ICR 18, S EAT   19
Carrington v Helix Lighting Ltd [1990] ICR 125; [1990]
  IRLR 6, EAT   72, 73
Carryfast Ld v Dawkins (unreported) EAT 290/83   201
Carter v Credit Change Ltd [1979] ICR 908; [1979]
  IRLR 361, CA   221
Cartiers Superfoods Ltd v Laws [1978] IRLR 315, EAT   177, 178
Chapman v Goonvean and Rostowrack China Clay Co
  Ltd [1973] ICR 50; [1972] IRLR 124, NIRC   17, 47
Chattopadyhyay v Headmaster of Holloway School
  [1982] ICR 132, [1981] IRLR 487, EAT   33, 162
Chelsea Football Club and Athletic Co Ltd v Heath
  [1981] ICR323; [1981] IRLR 73, EAT   131
Chocoladefabriken Lindt & Sprungli AG v Nestle Co
  Ltd [1978]RPC 287, ChD   90
Churchill v Yeates & Son Ltd [1983] ICR 380; [1983]
  IRLR 187, EAT   39
Clwyd County Council v Leverton [1985] IRLR 197,
  EAT   95
Cocking v Sandhurst (Stationers) Ltd [1974] ICR 650   18, 67, 68
Colchester Estates (Cardiff) v Carlton Industries plc
  [1984]3 WLR 693; [1986] Ch 80   31, 220
Colonial Mutual Life Assurance Society Ltd v Clinch
  [1981] ICR 752, EAT   74, 75
Commission of the European Communities v United
  Kingdom [1982] ICR 578; [1982] IRLR 333   190
Commissioner of Metropolitan Police v Locker [1993]
  ICR 440, EAT   192
Conway v Rimmer [1968] AC 910, HL   88
Cooper v Weatherwise (Roofing and Walling) Limited
  [1993] ICR 81, EAT   122
Coral Squash Clubs Ltd v Matthews [1979] ICR 607;
  [1979] IRLR 390, EAT   161, 168
Costellow v Somerset County Council [1993] 1 WLR
  256; [1993]1 All ER 952, CA   223
Courage Take Home Trade Ltd v Keys [1986] ICR 874;
  [1986] IRLR 427, EAT   130, 131
Craig v British Railways (Scottish Region) (1973) 8 ITR
  636   160
Cutts v Head [1984] Ch 290, CA   89

D v NSPCC [1977] 1 All ER 589, HL   87
DHSS v Sloan [1981] ICR 313, EAT   91
DHSS v Sloan (No 2) unreported EAT 342/81   91
Dada v Metal Box Co Ltd [1974] ICR 559; [1974] IRLR
     251, NIRC   108, 109
Danfoss case [1991] ICR 74; [1989] IRLR 532, ECJ   188
Davidson v John Calder (Publishers) Ltd and Calder
     Educational Trust Ltd [1985] ICR 143; [1985] IRLR
     97, EAT   179, 180
Dedman v British Building and Engineering Appliances
     Ltd [1974] ICR 53; [1973] IRLR 379, CA   29, 40
Dennehy v Sealink UK Ltd [1987] IRLR 120, EAT   190
Department of Education and Science v Taylor and
     Others [1992] IRLR 308, QBD   111
Derby & Co Ltd v Weldon (No 8) [1991] 1 WLR 73,
     CA   92
Derby City Council v Marshall [1979] ICR 731   160
Devis Ltd v Atkins [1977] ICR 662; [1977] IRLR 314,
     HL   162
Dexine Rubber Co Ltd v Alker [1977] ICR 434, EAT   225
Dibro Ltd v Hore [1990] ICR 370; [1990] IRLR 120,
     EAT   190
Dietmann and Wahlstrom v London Borough of Brent
     [1987] IRLR146, CA   106
Douglas Water Miners Welfare Society Club v Grieve
     (unreported) EAT/487/84   205
Drinkwater Sabey Ltd v Burnett [1995] ICR 328; [1995]
     IRLR 238, EAT   17
Eke v Commissioners of Customs and Excise [1981]
     IRLR 344, EAT   33
Emmott v Minister for Social Welfare [1993] ICR 8;
     [1991] IRLR 387, ECJ   25, 27
Enderby v Frenchay Health Authority and Secretary of
     State for Health [1994] ICR 112; [1993] IRLR 591,
     CA and ECJ   77, 124, 188
Estorffe v Smith [1973] ITR 627, NIRC   213
E T Marler Ltd v Robertson [1974] ICR 72, NIRC   177, 178
Etherson v Strathclyde Regional Council [1992] ICR
     579; [1992] IRLR 392, S EAT   30, 31
Evans' Executors v Metropolitan Police Authority
     [1993] ICR 151; [1992] IRLR 570, CA   112
FDR Ltd v Holloway [1995] IRLR 400, EAT   95
Fayed v Al-Tajir [1987] 2 All ER 396, CA   88
Fforde v Black (unreported) EAT 68/80   204
Financial Times v Byrne (No 2) [1992] IRLR 163, EAT   124, 187, 200
Fire Brigades Union v Knowles (unreported) EAT 123/
     94   223
Flint v Eastern Electricity Board [1975] ICR 395; [1975]
     IRLR 277, QBD   205, 206

Ford v Stakis Hotels and Inns Ltd [1987] ICR 943;
  [1988] IRLR 46, EAT   35
Ford Motor Co Ltd v Nawaz [1987] ICR 434; [1987]
  IRLR 163, EAT   91
Freeman v Sovereign Chicken Ltd [1991] ICR 853;
  [1991] IRLR 408, EAT   135
Gascol Conversions v Mercer [1974] ICR 420; [1974]
  IRLR 155, CA   52
General Council of British Shipping v Deria [1985] ICR
  198, EAT   206
George A Palmer Ltd v Beeby [1978] ICR 196   167
George Ballantine & Son Ltd v F E R Dixon & Son Ltd
  [1974] 2All ER 503, ChD   84
Gilbert v Kembridge Fibres Ltd [1984] ICR 188; [1984]
  IRLR 52, EAT   134
Gill v Harold Andrews Sheepbridge Ltd [1974] ICR
  294; [1974]IRLR 109, NIRC   156, 160
Gillick v BP Chemicals Ltd [1993] IRLR 437, S EAT   17, 68
Gosport Working Men's and Trade Union Club Ltd v
  Taylor (1978) 13 ITR 321, EAT   46, 50
Grant v Southwestern and County Properties Ltd [1974]
  2 All ER 465, ChD   84
Great Atlantic Insurance Co v Home Insurance Co
  [1981] 1 WLR529, CA   93
Green v Hampshire County Council [1979] ICR 861,
  ChD   124, 161
Green & Symons Ltd v Shickell and Another
  (unreported) EAT/528/83   213
Greenaway Harrison Ltd v Wiles [1994] IRLR 380,
  EAT   7, 168
Grieves v Coldshield Windows Ltd (unreported) EAT
  218/82   205
Grimes v Sutton London Borough Council [1973] ICR
  240   29
Habib v Elkington & Co Ltd [1981] ICR 435; [1981]
  IRLR 344, EAT   8, 150
Halford v Sharples [1992] ICR 146, EAT; [1992] ICR
  583, CA   86, 87, 88, 113, 150,
                                                        151, 192

Hammersmith and Queen Charlotte's Special Health
  Authority v Cato [1988] ICR 132; [1987] IRLR
  483, EAT   187
Hammond v Haigh Castle & Co Ltd [1973] ICR 148;
  [1973] IRLR 91, NIRC   40
Hampson v Department of Education and Science
  [1988] ICR 278; [1988] IRLR 87, EAT   224
Hancock v Middleton [1982] ICR 416, EAT   210
Hanks v Ace High Productions Ltd [1978] ICR 1155;
  [1979] IRLR 32, EAT   174
Hannan v TNT-IPEC (UK) Ltd [1986] IRLR 165, EAT   61

Harber v North London Polytechnic [1990] IRLR 198,
  CA   207
Harrod v Ministry of Defence [1981] ICR 8, EAT   222
Hawker Siddeley Power Engineering Ltd v Rump [1979]
  IRLR 425, EAT   157
Hayward v Cammell Laird Shipbuilders Ltd [1985] ICR
  71; [1984] IRLR 463, IT   194, 198
Help the Aged Housing Association (Scotland) Ltd v
  Vidler [1977] IRLR 104, EAT   205
Hennessy v Craigmyle & Co Ltd and ACAS [1986] ICR
  461; [1986] IRLR 300, CA   134
Hereford and Worcester County Council v Neale [1986]
  ICR 471; [1986] IRLR 168, CA   220
Hetton Victory Club Ltd v Swainstone [1983] ICR 341;
  [1983] IRLR 164, CA   35
Hollister v National Farmers Union [1979] ICR 542;
  [1979] IRLR 238, CA   221
Hotson v Wisbech Conservative Club [1984] ICR 859   160
House v Emerson Electric Industrial Controls [1980]
  ICR 795, EAT   29, 227
Houston v Lightwater Farms Ltd [1990] ICR 502; [1990]
  IRLR 469, EAT   164, 225
Hutchinson v Westwood Television Ltd [1977] ICR
  279; [1977] IRLR 69, EAT   43
Iggesund Converters Ltd v Lewis [1984] ICR 544; [1984]
  IRLR 431, EAT   155
IMI Yorkshire Imperial Ltd v Olender [1982] ICR 69,
  EAT   222
Independent Research Services Ltd v Catterall [1993]
  ICR 1 EAT   89, 90
International Computers Ltd v Whitley [1978] IRLR
  318, EAT   74
J Sainsbury plc v Moger [1994] ICR 800, EAT   229
J Sainsbury plc v Savage [1981] ICR 1; [1980] IRLR
  109, CA   41
Jacobs v Norsalta Ltd [1977] ICR 189, EAT   122, 125
James v Radnor County Council (1890) 6 TLR 240,
  QBD   74
James W Cook & Co (Wivenhoe) v Tipper [1990] iCR
  716; [1990]IRLR 386, CA   39, 42
Jean Sorelle Ltd v Rubak [1991] ICR 127; [1991] IRLR
  153, EAT   40
Jenkins v Kingsgate Ltd [1981] ICR 592; [1981] IRLR
  228, ECJ   185, 190, 188
JMCC Holdings Ltd v Conroy [1990] ICR 179, EAT   125
Johnson t/a Richard Andrew Ladies Hairstylists v
  Baxter [1984] ICR 675; [1985] IRLR 96   182
Johnston v RUC [1987] ICR 83, [1986] IRLR 263, ECJ   121
Jones v Enham Industries [1983] ICR 580n   152
Kapur v Shields [1976] ICR 26 QBD   69

Knapp v Harvey [1911] 2 KB 725, CA 84
Kumchyk v Derby County Council [1978] ICR 1116,
    EAT 227
Ladd v Marshall [1954] 1 WLR 1489 227
Ladup Ltd v Barnes [1982] ICR 107; [1982] IRLR 7,
    EAT 206, 208
Lamont v Fry's Metals Ltd [1985] ICR 566; [1985]
    IRLR 470, CA 175
Landauer Ltd v Comins & Co (1991) Times 7 August,
    CA 83
Laurie v Holloway [1994] ICR 32, EAT 159
Levy v Marrable & Co Ltd [1984] ICR 583, EAT 174
Lewis v Motorworld [1986] ICR 157; [1985] IRLR 465,
    CA 54
Linbourne v Constable [1993] ICR 698, EAT 18, 68
Lindsay v Ironsides, Ray and Vials [1994] ICR 384;
    [1994] IRLR 318, EAT 32, 206
Littlewoods Organisation plc v Traynor [1993] IRLR
    154, EAT 32
Livingstone v Hepworth Refractories plc [1992] ICR
    287; [1992] IRLR 63, EAT 25, 134, 137, 186, 188
Lloyd v McMahon [1987] AC 625 159
Lloyds Bank plc v Fox [1989] ICR 80; [1989] IRLR 103 198
London International College Ltd v Sen [1993] IRLR
    3339, CA 40
Lothian Health Board v Johnstone [1981] IRLR 321 178, 182
Lupeti v Wrens Old House Ltd [1984] ICR 348, EAT 32
M & W Grazebrook Ltd v Wallens [1973] ICR 256;
    [1973] IRLR 139, NIRC 90
Machine Tool Industry Research Association v Simpson
    [1988] ICR 558; [1988] IRLR 212, CA 39
Marley (UK) Ltd v Anderson [1994] IRLR 163; [1996]
    IRLR 163, CA 39, 40, 42
Marshall v Alexander Sloan & Co Ltd [1981] IRLR
    264, EAT 104
Marshall v Harland & Wolff Ltd [1972] ICR 97; [1972]
    IRLR 90 223
Martin v MBS Fastenings (Glynwed) Distribution Ltd
    [1983] ICR 511; [1983] IRLR 198 174
Mcarthys Ltd v Smith (No 2) [1980] ICR 672; [1980]
    IRLR 209, CA 187
McIvor v Southern Health and Social Services Board
    [1978] 1 WLR 757; [1978] 2 All ER 625, HL 90
McPherson v Rathgael Centre for Children and Young
    People [1991] IRLR 206, NI CA 187
Meek v City of Birmingham District Council [1987]
    IRLR 250, CA 174
Metropolitan Police Commissioner v Locker [1993] ICR
    440; [1993] IRLR 319, EAT 88

Migwain Ltd (in Liquidation) v TGWU [1979] ICR
597, EAT   203
Milestone School of English Ltd v Leakey [1982] IRLR
3, EAT   68
Milne v Waldren [1980] ICR 138, EAT   152
Moore v Duport Furniture Products Ltd [1982] ICR 84;
[1982] IRLR 31, HL   133
Morris v Griffiths [1977] ICR 153   204
Mulvaney v London Transport Executive [1981] ICR
351, EAT   111, 138
Munir v Jang Publications Ltd [1989] ICR 1; [1989]
IRLR 224, CA   119, 161
Nasse v Science Research Council [1979] ICR 921;
[1979] IRLR465, HL   192
National Grid Co Ltd v Virdee [1992] IRLR 555, EAT   83
Nea Karteria Maritime Co Ltd v Atlantic and Great
Lakes Steamship Corp [1981] Com LR 139, QBD   93
Neilson v Laugharne [1981] QB 736, CA   88
New Victoria Hospital v Ryan [1993] ICR 201; [1993]
IRLR 202, EAT   89
Nial v Baxters (Butchers) Ltd (1985) Times 9 February,
EAT   180
Nikitas v Metropolitan Borough of Solihull [1986] IRC
291, EAT   208
O'Kelly v Trusthouse Forte plc [1983] ICR 728; [1983]
IRLR 369, CA   228
O'Laoire v Jackel International Ltd [1990] ICR 197;
[1991] IRLR 70, CA   161, 216
Odeco (UK) Inc v Peachman [1979] ICR 823, EAT   11
Owen v Crown House Engineering Ltd [1973] ICR 511;
[1973] IRLR 233, NIRC   41
Owusu v London Fire and Civil Defence Authority
[1995] IRLR 574, EAT   32
Oxford v DHSS [1977] ICR 884   160
P & O European Ferries (Dover) Ltd v Byrne [1989]
IRLR 254, CA   75
P J Drakard & Sons Ltd v Wilton [1977] ICR 642, EAT   210
Paine & Moore v Grundy (Teddington) Ltd [1981]
IRLR 267, EAT   105
Palmer v Southend-on-Sea Borough Council [1984] ICR
372; [1984] IRLR 119, CA   37, 41
Paramount Airways [1994] ICR 395, CA   19
Peach Grey & Co (a firm) v Sommers [1995] IRLR 363,
DC   3
Perera v Civil Service Commission [1980] ICR 699;
[1980] IRLR 233, EAT   94
Peter Simper & Co Ltd v Cooke [1986] IRLR 19, EAT   168
Pickstone v Freemans plc [1987] ICR 867; [1987] IRLR
281, CA; [1988] ICR 697; [1988] IRLR 357, HL   1, 120, 185–186, 188

Piggott Brothers & Co v Jackson [1992] ICR 85; [1991]
  IRLR 309, CA   221, 224
Port of London Authority v Payne [1994] ICR 555,
  [1994] IRLR9, CA   151
Porter v Bandridge Ltd [1978] ICR 943; [1978] IRLR
  271   36
Post Office Counters Ltd v Heavey [1990] ICR 1; [1989]
  IRLR 513   156
Post Office Counters Ltd v Malik [1991] ICR 355   119, 120
Post Office v Moore [1981] ICR 623, EAT   48
Powdrill v Watson [1994] ICR 395, CA; [1995] 2 AC
  394; [1995] ICR 1100; [1995] IRLR 269, HL   19
Presley v Llanelli Borough Council [1979] ICR 419;
  [1979] IRLR 381, EAT   29
Pruden v Cunard Ellerman Ltd [1993] IRLR 317, EAT   33, 34
R v Chief Constable of West Midlands Police ex p
  Wiley [1995] 1 AC 274, HL   88
R v Gough [1993] AC 646, HL   7, 149, 169
R v Madan [1961] 2 QB 1, CA   91
R v Secretary of State for Employment ex p EOC
  [1994] ICR 317; [1994] IRLR 176, HL   26, 27
R v Secretary of State for Employment ex p Seymour-
  Smith andPerez [1995] ICR 889; [1995] IRLR 464,
  CA   25, 26, 27
RJB Mining (UK) Ltd v NUM [1995] IRLR 556, CA   33
Rankin v British Coal Corporation [1995] ICR 774;
  [1993] IRLR 69, EAT   27
Raybright TV Services Ltd v Smith [1973] ICR 640,
  NIRC   209
Ready Case Ltd v Jackson [1981] IRLR 312, EAT   64, 69
Red Bank Manufacturing Co Ltd v Meadows [1992]
  ICR 204; [1992] IRLR 209, EAT   169
Reddington v S Straker & Sons Ltd [1994] ICR 172,
  EAT   58, 70, 104, 113, 208
Reed Packaging Ltd v Boozer and Everhurst [1988] ICR
  391; [1981] IRLR 333, EAT   194
Rewe-Zentralfinanz eG and Rewe-Zentral AG v
  Landswirtschaftskammer für das Saarland (No 33/
  76) [1976] ECR 1989, [1977] CMLR 533, ECJ   25
Riley v Tesco Stores [1980] ICR 323; [1980] IRLR 103,
  CA   40, 42, 104
Rogers v Bodfari (Transport) Ltd [1973] ICR 325; [1973]
  IRLR172, NIRC   29
Rolls Royce Motor Cars Ltd v Mair and Others
  (unreported) EAT/794/92   85, 95
Rosedale Mouldings Ltd v Sibley [1980] ICR 816, EAT   160
Russell v Elmdon Freight Terminal Ltd [1989] ICT 629,
  EAT   227
Sandhu v Department of Education and Science [1978]
  IRLR 208, EAT   103

Science Research Council v Nasse [1980] AC 1028;
  [1979] ICR 921; [1979] IRLR 465, HL   83, 85
Secretary of State for Education v Birchall [1994] IRLR
  630, EAT   119
Secretary of State for Employment v Atkins Auto
  Laundries Ltd [1972] ICR 76, NIRC   29
Secretary of State for Scotland and Greater Glasgow
  Health Board v Wright and Hannah [1991] IRLR
  187, EAT   1, 185
Seldun Transport Services Ltd v Baker [1978] ICR 1035,
  EAT   56
Selvarajan v Inner London Education Authority [1980]
  IRLR 313, EAT   94
Sheffield Metropolitan District Council v Siberry [1989]
  ICR208   193
Slack v Greenham (Plant Hire) Ltd [1983] ICR 617;
  [1983] IRLR 271, EAT   135
Smith v Automobile Pty Ltd [1973] ICR 306, NIRC   46
Snowball v Gardner Merchant Ltd [1987] ICR 719;
  [1987] IRLR 397, EAT   163
Sougrin v Haringey Health Authority [1991] ICR 791;
  [1991] IRLR 447, EAT   32
South Shropshire District Council v Amos [1986] 1
  WLR 1271, CA   90
St Basil's Centre v McCrossan [1992] ICR 140; [1991]
  IRLR 455, EAT   37
St Mungo Community Trust v Colleano [1980] ICR
  254, EAT   57
Stein v Associated Dairies Ltd [1982] IRLR 447, EAT   178
Stevenson v Golden Wonder Ltd [1977] IRLR 474, EAT   201
Stevensons (Dyers) Ltd v Brennan [1974] ICR 194,
  NIRC   209
Stokes v Hampstead Wine Co Ltd [1979] IRLR 298,
  EAT   160, 167
Stonehill Furniture Ltd v Philippo [1983] ICR 556, EAT   213
Sun Life Assurance v Jervis [1994] AC 111, HL   222
Swithland Motors plc v Clarke [1994] ICR 231; 1994
  IRLR 275, EAT   32
T and D Transport (Portsmouth) Ltd v Linburn [1987]
  ICR 696, EAT   203
Taplin v C Shippam Ltd [1978] ICR 1068; [1978] IRLR
  450, EAT   101
Telephone Information Services Ltd v Wilkinson [1991]
  IRLR 148, EAT   111, 131
Tennants Textile Colours Ltd v Todd [1989] IRLR 3,
  NI CA   198
Thomas v NCB [1987] ICR 757; [1987] IRLR 451, EAT   187
Throsby v Imperial College of Science and Technology
  [1987] ICR 357; [1977] IRLR 337, EAT   30
Times Newspapers Ltd v Fitt [1981] ICR 637, EAT   139

Tracey and Others v Crosville Wales Ltd (1995) 31 July
  CA (unreported)   220
Trimble v Supertravel Ltd [1982] ICR 440; [1982] IRLR
  451, EAT   207, 212
Trollope & Colls v Sharpe EAT/812/92   173
Trust House Forte (UK) Ltd v Halstead (unreported),
  EAT 213/86   43
University College of Swansea v Cornelius [1988] ICR
  735   150
Vauxhall Motors Ltd v Henry [1978] ITR 332, EAt   206
Vyas v Leyland Cars   85
Walker v Josiah Wedgwood & Sons Ltd [1978] ICR
  744, [1978] IRLR 105   167
Walker v Wilsher (1889) 23 QBD 335, CA   91
Walls Meat Co Ltd v Khan [1979] ICR 52; [1978] IRLR
  499, CA   36, 38
Warnock v Scarborough Football Club [1989] ICR 489,
  EAT   124
West Midlands Passenger Transport Executive v Singh
  [1988] ICR 614; [1988] IRLR 186, CA   95, 96
White v University of Manchester [1976] ICR 419;
  [1976] IRLR218, EAT   74
Whitmore and Others v Frayling Furniture (unreported)
  1985 COIT 1680/204   196
Wiggin Alloys Ltd v Jenkins [1981] IRLR 275   180
Wileman v Minilec Engineering Ltd [1988] ICR 318;
  [1988] IRLR 144, EAT   205, 227
William Hill Organisation Ltd v Gavas [1990] IRLR
  488, CA   223
William P Harrower Ltd v Hogg (unreported) EAT
  215/78   213
Williams v Greater London Citizens Advice Bureaux
  Service [1989] ICR 545, EAT   73
Wise v Borneman [1971] AC 297   160
Worringham v Lloyds Bank [1981] ICR 558; [1981]
  IRLR 178, ECJ   185
Yorkshire Engineering and Welding Co Ltd v Burnham
  [1974] ICR 77; [1973] IRLR 316, NIRC   206, 208
Zucker v Astrid Jewels [1978] ICR 1088; [1978] IRLR
  385, EAT   102

Table of statutes

Administration of Justice	
Act 1985	
s 9	219
Arbitration Act 1950	
s 13A(2)	112
Bankers' Books Evidence	
Act 1879	84
Companies Act 1985	
s 691	11
Contempt of Court Act	
1981	3
Court of Session Act 1988	
s 40	3
Courts and Legal Services	
Act 1990	
s 4	181
s 71	3, 4
Criminal Evidence Act	
1995	161
Criminal Procedure	
(Scotland) Act 1995	
s 274(2)	153
Disability Discrimination	
Act 1995	133–136
s 8	15
s 9(2)	135
Sch 3 para 3	15, 28, 43
Employment Protection	
Act 1975	132
Employment Protection	
(Consolidation) Act	
1978	
s 46(3)(a)	31

Employment Rights Act	
1996	134–136
s 11(1)	15
s 11(2)	15
s 11(4)	15, 29, 31
s 23	6, 15
s 23(2)	15, 33
s 23(3)	33
s 34	15
s 34(2)	15
s 45	15
s 45(1)	33
s 48(3)	15
ss 48–55	217
s 50	15
s 50(2)	15
s 52	15
s 54(2)	15
s 55	15
s 57(2)	15
s 64	16
s 67	16
s 70(2)	16
s 87	217
s 88	217
s 92(1)	16
s 92(1)(c–e)	100
s 93	16, 100
s 94	16, 27
s 95	156
s 95(1)	155
s 95(1)(c)	29
s 96	63
s 97(1)	29, 30

s 97(4)	30	s 1(3)	77, 119, 158, 187, 194
s 98	61, 159		
s 98(1)	60, 156	s 1(5)	188, 190, 195
s 98(2)	60, 156		
s 98(4)	155, 156, 157	s 1(6)	186
		s 2	12, 30
s 100	31, 100	s 2(4)	12, 15, 28, 29, 30, 31
s 104	100		
s 104(2)	29	s 2A(1)	189, 199
s 111	16	s 2A(1)(a)	193, 195
s 111(2)	27, 36, 42	s 2A(1)(b)	193
s 113	215, 216	s 2A(2)	187, 189
s 117	215	s 2A(2)(b)	189
s 118	216	s 2A(3)	189
s 122(2)	155	s 2A(4)	195
s 123(6)	155	Fair Employment Acts 1976–89 (NI)	10
s 124(3)	216		
s 128	6, 16, 28, 31, 100	Health and Safety at Work etc Act 1974	34, 172
s 128(2)	16	s 24	12
s 131	6	s 24(2)	12
s 132	6	s 80	12, 28
s 145	30	Industrial Training Act 1964	1
s 159	217		
s 163	16, 24	Industrial Training Act 1982	
s 163(2)	157	s 12	13
s 164	16, 30	Industrial Tribunals Act 1996	
s 164(3)	29	s 3	6, 16
s 170	16	s 4	5, 7
s 171	24	s 4(3)	6
s 175	217	s 4(5)	6
s 182	6, 16	s 5(3)	184
s 188(2)	16	s 7(4)	83, 94, 108
s 193(2)	88		
s 195	88	s 10(1)	151
s 197	129	s 11	152
s 199	217	s 11(2)	152
s 203	129	s 11(3)	153
s 203(3)	135	s 11(6)	153
s 203(4)	135	s 15(1)	215
Pts I, III, V–XII,	217	s 15(2)	215, 216
Equal Pay Act 1970	21, 52–53, 119, 120, 132, 185– 188, 190, 196	s 16	8
		s 18	132, 134
		s 18(1)(d)	134
		s 18(4)	133
		s 18(7)	90
s 1(2)(a)	185, 188	s 20	218
s 1(2)(b)	185, 188, 189	s 20(3)	2, 219
s 1(2)(c)	185, 189	s 21	16, 220
		s 22	219

s 28	220
s 28(2)	219
s 28(3)	219
s 28(4)	219
s 33	112, 225
Insolvency Act 1986	
s 11(3)	19
s 19	19
s 44	19
s 130(2)	19
Insolvency Act 1994	19
Interpretation Act 1978	33
s 7	203
Judgments Act 1838	216
Limitation Act 1980	
s 5	24–25
Medical Reports Act 1988	91
Pension Schemes Act 1993	
s 11(5)(e)	15
s 113(1)	15
Pensions Act 1995	
s 62	15
s 63(4)	15
Police and Criminal Evidence Act 1984	88
Race Relations Act 1976	8, 17, 23, 70, 71, 94, 134–136, 150, 172, 207
s 2	54
s 54	13
s 59	13, 28
s 59(1)	13
s 63(3)(a)	13
s 64	13
s 65(1)	21, 70
s 65(2)(b)	72
s 65(5)	71
s 68(1)	13
s 68(4)	13
s 68(5)	13
s 68(6)	28, 43
s 68(7)(a)	32
s 68(7)(b)	31
s 72	129, 135
Sexual Discrimination Act 1975	23, 70, 71, 134–136, 150, 172
s 1(1)(b)	54, 190
s 1(1)(b)(ii)	64
s 63	12, 13
s 64(1)	193
s 68	12, 28
s 68(1)	12
s 72(2)	12
s 72(4)	12
s 73	12
s 74(1)	21, 70
s 74(2)(a)	71
s 74(2)(b)	72
s 76(1)	12, 13
s 76(3)	12
s 76(4)	12
s 76(5)	13, 28, 43
s 76(6)(b)	31, 32
s 77	12, 129, 135
s 77(1)	25
Sexual Discrimination Act 1986	17
s 6(4A)	12, 13, 25
Sexual Offences (Amendment) Acts 1976 and 1992	153
State Immunity Act 1978	
s 12(2)	57
Supreme Court Act 1981	
s 9	2
s 51	181
Trade Union and Labour Relations (Consolidation) Act 1992, as amended	134–136
s 3	218
s 4	218
s 66(1)	13
s 66(2)	13
s 66(3)	28
s 67	28
s 67(1)	13
s 67(2)	13, 218
s 67(3)	13
s 68A	13
s 68A(1)	13
s 95	218
s 104	218
s 116(4)	14
s 116(5)	14
s 137(2)	14
s 138(2)	14

s 139(1)	14	s 176	215
s 146(5)	14	s 176(2)	14, 218
s 147	14	s 176(3)	14, 28
s 147(a)	31	s 189(1)	14
s 150	104	s 189(5)	14
s 150(2)	104	s 192(1)	14
s 152	14, 31, 100	s 192(2)	14
s 153	100	s 209	132
s 160	104	s 238	14
s 160(2)	104	s 238(2A)	14
s 161	6, 31, 100	s 239(2)	14
s 161(1)	14	s 248	132
s 161(2)	14, 28	s 288	135
s 162	100, 101	s 290	132
s 163	101	s 291(2)	220
s 163(6)	102	Trade Union Reform and	
s 165	6, 102	Employment Rights	
s 166	6, 102, 215	Act 1993	
s 168(4)	14	s 39	136
s 169(5)	14	s 40	152
s 170(4)	14	Tribunals and Inquiries	
s 171	14	Act 1992	
s 174	28	s 10	164
s 174(5)	14	s 11	219
s 175	14	Sch 1	219

Table of statutory instruments

Civil Legal Aid (General) Regulations 1989 SI No 339
reg 149   220
County Court Rules 1981 SI No 1687
Ord 6
r 7   74
Ord 14   80
r 1–9   82
r 5   89
r 8(1)   82, 85
r 11   77
Ord 17
r 10   113
r 11   80
Ord 20
r 12A   164
r 27, 28   144
Ord 25
r 12   216
Ord 38
r 2   184
Employment Appeal Tribunal Rules 1993 SI No 2854   218, 222
r 3   223
r 3(2)   16
r 4   228
r 20   223
r 21   223
r 23   226
r 24   224
r 24(5)   224
r 26   225
r 27   225
r 3(2)   16
r 33   229
r 37   223

Employment Protection (Recoupment of Unemployment
Benefit and Supplementary Benefit) Regulations
1977 SI No 674   8, 128
Employment Protection (Recoupment of Unemployment
Benefit and Supplementary Benefit) Regulations
1980 SI No 1608   8
Employment Protection (Recoupment of Unemployment
Benefit and Supplementary Benefit) Regulations
1988 SI No 419   8
Industrial Training (Northern Ireland) Order 1984
art 31   3, 218
Industrial Tribunals Awards (Enforcement in Cases of
Death) Regulations 1976 SI No 663   217
Industrial Tribunals (Constitution and Rules of
Procedure) Regulations 1993 SI No 2687
    reg 2   138
    reg 2(1)   35, 152
    reg 2(2)   152, 172, 208
    reg 2(5)   172
    reg 3(1)   3, 4
    reg 3(3)   4
    reg 5(1)(a)   4
    reg 7(3)   151
    reg 8   194
    reg 8(2)   186
    reg 8(3)   11
    reg 9   49, 172
    reg 10(a)   216
    reg 13(10)   4
    Sch 1
      r 1(1)   34, 46, 48
      r 1(2)   49
      r 1(3)   49
      r 2(1)   38
      r 2(1)(a)   49
      r 2(1)(b)   49
      r 2(1)(c)   49
      r 2(2)   49
      r 3(1)   58
      r 3(2)   59, 153
      r 3(2)(a)   58
      r 3(2)(b)   5, 56, 58, 75
      r 3(2)(c)   59, 203
      r 3(2)(d)   59
      r 3(2)(e)   59
      r 3(3)   57
      r 3(5)   57
      r 4(1)   76, 83
      r 4(1)(a)   46, 56, 76
      r 4(1)(a)(i)   46

r 4(1)(b)	82
r 4(2)	108, 154
r 4(2)(a)	93, 149
r 4(2)(b)	93
r 4(3)	77, 78, 84, 154
r 4(4)	78
r 4(5)	76, 78, 83, 108
r 4(6)	83, 94
r 4(7)	76, 79, 83, 112, 153, 208
r 5(1)	203
r 5(2)	142
r 6	5, 7, 114
r 6(1)	119
r 7	113
r 7(1)	115
r 7(4)	115, 116
r 7(6)	116
r 7(7)	116
r 7(9)	117
r 8(2)	143, 151
r 8(3)	143, 151
r 8(5)	143, 154
r 8(6)	153
r 9	5
r 9(1)	1, 158, 159
r 9(2)	153, 158, 170
r 9(3)	154, 160
r 9(4)	163
r 10	5
r 10(1)	151, 175
r 10(2)	172, 173, 202
r 10(3)	164, 172, 202
r 10(4)	172
r 10(6)	172
r 10(9)	174
r 10(10)	202
r 10(12)	172, 202
r 11	5, 174
r 11(1)	202
r 11(1)(a)	214
r 11(1)(b)	203, 210, 214
r 11(1)(c)	203, 210, 211, 214
r 11(1)(d)	205, 206, 211, 212, 214
r 11(1)(e)	138
r 11(2)	209, 211
r 11(3)	209
r 11(4)	210
r 11(5)	210
r 11(6)	211
r 11(6)(a)	211

Industrial Tribunals Regulations 1993 – cont.

r 11(6)(b)	211
r 11(7)	213
r 12	154, 184
r 12(1)	22, 126, 179, 180, 183
r 12(1)(a)	180
r 12(1)(b)	180
r 12(2)	154
r 12(3)	183
r 12(4)	122, 126
r 12(5)	154, 179
r 12(6)	183
r 12(7)	117
r 12(8)	117
r 13(1)	1, 57, 67, 122, 149
r 13(2)	69, 208
r 13(2)(a)	5, 138
r 13(2)(b)	138, 173
r 13(2)(c)	143, 154
r 13(2)(d)	5, 110, 208
r 13(2)(e)	108, 110
r 13(2)(f)	112
r 13(3)	110, 113
r 13(5)	83, 104
r 13(6)	49, 153, 172
r 13(7)	5, 122
r 13(8)	5, 76, 78, 83, 108, 115, 119, 211
r 13(8)(c)	211
r 14(3)	152
r 15	5, 122
r 15(1)	57, 57, 209, 210, 214
r 16	5
r 16(1)	113
r 16(2)	113
r 17	5, 104, 105
r 17(1)	17, 103, 104
r 17(2)	103, 133
r 17(3)	103
r 18	5, 106, 107
r 18(1)	105, 106
r 18(2)	106
r 18(3)	106
r 20(2)	48
r 20(3)	203
r 20(4)	50, 51, 59, 62
r 20(7)	133
Sch 2	186, 191
r 4(2)	198
r 4(2A)	192, 196

r 7	192
r 8A	195
r 8A(2)	195
r 8A(3)	195
r 8A(4)	196
r 8A(6)	196
r 8A(9)	196
r 8A(10)	196
r 8A(11)	197
r 8A(12)	198
r 8A(13)	197, 198
r 8A(14)	197
r 8A(15)–(17)	197
r 8A(18)	198
r 9(1)	196
r 9(2A)	198
r 9(2B)	198
r 9(2E)	194
r 10(4A)	173
r 12	181
r 13(2)(d)	192
r 13(6A)	193
r 13(7)	193
r 18(1)	192
Schs 3–5	158
Industrial Tribunals (Constitution of Rules of Procedure) Regulations 1994 S No 536	
reg 6	194
Industrial Tribunals (Extension of Jurisdiction) (England and Wales) Order 1994 SI No 1623	124
reg 7	16
Industrial Tribunals (Extension of Jurisdiction) (Scotland) Order 1994 SI No 1624	124
Industrial Tribunals (Interest) Order 1991 SI No 479	216
Industrial Tribunals (Rules of Procedure) Regulations 1985 SI No 16	
r 11(1)	177
Industrial Tribunals (Rules of Procedure) (Equal Value Amendment) Regulations 1983	191
Occupational Pension Schemes (Contracting-out) Regulations 1984 SI No 380 (amended by SI No 1323 and SI 1986 No 1716	15
Occupational Pension Schemes (Disclosure of Information) Regulations 1986 SI No 1046	
reg 10	15
Occupational Pension Schemes (Equal Treatment) Regulations 1995 SI No 3183	15
Race Relations (Interest on Awards) Regulations 1994 SI No 1748	217

Race Relations(Questions and Replies) Order 1977 SI

    No 842   71

        Art 5   72

        Pt IV   72

Rules of Supreme Court 1965 SI No 1776

    Ord 3

        r 1   33

        r 2   33

        r 4   33

    Ord 6

        r 7   74

    Ord 18

        r 12   74

    Ord 24   80

        r 2   85

    Ord 26   77

    Ord 38

        r 2A(1)   164

        r 2A(2)   164

        r 14   108

        r 36   144, 198

        r 37   144, 198

        rr 38–44   144

    Ord 52

        r 1   219

    Ord 55

        r 4   219

    Ord 62

        r 2   181

    Ord 94

        r 8(3)   16

    Ord 114   121

Rules of Supreme Court (Northern Ireland) 1980

    Ord 61   3, 218

Safety Representative and Safety Committee

    Regulations 1977 SI No 500

        reg 11(1)   12

        reg 11(2)   12, 28

Sex Discrimination and Equal Pay (Miscellaneous

    Amendments)Regulations 1996 SI No 438   195

Sex Discrimination and Equal Pay (Remedies)

    Regulations 1993 SI No 2798   217

Sex Discrimination(Questions and Replies) Order 1975

    SI No 2048, as amended   71

        Art 5   72

        Pt IV   72

Transfer of Undertakings (Protection of Employment)

    Regulations 1981 SI No 1794 as amended   60

        reg 11(1)   13

        reg 11(5)   13

        reg 11(8)(a)   13

Proposals for change

On 17 July 1996 the government published a draft Employment Rights (Dispute Resolution) Bill. The Bill contains measures aimed at improving existing tribunal procedures and, more radically, introduces proposals for the promotion of alternative means of resolving disputes. The consultation documents also highlighted further proposals, relating to the extension of tribunals' powers to dismiss cases and award costs, which are expected to be introduced by way of further secondary legislation in due course. The principal changes suggested affect the parts of this book dealing with the matters set out in the table on pxxxviii.

Jurisdiction for handling discrimination at work on the grounds of disability is to be given to tribunals throughout the United Kingdom when the Disability Discrimination Act 1995 comes into effect on 2 November of 1996 and racial discrimination is to be outlawed in Northern Ireland.

Table of government proposals for change: July 1996

title	to change the name to Employment Tribunals	p1
compromise agreements	to recognise that solicitors are insured, and to extend the power to make agreements to union officials and other non-lawyers who are insured	p137 p276
attempts to raise grievances and settle complaints	to require tribunals to consider in assessing compensation whether employees have tried to resolve disputes with their employer before making a claim	p128
alternatives to tribunals	to allow for voluntary binding arbitration	p130
dismissing claims	to allow tribunals to dismiss hopeless cases at an early stage; and for some cases to be decided on written evidence where all parties consent	p115
applicants claiming unfair dismissal	to require applicants to state on the originating application whether they have a new job and at what rate of pay	p52
chairman-only cases	to extend the range of cases which can be heard by a chairman alone without lay members	p5
legal officers	to create a new tribunal post to deal with many interlocutory decisions	p7
ACAS	to allow ACAS to conciliate in redundancy pay cases	p132
costs	to allow tribunals to award costs if a party has unreasonably turned down an offer of settlement and to increase the maximum award above £500	p131, p177
agency status	to place tribunals under agency status (from 1 April 1997)	–
tribunal offices	to require registration of claims in the appropriate office for each postal district in England and Wales (September 1996)	p3

Abbreviations

ACAS	Advisory, Conciliation and Arbitration Service
CCR	County Court Rules
COIT	Central Office of Industrial Tribunals
CRE	Commission for Racial Equality
CROTUM	Commissioner for the Rights of Trade Union Members
DC	Divisional Court
DDA	Disability Discrimination Act 1995
EAT	Employment Appeal Tribunal
EAT Rules	Employment Appeal Tribunal Rules 1993 SI No 2854
EDT	effective date of termination
EOC	Equal Opportunities Commission
EPCA	Employment Protection (Consolidation) Act 1978
EqPA	Equal Pay Act 1970
ERA	Employment Rights Act 1996
GMF	genuine material factor
HSWA	Health and Safety at Work Act 1974
IE	independent expert
IT	industrial tribunal
ITA	Industrial Tribunals Act 1996
JES	job evaluation study
NIRC	National Industrial Relations Court
OIT	Office of Industrial Tribunals
PD	Practice Direction 1996
Regulations (reg)	Industrial Tribunals (Constitution and Rules of Procedure) Regulations 1993 SI No 2687
ROIT	Regional Office of Industrial Tribunals
RRA	Race Relations Act 1976
RSC	Rules of the Supreme Court
Rules (r)	Industrial Tribunals Procedure Rules 1993 (Sch 1 to Regulations) as amended 1996
Sch 2 Rules	Complementary Rules of Procedure (Sch 2 to Regulations)
SDA	Sex Discrimination Act (1975 unless otherwise stated)

SEAT   Employment Appeal Tribunal (Scotland)
TULRCA   Trade Union and Labour Relations (Consolidation) Act
           1992
TUPE   Transfer of Undertakings (Protection of Employment)
           Regulations 1981 SI No 1794

CHAPTER 1

Constitution

General

Industrial tribunals were first established by the Industrial Training Act 1964. Since that time, the role of industrial tribunals has changed dramatically and they now have jurisdiction to hear many types of claim (p10), but the vast majority of cases involve unfair dismissal or redundancy pay.

Although performing a judicial function, tribunals are creatures of statute. Unlike the courts, they have no inherent jurisdiction: if a tribunal is to exercise a particular power, it is necessary to find out which statute creates the power. There is no general power, except that a tribunal is required to give effect to European Union law.[1]

The aim of industrial tribunals has always been to provide 'an easily accessible, speedy, informal and inexpensive procedure for the settlement of . . . disputes . . . and to remove the . . . multiplicity of actions'.[2] To some extent these goals have been achieved: tribunals are not bound by the rules of evidence or procedure which govern most courts. Instead they can moderate their own procedure as they see fit (Industrial Tribunals Procedure Rules 1993 ('Rules') rr9(1) and 13(1)). Equally, there is no monopoly on rights of audience before tribunals, so anyone can represent a party or can choose to represent themselves, and no-one wears wigs or gowns. The tribunal, representatives and witnesses remain seated for the hearing and modes of address are relatively informal: 'Sir' or 'Madam' are acceptable and usual, without being too obsequious;

---

1 *Secretary of State for Scotland v Wright* [1991] IRLR 187, EAT, applying *Pickstone v Freemans plc* [1987] ICR 867; [1987] IRLR 218, CA.
2 Royal Commission on Trade Unions and Employers' Associations under Lord Donovan 1968, Cmnd 3623, para 578.

Mr, Ms for representatives, parties and witnesses.

On the other hand, for most litigants in person and many lay representatives, tribunals will seem highly formal and legalistic. Evidence is usually given on oath or affirmation, witnesses are cross-examined, legal language is used and legal submissions are made. At times the issues before the tribunal will be complex and involve quite complicated legal analysis. Frequently parties will employ legal professionals who are trained in and used to the greater formality of the courts. All this increases the formality and costs of the proceedings, and sometimes causes delays.

In the vast majority of cases the issues are quite simple ones of fact and there is no reason why the tribunal should not be able to adjudicate upon these cases without the 'assistance' of detailed rules of evidence and procedure and lawyers.

Position of industrial tribunals in the legal system

Industrial (or employment) tribunals are the first stage in the legal process for enforcing most statutory employment rights. The decisions of one tribunal are not binding on any other tribunal or court, although they may be persuasive.

The next stage is the Employment Appeal Tribunal ('EAT'), to which an appeal lies from decisions of industrial tribunals. There are divisions of the EAT in England and Wales (sitting in London) and in Scotland (sitting in Edinburgh). It has the status of a court of record, which means its decisions are binding on industrial tribunals, and on county courts in England and Wales and sherriff courts in Scotland and create legal precedents which should be followed.[3]

The EAT in England and Wales is a branch of the High Court and hearings are presided over by a High Court judge or a circuit judge appointed under Supreme Court Act 1981 s9, sitting with two (or, exceptionally, four) lay members drawn from separate panels nominated by the different sides of employment relations, appointed by the Lord Chancellor in conjunction with the Secretary of State (the President of the Board of Trade). In Scotland, EAT cases are heard by a judge of the Court of Session sitting with two lay members appointed by the same system.

Appeals from the EAT in England and Wales lie to the Court of Appeal (Civil Division) and in Scotland they go to the Court of

3 Industrial Tribunals Act (ITA) 1996 s20(3).

Session (Inner House). Appeals must be on points of law (not fact) and can only be made with the leave (consent) of the EAT or, if it refuses, the Court of Appeal or Court of Session. From there they go to the House of Lords. Leave is required in England and Wales and Northern Ireland but not in Scotland.[4]

Appeals from tribunals sitting in Northern Ireland, where there is no EAT, are heard by the Northern Ireland Court of Appeal, by way of case stated.[5] Appeal from this court lies to the House of Lords.

Contempt

Although tribunals are not courts of record, for the purposes of the Contempt of Court Act 1981 and RSC Order 52, which provide the power for the Divisional Court to punish contempt of other courts, they are inferior courts and any person acting in contempt of them can be punished by imprisonment: *Peach Grey & Co (a firm) v Sommers* [1995] IRLR 363, DC. In this case, the applicant to the tribunal proceedings had indirectly tried to persuade a witness to withdraw his evidence. The court held that it did have the power to commit the applicant to prison for that contempt of the proceedings of the tribunal as an inferior court.

Location and administration

There is a Central Office of Industrial Tribunals ('COIT') for England and Wales based at Southgate Street, Bury St Edmunds, Suffolk IP33 2AQ. The role of the COIT is administrative. There are also 11 Regional Offices of Industrial Tribunals ('ROITs'). The postal address of the applicant's workplace determines to which of the 20 offices the application is made and by which it is administered (see list of addresses at p237). Any hearing in a case will take place at the relevant ROIT or an Office of the Industrial Tribunals ('OIT') within one of the regions.

The head of all industrial tribunals in England and Wales is the President of Industrial Tribunals, who must have held a 'general qualification' for at least seven years.[6] This will mean a barrister or

---

4 Court of Session Act 1988 s40.
5 Industrial Training (Northern Ireland) Order 1984 article 31 and Rules of Supreme Court (Northern Ireland) 1980 Order 61.
6 Industrial Tribunals (Constitution and Rules of Procedure) Regulations 1993 SI No 2687 ('regs') reg 3(1), and Courts and Legal Services Act 1990 s71.

solicitor with rights of audience in part of the Supreme Court and the county courts, appointed by the Lord Chancellor. S/he may hold office until the age of 72[7] (age 70 for appointments in and after 1995). Recently the presidents have been circuit judges. The chief administrative officer of the COIT is the Secretary of Tribunals. The secretary is the named officer to whom all originating applications must be first presented at the address of the appropriate tribunal offices. At each tribunal office there is a Regional Secretary, who may exercise any of the functions of the Secretary of Tribunals.[8]

There are 11 Regional Chairmen, one at each ROIT, who take charge of the administration of cases by the tribunals in their regions and also hear cases.

In Scotland there is a separate COIT, based at St Andrews House, 141 West Nile Street, Glasgow G1 2RU and three Offices of Industrial Tribunals ('OITs') (see addresses p393). Presiding over the Scottish tribunals is a President appointed by the Lord President of the Court of Session.[9]

The equivalent to the COIT in Northern Ireland is the Office of the Industrial Tribunals and the Fair Employment Tribunal, Long Bridge House, 20–24 Waring Street, Belfast BT1 2EB.

Composition of tribunals

Chairman

A legally qualified chairman presides over the hearing and advises his/her lay colleagues on the tribunal on the relevant law and its application. The chairman must be a barrister (in Scotland, an advocate) or solicitor holding a 'general qualification' (within the meaning of Courts and Legal Services Act 1990 s71, see reg 5(1)(a)) of at least seven years' standing in part of the Supreme Court and the county courts. S/he is appointed by the Lord Chancellor or, in Scotland, by the Lord President. Part-time chairmen are also appointed who undertake to serve at least 30 days each year; in practice, they sit on about one third of all tribunals.

It is the chairman's role to set out the tribunal's decision in any case and give the reasons for that decision. The chairman does not,

7 reg 3(3).
8 reg 13(10).
9 reg 3(1).

however, carry any more weight on the tribunal than his/her colleagues: s/he can be outvoted by the lay members of the tribunal and will then give the majority decision of the lay members and his/her own minority decision. The majority decision is binding.

Tribunal chairmen can, however, make certain decisions alone, either considering the relevant application on the papers or sitting alone with the parties present. The chairman's power to make decisions without lay members present is strictly limited and, subject to the following exceptions, does not extend to making final decisions upon substantive questions of fact or law, or to reviewing a decision of the tribunal.[10]

Chairman sitting alone

In an increasing number of cases the tribunal consists of the chairman without lay members. This is achieved by one of two routes.

1) By r13(8), 'any act' required to be done by a tribunal may be done by a chairman alone except:

   - hearing an originating application;
   - acts incidental to the hearing of an originating application by a full tribunal as implied by rr9 and 10;
   - the review of a tribunal decision under r11; and
   - the ordering of a re-hearing.

   In practice this means that all interlocutory stages (including jurisdiction decisions under r6 about entitlement to bring proceedings) and pre-hearing reviews are conducted by a chairman sitting alone. The powers also include:

   - dismissal of proceedings on withdrawal by the applicant (r13(2)(a));
   - a decision in accordance with the written agreement of the parties (r3(2)(b));
   - striking out of proceedings (r13(2)(d));
   - postponement or adjournment (r13(7)) and extension of time (r15));
   - giving directions (r16);
   - joining and creating representative actions (rr17 and 18).

2) In addition to these general powers, financial constraints have gradually slimmed down the number of cases which must or may be heard by a full tribunal. By ITA 1996 s4 the following

10 r13(8).

proceedings 'shall' be heard by a chairman alone, subject only to the caveat in s4(5) (see below):

- applications for interim relief in trade union membership, health and safety and other cases (Employment Rights Act (ERA) 1996 ss128, 131 and 132 and Trade Unions and Labour Relations (Consolidation) Act 1992 (TULRCA) ss161, 165 and 166);
- applications under the insolvency provisions (ERA 1996 s182);
- complaints relating to unlawful deductions from wages (ERA 1996 s23);
- claims for breach of the contract of employment (ITA 1996 s3);
- proceedings where the complainant has given written notice withdrawing his/her claim;
- proceedings where the parties have given written consent to the case being heard by a chairman alone (even if they subsequently withdraw it);
- proceedings where the respondent no longer contests the case.

These cases are subject to the caveat in ITA 1996 s4(5) that they *may* be heard by a full tribunal following a decision by a chairman sitting alone, who must have regard to:

- the likelihood of a dispute arising on the facts which makes it desirable for the hearing to be in front of a full tribunal;
- whether there is a likelihood of an issue of law arising which would make it desirable for the case to be heard by a chairman alone;
- any views expressed by the parties; and
- whether there are other proceedings concurrently being heard which must be heard by a full tribunal.

As a matter of policy, tribunals regard the statute as requiring chairmen to sit alone in those cases set out in ITA 1996 s4(3), unless a specific *exception* has been made, judicially, by a chairman. There appears to be no requirement to consult the parties, but if they are consulted, their representations must be considered. This might usefully be done at a directions hearing (see p113). The notice of hearing indicates that the case will be heard a chairman alone and if a party wants a hearing by a full tribunal, representations should be made at the time the notice is received.

Although a preliminary point on jurisdiction under r6 can be heard by a chairman sitting alone, considering a preliminary point of law is held to be the hearing of an originating application, or an integral part of it, and so is regulated by ITA 1996 s4, which indicates whether either a chairman sitting alone or a full tribunal is appropriate.

Lay members

As stated above, the chairman of a tribunal usually sits with two lay members, drawn from two panels of people representing employers and employees. Lay members are appointed to serve on tribunals by the Secretary of State after consultation with representative bodies such as the Confederation of British Industry and the Trades Union Congress. They are entitled (and encouraged) to utilise their industrial knowledge and experience in assessing tribunal cases and are seen as forming (together with the chairman) the 'industrial jury'.

If any member (including the chairman) of a tribunal has a personal or financial interest in a particular case, s/he should declare that interest to the parties and should not sit on that case unless all parties consent. All those coming before tribunals should be able to have complete confidence in the independence and integrity of those hearing the case. Any direct interest in the case will automatically exclude a member from sitting.[11] The occasions when the question of bias might arise are considered in more detail in chapter 17, which also sets out guidance for parties who need to raise the question during the course of the hearing.

In these circumstances, or if one of the lay members is absent for any other reason, and the parties both consent, the chairman may sit with just one lay member. While lay members are expected to give fair consideration to all cases whichever panel representing whichever side of employment relations they are drawn from, the whole purpose of the composition of a tribunal is to try and ensure that both perspectives are present. Clearly this is not achieved if the chairman sits with just one lay member. In such circumstances, it is always a party's right to insist that a tribunal is fully constituted.

---

11 *R v Gough* [1993] AC 646, HL (and, in the employment law context, *Greenaway Harrison Ltd v Wiles* [1994] IRLR 380, EAT).

Equal pay and sex and race discrimination claims

There is no requirement that members of a particular sex or ethnic background sit on tribunals considering these cases, nor that any member hearing such a case has any specialised knowledge. In these classes of case, however, selection of the tribunal will generally be made by the ROIT so as to have a representative membership or at least one member with specialised knowledge or training. This is a particular concern in cases involving allegations of race discrimination following the government's undertaking at the time of passing the Race Relations Act 1976 to take steps to appoint persons to the panels of lay members with specialised knowledge or experience of race relations matters. It remains, however, a goal, not a legal requirement.[12]

Tribunal clerks

A tribunal clerk is appointed for each hearing. S/he will introduce him/herself to the representatives or parties and take details of witnesses (their full name, position, which oath or affirmation they will take) and observers, and collect any additional documents and the legal authorities which will be referred to during the course of the hearing. If the applicant has been claiming unemployment benefit, jobseekers' allowance or income support, the clerk will also take details of the benefit office concerned. Any subsequent award of compensation will be notified to that office should the recoupment provisions apply to an award of compensation.[13]

The clerk to the tribunal also sits in at the beginning of most cases to administer the oath/affirmation but tends not to stay throughout. Limited assistance can be sought from tribunal clerks before and during the course of a hearing but their primary function is to assist the tribunal.

Tribunal consultative groups

Most ROITs now have consultative groups which meet about once each legal term and liaise with regular users of tribunals in the

---

12 *Habib v Elkington & Co Ltd* [1981] ICR 435; [1981] IRLR 344, EAT.
13 Employment Protection (Recoupment of Unemployment Benefit and Supplementary Benefit) Regulations SI 1977 No 674, 1980 No 1608 and 1988 No 419; ITA 1996 s16.

relevant area. An adviser with a general query on the practices or procedures in a particular ROIT may find it helpful to contact the appropriate representative on the consultative group (eg, the law centre/CAB representative) to ask him/her to raise the issue. If there appears to be no such representative to approach, advisers should contact the secretary to the relevant ROIT with any query.

CHAPTER 2

Types of claim

Jurisdiction: general

Tribunals are created by statute and have no powers other than those given them by parliament. If a case falls outside a tribunal's jurisdiction, it is not permitted to consider the matter. Even if the parties do not raise the point, the tribunal must always be satisfied that it has the power to hear a particular case before it goes on to do so: '[it] cannot merely by silence confer upon [itself] a jurisdiction which [it does] not have'.[1] Furthermore, even if the point is not taken before the tribunal, lack of jurisdiction can always be raised on review or appeal.

Not all jurisdictional questions are dealt with in this book, as many give rise to questions of substantive law rather than procedure. Reference should be made to other texts (and the relevant Acts) to ensure that a particular applicant has the right to bring a complaint before a tribunal. Where the jurisdictional issue is of a procedural nature it is referred to in this chapter or in chapter 4 on time limits.

On p12 is a list of rights in which legislation provides that industrial tribunals have jurisdiction in England and Wales; there is not room in this book for a complete list for Scotland and Northern Ireland, but the headings are roughly the same, except that Northern Ireland tribunals will have jurisdiction to hear complaints of race discrimination only when legislation is introduced following government commitments made in 1995. In Northern Ireland the Fair Employment Tribunal already has a parallel jurisdiction under the Fair Employment (NI) Acts 1976-89 in cases of religious and political discrimination which does not exist for tribunals in Great Britain.

1 *British Midland Airways v Lewis* [1978] ICR 782, EAT.

Territorial jurisdiction

Tribunals in England and Wales are permitted to hear claims only where:

- any respondent resides or carries on a business in England or Wales; or
- if the claim could have been determined by a county court, the cause of action would have arisen wholly or in part in England or Wales; or
- the proceedings are to determine a question which has been referred to the tribunal by a court in England or Wales.[2]

A company with a registered office in England or Wales is within these territorial limits.[3] A check on the registered address of a company (as required to be notified by Companies Act 1985 s691) can be made by a search of its records at Companies House.

Even if a company has no registered office in England or Wales but the cause of action arises within the jurisdiction, eg, the employee is dismissed in England or Wales, a tribunal will have jurisdiction to hear that claim.

Similar provisions apply to tribunals in Northern Ireland and in Scotland except that there is no reference to county courts and in Scotland jurisdiction also arises if the contract of employment is executed or performed in Scotland.

2 reg 8(3).
3 *Odeco (UK) Inc v Peacham* [1979] ICR 823, EAT.

INDUSTRIAL TRIBUNAL JURISDICTION AND TIME LIMITS

Statutory right	Time limit
Equal Pay Act 1970	
s2: breach of equality clause	6 *whole* months from termination of employment (s2(4))
Health and Safety at Work etc Act 1974	
s24: appeal against improvement or prohibition notice	As specified in the notice (s24(2))*
s80: Safety Representatives and Safety Committee Regulations 1977 SI No 500 reg 11(1): time off with pay for safety representative	3 *whole* months from failure to pay (reg 11(2))
Sex Discrimination Act 1975	
s63: discrimination on the ground of sex or against a married person	3 months (s76(1))**
s68: appeal against non-discrimination notice	6 *whole* weeks from service of notice (s68(1))
s72(2) and s72(4): application by EOC relating to discriminatory advertisement, etc	6 months or 5 years (s76(3))**
s73: preliminary action by EOC relating to persistent discrimination, advertisements, etc	6 months (s76(4))**
s77: complaint that contract, rule, collective agreement is void	none (SDA 1986 s6(4A))

Race Relations Act 1976

s54:	discrimination on the ground of race	3 months (s68(1))**
s59:	appeal against non-discrimination notice	6 *whole* weeks from service of notice (s59(1))
s63(3)(a):	application by CRE relating to discriminatory advertisements, etc	6 months or 5 years (s68(4))**
s64:	preliminary action by CRE relating to persistent discrimination, advertisements, etc	6 months (s68(5))**

Transfer of Undertakings (Protection of Employment) Regulations 1981, as amended 1987 and 1995

reg 11(1):	failure to inform or consult appropriate representatives of employees about transfer of undertaking	3 months (reg 11(8)(a))*
reg 11(5):	failure to pay compensation	3 months of order (reg 11(8)(a))*

Industrial Training Act 1982

s12:	appeal by employer against assessment of industrial training levy	As specified by the relevant levy order

Sex Discrimination Act 1986

s6(4A):	invalidity of discriminatory collective agreements and other rules	6 months (1975 Act ss63, 76(1), (5))**

Trade Union and Labour Relations (Consolidation) Act 1992, as amended 1993 and 1996

s66(1):	union member not to be unjustifiably disciplined	3 months (s66(2))* (and extended where internal appeal)
s67(1) and (2):	compensation for unjustifiable discipline	4 weeks to 6 months from declaration (s67(3))
s68A:	unauthorised or excessive union subscription deducted from wages	3 months (s68A(1))*

INDUSTRIAL TRIBUNAL JURISDICTION AND TIME LIMITS *(contd)*

Statutory right		Time limit
s116(4):	trade union's secret ballot on employers' premises (repealed from 1 April 1996)	3 months (s116(5))*
s137(2):	refusal of employment on ground related to union membership or non-membership	3 months (139(1))*
s138(2):	refusal of service by employment agency on ground related to union membership	3 months (s139(1))*
s146(5):	action short of dismissal relating to union membership and activities	3 months (s147)*
ss152 and 161(1):	interim relief in dismissal cases relating to union membership or non-membership	7 days following termination (s161(2))
s168(4):	time off for union duties	3 whole months (s171)*
s169(5):	time off with pay for union duties	3 whole months (s171)*
s170(4):	union member's time off for union activities	3 months (s171)*
s174(5):	exclusion or expulsion from union	6 months (s175)*
s176(2):	compensation for unlawful exclusion/expulsion	4 weeks to 6 months from declaration (s176(3))
s189(1):	failure to consult or inform employee representative/union/employee on redundancies	Before the date of the last dismissal and 3 months thereafter (s189(5))*
s192(1):	remuneration under protective award	3 months (s192(2))*
s238:	unfair dismissal during certain official industrial action (including maternity or health and safety grounds s238(2A))	6 months (s239(2))*

Pension Schemes Act 1993

Section	Description	Time limit
s11(5)(e):	with Occupational Pension Schemes (Contracting-out) Regulations 1984 SI No 380 (amended by SI No 1323 and SI 1986 No 1716): contracting out	None
s113(1):	with Occupational Pensions Schemes (Disclosure of Information) Regulations 1986, SI No 1046 reg 10: questions whether union is recognised	None

Pensions Act 1995

Section	Description	Time limit
s62:	with Occupational Pension Schemes (Equal Treatment) Regulations 1995 SI No 3183, equal treatment rules in pension schemes for persons of different sex and family or marital status	6 whole months from termination of employment (Equal Pay Act 1970 s2(4) as amended by Pensions Act 1995 s63(4))

Disability Discrimination Act 1995

Section	Description	Time limit
s8:	discrimination/detriment on grounds of disability	3 months** (Sch 3 para 3)

Employment Rights Act 1996

Section	Description	Time limit
s11(1)–(2):	reference of question relating to written statement of particulars of employment (s1) and itemised pay statement (s8)	while employed and for 3 months beginning with termination of employment (s11(4))*
s23:	unlawful deduction from wages	3 months from deduction or last in series (s23(2))*
s34:	guarantee payment	3 months (s34(2))*
s45:	detriment in health and safety/shop workers/betting workers/Sunday trading cases	3 months (s48(3))*
s50:	time off for public duties	3 months (s50(2))*
s52:	time off to look for work or make arrangements for training	3 months (s54(2))*
s55:	time off for ante-natal care	3 months (s57(2))*

INDUSTRIAL TRIBUNAL JURISDICTION AND TIME LIMITS (*contd*)

	Statutory right	Time limit
s64:	remuneration on suspension on medical grounds	⎫
s67:	alternative work on maternity grounds/medical grounds	⎬ 3 months (s70(2))*
		⎭
s92(1):	written statement of reason for dismissal	3 months from EDT (s93, 111)
s94:	unfair dismissal	3 months from EDT (s111)*
s128:	interim relief in dismissal cases relating to certain health and safety issues	7 days after EDT (s128(2))
s163:	reference of question relating to failure by employer to make redundancy payment	6 months (s164)
s170:	reference of question relating to payment equivalent to redundancy rebates in respect of civil servants, etc	None
s182:	payment by Secretary of State on insolvency of employer	3 months (s188(2))*

Industrial Tribunals Act 1996 and Industrial Tribunals (Extension of Jurisdiction Order) 1994

s3 and reg 7:	contract claims	3 months*

Industrial Tribunals Act 1996 and EAT Rules 1993 (and RSC Order 94 r8(3))

s21 and EAT Rules r3(2): appeal to EAT (or High Court)		42 days from promulgation of IT decision

NOTES: Time limit extendable if   EDT = effective date of termination
* 'not reasonably practicable'   The right to consultation and information about collective redundancies and transfers is extended to
** 'just and equitable'   'appropriate representatives' of the employees

CHAPTER 3

Stages before the originating application

The correct respondent

After checking to make sure that the tribunal has jurisdiction to hear the case, the applicant needs to consider who is the correct respondent to name on the originating application. This will generally be the employer but it may also be a fellow employee or other individual, in claims under the Sex Discrimination Acts (SDA) 1975–86 or Race Relations Act (RRA) 1976, or possibly a trade union.

Sometimes it will not be clear who the relevant employer is, eg, in cases arising out of transfer of a business or where there is a complicated arrangement of associated companies. Difficulties in naming the correct respondent may sometimes be resolved by a reply given to a letter before action (p20). If in doubt, the applicant should name all possible respondents and explain the reasons for doing so in the details of the complaint.

Where a purely technical error has been made in the naming of a respondent and no prejudice has been caused, the tribunal may take a pragmatic approach, allowing an amendment late on in the proceedings.[1]

A tribunal is given a broad discretion to join a party to proceedings as a respondent 'at any time',[2] and can do so even after the time limit for presenting a claim against a new respondent has expired.[3] It can also be done after a decision on the merits of the

---

1 *Chapman v Goonvean and Rostowrack China Clay Co Ltd* [1973] ICR 50; [1972] IRLR 124, NIRC.
2 r17(1).
3 *Drinkwater Sabey Ltd v Burnett* [1995] ICR 328; [1995] IRLR 238, EAT, following *Gillick v BP Chemicals Ltd* [1993] IRLR 437, S EAT.

case has been given: in *Linbourne v Constable*[4] the EAT held that an amendment should be allowed to substitute a respondent even after a decision had been given. The guidelines to be taken into consideration by the tribunal in such cases were set out by the NIRC in *Cocking v Sandhurst (Stationers) Ltd:*[5]

- Did the unamended application comply with the rules relating to the presentation of originating applications (see p35) and was it presented within the relevant time limit? If not, there is no power to amend and a new originating application must be presented within the relevant time limit.
- If it did comply with the rules on presentation, the tribunal has a discretion to allow an amendment which would add or substitute a new party. It should do so only if satisfied that the mistake sought to be corrected was a genuine mistake and was not misleading or such as to cause reasonable doubt as to the identity of the person intending to claim or, as the case may be, to be claimed against.
- In deciding whether or not to exercise its discretion, the tribunal should have regard to all the circumstances of the case, including any injustice or hardship which may be caused to any of the parties or potential parties if the amendment were allowed or refused. If allowing the amendment might cause unnecessary additional cost to one party, the tribunal might properly conclude that this was an appropriate case for the amending party to be ordered to pay the additional costs caused by the late amendment (see p177 on costs).

When an amendment is allowed after a decision has been given, as in the *Linbourne* case (above), the tribunal will give the new respondent an opportunity to be heard on the merits of the case unless there would be no prejudice by not doing so.

Unincorporated associations

One word of warning: proceedings must be commenced against some legal 'person' or body, whether that 'person' is an individual, a collection of individuals or a company. If the employer is an unincorporated association, the claim cannot be made against the association in the abstract, as it is not a legal body. The correct respondent in these cases is the individual or individuals with

4 [1993] ICR 698.
5 [1974] ICR 650.

effective day-to-day control of the association, often the chairman or members of the management or executive committee.[6]

Insolvent employers

As with court proceedings, tribunal proceedings may be commenced or continued against a company in administration only with the leave of the High Court or the administrator.[7] The administrator is an interested party and may be joined to the proceedings. However, failure to obtain the leave of the court does not make the originating application a nullity. The proper course is for the tribunal to stay (*sist*, in Scotland) the proceedings while the leave of the court is obtained.[8] It is highly likely that a similar approach would be taken where the company is in compulsory liquidation under Insolvency Act 1986 s130(2).

If the administrator adopts the contracts of employment of a company's employees, s/he will be liable to be sued personally, so leave of the court is not required. The Insolvency Act 1986 ss19, 44 were amended by the Insovency Act 1994 with effect from 15 March 1994 to limit the responsibilities of administrators, which in *Powdrill v Watson*[9] had been held to be unlimited once the administrator adopts or is deemed to adopt a contract of employment.

If one of the parties is bankrupt, the trustee in bankruptcy will have a clear interest in the outcome of the proceedings and would be entitled to apply to be joined as a party.

In these cases a directions hearing (p113) may assist in clarifying the position of the insolvent party and the interests of others who may wish to be joined in the proceedings.

The Secretary of State is likely to be interested in most claims against insolvent employers, since there is likely to be a payment out of the National Insurance Fund under ERA 1996 s182. The tribunal will notify the department of these claims and the Secretary of State may be joined as a party.

---

6 *Bradley Egg Farm v Clifford* [1943] 2 All ER 378.
7 Insovency Act 1986 s11(3), applied in *Carr v British International Helicopters Ltd (in administration)* [1994] ICR 18, S EAT.
8 *Carr*, above.
9 [1995] 2 AC 394; [1995] ICR 1100; [1995] IRLR 269, HL, confirming [1994] ICR 395, CA (the Paramount Airways case).

Letter before action

Whilst applicants are under no obligation to notify their employers of a claim before presenting it to a tribunal, a letter before action can serve to resolve some of the issues between the prospective parties before tribunal proceedings are commenced and may even render such proceedings unnecessary if the employer makes the payment or takes the action sought by the employee. If there is no risk of time limits being missed, it is generally worth writing a letter notifying the prospective respondent of the complaint which may be made.

This is particularly helpful where the employee is unsure as to the precise identity of the employer. If, subsequently, an application has to be made to change the name of the respondent after tribunal proceedings have been commenced (p17), the fact that the first named respondent took no steps to correct the mistake on receipt of the letter before action, or that the correct respondent had already been put on notice by such a letter, will assist the employee making the application.

The letter before action should set out the broad nature of the complaint and indicate that the writer will commence proceedings in the tribunal unless steps are taken to remedy the situation within a specified period of time. Obviously, a prospective applicant should have in mind at this stage what s/he hopes to get out of the proceedings and the limitations on tribunals' remedies. The letter should be 'open': it should express the full claim and not deal with proposals for settling the claim as a form of compromise. Such proposals, if made, should be contained in separate correspondence, specifically marked 'without prejudice'.

It is not necessary to go into much detail at this stage and it would be unwise to do so without full instructions and advice. Be warned: respondents will often seek to cross-examine on the basis of any inconsistencies, however slight, between correspondence before action and the case as stated in the course of the proceedings. On the other hand, if the applicant is confident that a full account can be given at this stage, the fact it has been given even before proceedings are commenced can make the case easier to sustain subsequently in the tribunal. This is especially true in constructive dismissal and discrimination cases, where the applicant's contemporary perception of events and feelings is very important.

Further, if there is no reasonable defence to the complaint and the case is one where there is a real chance of the applicant obtaining an order for costs against the respondent (p115), the fact that the nature of the complaint and the relief sought has been detailed prior to the commencement of tribunal proceedings will be a relevant factor in any application for costs against a respondent who failed to take that opportunity to resolve the matter.

Questionnaires

In race and sex discrimination cases, information can be requested of an employer or other respondent by use of a questionnaire *before* any claim is presented to a tribunal: SDA 1975 s74(1) and RRA 1976 s65(1).

The questionnaire enables a prospective applicant to find out background information which may assist the claim, for example, the relative numbers of men and women or the racial background of employees in each grade within the workplace; and to question the prospective respondent on the reasons for the action which has led to the grievance. It may also lead to the provision of relevant statistical evidence, even if the employer has to create documentation in order to provide such information. As a respondent cannot otherwise be ordered to create documents not already in existence, this is an unusual and potentially very useful procedure.

Copies of the prescribed forms for the questionnaire and reply are set out at Appendix 1.16, p259. Chapter 8 deals with the procedure.

Questionnaires are not available for use in Equal Pay Act cases but it is always possible to draft a question which arguably relates to the SDA even if the claim is about pay.

Financing a case and costs implications

Legal aid is not available for representation at tribunals.[10] A prospective applicant may, however, be eligible to receive legal assistance (which may include representation) from the following sources:

- a trade union or professional association;
- in sex discrimination or equal pay cases, the Equal Opportunities Commission (EOC);
- in race discrimination cases, the Commission for Racial Equality (CRE);

---

10 1996 proposals do not include this; see pxxxvii.

- in cases against trade unions, from the Commisioner for the Rights of Trade Union Members (CROTUM);
- law centres or CABx;
- solicitors under the legal aid green form scheme[11] (for advice and all steps other than actual representation);
- under an insurance scheme – increasingly a feature of many household insurance policies;
- ACAS (basic, non-partisan advice only).

Respondents may also be eligible for assistance from the above sources, although company respondents are less likely to be in need of financial assistance in obtaining legal advice or representation. Respondents who are members of particular trade associations may be entitled to free advice and representation under the terms of their membership.

Both lay and professional advisers may also refer appropriate cases to the EOC or CRE or act as a referral agency to the Free Representation Unit (FRU), which may be able to provide preliminary advice and representation at the hearing. Addresses for some of the above organisations are set out at Appendix 4.

Although anyone can appear at an tribunal, it stands to reason that the more and the better informed the advice and assistance that a party receives before or during the hearing, the better prepared s/he is likely to be.

The successful party in a tribunal case is, however, unlikely to be able to reclaim from the other side any legal costs incurred in fighting the proceedings. The general rule in tribunals is that costs will not be awarded unless a party has acted frivolously, vexatiously, abusively, disruptively or otherwise unreasonably.[12] If one party believes that there may be a good argument for obtaining costs against the other, it is worth bringing this to the other side's attention in writing before making the application. If the other side continues to act in the same frivolous, vexatious or unreasonable manner, the letter will assist any application to the tribunal for costs. On the other hand, letters threatening applications for costs in tribunals are often made where there is really no ground for such an application. The recipient of such a letter should consider its contents seriously and take further advice if necessary, but should not be deterred from bringing or defending a claim by a groundless threat.

11 Pink in Scotland.
12 r12(1).

The subject of costs orders is dealt with in more detail in chapter 19 p176.

CHECKLIST: PRE-ACTION CONSIDERATIONS

- Is the applicant eligible for legal aid green form assistance or any other financial aid in respect of the claim?
- Do questions of sex or race discrimination arise or of equal pay where advice and assistance might be obtained from the EOC or CRE?
- Is the complaint one which a tribunal can properly hear or should it be brought in the county court or some other court or tribunal?
- Does the tribunal have the appropriate territorial jurisdiction?
- Does the applicant meet the other jurisdictional conditions in relation to pursuing a particular claim in a tribunal?
- Is the correct respondent named?
- Are any of the parties insolvent?
- Has a letter before action been sent to give the respondent the opportunity of meeting the claim without the necessity of tribunal proceedings?
- In cases under SDA 1975 and RRA 1976, has the appropriate questionnaire been served?

Time limits

General principles

The table on p12 sets out the time limits applicable to the inititation of all of the 50-odd statutory claims which may be made before a tribunal. Different considerations apply to time limits for presenting a notice of appearance, which are less strict, and for complying with interlocutory orders. There are three general principles:

1) There is a time limit for most statutory claims.
2) Most statutory claims are subject to an escape clause allowing the claim to be presented within a further time limit by the exercise of the tribunal's discretion.
3) All time limits operate according to rigid rules based on a determination of the precise relevant date. These time limits are matters of jurisdiction, and not of discretion or procedure.

Time limits in general

Almost all statutory rights are subject to a time limit, but the following require particular attention:

1) Reference under ERA 1996 s163 of a question relating to a failure by an employer to make a redundancy payment. The reference is to the Secretary of State, who may make a payment out of the National Insurance Fund. There is no time limit on this reference by a former employee.
2) Reference of a question relating to payment of the equivalent of a redundancy payment to civil servants and other public office holders, under ERA 1996 s171. These are subject to the normal contractual limitation period of six years (Limitation Act 1980

s5). This is because the claim arises not under statute but under contract and the mechanism for resolving this particular contractual issue is reference of a question to the tribunal.

3) A complaint under SDA 1975 s77(1) and SDA 1986 s6(4A) that a term in a contract, or a rule, or a collective agreement is void on the grounds that it is discriminatory. No time limit is prescribed.

4) Claims where European Union law affects United Kingdom claims. This subject must be regarded as unclear until after appeals have been heard in *Biggs* and *Ex parte Seymour-Smith* (below), but a brief summary appears to be as follows.

- Claims based directly on the Treaty of Rome, eg, article 119 (equal pay) and article 148 (free movement of workers), are not subject to any specific time limit under the Treaty. The European Court has held that such matters are for the member states' own jurisdictions to apply as matters of procedure.[1] This was followed in relation to time limits for enforcing claims under a directive which was intended to be directly effective (ie, not the Treaty itself) in *Emmott v Minister for Social Welfare*,[2] a case from the Irish Republic where the ECJ held:

In the absence of Community rules on the subject, it is for the domestic legal system of each member state to determine the procedural conditions governing actions at law intended to ensure the protection of the rights which individuals derive from the direct effect of Community law, provided that such conditions are not less favourable than those relating to similar actions of a domestic nature nor framed so as to render virtually impossible the exercise of rights conferred by community law. (See para 16 of the judgment).

- In *Livingstone v Hepworth Refractories plc*[3] it was held that analogous time limits to those in domestic procedures should be applied to claims under article 119. In that case a time limit of three months was appropriate for a sex discrimination claim under article 119 as that is the time provided by the SDA 1975.

- In *Biggs v Somerset County Council*[4] the Court of Appeal held

---

1 *Rewe-Zentralfinanz eG and Rewe-Zentral AG v Landswirtschaftskammer für das Saarland* (No 33/76) [1976] ECR 1989, [1977] CMLR 533, ECJ.
2 [1993] ICR 8; [1991] IRLR 387, ECJ.
3 [1992] ICR 287; [1992] IRLR 63, EAT.
4 [1996] IRLR 203, CA.

that rights under the Treaty are not justiciable as free-standing claims in tribunals. Tribunals have jurisdiction only when given it by statute. Although they must apply EU law in the application and enforcement of domestic law, and even dis-apply domestic law inconsistent with it, they cannot hear cases founded solely on directly effective European provisions. The claim was made by a woman part-time teacher dismissed in 1976 who thought she must have a claim for unfair dismissal once she read of the judgment of the House of Lords in *R v Secretary of State for Employment ex p EOC*.[5] She argued that the exclusion of part-timers from the right to claim unfair dismissal was discriminatory (as had been held in that case) and that she should be entitled to bring a claim within three months of the Lords' judgment.

The Court of Appeal held that this was a matter of domestic law and procedure, as unfair dismissal was not within the Treaty, nor had the Equal Treatment Directive (EEC/76/107) then (1976) become operative. There was no free-standing right of unfair dismissal in EU law which could be taken before a tribunal. Further, it was possible for the applicant to have lodged a claim of unfair dismissal in 1976 and fought the battle then.

In the light of the acceptance at many judicial levels of an individual's right to commence proceedings in the tribunal this judgment is surprising. In view of this difficulty, as a safe rule three months should be considered the appropriate limitation from the date of the relevant act by the employer. Where unfair dismissal is claimed, this might start to run from the date of dismissal or from the date of a significant court decision, eg, the date of any ruling in the House of Lords in *Biggs* or *ex p Seymour-Smith*.

It is also submitted that the Court of Appeal was wrong to dismiss the right of individuals to bring claims in the tribunal based on EU law. Since the domestic procedures must not make it more difficult for individuals to enforce European rights than similar rights in domestic law, it cannot be right for an individual to have to use the courts rather than the more accessible tribunals for such enforcement.

– If there is a right to bring a claim under directly effective EU provisions, the same principles apply to claims brought under relevant directives, eg, the Equal Treatment Directive, as to claims directly under the Treaty of Rome, with the exception that time runs only from the date when a directive is properly and fully transposed into United Kingdom law: *Emmott* (above).

– For claims based on the Treaty the date appears to run from 'the date upon which it could reasonably be said to be clear to any person affected . . . that such a claim could properly be made'.[6] One interpretation is to make time run for equality of redundancy pay (and arguably pensions) from the date of the judgment of the European Court in *Barber v Guardian Royal Exchange Assurance Group*.[7] This seems to treat judgments of the European Court in a different way from judgments of the High Court in the UK, where the principle is maintained that judgments of, for example, the House of Lords do not change the law, but simply make clear what the law always was.

– It is always necessary to apply domestic legislation with its own time limit and other procedural restrictions to cases where there is no directly effective EU right. According to the Court of Appeal, the existence of a statutory bar is not a good reason for contending that it was not reasonably practicable to present a claim, or that it is just and equitable to extend time.[8]

Time limits and escape clauses

Most of the time limits are softened by words such as those relating to unfair dismissal complaints (ERA 1996 s94), which introduce a secondary time limit (see s111(2)):

. . . an industrial tribunal shall not consider a complaint . . . unless it is presented to the tribunal –
(a) before the end of the period of three months beginning with the effective date of termination, or

6 See *Rankin v British Coal Corporation* [1995] ICR 774; [1993] IRLR 69.
7 [1990] ICR 616; [1990] IRLR 240.
8 See *Biggs v Somerset County Council* (above) (unfair dismissal claim refused to part-time worker 18 years late), *R v Secretary of State for Employment ex p EOC* [1994] ICR 317; [1994] IRLR 176, HL (the part-time workers' case), and *R v Secretary of State for Employment ex p Seymour-Smith and Perez* [1995] ICR 889; [1995] IRLR 464, CA, leave given to appeal to HL.

(b) within such further period as the tribunal considers reasonable in a case where it is satisfied that it was not reasonably practicable for a complaint to be presented before the end of the period of three months.

A different formulation applies in relation, for example, to complaints of disability, race and sex discrimination:

A court or tribunal may nevertheless consider any such complaint . . . which is out of time if, in all the circumstances of the case, it considers that it is just and equitable to do so. (SDA 1975 s76(5), RRA 1976 s68(6), DDA 1995 Sch 3 para 3).

These latter claims have only one limitation period. Claims which are subject to an escape clause carry with them their own limitation periods, each of which is capable of shutting out an applicant.

Provisions which do not give the tribunal any flexibility are:

1) Claims under the Equal Pay Act 1970 s2(4).
2) A claim for time off with pay for a safety representative: Health and Safety at Work Act 1974 s80 and Safety Representative etc Regulations 1977 reg 11(2).
3) Appeals against non-discrimination notices under SDA 1975 s68 and RRA 1976 s59.
4) An application for interim relief (TULRCA 1992 s161(2) and ERA 1996 s128).
5) Complaints by union members for a declaration following findings of unjustifiable discipline (TULRCA 1992 s66(3)) and expulsion/exclusion (TULRCA 1992 s176(3)).
6) Applications for compensation following findings of unjustifiable discipline or unlawful expulsion/exclusion from a trade union (TULRCA 1992 ss67, 174).

Jurisdiction

Almost all of the statutory rights which are subject to a time limit are affected by a jurisdictional bar. Tribunals have no jurisdiction to hear a case brought outside the time limit.[9] This means that the parties cannot waive a time limit, eg, by agreeing to have the case heard even though a complaint was not made within time. It also means that the tribunal itself can and should take the point if it is

9 *Biggs v Somerset* CC [1996] IRLR 203; [1996] ICR 364, CA.

aware of it.[10] Further, a new point relating to jurisdiction may be taken on appeal to the EAT even though not raised at the tribunal.[11] The vast majority of statutory rights are qualified by words such as 'an industrial tribunal shall not consider a complaint . . . unless it is presented . . .' within the appropriate period.[12]

A similar bar in different words appears in the Equal Pay Act 1970 s2(4) and ERA 1996 s11(4) (claims for written particulars). Although the NIRC in *Grimes v Sutton London Borough Council*[13] felt the latter provision was not jurisdictional, the better view, it is submitted, is now found in *Rogers* (above) and *Secretary of State for Employment v Atkins Auto Laundries Ltd*,[14] which related to the comparable provision on redundancy pay now in ERA 1996 s164(3).

Time limits, therefore, are rigid and jurisdictional.

When does time start running?

All the statutory rights depend on the identification of a relevant event from which time begins to run. Once that date is clear, the rules relating to the counting of time can be applied.

Unfair dismissal

Time runs from the effective date of termination (EDT) as defined in ERA 1996 s97(1). A specific exception is provided by ERA s104(3) so that an applicant can present a claim after notice has been given but before the EDT. The same goes for an applicant claiming constructive dismissal under ERA 1996 s95(1)(c) who, instead of terminating summarily (as s/he would be entitled to do), gives notice and between the giving of notice and the EDT lodges a complaint.[15]

Since the termination of a fixed term contract on its due date is not a termination by notice, a complaint presented before the due

---

10 *Rogers v Bodfari (Transport) Ltd* [1973] ICR 325; [1973] IRLR 172, NIRC and *Dedman v British Building and Engineering Appliances Ltd* [1974] ICR 53; [1973] IRLR 379, CA.
11 *House v Emerson Electric Industrial Controls* [1980] ICR 795, EAT.
12 ERA 1996 s104(2) (on unfair dismissal).
13 [1973] ICR 240.
14 [1972] ICR 76, NIRC
15 *Presley v Llanelli Borough Council* [1979] ICR 419; [1979] IRLR 381, EAT.

date does not fall within the exception in ERA 1996 s97(4).[16] If you know the contract is not going to be renewed, you must wait until after it has expired before presenting a claim.

Redundancy pay

A claim for redundancy pay must be made within six months of the 'relevant date'. This is defined by ERA 1996 s145 and is a slightly expanded version of that applying to unfair dismissal under s97(1). A claim is in time if within the six months counting the EDT:[17]

- a redundancy payment has been agreed and paid;
- the employee has made a claim in writing to the employer for redundancy pay;
- a question has been referred to a tribunal by originating application; or
- an unfair dismissal complaint has been presented in time, ie, within three months.

This means that the applicant need not present a claim to the tribunal but can stop time running by writing to the employer and claiming redundancy pay.

Extension of time can be granted by the tribunal if during a *further* limitation period of six months the employee does the second, third or fourth things above *and* the tribunal considers it just and equitable in all the circumstances to allow the complaint to go ahead, having regard to the reason for the failure to take any of the above steps in the original six-month limitation period.

Equal pay

Claims under the Equal Pay Act 1970 s2 for breach of an equality clause should be brought during the existence of the contract, or within six months of the employee leaving: s2(4).

There are, however, conflicting authorities on this point.[18] They deal with the meaning of 'the reference' of a question under s2(4).

---

16 *Throsby v Imperial College of Science and Technology* [1978] ICR 357; [1977] IRLR 337, EAT.
17 ERA 1996 s164.
18 *British Railways Board v Paul* [1988] IRLR 20, EAT (Sir Ralph Kilner Brown); *Etherson v Strathclyde Regional Council* [1992] ICR 579; [1992] IRLR 392, S EAT (Lord Coulsfield).

Etherson decided that there is a six-month limit. It is submitted that this is the correct view. As a matter of construction, the term 'refer' in s2(4) is wide. And by the doctrine in *Colchester Estates (Cardiff) v Carlton Industries plc*,[19] *Etherson* should be followed, since it dealt fully with the arguments and decided not to follow the earlier decision.

Written particulars

Claims under ERA 1996 s11(4) seeking written particulars of contractual terms, or an itemised pay statement, must be brought during the existence of the contract or within three months of the employee leaving.

Interim relief

Claims for interim relief in cases of dismissal on the grounds of trade union activity or membership, or health and safety complaints (ERA 1996 ss100 and 128; TULRCA 1992 ss152, 161) must be brought at any time up to seven days after the EDT. A claim can be brought *before* the EDT, and the period of seven days runs from the day *after* the EDT, so a dismissal with or without notice taking effect on a Tuesday would require presentation of a claim by the end of the following Tuesday.

None of these claims attracts an escape clause giving the tribunal discretion to extend the deadline.

Discrimination

Special time limits apply to bringing discrimination claims. These are generally where the act complained of extends over a period of time. Time runs from the date of the act complained of. But 'any act extending over a period shall be treated as done at the end of that period' (SDA 1975 s 76(6)(b) and RRA 1976 s68(7)(b)). Discrimination against someone on the grounds of raising health and safety issues is actionable within thre months of the act complained of, or '. . . where that act . . . is part of a series of acts . . . the last of them' (EPCA 1978 s46(3)(a)). A similar provision applies in respect of action short of dismissal on trade union grounds (TULRCA 1992 s147(a)).

---

19 [1984] 3 WLR 693 (where there are two conflicting decisions of equal authority, the later is to be preferred if it gave full consideration to the earlier).

When a contractual term is unlawful by way of discrimination, it is treated as extending throughout the duration of the contract (SDA 1975 s76(6)(b) and RRA 1976 s68(7)(a)). Where discrimination arises in respect of other matters than terms of the contract, it continues throughout the duration of the regime in which the discrimination is carried on. In *Barclays Bank plc v Kapur*[20] Asian workers, formerly employed by the bank in East Africa, who joined the bank's pension scheme in England in 1970 were denied recognition of their previous service in Africa, arguably on discriminatory grounds. This was held not to be a one-off act of discrimination but a continuing regime providing unfavourable pension rights as long as the employees remained in employment (although, having succeded in the preliminary procedure, the employees lost at the hearing of the substantive claim).[21] Similarly, a failure to take proper remedial action following an act of discrimination has a continuing effect until that remedial action is taken.[22] The critical distinction is between a single act such as a decision on grading, and a general regime which has a continuing discriminatory effect.[23]

For deliberate omissions which are claimed to be discriminatory, time runs from the date on which a 'decision' is taken 'at a time and in circumstances when [the employer] was in a position to implement that decision'. So when a car dealership seeking to take over the assets of a dealership which went into receivership interviewed but refused to appoint male car salesmen, allegedly on discriminatory grounds, it made the 'decision' not at the time of the interview but at the time of the takeover when it was in a position to implement the decision.[24] But where the discrimination takes the form of *dismissal*, the time limit runs from the date of the expiry of the notice (if given) and not the date of the decision to dismiss or the giving of the notice.[25]

Even if acts outside the three-month period do not constitute part

---

20 [1991] ICR 208; [1991] IRLR 136, HL.
21 [1995] IRLR 87, CA.
22 *Littlewoods Organisation plc v Traynor* [1993] IRLR 154, EAT.
23 *Sougrin v Haringey Health Authority* [1991] ICR 791; [1991] IRLR 447, EAT; *Owusu v London Fire and Civil Defence Authority* [1995] IRLR 574, EAT. See also *Lindsay v Ironsides, Ray and Vials* [1994] ICR 384; [1994] IRLR 318, EAT: preliminary issue should be tried as to whether a single discriminatory act is out of time.
24 *Swithland Motors plc v Clarke* [1994] ICR 231; 1994 IRLR 275, EAT.
25 *Lupeti v Wrens Old House Ltd* [1984] ICR 348, EAT.

of a series of discriminatory acts or a continuing regime, they may nevertheless be adduced as evidence of discrimination occurring within the time limit.[26] Similarly, acts probative of discrimination occurring *after* the presentation of a valid claim may also be adduced.[27]

Wages protection and Sunday trading cases

Claims relating to unlawful deductions from wages in respect of a series of deductions must be made within three months of the *last* deduction (ERA 1996 s23 (2) and (3)).

Claims of detrimental treatment for refusing to do Sunday shop work following a series of acts must be brought within three months of the *last* of them (ERA 1996 s45(1)).

The rules on counting time

Having identified the date of the relevant event which triggers a claim, complaint, application or appeal to a tribunal, by reference to the appropriate statute, one can determine the time limit for presentation of the originating application. The rules for calculating time were comprehensively summarised in *Pruden v Cunard Eller-man Ltd.*[28] Following citation of relevant authorities and reference to the Interpretation Act 1978, Wood J said:

> Where time is specified to run from a particular date, the word 'date' means the whole of the period of 24 hours from midnight to midnight, and the law takes no account of a fraction of a day unless special reasons require it. . . . Where a complaint is required to be presented within a specific period – 'from', 'after' or 'of' – a particular date, that date is to be excluded from the calculation. . . . However, where a complaint is required to be presented within a specified period beginning with 'a particular date' that date is to be *included* in the calculation. . . . Those principles are well established. (at para 6)

An expanded analysis appears in RSC Order 3 rr1, 2, 4 and the accompanying notes. In the table on p12 the expression 'whole' weeks or months refers to time periods which begin from, after or

---

26 *Eke v Commissioners of Customs and Excise* [1981] IRLR 344, EAT.
27 *Chattopadyhyay v Headmaster of Holloway School* [1982] ICR 132, [1981] IRLR 487, EAT.
28 [1993] IRLR 317, EAT. See also *RJB Mining (UK) Ltd v NUM* [1995] IRLR 556, CA.

of a particular date. For example, a dismissal for trade union activities occurring on a Tuesday triggers a limitation period of seven whole days so that an originating application must be presented on or before the following Tuesday. A claim for equal pay by a woman who left her job on 15 June must be presented on or before 15 December.

However, most claims under employment protection legislation must be brought 'before the end of the period of three months beginning with [the relevant event]', eg, unfair dismissal, a claim for which must be brought within the period of three months beginning with the effective date of termination. In such a case a claim for a dismissal arising on 15 June must be presented on or before 14 September. The date of the relevant event, in this case dismissal, is day 1 of the limitation period.

The EAT in *Pruden* (above) resolved the problem which arises when the trigger event is the last day of a month, because months consist of different numbers of days, ie, 28, 29, 30 or 31. Only four months have the same number of days as the corresponding month three months later (May, June, July, October). For all other months, the approach in *Pruden* will produce the correct answer. In that case, an originating application presented on 30 November in respect of a dismissal on 31 August was within time. If there is no corresponding date in the month in which limitation occurs, take the next earlier date. So a dismissal on 30 November must generate an originating application by 28 February in the succeeding year (or 29 February in a leap year).

The only slight surprise in applying these rules is that a dismissal on the last day of the month of February (ie, 28) must generate an originating application on 27 May, which is, of course, four days before the end of the month. However, a dismissal on the next day, 1 March, must generate an originating application by 31 May, four days later.

Commencement of proceedings

Time ceases to run when proceedings are properly commenced. By r1(1), proceedings 'shall be instituted by the applicant presenting to the Secretary an originating application . . .' (although some proceedings are commenced by an *appellant* with a notice of appeal, eg, those under the Health and Safety at Work Act (HSWA) 1974). Presentation is a unilateral act. It does not require any response by the tribunal office.[29] As long as the originating application is physically delivered to the relevant office before midnight at the end of the last day in the limitation period, the application is validly presented. So if a letter box is available at the office, posting through it will be effective presentation. If there is no provision for postal delivery through a letter box at the relevant office, service can be effected on the next available date when the office is open.[30]

Presentation must be made to 'the Secretary'. This means the Secretary of the Tribunals in England and Wales at Bury St Edmunds and in Scotland at Glasgow. The regulations provide for regional offices with regional secretaries who are established 'under the Office of the Tribunals for an area specified by the President' of the Tribunals.[31] Presentation at a regional office is valid and there seems to be no reason why this definition should not extend also to sub-offices within a region, eg, Stratford, part of London North Region.

Presentation may be effected by fax. In such a case the IT1 expressly discourages following this up with a hard copy, but it would be prudent to do so with a covering letter as soon as practicable. There is of course always a risk that there may be a fax transmission problem, or some simple practical problem such as lack of paper, which means that the fax is not 'presented' at the tribunal. Arguably, a claim is validly presented if it is transmitted and stored electronically at the tribunal awaiting paper and printout.

If it is impossible to 'present' the originating application within the timescale, for example because there is no letter box at the tribunal office available for use when the office is closed, as on a week-end, or possibly where a fax machine malfunctions, *either* the deadline is extended until the next working day *or* it would be possible to argue that it was not 'reasonably practicable' to present the claim on time and to make use of the secondary limitation period (see below).

Extending the deadline

Extensions of time can be granted in the two categories of case cited on p28. For those situations where power is given to the tribunal to

29 *Hetton Victory Club Ltd v Swainstone* [1983] ICR 341; [1983] IRLR 164, CA.
30 *Ford v Stakis Hotels and Inns Ltd* [1987] ICR 943; [1988] IRLR 46, EAT.
31 reg 2(1).

extend the deadline on the grounds that 'it was not reasonably practicable' to present the claim on time, a *further* limitation period applies which is itself subject to legal constraint. So, for unfair dismissal, the tribunal must make a finding in relation to the limitation period that it was not reasonably practicable to present the claim on time, and then go on to consider whether the claim was presented 'within such further period as the tribunal considers reasonable . . .' (ERA 1996 s111(2)).

Failure to meet the deadline: 'not reasonably practicable'

The limitation period may be extended by reason of an 'escape clause'. The following general principles were laid down in *Walls Meat Co Ltd v Khan:*[32]

> The performance of an act . . . is not reasonably practicable if there is some impediment which reasonably prevents, or interferes with, or inhibits, such performance. The impediment may be physical, for instance the illness of the complainant or a postal strike; or the impediment may be mental, namely, the state of mind of the complainant in the form of ignorance of, or mistaken belief with regard to, essential matters. Such states of mind can, however, only be regarded as impediments making it not reasonably practicable to present a complaint within the period of three months, if the ignorance on the one hand or the mistaken belief on the other, is itself reasonable. Either state of mind will, further, not be reasonable if it arises from the fault of the complainant in not making such enquiries as he should reasonably in all the circumstances have made, or from the fault of his solicitors or other professional advisers . . . .

Each of these triggers for the operation of the escape clause is considered below.

Onus of proof
Since the issue relates to jurisdiction, it is for the applicant to prove the facts necessary for establishing jurisdiction and for establishing it was not reasonably practicable to comply with the deadline.[33]

Physical inability
Physical illness and mental depression may well make it not reasonably practicable for the applicant to make a claim in time. But if the

---

32 [1979] ICR 52; [1978] IRLR 499, CA per Brandon LJ at ICR p60.
33 *Porter v Bandridge Ltd* [1978] ICR 943; [1978] IRLR 271, followed in *Walls Meat v Khan* (above): '. . . the burden of proof being on the employee . . .'.

applicant is in touch with an adviser, it seems the applicant will be assumed to have passed the responsibility for ensuring the necessary steps are taken to the adviser and may not rely on his/her own incapacity.

Postal delays

If the originating application is correctly addressed but is either lost or delayed in the post, it may not be reasonably practicable to have presented it on time. Evidence must be produced by the applicant or his/her adviser to show that the originating application was posted and was correctly addressed. Evidence can be brought to show that a letter posted first class one day will be delivered to the same town the next. But in *St Basil's Centre v McCrossan*[34] it was suggested that the timescale set out in the practice direction applying in the High Court for the service of documents[35] should apply. This says that in the normal course of post documents are deemed to have been served (a) in the case of first class mail, on the second working day after posting and (b) in the case of second class mail, on the fourth working day after posting.

This is a slightly odd approach to the meaning of 'practicable' and is more akin to 'feasible', the equivalent meaning attached to it by the Court of Appeal in *Palmer v Southend-on-Sea Borough Council*.[36] It is likely that the timescale specified in the practice direction will be held to be 'reasonable' as an expectation by the applicant and her advisers. A shorter period may also be reasonable in the circumstances. What is unlikely to be reasonable, however, is a delay between the preparation of the originating application and its being taken to the post. A postal delay may excuse the presentation of the application within time, but will not excuse a failure to take the prepared originating application to the post, since it cannot be said that it was 'not reasonably practicable' to present the claim within time. The lesson is: don't delay.

Objective circumstances which might provide justification for the escape clause may be affected by the applicant's actions during that time so as to defeat the escape clause. In *Capital Foods Retail Ltd v Corrigan*[37] the EAT held that part and parcel of the reasonableness of the applicant complying with the deadline is a duty to follow up

34 [1992] ICR 140; [1991] IRLR 455, EAT.
35 [1985] 1 All ER 889.
36 [1984] ICR 372; [1984] IRLR 119, CA.
37 [1993] IRLR 430.

the presentation of a complaint which has been unacknowledged. Rule 2(1) requires the tribunal office to notify the parties (including the applicant) of the case number and address for further communications 'upon receiving an originating application'. Failure to do anything about an unacknowledged originating application may jeopardise the escape clause in the limitation period. In other words, if you post an originating application which ought to arrive with one month to spare, hear nothing for two weeks and yet do nothing further until after the deadline, you cannot complain that it was not 'reasonably practicable' to present the claim on time, since with due diligence the failure to acknowledge could have been investigated and a new claim presented within time.

Ignorance of rights and facts

This comes within the category of 'mental impediment – namely the state of mind of the complainant' as Brandon LJ put it:[38]

> . . . if . . . an employee was reasonably ignorant of either (a) his right to make a complaint for unfair dismissal at all, or (b) how to make it, or (c) that it was necessary for him to make it within a period of three months from the date of dismissal, an industrial tribunal could and should be satisfied that it was not reasonably practicable for his complaint to be presented within the period concerned.

In *Walls Meat* itself, the applicant was under the impression that his claim for unfair dismissal was being handled by the tribunal adjudicating his claim for unemployment benefit. His mistake was held to be reasonable. The escape clause will be more readily available to someone who was totally ignorant of all these factors, than to someone who knew of the right to claim unfair dismissal but was unclear as to how and when to exercise it. In the latter case, the applicant would be on notice and would find it more difficult to make out the justification for a late claim.

In assessing the reasonableness of the applicant's belief, the tribunal will find such a claim more difficult to accept if it comes from a highly articulate applicant. In *Avon County Council v Haywood-Hicks*[39] it was held that an intelligent and well educated applicant ought to have investigated his rights within the time limit. Clearly, since compensation for unfair dismissal has been in existence since 1971, it will be increasingly difficult to claim ignorance of the right to claim and of the need to seek advice.

---

38 *Walls Meat v Khan* (p36 above) at 61.
39 [1978] ICR 646; [IRLR] 118, EAT.

To ignorance of rights can be added an extra category: ignorance of a material fact. In *Machine Tool Industry Research Association v Simpson*[40] an employee accepted her redundancy but after the deadline for claiming unfair dismissal had expired discovered some facts which led her to believe she had not been dismissed for redundancy and claimed unfair dismissal. Her claim was allowed to proceed. Purchas LJ said (at p564):

> ... 'reasonably practicable' imports three stages, the proof of which rests on the employee. The first proposition ... is that it was reasonable for the employee not to be aware of the factual basis on which she could bring an application to the tribunal during the currency of the three months limitation period. ... [I]f that is established, it cannot be reasonably practicable to expect an applicant to bring a case based on facts of which she is ignorant. Secondly, the applicant must establish that the knowledge which she gains has, in the circumstances, been reasonably gained by her and that that knowledge is either crucial, fundamental or important ... to her change of belief ... [T]hat concept ... is an objective qualification of reasonableness, in the circumstances, to a subjective test of the applicant's state of mind. The third ground ... is that the acquisition of this knowledge had to be crucial to the decision to bring a claim in any event.

So the discovery of facts which for the first time enable the applicant to put forward a claim justifies escape from the limitation period.
Illustrations of this approach are found in:

- *James W Cook & Co (Wivenhoe) v Tipper*,[41] where employees made redundant were entitled to bring their claims for unfair dismissal when, after the deadline, they realised that all chances of getting their jobs back disappeared on the closure of the yard they were working in. It was not reasonably practicable to bring proceedings during the relevant period.
- *Churchill v Yeates & Son Ltd*[42] where it was held that it was not reasonably practicable for an employee to bring a complaint 'until he is aware of a fundamental fact which renders his dismissal unfair'. There was doubt as to the correctness of the employer's reason for dismissal as being, inter alia, redundancy.

In all cases of timing, the essential ingredient is the employee's reasonable and genuine belief. It is not necessary for the applicant

40 [1988] ICR 558; [1988] IRLR 212, CA.
41 [1990] ICR 716; [1990] IRLR 386, CA.
42 [1983] ICR 380; [1983] IRLR 187, EAT, approved in *Marley* (n43 below).

to establish the truth of the new fact, only the reasonableness of a belief in it.[43]

Advisers: wrong advice or delay

The general rule is that you cannot use the escape clause where your advisers have been at fault. As Lord Denning MR said:

> If a man engages skilled advisers to act for him – and they mistake the time limit and present [the claim] too late – he is out. His remedy is against them.[44]

Within this category are solicitors, CABx, trade union full time and lay officers including shop stewards, and representatives of trade, employers' and professional associations.[45] In *Riley v Tesco Stores*[46] the applicant received incorrect advice from a CAB but was not excused.

But a different test is applied to employees of tribunals and job centres. In *Jean Sorelle Ltd v Rybak*[47] it was held that a tribunal could decide that information given by an employee of the tribunal office did not fall within the category of skilled advice, so that if it were incorrect and relied on by the applicant so that she missed the deadline, she would be saved by the escape clause. The distinction between advisers retained by the applicant and staff of official bodies was also drawn in *London International College Ltd v Sen*.[48] Here the applicant received advice from a solicitor and also contacted the tribunal office. It was held that the fact the applicant had consulted a solicitor did not automatically make it reasonably practicable for the applicant to present an originating application in time. The proper approach is to ask what was the substantial cause of the late application, and since in *Sen* this was the information given by the tribunal office, the escape clause was operated in favour of the applicant.

Of course, failure by a skilled adviser to ensure that the claim posted on time has been received in time remains inexcusable, and unreasonable conduct during the intervening time might exclude the operation of the escape clause.[49]

---

43 *Marley (UK) Ltd v Anderson* [1996] IRLR 163, CA.
44 *Dedman v British Building and Engineering Appliances Ltd* [1974] ICR 53; [1973] IRLR 379, CA.
45 See *Hammond v Haigh Castle & Co Ltd* [1973] ICR 148; [1973] IRLR 91, NIRC.
46 [1980] ICR 323; [1980] IRLR 103, CA.
47 [1991] ICR 127; [1991] IRLR 153, EAT.
48 [1993] IRLR 3339, CA.
49 See *Capital Foods (Retail) Ltd v Corrigan* [1991] IRLR 430, EAT.

Delay caused by internal appeals

It is often thought by applicants, particularly those in jobs where there is a sophisticated appeal and disciplinary machinery, that time does not begin to run against them until the exhaustion of the relevant appeal procedures. This is wrong. In most cases, the decision of management to dismiss causes an effective date of termination for the purposes of the commencement of a relevant limitation period, and is not affected by any internal appeal machinery. Naturally, in such cases, if the applicant is successful at the internal appeal, reinstatement occurs and there has been no dismissal.[50] If the effective date of termination starts the limitation period running, however, an internal appeal can have no effect on it; nor is it a sufficient ground for finding that presentation of a complaint of unfair dismissal was not reasonably practicable.[51]

This approach was approved in *Palmer v Southend-on-Sea Borough Council*.[52] There, two local government workers were convicted of stealing petrol and dismissed, but the council's appeal committee indicated that should their conviction be overturned, the dismissals might be reconsidered. The Court of Appeal did overturn their convictions but the council refused to reinstate them. The tribunal's decision that it had been reasonably practicable to present claims to the tribunal within three months was upheld.

The moral is that if there is an internal appeal procedure, a claim for unfair dismissal should still be lodged in any event. The tribunal hearing can always be postponed on the ground that an internal procedure is operating and will imminently decide the matter. Most employers would accept the lodging of an originating application in such circumstances as simply a protective measure and not in any way an attempt to threaten them or short-circuit existing procedures.

The only clear case in which it is likely that the escape clause will be operated in favour of the applicant is when the employer itself encourages the applicant to forego making a claim in time. In *Owen v Crown House Engineering Ltd*,[53] negotiations took place with the applicants' union following redundancy notices. The employers invited the union official to 'hold his hand' in submitting claims to the tribunal so that the employers' board could consider the matter

---

50 See *J Sainsbury Ltd v Savage* [1981] ICR 1; [1980] IRLR 109, CA.
51 *Bodha v Hampshire Area Health Authority* [1982] ICR 200.
52 [1984] ICR 372; [1984] IRLR 119, CA.
53 [1973] ICR 511; [1973] IRLR 233, NIRC.

in more detail. The NIRC upheld the 'vital importance of attempting to settle all differences by amicable negotiation' and that had claims been made 'it would almost certainly have killed any hope of a fruitful outcome to the negotiations', per Sir Hugh Griffiths at p516. So, action by employers causative of the applicant missing the deadline can give rise to the operation of the escape clause. For safety's sake, however, it is still advisable to present the originating application within the time-scale.

Criminal or other proceedings

It can sometimes be reasonable to misunderstand the nature of proceedings where a similar issue is being judged by social security and industrial tribunals: see *Riley v Tesco* (p40). A safe rule is to make a claim in time. The existence of criminal proceedings will certainly affect many tribunal claims for unfair dismissal based on dishonesty, and the appropriate course is to apply for a stay of the tribunal hearing. In such a case it is more likely than not that the applicant will have or have access to legal advice. This advice should include advice on, at the very least, time limits for presenting an unfair dismissal claim. In these circumstances, it is unlikely that the escape clause would be operated in favour of the applicant if no claim were lodged at the industrial tribunal.

Failure to meet the deadline: time limits on the escape clause

When the tribunal is satisfied that it was not reasonably practicable to present the originating application during the limitation period (eg, three months), it must then go on to decide whether it was presented 'within such further period as the tribunal considers reasonable . . .' (ERA 1996 s111(2)). A broader discretion is thus given to the tribunal than in respect of the original limitation period. The length of time permitted is strictly a matter of fact for the tribunal to determine. In *Marley (UK) Ltd v Anderson*,[54] the EAT held that, although the Court of Appeal in *James W Cook*[55] did express views about the time-scales in that particular case (four to six weeks 'were simply too long'), there was an error of law when the tribunal felt itself *bound* by that approach. Similarly, the

---

54   [1994] IRLR 152.
55   Note 42 above.

tribunal must not simply consider the length of the delay, but also the circumstances in which the delay occurred and the reasons for it extending beyond the limitation period.

Failure to meet the deadline: 'just and equitable'

Sex, race and disability discrimination cases

Questions of reasonable practicability do not arise in relation to claims of sex, race and disability discrimination, since the limitation period of three months may be set aside if 'in all the circumstances of the case [a tribunal] considers that it is just and equitable to do so' (SDA 1975 s76(5); RRA 1976 s68(6); DDA 1995 Sch 3 para 3). Because of the wide discretion given to tribunals, it is unlikely that a decision can successfully be appealed. The 'circumstances of the case' appear to be those related to the reason for the delay, and tribunals are not required to investigate them in full.

That different statutory considerations apply is apparent from *Trust House Forte (UK) Ltd v Halstead*,[56] where late claims were made in respect of unfair dismissal and racial discrimination. The tribunal gave the applicant the benefit of the escape clause in respect of both claims. On appeal, the EAT refused to uphold the unfair dismissal claim, but did not interfere with the exercise of discretion in relation to the discrimination claim.

Given the breadth of the discretion, it would be appropriate to call evidence relating to the degree of prejudice should the tribunal exercise its discretion, eg, whether the length of the delay and the circumstances attending it make it more difficult for the employer to defend the case, and whether the employer has in any way contributed to the delay or acquiesced in it. In general, though, the approach is that the tribunal can take account of anything it considers relevant.[57]

It is worth recalling that time does not begin to run until the *end* of a period during which a continuing act of discrimination has occurred, or the last of a series of acts of discrimination, and may not have begun to run in respect of a continuing policy which is held to be discriminatory. A claim can be made at any time during its currency.

---

56 Unreported, EAT 213/86.
57 *Hutchinson v Westwood Television Ltd* [1977] ICR 279; [1977] IRLR 69, EAT.

Redundancy pay

A *further* limitation period applies in respect of redundancy payments (see p30).

CHAPTER 5

The originating application

Introduction

The originating application is the title given to the document which starts tribunal proceedings: the means by which an applicant actually makes his/her claim and the first formal step in the tribunal complaint procedure. In this respect it is the tribunal equivalent of a statement of claim in the High Court or particulars of claim in the county court, but it is not a formal 'pleading' (see below) and should not be treated as such.

The time limits within which proceedings must be brought in the tribunal have been dealt with in chapter 4 and any potential applicant should pay particular attention to these.

Minimum requirements and Form IT1

Generally the originating application takes the form of the COIT's Form IT1 (see Appendix 1). This can be obtained from any local office of the Employment Service, including jobseekers' allowance offices and job centres, and from most advice centres. An explanatory booklet ('ITL 1') can also be obtained from the same sources. In Scotland, the IT1 is known as the 'IT1 (Scot)' and in Northern Ireland, the 'IT1 (NI)', where the explanatory booklet is referred to as the 'IT1 (L) (NI)'. In Northern Ireland, forms and booklets may be obtained from any local training and employment agency.

Using Form IT1 is by far the easiest way of submitting a claim to the tribunal: by completing it properly, an applicant can be sure that s/he has provided all the information necessary to commence a claim. Tribunal proceedings may, however, be commenced by

45

other means: by using a home-made form or even by a letter sent to the COIT.[1] Any claim made, whether by IT1 or by any other document, must be in writing and should contain the following details:

- the applicant's name and address and, if different, an address within the United Kingdom to which notices and other documents relating to the claim can be sent;
- the names and addresses of the person or persons against whom relief is sought; and
- the grounds, with particulars, on which relief is sought.[2]

Although an originating application to a tribunal should meet all these requirements, a fairly flexible approach has been taken to claims presented which fail to comply with these conditions.

In *Burns International Security Services (UK) Ltd v Butt*,[3] where the applicant had failed to give any particulars of the grounds of his unfair dismissal complaint, the EAT stated that this was not fatal, the only mandatory requirement being that the application must be made in writing and the other requirements being of a directory rather than a mandatory nature. In particular, the EAT pointed out that under the predecessor rule to r4(1)(a)(i) the tribunal could order further particulars of a complaint to be provided if necessary so that failing to give full particulars in the originating application was a rectifiable omission. This reasoning is strengthened under the 1993 Rules (r4(1)(a)), which provide that a tribunal can, of its own motion, order that such further particulars be provided.

Similarly, in *Gosport Working Men's and Trade Union Club Ltd v Taylor*,[4] the fact that the applicant had merely given his name and telephone number but not his address was held not to be fatal, as he had provided sufficient details to enable him to be identified. As the bare minimum, it seems that if the originating application is in writing and contains sufficient details to identify the person making the claim and the person or persons against whom the claim is made, it will be allowed, although the applicant may be required to provide further particulars of the claim.

1   *Smith v Automobile Pty Ltd* [1973] ICR 306, NIRC.
2   r1(1).
3   [1983] ICR 547; [1983] IRLR 438.
4   (1978) 13 ITR 321, EAT.

The originating application distinguished from pleadings

This flexible approach to the originating application is consistent with the distinction between it and the formal pleadings required in the High Court or county courts. An applicant should not be held to the particulars given in the originating application at any later hearing in the case, although obvious inconsistencies may be the subject of adverse inference. If a respondent has failed to ask for further particulars of the complaint, then the applicant cannot be criticised too greatly for failing to provide them; if the factual basis for making a complaint of, eg, unfair dismissal is included in a claim expressly stated to be of race or sex discrimination, then the applicant should be allowed to make that complaint as well: failure to provide full details from the start should not be fatal.

The correct approach for the tribunal in cases where the originating application provides little (if any) detail of the complaint (or one of the complaints) that the applicant seeks to make at the substantive hearing will often be to allow an amendment to be made, and to consider any representations the respondent wishes to make in respect of the need for an adjournment in the light of the amendment and/or in respect of the additional costs incurred due to the amendment (see chapter 7).

Furthermore, whilst the rules require an applicant to set out the grounds of complaint in respect of which relief is sought, there is no requirement to specify the relief itself. If the facts particularised in the originating application lead the tribunal to conclude that the applicant's dismissal was by reason of redundancy but was unfair in all the circumstances, then it will not be fatal to a finding of unfair dismissal that the applicant has indicated that she is claiming only a redundancy payment on the face of the originating application. In *Chapman v Goonvean and Rostowrack China Clay Co Ltd*[5] Sir John Donaldson (P) said:

> [if there were] the slightest doubt whether an applicant's claim is or should be for a redundancy payment or for compensation for unfair dismissal, or for both . . . the applicant should be encouraged to put forward or maintain both such claims until all the facts are known.

This view was affirmed by the Court of Appeal.[6]

---

5 [1973] ICR 50; [1973] IRLR 124, NIRC.
6 [1973] ICR 310.

Presentation of the originating application

This subject is dealt with in full in chapter 4. The originating application should be 'presented' to the Secretary of Tribuanals at the COIT (r1(1)). It can be delivered by hand, sent by post or faxed but the time limits for presentation must be complied with. Originating applications which are sent to ROITs or OITs appear to be accepted as having been duly 'presented', provided the Assistant Secretary at the appropriate ROIT accepts it by forwarding it to the COIT.[7]

Those acting for applicants should take all steps to make sure that the originating application has been received by the tribunal in time.

- If it is sent by post, it appears that the onus is on representatives to telephone the COIT to make sure that it has been received.[8]
- If it has been sent to an OIT or ROIT and returned, it may not have been accepted as validly presented to the Secretary and should be sent to the COIT within the relevant time limit.

Action on receipt of the originating application

As soon as an originating application is received at the COIT, or at a ROIT or OIT, it is date-stamped. As a matter of evidence, this will generally be taken to be the date on which the application was 'presented'. The relevant date is, however, not the date of 'receipt' but the date of actual 'presentation' and if there is evidence that the application was presented, eg, by the applicant putting it through the letter box of the COIT in person the day before, then this will be the crucial date in respect of any time limit.[9]

Initial vetting procedure

If an originating application is received which the secretary to the tribunal believes seeks relief which is outside the jurisdiction of the tribunal, then notice will be sent to the applicant to that effect, indicating the reasons for that view and stating that the originating

---

7 r20(2) and *Bengey v North Devon District Council* [1977] ICR 15, EAT.
8 See *Capital Foods (Retail) Ltd v Corrigan* [1993] IRLR 430, EAT (p37 above).
9 *Post Office v Moore* [1981] ICR 623, EAT.

application will not be registered unless written indication of an intention to proceed with the claim is received from the applicant (r1(2)).

As the secretary to the tribunal performs an administrative, not a judicial function, this step should not be seen as a form of striking out and is in fact rarely used. It would be appropriate in obvious cases of mistaken forum, for example, a claim for damages for personal injury sustained at the work-place made to the tribunal. Indeed, even if the applicant has manifestly made such a mistake, if s/he states that s/he wishes to proceed despite the notice sent by the secretary, then the application will be duly registered and will proceed as normal (r1(3)), although it may subsequently be the subject of a pre-hearing review or an application for costs.

The register

Within 28 days of receiving the originating application, or as soon as reasonably practicable thereafter, particulars of the application will be entered in the register (r2(2)). The register is a public record of all tribunal applications, appeals and decisions which is open to inspection (reg 9) and which is often used by members of the press to obtain prior information on the nature of particular tribunal cases. Due to the public nature of the register, where an application appears to involve allegations of the commission of a sexual offence, any particulars which might allow the identification of the person making the allegation, or affected by it, must be omitted (rr2(2) and 13(6)).

Informing others of the originating application

As well as entering particulars of the originating application in the register, the secretary will send a copy of it to the respondent with a notice stating the means and time for entering an appearance, the consequences of failing to do so and the right to receive a copy of the decision (r2(1)(a) and (c)) (see appendix 1). When an application is entered in the register, it is allocated to a ROIT and given a case number. These details are sent to all parties to the proceedings (r2(1)(b)).

The contents of the originating application

While the essential requirements for a valid originating application may be minimal, it is always preferable to give the details specified in the Rules so far as this is possible, including sufficient particulars to enable the nature of the complaint being made to be clearly identified. If at all possible:

- use a Form IT1.
- type in the entries on the IT1 and complete all parts after reading the notes accompanying it.

Box 1: Type of complaint

Specify the type of complaint made, eg, 'Unfair dismissal' or 'Entitlement to a redundancy payment'.

If more than one complaint is being made, list each complaint separately, eg, '(1) Unfair dismissal; and/or (2) Entitlement to a redundancy payment.'

If different complaints are being made in respect of different respondents, say so, eg, (in a TUPE case) 'In respect of the First Respondent: (1) Unfair dismissal; and/or (2) Entitlement to a redundancy payment. In respect of the Second Respondent: (1) Unfair dismissal; and/or (2) Declaration of terms and conditions and unlawful deductions'.

Box 2: The applicant's details

Although not all the items set out in the IT1 are required under the Rules, as much information should be included as possible; the applicant's date of birth, for example, will often be relevant in determining the calculation of any basic award or redundancy payment due.

If the applicant is not represented, the address given here will be that to which all subsequent notices and other correspondence relating to the proceedings will be sent. It is for the applicant to ensure that the correct information is supplied. Any changes to the contact address should be notified to the tribunal and all other relevant parties (r20(4)).

While more than one applicant can make an application on the same IT1[10] it is obviously preferable for separate applications to be completed and individual details given.

10 *Gosport Working Men's and Trade Union Club Ltd v Taylor* (1978) 13 ITR 321, EAT.

Box 3: Details of the applicant's representative

If the aplicant is represented, then the address given here will be the one to which the tribunal will send all notices and other documents relating to the proceedings. Any adviser who is 'on the record' on the IT1 must be prepared to keep his/her client properly informed as to the conduct of the proceedings and as to the times and dates of any hearings. Any changes to the named representative or to the contact address should be notified to the tribunal and all other relevant parties (r20(4)).

Box 4: Dates of employment

The details given here may give rise to questions relating to the tribunal's jurisdiction to hear the complaint in question and may be used in any calculation of basic award or redundancy payment and should therefore be completed as accurately as possible. The start date should be the date the applicant's continuous employment commenced (whether it was with a previous employer or under a different contract of employment) and the date of termination will be the date on which notice expired or (if no notice was given or if the applicant was paid in lieu) the actual date on which the applicant left the employment. Regard should be had to the relevant statutory provisions applicable to a particular complaint where the start or leaving date of employment might be in issue.

Box 5: Details of the respondent

Sufficient details should be given to enable the tribunal to identify and communicate with the appropriate respondent. More than one respondent can be named, eg, in a transfer of undertakings case or where the allegation is one of discrimination and the complaint is made, for example, both against the individual discriminator and vicariously against the employer.

If an applicant is unsure of the correct identity of the respondent (ie, where the employer is one of a group of companies or in a transfer of undertakings case), then all possible respondents should be identified and the reasons for so doing set out in the particulars of the complaint; a complaint against a particular respondent can always be withdrawn at a later date. Mistakes over the identity of the correct respondent should not be fatal, as an application to amend the identity of the respondent can be made at a later date (see chapter 7).

Box 6: Connection with the respondent

Generally this will be the applicant's job title, although if the relationship is other than that of employer/employee (eg, where the applicant is complaining of discrimination in her application for a job or where the respondent is a colleague who is alleged to have committed acts of discrimination against the applicant) then the connection which has led the applicant to make the application to the tribunal should be explained.

Box 7: Normal basic hours

Although not required by the Rules, this information will indicate whether there might be a problem relating to the calculation of any payments claimed.

Generally speaking the 'normal working hours' will be the contractual minimum hours the applicant was required to work, and this may include overtime where there is a contractual obligation to work it.[11]

Box 8: Details of earnings

This information may be used in establishing, eg, any basic award or redundancy payment or compensatory award and should be given as accurately as possible, although an applicant will not be held to a mistaken weekly rate if s/he later seeks to amend these details. The 'basic wage/salary' is the gross amount the applicant was due, the 'average take home' is the net amount (ie, after deduction of tax and national insurance). It is up to the applicant whether to give weekly, monthly or yearly figures, but it helps if the information is given for a consistent period throughout. If the applicant's wage varied from week to week, the average amount for the last 12 calendar weeks of the employment should be taken. Under 'bonuses/benefits', all additional 'perks' should be listed, including any pension benefit etc. Whilst these will not be included as part of a 'week's pay' for the purposes of a basic award or redundancy payment, they are part of the applicant's loss in terms of any compensatory award or equal pay order.

Box 9: Date of action complained of other than dismissal

This will generally apply in relation to discrimination cases (race, sex, disability and trade union), wage protection complaints, Equal

11 *Gascol Conversions v Mercer* [1974] ICR 420; [1974] IRLR 155, CA.

Pay Act cases and applications for a declaration of terms and conditions. This information may also give rise to an issue relating to the tribunal's jurisdiction to hear the complaint (ie, as to whether the claim has been presented in time) and should be completed carefully.

If it is difficult to specify one date, eg, where the complaint relates to a continuing course of conduct in a discrimination case (p31), then this can be clarified in the more detailed particulars of complaint.

Box 10: Remedy sought in unfair dismissal cases

This is not a requirement of the Rules and can be left blank without rendering the application a nullity. It does, however, give a clear indication to the respondent of the relief sought by the applicant and, consequently, of its potential liability. Whatever the applicant states under this head will not be binding on him/her and the tribunal should address the question again when it considers remedies at the full hearing of the complaint.

Preference for chairman alone or full tribunal

Again, not a requirement under the Rules, but it appears on some obsolete forms still in use. Once both parties have given their consent in writing it cannot be withdrawn. (See p5 for the types of case which might be heard by a chairman sitting alone and for discussion of the arguments for and against.) Generally speaking, the stage at which the IT1 is completed is usually too early to give any firm indication and an applicant would generally be well advised at this stage to state a preference for a full tribunal; a change of preference can always be notified to the tribunal after consideration of the respondent's notice of appearance, when the issues between the parties have been clarified.

Box 11: Details of complaint

This is the applicant's opportunity to set out the nature of his/her case and it will generally be the first document the tribunal members hearing the case actually read in relation to the complaint: care should therefore be taken to present the details to the applicant's best advantage (which may mean setting out the details on a separate sheet attached to the IT1 rather than trying to work within the confined space given on the form). While there may be some advantage in keeping certain matters open, for example, in an unfair dismissal case, in not admitting the reason given for dismissal straight away but putting the respondent to proof, the purpose of the originating application is to set out the case the respondent has to meet and to make it clear what is and what is not in issue. It is often useful to give detailed particulars where the burden of proof is on the applicant, for instance in constructive dismissal and race and sex discrimination cases.

In cases where the applicant is relying on a number of different incidents (eg, where there has been on-going harrassment or in a 'last straw' constructive dismissal case),[12] it is advisable to set out details of all incidents which are relied upon; in this way the applicant cannot be accused of raising them for the first time at the hearing of the claim.

It is not necessary to set out the relevant law in the originating application, although reference to the relevant sections can assist in making the nature of the claim clear to those reading the document (eg, in specifying that the claim is one of indirect sex discrimination under SDA 1975 s1(1)(b), of unlawful racial discrimination on the grounds of victimisation under RRA 1976 s2, etc). Furthermore, the relevant law should be borne in mind when completing the originating application to ensure that important points are not left out, eg, the size and administrative resources of the respondent in an unfair dismissal case.

It is not helpful to include background detail if this is not relevant to the type of claim being made: if the issue in an unfair dismissal by reason of redundancy case is the fairness of the selection procedure, details of the applicant's views on the need for redundancies and the business decisions which led to the redundancy situation in the first place are unlikely to assist the tribunal.

On the other hand, where information is relevant and may later form the subject of a request for further particulars or for written answers, it will help to expedite the applicant's claim to provide the details from the start: where relevant, name names, give dates, set out the gist of conversations relied upon and so on.

Examples of details of complaints which might by used in originating applications are set out in Appendix 2.

12 *Lewis v Motorworld* [1986] ICR 157; [1985] IRLR 465, CA.

CHAPTER 6

Notice of appearance

The notice of appearance is the respondent's 'defence' to any application to the tribunal and provides the opportunity for the respondent to set out its case and to state where there are specific points of dispute or agreement. With the originating application, this will generally be one of the first documents read by the tribunal and will form the starting point for any consideration of the respondent's case.

Minimum requirements and Form IT3

Generally the notice of appearance takes the form of the COIT's Form IT3 (see example at Appendix 1). A copy will be sent to the respondent(s) to an application to the tribunal with a copy of the originating application.

As with the originating application, use of Form IT3 is the recommended although not the only means of entering a notice of appearance. Generally speaking, completing the IT3 will be the most convenient means open to a respondent to state its case. It will give a clear indication of precisely which information the tribunal requires to be able to consider how best to progress the claim further.

A respondent may choose to enter a notice of appearance by other means providing it meets the basic requirements provided for in r3, ie, it must be in writing and should contain the following details:

– the respondent's full name and address and, if different, an address within the United Kingdom to which notices and other documents relating to the claim can be sent;

- whether or not the respondent intends to resist the application; and
- if the respondent does intend to resist the application, sufficient particulars to show on what grounds the application is resisted.

As with the originating application, apart from the necessity of submitting a written notice of appearance, the other requirements are of a directory rather than mandatory nature. This has been held to be the case in relation to the requirement to set out particulars of the grounds which the application will be resisted.[1]

While the rules may not set out absolute standards for the notice of appearance, reasonably full particulars are to be encouraged; although the EAT in *Seldun* recognised that a lack of detail could be corrected by ordering further particulars to be provided of the grounds of resistance, it did not thereby seek to encourage this course of action.

Like the originating application, the notice of appearance in tribunal proceedings is not to be considered as a formal 'pleading' in the same way as a defence in a High Court or county court action. While some corporate respondents may be able to utilise the services of lawyers in drafting the notice of appearance, it is recognised that many respondents are not in this position and that the notice of appearance may well have been completed by someone entirely unfamiliar with court or tribunal proceedings.

If the respondent believes that it is unable to answer the case set out by the applicant in the originating application because insufficient details have been presented, the proper course is to write to the applicant asking for further particulars of the originating application and also to write to the tribunal enclosing details of the request made and formally applying for an extension of time to enter the notice of appearance. If the request is not satisfactorily answered on a voluntary basis, an application can be made for the applicant to be ordered to respond under r4(1)(a) – see r3(2)(b) and chapter 8 on requests for further particulars.

This is not a course of action which should be lightly embarked upon by a respondent: a tribunal may well take a different view as to the sufficiency of detail required in the originating application (particularly on a fairly straightforward unfair dismissal claim) before the respondent is able to enter a notice of appearance. The safer course of action in most cases will be for the respondent to

1 *Seldun Transport Services Ltd v Baker* [1978] ICR 1035, EAT.

enter a notice of appearance on Form IT3 and state under part 8 of the form that insufficient details of the applicant's case have been given to enable the respondent to give details of the grounds of resistance, but that further particulars have been sought and fuller details of the respondent's case will be given once these further particulars are received. This type of 'holding IT3' may often be preferable to seeking to extend time for presentation of the notice of appearance altogether, and protects the respondent from any of the adverse consequences which can flow from not having entered a notice of appearance (see p58).

Time limits

The notice of appearance should be submitted within 21 days after a copy of the originating application has been received from the ROIT (r3(1)), except where the claim made is against a foreign state, where the time limit is two months by virtue of the provisions of State Immunity Act 1978 s12(2). Unlike originating applications, this time limit is not rigidly adhered to and there is usually great flexibility allowed to respondents in entering a notice of appearance. An extension of time can be sought under r15(1), although a notice of appearance presented after the expiry of the 21-day time limit is expressly deemed to include such an application for an extension of time by virture of r3(3) provided grounds have been given in support of the application. Whether an extension of time is granted is a matter for the discretion of the tribunal, but a chairman can grant an application, and can order costs to be paid if it was reasonably practicable to present the IT3 within 21 days (r3(4)).

Neither r3(3) nor r15(1) imposes a time limit on an application for an extension of time. A tribunal therefore has the power to consider an application for an extension of time in which to enter a notice of appearance (under either rule) at any stage, even after the registration of the tribunal's substantive decision in the case,[2] although in *St Mungo* the EAT observed: 'There must inevitably be a very heavy burden on a respondent who applies for an extension of time, after notice of the proceedings and after judgment, to justify the application'.

The decision to grant an extension of time can be made without any

2 *St Mungo Community Trust v Colleano* [1980] ICR 254, EAT.

consultation with the applicant or other parties to the proceedings. Any order made without notice to the other side has been said to be provisional in nature and open to further consideration, because it is always open to the absent party to challenge it.[3]

The question of the time limit in relation to a notice of appearance is a procedural not a jurisdictional matter. In practice, tribunals are encouraged to be flexible in extending time for respondents, as the consequences of not doing so would mean that a respondent would be debarred from defending the claim. Where a respondent fails to enter a notice of appearance within the 14-day time limit, a further copy of the originating application will again be sent, this time by recorded delivery, with a reminder of the consequences of not entering a notice of appearance and a notice giving a futher seven days' extension of time. Even where the application for an extension of time is made late on in the proceedings, a tribunal may well still allow the late notice of appearance to be presented, provided serious prejudice is not then suffered by the applicant (ie, prejudice other than merely having to prove a case which is disputed).

Action on receipt of a notice of appearance

As the case will have been assigned to a ROIT after the receipt and registration of the originating application, the respondent will be asked to return the notice of appearance to the secretary to that ROIT rather than the COIT. Once a notice of appearance has been received, the secretary sends a copy of it to all the other parties to the proceedings (r3(1)).

The consequences of not entering a notice of appearance

A respondent which fails to enter a notice of appearance is, except in five respects, debarred from taking any further part in the proceedings. The five exceptions are as follows:

– to apply for an extension of time for entering a notice of appearance (r3(2)(a));
– to apply for further particulars of the originating application (r3(2)(b));
– to apply for a review of the tribunal's decision on the ground

3 *Reddington and Others v S Straker & Sons Ltd and Others* [1994] ICR 172, EAT.

that the respondent never received notice of the proceedings
(r3(2)(c));
- to be called as a witness by another person (r3(2)(d)); and
- to be sent a copy of the tribunal's decision (r3(2)(e)).

Except for the actions specified in these exceptions, the respondent
concerned is no longer considered to be a 'party' to the proceedings
(r3(2)).

Contents of the notice of appearance

Although the essential requirements for a valid notice of appearance
may be minimal, it is always preferable to give the details specified
in the rules so far as this is possible, including sufficient particulars
to enable the nature of the grounds upon which the claim is resisted
to be clearly identified. If at all possible:

- use a Form IT3;
- type in the entries on the IT3 and complete all parts after reading
  the contents of the originating application.

Box 1: The respondent's details
While not all the items requested in Form IT3 are required under
the rules, as much information should be given as possible. If the
respondent is not represented, the address given here will be that to
which all subsequent notices and other correspondence relating to
the proceedings will be sent. It is for the respondent to ensure that
the correct information is supplied. Any changes to the contact
address should be notified to the tribunal and all other relevant
parties (r20(4)).

Box 2: Whether the application is resisted
Even if the respondent does not wish to contest all or part of the
claim, it is advisable still to complete a notice of appearance, as
there are a number of adverse consequences which arise for a
respondent who has failed to enter a notice of appearance. In
circumstances where liability is not contested but the remedy is, the
appropriate course is to tick the second box under this part of the
form, but make it clear that there remains a dispute as to remedy;
the case will then be listed for a hearing before the tribunal on the
question of remedy only.

Box 3: Whether dismissal is admitted and, if so, the reason for that dismissal

In certain cases (most obviously claims of unfair dismissal), the applicant's case will depend on the tribunal first establishing that there was in fact a dismissal. If this is admitted by the respondent, as indicated by ticking the relevant box under this part of the form, the tribunal will move straight away to consider the fairness or otherwise of that dismissal. If dismissal is not admitted (eg, in a constructive dismissal claim or in a case where the meaning of the words taken by the applicant to terminate the employment is in dispute), this should be made clear on the face of the IT3. The tribunal can then go on either to consider the question of dismissal as a preliminary point or to identify this as an issue to be determined as part of the substantive hearing into the whole claim. The latter course may be the most appropriate in a constructive dismissal case where the issues relating to the question of whether there was a dismissal are likely also to determine the question of the fairness of the dismissal if so found.

Where dismissal is admitted, the respondent is invited to state the reason for that dismissal. ERA 1996 s98(1) and (2) sets out the reasons for dismissal which will be found to be prima facie fair and the respondent should consider that section before completing this part of the IT3 in an unfair dismissal case. In a case involving a dismissal arguably in connection with the transfer of an undertaking, particular regard should be had to the Transfer of Undertakings (Protection of Employment) Regulations 1981 (TUPE) before completing the IT3.

A respondent should try to state clearly the reason (or principal reason) for any dismissal in this part of the IT3. The important point is to ensure that the facts and matters set out at box 8 (details of grounds of resistance) accurately reflect the respondent's case on the reason for the decision to dismiss. A respondent should not be penalised for using the wrong 'label' if it is clear throughout which matters are actually relied upon as having given rise to the dismissal in any particular case, although it will still be necessary to apply to amend the reason given in the IT3 if the wrong label has been used initially. In *Blue Star Ship Management Ltd v Williams*[4] it was held that an amendment to allege a different reason for a dismissal would generally not be allowed at a late stage in the proceedings unless 'it can genuinely be said that the amendment is no more than

4 [1978] ICR 770; [1979] IRLR 16, EAT.

for the purpose of giving an appropriate label to a fully established set of facts'.

Where the facts and matters relied on for the dismissal are clearly put forward by the respondent, the tribunal may even find that the dismissal was fair, although for a different reason under ERA 1996 s98 than the label given by the respondent, provided the grounds relied upon are those set out by the respondent. A tribunal will not be entitled to find a dismissal fair on a ground not 'pleaded' or argued for by the respondent where the difference in grounds goes to the facts or substance of the dismissal or where there might have been some difference in the way in which the applicant conducted the case in the light of the reason relied upon. If, however, the different grounds are in fact just different labels and there was no basis for thinking that the applicant has been prejudiced in the presentation of his/her case, it will be open to a tribunal to find the dismissal fair for a different reason to that stated by the respondent.[5] In *Hannan*, the tribunal held that the dismissal was not by reason of redundancy (as had been argued by the respondent), but was by reason of some other substantial reason ('SOSR') which was fair in all the circumstances of the case. As the grounds relied upon by the tribunal for this conclusion were the same as those initially relied upon by the respondent in seeking to claim that the dismissal was by reason of redundancy and as there was no reason to think that the applicant's case would have been differently conducted had 'SOSR' been the label used by the respondent on the IT3, the EAT refused to allow the employee's appeal against the tribunal's decision.

Alternative reasons should be given when appropriate, eg '(1) Redundancy or (2) business reorganisation amounting to some other substantial reason of a kind such as to justify the dismissal of an employee holding the position which the applicant held'. Further, where the respondent's primary case is that there was no dismissal, it is still advisable to put forward a reason for the termination of the applicant's employment by way of alternative.

Box 4: The dates of the applicant's employment

The dates given here may give rise to questions relating to the tribunal's jurisdiction to hear the complaint in question and may be used in any calculation of a basic award or redundancy payment and should therefore be completed as accurately as possible. The start date should be the date on which the applicant's period of

5 *Hannan v TNT-IPEC (UK) Ltd* [1986] IRLR 165, EAT

continuous employment commenced (whether it was with a previous employer or under a different contract of employment) and the date of termination will be the date on which notice expired or (if no notice was given or if the applicant was 'paid in lieu') the actual date on which the applicant left the employment. Attention should be paid to the relevant statutory provisions applicable to a particular complaint when the start or end date of employment might be in issue.

Box 5: Details of the respondent's representative

If the respondent is represented, the address given here will be the one to which the tribunal will send all notices and other documents relating to the proceedings. Any adviser who is 'on the record' on the IT3 must be prepared to keep the client properly informed of the conduct of the proceedings and on the times and dates of any hearings. Any changes to the named representative or to the contact address should be notified to the tribunal and all other relevant parties (r20(4)).

Box 6: Details of the applicant's earnings

This information may be used in establishing any basic award or redundancy payment or compensatory award. If the respondent disagrees with the information supplied by the applicant, this should be made clear by ticking the appropriate box and supplying the information the respondent believes to be correct. Often the respondent may be in a better position to supply details relating to net earnings, pension contributions etc and it is helpful to all concerned if the information is provided at this early stage. If it remains in dispute, at least all parties then know of the issue between them and can endeavour to find material (eg, actuarial evidence etc) to support their particular position. The information should be given as accurately as possible, although a respondent will not be held to a mistaken weekly rate if it later seeks to amend these details.

The 'basic wage/salary' is the gross amount the applicant was due, the 'average take home' is the net amount (ie, after deduction of tax and national insurance). It is up to the respondent whether weekly, monthly or yearly figures are given but it helps if the information is given for a consistent period throughout and in such a way as would provide a ready comparison with the details supplied by the applicant.

If the applicant's wage varied from week to week, the average amount for the last 12 calendar weeks of the employment should be taken. Under 'bonuses/benefits', all additional 'perks' should be listed, including any pension benefit, etc. While these will not be included as part of a 'week's pay' for the purposes of a basic award or redundancy payment, they are part of the applicant's loss in terms of any compensatory award.

Box 7: Details in relation to maternity rights cases

This part of the form needs to be completed only where an employee is claiming a right to return to her job after maternity leave, as there are implications for a claim of unfair dismissal where this right is denied in circumstances where the number employed by the respondent (or any associated companies) does not exceed five (ERA 1996 s96).

Preference for chairman alone or full tribunal

There is no box corresponding to the question on some versions of the IT1. See p5 for the types of case which might be heard by a chairman sitting alone and for discussion of the relevant factors.

Box 8: Details of the grounds of resistance

This is the respondent's first opportunity to set out the nature of the defence and will generally be the first document relating to the respondent's case read by the members of the tribunal: care should therefore be taken to present the details to the respondent's best advantage (which may mean setting out the details on a separate sheet attached to the IT3 rather than trying to work within the confined space given on the form).

The purpose of the notice of appearance is to set out the respondent's case in answer to the allegations made by the applicant in the originating application and to make it clear what is and what is not in issue.

Where the respondent bears the burden of proof, it is particularly important to make sure the case set out in the notice of appearance accurately reflects the way in which the respondent in fact wishes to present the case.

Sufficient details should be given to show how the respondent views the facts and matters which led to the decision to dismiss or take the other action complained of, eg, if there was a history of warnings and/or a number of disciplinary meetings, details should be provided so that the applicant knows in advance the events on which the respondent intends to rely.

Even where dismissal is not admitted, if it is subsequently found that the applicant was in fact dismissed, the tribunal will go on to consider whether that dismissal was fair. In such cases the respondent should consider 'pleading' in the alternative grounds upon which it might be considered that any dismissal found was in fact fair. In particular, if a respondent intends to continue to contest liability once it is found that there was a dismissal, a reason should be put forward for that dismissal as an alternative to the respondent's primary case as soon as possible. Although a respondent can subsequently apply to amend and put forward a reason for the dismissal, leave will not be given if this would require further evidence to be adduced and considered or an adjournment of the hearing.[6]

It is not necessary to set out the relevant law in the notice of appearance, although reference to the relevant sections can assist in making the nature of the defence clear to those reading the document (eg, by specifying that a claim of indirect sex discrimination is contested on the basis of a defence of justification under SDA 1975 s1(1)(b)(ii)). Furthermore, the relevant law should be borne in mind when completing the notice of appearance to ensure that important points are not left out, eg, the size and administrative resources of the respondent in an unfair dismissal case.

It is not helpful to include background detail if this is not relevant to the type of claim being made, eg, if the issue in an unfair dismissal by reason of redundancy case is the fairness of the selection procedure, details of the applicant's capability will only be relevant if this formed part of the selection criteria.

On the other hand, where information is relevant and may later form the subject of a request for further particulars or for written answers, it will assist to provide the details from the start and will avoid the possibility that the respondent will be accused of having raised matters for the first time at the substantive hearing of the case. Where relevant, name names, give dates, set out the gist of conversations relied upon and so on.

Incorrect identification of the respondent

If the body named as respondent by the applicant is in fact wrong (or, at least, it intends to argue that this is the case), this should be detailed as a preliminary matter in the body of the notice of appearance. If identification of the correct respondent requires

6   *Ready Case Ltd v Jackson* [1981] IRLR 312, EAT

resolution of some preliminary legal or factual point (eg, when there might have been a transfer of an undertaking), the tribunal is likely to consider this at a preliminary hearing under r6 (see chapter 13). The tribunal has a broad discretion to join other parties as respondents and/or to allow an amendment to the identification of the respondent in the originating application (see p17).

Jurisdictional points

If a jurisdictional point is apparent to a respondent on receipt of the originating application (eg, the application was presented out of time or the applicant fails to meet the qualifying requirements for the type of claim submitted), the best course is to raise this as a preliminary point in the notice of appearance, before going on to set out the details of the grounds upon which the claim is resisted. If appropriate, the respondent should also apply for the jurisdictional point to be determined at a preliminary hearing under r6.

As a jurisdictional point cannot be waived by a party or by the tribunal, it would in fact be open to the respondent to raise the matter not in the notice of appearance but at some subsequent stage in the proceedings, even as late as an appeal. If the respondent is aware of the point at the stage of completing the notice of appearance, however, there is no good reason why it should not be raised in that document, particularly if leaving it to some later stage (eg, just before the hearing) might take the applicant by surprise and lead to an adjournment or postponement of the case. Where a respondent was intending to raise a jurisdictional issue in a case at the time of completing the notice of appearance and yet failed to raise it until shortly before the hearing, thereby necessitating an adjournment or postponement, it might well be open to the tribunal to conclude that such conduct was unreasonable and should result in the respondent being ordered to pay the wasted costs incurred by the applicant.

If liability is in dispute, a respondent should not seek to rely exclusively on a jurisdictional question but should look ahead to consider what might happen if the tribunal in fact finds that it does have jurisdiction to hear the complaint. The substantive defence to the claim should be put forward 'without prejudice' to the respondent's contention that the tribunal has no jurisdiction to hear the complaint.

Examples of details of grounds of resistance which might be used in notices of appearance are set out in Appendix 2.

The applicant's notice of appearance

Where an applicant makes a complaint of breach of contract, the respondent may well include a (counter-)claim in addition to the 'defence' entered by way of the notice of appearance. As the counter-claim will be a positive claim by the respondent, it obviously would help to clarify the issues between the parties if the applicant were to make his/her position clear in relation to the contentions of the counter-claim at an early stage in the proceedings. In order to enable the applicant to do this, Form IT3(c) will be sent to the applicant for completion with the notice of appearance when this raises a counter-claim.

CHAPTER 7

Amendment

Within its general power to regulate its own procedure under r13(1), a tribunal may at any stage of the proceedings consider an application to amend the originating application or notice of appearance. While there are no formal 'pleadings' in tribunals, the principal grounds on which a claim is to be brought or defended should be clear on the face of the originating application or notice of appearance. In so far as the initial document presented fails to set out the claim or defence relied on properly, the party concerned should seek to amend it as soon as possible.

The guidelines which will be considered by the tribunal when faced by an application to amend are set out below. Generally a tribunal will permit an amendment to be made providing the other side is not prejudiced thereby. A late amendment, even shortly before the commencement of the substantive hearing, may well be allowed: any prejudice suffered by the other side may be remedied by granting an adjournment of the hearing with an order for costs against the person applying to amend so late in the day.

Amendment of the originating application

The guidelines which tribunals should follow when considering any application to amend an originating application, whether to add or substitute respondents or to change the basis of the claim made, were set out by the NIRC in *Cocking v Sandhurst (Stationers) Ltd:*[1]

- Did the unamended originating application comply with the rules relating to the presentation of originating applications (see p45)

1 [1974] ICR 650.

and was it presented within the relevant time limit (see chapter 4)?

- If not, then there is no power to amend and a new originating application must be presented within the relevant time limit if this is still possible.
- If it was, the tribunal has a discretion to allow an amendment which would add or substitute a new party but should only do so if satisfied that the mistake sought to be corrected was a genuine mistake and was not misleading or such as to cause reasonable doubt over the identity of the person intending to claim or to be claimed against.
- In deciding whether or not to exercise its discretion, the tribunal should have regard to all the circumstances of the case, including any injustice or hardship which may be caused to any of the parties if the amendment were allowed or refused. If allowing the amendment might cause unnecessary additional cost to one party, the tribunal might properly conclude that this was an appropriate case for the amending party to be ordered to pay the additional costs of or occasioned by the amendment (see p176 on costs).

The NIRC's decision in *Cocking* has since been approved by the Court of Appeal in *British Newspaper Printing Corporation (North) Ltd v Kelly*.[2]

If a purely technical error is made in the naming of a respondent, *and* no prejudice has been caused, the tribunal may take a pragmatic approach, allowing an amendment late on in the proceedings, even after the issue of a consent order.[3] A tribunal is given a broad discretion to join a person to proceedings as a respondent and can do so at any time, even when the time limit for bringing a claim has expired by the time of the application to amend. The person whom it is sought to join should be given the opportunity to be heard on the application.[4] A new respondent may even by joined after a decision on the merits of the case has been given; although in that case, the new respondent must be afforded the opportunity to be heard, either by a re-hearing after the presentation of an IT3 or by review.[5]

2 [1989] IRLR 222.
3 *Milestone School of English Ltd v Leakey* [1982] IRLR 3, EAT.
4 *Gillick v BP Chemicals Ltd* [1993] IRLR 437.
5 *Linbourne v Constable* [1993] ICR 698, EAT.

Amendment of the notice of appearance

Similar principles apply to any application to amend the notice of appearance. The later a respondent seeks to amend the basis of the defence relied upon, the less likely it is that the tribunal will allow the amendment to be made. In particular, the tribunal will be reluctant to allow a respondent to amend in order to claim a new reason for a dismissal,[6] or to put forward a reason for a constructive dismissal where previously none was claimed,[7] unless the *substance* of the case was already contained within the original notice of appearance, ie, the amendment is no more than for the purpose of giving an appropriate label to a fully described set of facts.[8]

Amendment and striking out

By r13(2) a tribunal may (of itself or on application) order any part of an originating application or notice of appearance to be amended or struck out on the grounds that it is scandalous, frivolous or vexatious. See also pp58, 110 and 177.

6 *Kapur v Shields* [1976] ICR 26 QBD.
7 *Ready Case Ltd v Jackson* [1981] IRLR 312, EAT.
8 *Blue Star Ship Management Ltd v Williams* [1978] ICR 770; [1979] IRLR 16, EAT.

CHAPTER 8

Defining the issues: questionnaires, further particulars, written answers

Anyone contemplating or conducting tribunal proceedings needs to be able to make the best assessment possible of the prospects of success at all stages in the process. In chapter 3 the basic steps which can be taken to assess the strengths and costs of a case before commencing tribunal proceedings were described. This chapter builds on these steps, describing the special 'pre-action' procedure available in discrimination cases in the form of the questionnaire and detailing this and other interlocutory steps which can be used before a full hearing to learn as much as possible about the way in which the other side intends to fight the case.

An order made by an tribunal in respect of any of these procedures will be interlocutory in nature and, therefore, not open to review (see chapter 21). Where, however, an interlocutory order is initially made after considering representations from only one party, the order is essentially provisional and may be reconsidered by the tribunal upon application by an absent party.[1]

Questionnaires

Scope

A person considering bringing a complaint under SDA 1975 and/or RRA 1976 should use the questionnaire procedure (see p21) to decide whether to institute proceedings and, if so, to formulate and present the complaint in the most effective manner. SDA 1975 s74(1) and RRA 1976 s65(1) provide that the Secretary of State may

1 *Reddington v Straker & Sons Ltd* [1994] ICR 172, EAT.

by order prescribe the forms by which a potential complainant might question the respondent and by which the respondent might then reply. The relevant forms are to be found in the schedules to the Sex Discrimination (Questions and Replies) Order 1975 SI No 2048, as amended, and the Race Relations (Questions and Replies) Order 1977 SI No 842.

The forms provided consist of a questionnaire which the applicant or potential applicant may use to direct questions at the respondent about the reasons for doing any relevant act (ie, some act which might amount to unlawful discrimination under the SDA 1975 and/ or RRA 1976) or on any other matter which is or may be relevant, and a form of reply for the respondent to use by way of answer.

Use of the questionnaire procedure

Any applicant or potential applicant complaining of sex or race discrimination should be aware of the questionnaire procedure and the uses to which it can be put.

First, the questionnaire provides a means for a potential applicant to question the respondent prior to bringing a claim. It allows the complainant to obtain detailed information which might assist the presentation of the complaint and to find out more about the case the respondent is likely to present by way of a defence. In some cases (particularly those involving complaints of indirect discrimination), the answers provided to a well-formulated questionnaire might be the best means by which a complainant can assess the prospects of succeeding in a claim.

Furthermore, provided it has been served within the relevant time limits (see below), the questionnaire and any answers given by way of reply can be used as evidence in any tribunal proceedings. The replies given are admissible as evidence, whether or not the prescribed form has been used by the respondent.[2] If the respondent fails to answer or replies in an equivocal or evasive fashion, this might in itself be used as evidence of discrimination (see p72, 'Responding to the questionnaire').

In many discrimination cases, particularly those involving allegations of indirect discrimination, statistical information about the respondent's workforce may provide the best evidence available from which to draw an inference of discrimination. Where no existing document contains the statistical information sought,

2 SDA 1975 s74(2)(a) and RRA 1976 s 65(5).

discovery will be useless and an order for further particulars is unlikely to be considered appropriate in these circumstances.[3] Furthermore, some tribunals have indicated that they will not order that information be provided by way of written answers (see p77 below) where a questionnaire would the appropriate means for requesting the details concerned.

The basic form of questionnaire set out in the Questions and Replies Orders provides a useful starting point for any complainant. Part 4 allows for other questions to be included in the form and these will obviously depend on the particular circumstances of the case which is to be brought. As a general rule, details of the sex or racial breakdown of the relevant part of the work-force will provide useful background to the claim, as will any information on the maintenance and operation of any equal opportunities policy by the employer. Specialist assistance in the drafting of questionnaires may be obtained from the CRE or EOC, either from members of their staff or by way of reference to local advisers with relevant experience.

Responding to the questionnaire

The recipient of a questionnaire is not obliged to serve a reply nor can s/he be ordered to do so. If, however, the tribunal finds that a respondent has deliberately and without reasonable excuse omitted to reply to a properly presented questionnaire within a reasonable period of time, or that the replies given are evasive or equivocal, it may draw any inference from that fact that it considers just and equitable to draw, including an inference that the respondent committed an unlawful act (ie, an act of unlawful sex or race discrimination).[4] Any respondent on the receiving end of a question-naire would, therefore, be well advised to answer clearly and promptly.

Time limits on questionnaires

Article 5 of both Questions and Replies Orders provides for time limits within which the questionnaire must be served if it is to be utilised as evidence before a tribunal. These limits are as follows:

---

3 *Carrington v Helix Lighting Ltd* [1990] ICR 125; [1990] IRLR 6, EAT.
4 SDA 1975 s74(2)(b) and RRA 1976 s65(2)(b).

- If the questionnaire is served *before* the presentation of an originating application: three months beginning with the date of the act complained of.
- If the questionnaire is served *after* the presentation of an originating application: 21 days beginning with the day upon which the application was presented.

A questionnaire served outside these time limits must be served with the leave of the tribunal if it is to be admissible as evidence. Where leave is given by a tribunal to serve a questionnaire, the time limit within which it must then be served will be specified by the tribunal itself. If an applicant wishes to serve a questionnaire out of time, the best course is to send a copy to the respondent, giving notice that s/he intends to apply to the tribunal for leave to serve out of time. At the same time s/he should make her application to the tribunal, including with the application a copy of the proposed questionnaire together with all relevant correspondence. The tribunal which considers whether or not to grant leave will consider matters such as the length of any delay and the reasons for it and the possible prejudice to the respondent, as well as the relevance or oppressiveness of the questions included within the questionnaire itself.[5]

If on receipt of the reply to the original questionnaire it is apparent that further questions need to be asked, there is nothing to stop an applicant from applying to the tribunal for leave to serve further questionnaires, although s/he will be unable to ask for further particulars of the original questionnaire (see below). Indeed, the service of further questionnaires is a practice which the EAT has endorsed in appropriate circumstances as a 'sensible and necessary part of the procedure'.[6]

The service of further questionnaires must, however, be distinguished from the service of a request for further particulars of matters raised in the reply. Just as the tribunal cannot order that a respondent reply to a questionnaire, it has no power to order that further particulars of a reply be provided.

5 *Williams v Greater London Citizens Advice Bureaux Service* [1989] ICR 545, EAT.
6 *Carrington v Helix* (n3 above).

Further particulars

A party to tribunal proceedings may ask the other party to provide further particulars of the originating application or notice of appearance. Although there are no formal 'pleadings' in tribunal proceedings, the process is similar in many respects to requests for further and better particulars in High Court or county court cases under RSC Order 18 r12 or CCR Order 6 r7. The purpose of a request for further particulars is to ensure that a party is properly informed of its opponent's case so that it can be prepared to meet it at any hearing. If an employer's notice of appearance contains the allegation that the applicant was unable to perform his/her duties satisfactorily, the applicant would be entitled to further particulars as to which duties are referred to and the manner in which it is alleged his/her performance was unsatisfactory.[7] Or if an applicant claims s/he was treated in a way which was inconsistent with the treatment of other employees and with the general practice within that employment, the employer would be entitled to request further particulars of the general practice alleged, and citation of instances involving other employees.[8]

As a general rule, a party should not be required to supply further particulars in respect of an issue upon which the other side bears the burden of proof.[9] Where a party puts forward a postitive case, however, further particulars may be ordered of the allegations made even though s/he does not bear the burden of proof. For instance, in a case where dismissal is admitted (where the employer will bear the burden of proving the reason for that dismissal), it has been held that an applicant who speculates upon the real reason for the dismissal may be required to provide further particulars of any positive assertion made.[10]

The necessity of requesting further particulars arises when the other side has failed fully to particularise its case. If the replies given to a request are still not sufficiently particularised, a further request can be made: a request for further particulars of the further particulars. But requests should not develop into an attempt to carry out the trial of the issues on paper. Tribunals will not order further particulars requested solely for the purpose of ascertaining the

---

7 *White v University of Manchester* [1976] ICR 419; [1976] IRLR 218, EAT.
8 *International Computers Ltd v Whitley* [1978] IRLR 318, EAT.
9 *James v Radnor County Council* (1890) 6 TLR 240, QBD.
10 *Colonial Mutual Life Assurance Society Ltd v Clinch* [1981] ICR 752, EAT.

witnesses the other party is likely to call to give evidence.[11] Tribunals will also be reluctant to order that further particulars be provided which go solely to compensation when the issues on liability have not yet been determined, even though this might be useful for an employer seeking to make a realistic offer of settlement.[12]

Where an originating application is insufficiently particularised for a respondent to understand the nature of the case made by the applicant, even to the extent of being able to present a properly formulated notice of appearance, an order can be made for further particulars to be supplied even before a notice of appearance is served (r3(2)(b)). This is one of the few steps which can be taken by a respondent who has not entered a notice of appearance (see p59).

When responding to a request for further particulars, a party is not obliged to supply information which has not been sought, although it may be advisable to expand the answer if it is not otherwise possible to answer the request properly. At the same time, parties should be wary of requests which require 'all facts and matters relied on in support of the allegation that . . .'. An incomplete answer to such a request may result in an objection to the subsequent introduction of further matters relied upon in support of the allegation concerned but not specified in the reply. This is an attempt to use the further particulars as a means of defining the limits of the opponent's case. If, after responding to a request for further particulars, new information comes to light which adds to the case a party wishes to put forward, or if it has left out certain matters by mistake, it is better to raise these points either by amendment or by voluntary additional further particulars, rather than to wait until the hearing of the case.

In making a request for further particulars, or in responding to such a request, the basic principles to be applied should be borne in mind, as summarised by Wood J in *Byrne v Financial Times Ltd*:[13]

> General principles affecting the ordering of further and better particulars include that the parties should not be taken by surprise at the last minute; that particulars should only be ordered when necessary in order to do justice in the case or to prevent adjournment; that the order should not be oppressive; that particulars are for the purpose of identifying the issues, not for the production of the evidence; and that complicated pleadings battles should not be encouraged.

11 *P&O European Ferries (Dover) Ltd v Byrne* [1989] ICR 779; [1989] IRLR 254, CA.
12 *Colonial Mutual Life Assurance Society Ltd v Clinch* (n10 above).
13 [1991] IRLR 417 at 419, EAT.

The power to order further particulars

A request for further particulars should first be made directly to the other party without seeking an order from the tribunal. It is always better to try to obtain further details from the other side on a voluntary basis and this is certainly the practice encouraged by tribunals.

Rule 4(1)(a) sets out the tribunal's power to order that a party provide further particulars of the grounds on which that party relies, and of any facts and contentions relevant to those grounds. Such an order can be made on the application of a party or by the tribunal of its own motion. An application for an order under this rule is decided by a chairman sitting alone (r13(8)).

Whether made directly to the other party or by way of application to the tribunal, a request for further particulars should be in writing and should ideally set out the passage in respect of which the particulars are sought before stating the nature of the request made.

As with all interlocutory orders, a tribunal's decision whether or not to order further particulars will be largely a matter for its discretion and will be very difficult to overturn on appeal. This is also true of the tribunal's power to vary or set aside orders for further particulars and of any decision whether or not to strike out or debar for failure to comply with an order.

Application to vary or set aside an order

If an order requiring a person to supply further particulars is made by the tribunal in his/her absence, that person may apply to the tribunal to vary or set aside the order under r4(5). Such an application should be made by notice to the secretary before the date by which the tribunal has ordered that the particulars be supplied. Notice of the application to vary or set aside will then be sent to all other parties.

Failure to comply with an order

If a party does not comply with an order made under r4(1), the tribunal may, before or at the hearing, strike out the whole or part of the originating application or notice of appearance and can also debar a respondent from further defending the application. A tribunal cannot do so without having sent notice to the party in default giving him/her an opportunity to show cause why the tribunal should not do so (r4(7)). The notice cannot be sent out before expiry of the time limit ordered for the further particulars to be provided.[14]

Further particulars of questionnaires

A tribunal will not order a respondent to provide further particulars of a reply to a questionnaire. The proper course of action if a complainant wishes to ask further questions of the respondent in such cases, is to seek leave to serve a further questionnaire (see p73).

Equal pay cases

In an equal pay case, where the respondent seeks to rely on the genuine material factor defence provided by Equal Pay Act 1970 s1(3), an applicant can request precise details of the percentage pay differentials which are said to be explained by the material factor relied on.[15] The arguments previously relied on by respondents to resist any such request for further particulars of this defence[16] would now be contrary to the decision of the ECJ in *Enderby*.

Written answers

A further means of seeking information about another party's case is to ask that answers be given in writing to specific questions in respect of that case (r4(3)). Written answers are likely to be viewed in the same way as interrogatories in the High Court or county court and the same guidelines are likely to be applied.[17] Indeed, r4(3) is similar to the equivalent court rules on interrogatories in providing that such an order may be made if the tribunal 'considers (a) that the answer of the party to that question may help to clarify any issue likely to arise for determination in the proceedings, and (b) that it would be likely to assist the progress of the proceedings for that answer to be available to the tribunal before the hearing'.

Like interrogatories in court proceedings, written answers are unlikely to be ordered where other procedural processes would be

---

14 *Beacard Property Management and Construction Co Ltd v Day* [1984] ICR 837, EAT.
15 *Enderby v Frenchay Health Authority and Secretary of State for Health* [1994] ICR 112; [1993] IRLR 591, CA and ECJ.
16 *Byrne and Others v Financial Times Ltd* [1991] IRLR 417, EAT.
17 See RSC Order 26 and CCR Order 14 r11.

more appropriate, eg, where the answer could be sought by way of a request for further particulars or where it would be resolved on discovery. Some tribunals have indicated that they will not be prepared to order written answers to questions in sex or race discrimination cases where the information could be sought by using the questionnaire procedure (see p71). As with further particulars, tribunals will be reluctant to order that written answers be provided where the questions asked amount to an attempt to try the issues in the case on paper rather than at a hearing.

Written answers will be considered by the tribunal not as part of the 'pleading' process but as representations made by the party concerned as part of his/her case, as if made orally at any hearing on the matter (r4(3) and (4)).

The power to order written answers

The other party should first be asked to provide written answers on a voluntary basis. If this is refused, r4(3) provides that the party may be ordered to do so by the tribunal, either on the application of a party or of its own motion. If an application is made by a party, the tribunal may require it to send notice of the application to all other parties. When a tribunal makes an order, it will state the time within which the answers must be supplied and a copy of the order will be sent to all other parties by the secretary. A chairman sitting alone may decide the application of a party for an order under this rule, r13(8).

Application to vary or set aside an order to provide written answers

If an order requiring a party to supply written answers is made by the tribunal in his/her absence, r4(5) provides that the person may apply to the tribunal to vary or set aside the order. Such an application should be made to the secretary before the expiry of the date by which the tribunal has ordered that the particulars be supplied. Notice of the application to vary or set aside will then be sent to all other parties.

Failure to comply with an order

If a party does not comply with an order under r4(3), the tribunal may, before or at the hearing, strike out the whole or part of the originating application or notice of appearance and can also debar a respondent from defending the action further. A tribunal cannot strike out or debar, however, without having sent notice to the party in default giving him/her an opportunity to show cause why the tribunal should not do so (r4(7)); such notice must not be sent out before expiry of the time limit ordered for the written answers to be provided (by analogy with requests for further particulars).[18]

18 *Beacard Property Management and Construction Co Ltd v Day* [1984] ICR 837, EAT.

CHAPTER 9

Discovery

Introduction

The documentation relevant to a particular case will generally provide the best evidence to the issues in that case. It avoids the need to rely on selective recollection of events, and can provide a useful indication of the real view taken by a particular individual at the time an event occurred rather than that which s/he adopts when giving evidence after proceedings have commenced. Finding out about the existence of those documents and gaining sight of them is effected by *discovery and inspection* (recovery in Scotland). It may well be the most crucial step taken by the parties. The documents available in a case will often be the best weapon available and the earlier inspection of the documents takes place, the earlier a party can use the weapon to its advantage, whether by way of requests for further discovery, or further particulars, or for use in assessing the merits of the case generally and in settlement negotiations.

General principles

Unlike in High Court or county court proceedings (see RSC Order 24 and CCR Order 14 and Order 17 r11), there is no general duty to make discovery in tribunal proceedings. Unless a party requests discovery, the other side is not obliged to disclose any documents at all. Late production of documents, on the morning of the hearing, may, however, give good grounds for seeking an adjournment with an order for costs to be made against the party with previously undisclosed documents. Where the late discovery involves just one or two short documents, the tribunal may expect the hearing to go ahead after a short adjournment on the morning to enable the other party to read the new papers. The principle is that no party should be prejudiced by late disclosure of documents.

Such difficulties can be overcome to some extent by seeking discovery before the hearing. As there is no general duty to disclose all documents, this can often be a very imprecise procedural instrument. As an employee will not know all the documents in the employer's possession, *specific* requests may miss the most important document in the case. The crown jewels may be a board minute or confidential memo refering to him/her as a dangerous militant who will have to be removed (in a union reasons case), or stating that s/he does not fit in (in a race discrimination case). General requests for discovery of an employee's personnel file, or for all documents on which the other side intends to rely, may not produce the goods: damning policy documents, for instance, may not be specific to that employee. While tribunals dislike general orders for discovery, a request for all documents relevant to the issues in the case may be the best way to ensure at the hearing that all the cards are on the table.

A party who chooses to make *voluntary* disclosure of any documents must, however, disclose all of them and not be selective. The principles were set out by Waite J:

> Once ... a party has disclosed certain documents ... it becomes his duty not to withhold ... any further documents in his possession or power ... if there is any risk that the effect ... might be to convey to his opponent or to the tribunal a false or misleading impression as to the true nature, purport or effect of any disclosed document.
>
> ... [T]wo principles [are] to be borne in mind if injustice is not to be suffered ... the duty of every party not to withhold from disclosure any document whose suppression would render a disclosed document misleading is a high duty which the tribunals should interpret broadly and strictly.... Tribunals should ... ensure that if any party can be ... at risk of having his claim or defence unfairly restricted by the denial of an opportunity to become aware of a document ... material to the just prosecution of his case, he does not suffer any avoidable disadvantage as a result.[1]

Discovery actually means providing a list of documents; inspection, which may include the taking of copies, is what is required to see them. In practice, parties generally agree to conduct discovery by mutual exchange of copies of relevant documentation. Rarely, a charge is made for copying and, if it is reasonable, it must be paid.

1 *Birds Eye Walls Ltd v Harrison* [1985] ICR 278, [1985] IRLR 47, EAT.

Reliance on the more technical form of discovery by list arises where the great majority of documents are with one party, usually the employer, the request is generalised and providing extensive copies might be unduly burdensome. In these circumstances, or where the party in question is just being bloody-minded, discovery may well be by list, the other party being expected to request inspection of specific items or to undertake the copying itself.

Power to order discovery

The power to order discover is provided by r4(1)(b). A tribunal may, on the application of a party or of its own motion, order one party to grant to another such discovery or inspection of documents (including the taking of copies) as might be granted by a county court. The procedure of the county court is set out in CCR Order 14 rr1–9. A county court may order discovery of the documents which are or have been in the possession of a party and which relate to any question in the proceedings. The court may make either a general order or one limited to certain classes of documents, as it thinks fit. But a court should not make an order 'if and so far as it is of the opinion that discovery, disclosure or production, as the case may be, is not necessary either for disposing fairly of the action or matter or for saving costs' (Order 14 r8(1)).

Tribunals encourage parties to avoid the need for formal applications for discovery and inspection and, instead, to agree to the mutual exchange of documents and the creation of an 'agreed bundle' for use in any tribunal hearing. An agreed bundle does not mean that all parties agree on the relevance of the documents it contains or on the truth of their contents. All it means is that there is no live dispute about the existence and authorship of the documents involved, so the writer need not be called as a witness simply to prove s/he created the document. Of course, the writer should be called if there is dispute about the reasons for what is written. So a director who signed a disciplinary procedure agreement need not be called but the manager who wrote the dismissal letter under the procedure should be.

Although the tribunal's power in relation to discovery and inspection is quite limited, the notice of hearing, Form IT4 (p245), expressly suggests that mutual discovery by list take place voluntarily and that sufficient copies are provided for other parties, before the hearing, and for the tribunal members and the witness-table at the hearing.

A decision relating to discovery may be made by a tribunal

chairman sitting alone (r13(8)) and may arise from the tribunal acting of its own motion (r4(1)).

Before determining an application for discovery, a tribunal may require the party making the application to give notice of it to all other parties, giving particulars of the application and the address to which and the time within which any objection should be made (both of which will be specified by the tribunal) (r13(5)).

If the tribunal determines an application for discovery on the papers, or in the absence of any party, the absent party against whom any order is made may apply to the tribunal to vary or set aside the requirement (r4(5)). Any order for discovery is an interlocutory order and not a decision. There is no power for the tribunal to review it (see chapter 21) but it can be appealed.[2] The decision in any instance is, however, largely a matter for its discretion and it will be difficult for any party to appeal against that decision.

Failure to comply

If a party fails to comply with an order for discovery, the tribunal may, at or before the hearing, strike out the whole or part of the originating application or notice of appearance, and debar a respondent from defending the proceedings altogether. The tribunal cannot, however, strike out or debar unless prior notice has been sent to the party concerned giving an opportunity to show cause why the tribunal should not do so (r4(7)).

In considering whether to strike out or debar, the tribunal will take into account similar considerations to those applied in the High Court or county courts.[3] The main test is whether there is a real or substantial risk that, as a result of the default, a fair trial will no longer be possible.[4]

Failure to comply with an order for discovery, without reasonable excuse, may also render the party concerned liable on summary conviction to a fine not exceeding level 3 on the standard scale.[5]

No duty to create documents

Discovery applies only to existing documentation; there is no obligation under this procedure for a party to create a document. Where

2 *Science Research Council v Nasse* [1980] AC 1028; [1979] ICR 921; [1979] IRLR 465, HL.
3 *National Grid Co Ltd v Virdee* [1992] IRLR 555, EAT.
4 *Landauer Ltd v Comins & Co* (1991) *Times* 7 August, CA.
5 ITA 1996 s7(4) and r4(6).

statistics are sought which will have to be created for that case, the questionnaire in discrimination cases, or the written answer procedure under r4(3), might provide the only means of obtaining such information (see pp70 and 77).

Discovery and inspection: general principles

Documents

A 'document' is widely defined for the purposes of discovery. It is not limited to writing or print on paper but includes anything upon which information or evidence is recorded, eg, tape recordings,[6] photographs, videotapes, microfilms,[7] computer disks and so on.

In High Court and county court proceedings, the documents used at court hearings should be the originals whenever possible. This rule does not apply to tribunal proceedings, although the original should be available for inspection if any question is raised (or is likely to be raised) as to its authenticity, or its alteration.

Relevance

A document of which discovery is sought must first be shown to be material and relevant to the issues in the proceedings. A document is 'relevant' when:

> it is reasonable to suppose [it] contains information which *may*, not which *must*, either directly or indirectly enable the party [applying for discovery] either to advance his own case or to damage the case of his adversary [including] a document which may fairly lead him to a train of enquiry which may have either of these two consequences . . .[8]

A document is not 'relevant' if it is intended to be used merely to attack a witness's credibility;[9] nor if it is being sought to find out the names of the other side's witnesses.[10]

Relevance is not the only criterion. If the tribunal is satisfied that the documents are material and relevant to the case, it may still

6 *Grant v Southwestern and County Properties Ltd* [1974] 2 All ER 465, ChD.
7 Bankers' Books Evidence Act 1879.
8 *Compagnie Financière du Pacifique v Peruvian Guano Co* [1882] 11 QBD 55, CA.
9 *George Ballantine & Son Ltd v F E R Dixon & Son Ltd* [1974] 2 All ER 503, ChD.
10 *Knapp v Harvey* [1911] 2 KB 725, CA.

exercise its discretion to decide not to order disclosure. Similar principles will apply as in county court cases, that is to say:

> the court, if satisfied that the discovery, disclosure, production or supply sought is not necessary, or not necessary at that stage of the action or matter, may dismiss or adjourn the application and shall in any case refuse to make an order if and so far as it is of the opinion that discovery, disclosure, production or supply, as the case may be, is not necessary either for disposing fairly of the action or matter or for saving costs.[11]

Relevant to the tribunal's exercise of discretion are the following questions:

- Will refusing discovery hinder a fair hearing?
- Will refusing discovery cause delay and thereby increase costs?
- Would an order for discovery in the terms sought be oppressive?
- Are there any other relevant considerations, such as confidentiality, which need to be balanced against the question of relevance?

It is for the party applying for discovery to show that the document is relevant to an issue or issues already clearly defined in the proceedings, ie, it is not a fishing expedition and that discovery is necessary at that stage in the proceedings.[12]

Privilege

'Privilege' protects a document from disclosure or inspection in the interests of the administration of justice. For public policy reasons, a party will not be obliged to hand over certain classes of documents. Privilege may arise in a number of instances which are considered below.

Confidentiality

General guidelines as to confidentiality of documents and discovery in tribunal cases were set out by Lord Wilberforce in *Science Research Council v Nasse; Vyas v Leyland Cars*[13] and can be summarised as:

a) If a tribunal is satisfied that discovery of a document is necessary in order fairly to dispose of the proceedings, it must order

---

11 CCR Order 14 r8(1); and see RSC Order 24 r2.
12 *Rolls Royce Motor Cars Ltd v Mair and Others* (unreported) EAT/794/92.
13 [1980] AC 1028; [1979] ICR 921; [1979] IRLR 465, HL.

disclosure of the document, even though the document is confidential. There is no principle in law by which documents are protected from discovery by reason of confidentiality by itself.[14]

b) There is no presumption against disclosure of confidential documents.

c) Where there is an objection to disclosure of documents on the grounds of confidentiality, the tribunal should inspect the documents to decide whether disclosure is necessary for the fair disposal of the case or for saving expense.

d) In exercising its discretion as to whether to order disclosure, the tribunal should have regard to the fact that documents are confidential and should consider whether the necessary information can be obtained by other means, not involving a breach of confidence.

e) Confidentiality is a relevant factor in deciding whether to order discovery: relevance is not the only factor and general orders for discovery are not always appropriate in tribunal proceedings.

A party will not be able to claim privilege against disclosure solely on the ground that the document, or its contents, was supplied in confidence by a third party.[15]

It is for the tribunal in its discretion, rather than as a matter of strict entitlement by a party, to decide questions of confidentiality and discovery. It can decide them at some interlocutory stage or as they arise during the hearing.[16] Often the most appropriate course is to consider all arguments relating to discovery and the confidentiality of documents at a separate directions hearing. This has been particularly encouraged by the EAT for complex cases.[17]

If the tribunal, at whatever stage, considers it appropriate that there should be an examination of the documents, it should consider how the facts in the documents can be disclosed without divulging the confidential parts. As a general rule, names and addresses of those against whom comparison is being made (eg, in a case alleging discrimination at interview for a job) should not be disclosed, although qualifications may well be, as might other factors

14 *Alfred Crompton Amusement Machines Ltd v Customs and Excise Commissioners (No 2)* [1974] AC 405, HL.

15 *Alfred Crompton Amusement Machines Ltd v Customs and Excise Commissioners (No 2)* [1974] AC 405; [1973] 2 All ER 1169, HL.

16 *BRB v Natarajan* [1979] ICR 326; [1979] IRLR 45, EAT.

17 See *Brooks v British Telecommunications plc* [1991] ICR 286; 1991 IRLR 4, EAT (affirmed by the CA: [1992] ICR 414; [1992] IRLR 66) and *Halford v Sharples* [1992] ICR 146, EAT (affirmed by the CA: [1992] ICR 583).

necessary for the tribunal to make a proper assessment of the value of the evidence.

Public interest immunity

All claims of privilege rely on general principles of public policy. Public interest immunity goes further and asserts protection from discovery on the ground that disclosure would be injurious to the public interest. When public interest immunity is claimed, the tribunal will have to balance that claim against the importance of the documents to the proceedings, the extent of injustice caused by their non-disclosure and the public interest in fair administration of justice.[18] There is no 'right' to resist disclosure on such a ground but the party seeking to do so should be able to show some public duty which outweighs the public policy considerations in favour of disclosure.

The circumstances in which public interest immunity might arise have been identified as falling within two types: immunity extending to a whole class of documents and immunity simply in relation to the contents of a particular document. The distinction has been described by Lord Wilberforce as follows:

> ... with a 'class' claim it is immaterial whether the disclosure of the particular contents of particular documents would be injurious to the public interest – the point being that it is the maintenance of the immunity of the 'class' from disclosure in litigation that is important; whereas in a contents claim, the protection is claimed for particular 'contents' in a particular document. A claim remains a 'class' even though something may be known about the contents; it remains a 'class' even if parts of the documents are revealed and parts disclosed.[19]

Where immunity is claimed on a 'class' basis, an order for inspection should be made with extreme care and should not be exercised before giving the party claiming the immunity the opportunity to appeal.[20]

If a claim of 'class' immunity is accepted and documents are excluded on that basis, no use whatever can be made of the documents and no reliance placed on anything contained in them by any of the parties to the proceedings.

18 *D v NSPCC* [1977] 1 All ER 589, HL.
19 *Burmah Oil Co Ltd v Bank of England* [1980] AC 1090 at 1111, HL.
20 *Halford v Sharples* [1992] ICR 146 at 155–158, EAT and [1992] ICR 583 at 609–610, CA.

Police complaints files containing documents prepared under the Police and Criminal Evidence Act 1984, and files compiled under the police disciplinary regulations, are discoverable as a 'class'. But immunity or other kinds of privilege may be claimed in respect of the contents of *particular* documents within those categories.[21]

'Class' immunity has also been held not to apply to files held by the Association of Chief Police Officers consisting of confidential reports kept on each individual chief officer[22] (subject to the exclusion of particular documents relating to positive vetting and the private lives of individual officers). Nor does it apply to statements made in the course of police grievance proceedings.[23]

National security

Where the disclosure of any information would, in the opinion of a minister, be contrary to the interests of national security, any disclosure of that information will be prohibited.[24] Even without this statutory prohibition, which could be applied in most proceedings before a tribunal (ERA 1996 s193(2)), whenever public interest immunity is claimed, courts and tribunals will generally not look behind that certificate to assess the likely danger themselves. In *Balfour v Foreign and Commonwealth Office*[25] the Court of Appeal held that whilst a tribunal should be vigilant to ensure that a claim of public interest immunity was raised only in appropriate circumstances, and was particularised, once a certificate of a minister demonstrated that the disclosure of documentary evidence posed an actual or potential risk to national security, the tribunal should not exercise its right to inspect that evidence.[26]

Diplomatic privilege

Embassy documents are protected by absolute privilege.[27]

---

21 *R v Chief Constable of West Midlands Police ex p Wiley* [1995] 1 AC 274, overruling *Neilson v Laugharne* [1981] QB 736, CA.
22 *Halford v Sharples* [1992] ICR 146, EAT.
23 *Metropolitan Police Comr v Locker* [1993] ICR 440; [1993] IRLR 319, EAT.
24 ERA 1996 s195.
25 [1994] ICR 277.
26 Also see *Conway v Rimmer* [1968] AC 910, HL.
27 *Fayed v Al-Tajir* [1987] 2 All ER 396, CA.

Legal privilege

Legal privilege falls under two heads:

a) *Legal advice privilege*: communications between client and legal adviser which are confidential and made for the purpose of obtaining or providing legal advice. These include documents which come into being in contemplation of litigation, but are not limited to that classification. The basis of the privilege is the principle that any person should be entitled to seek and obtain legal advice at any time without fear that it might later be disclosed to another; the privilege is therefore owned by the client, not the lawyer, and continues indefinitely.

b) *Legal proceedings privilege*: communications between client, legal adviser and third parties which are made for the purpose of existing or contemplated legal proceedings. This privilege is more limited in nature and has a restricted life. It can no longer be relied on once the litigation concerned has come to an end.

'Legal adviser' is defined as a qualified lawyer: a barrister, advocate, solicitor or salaried legal executive, whether in independent practice or employed 'in-house': see notes to CCR Order 14 r5. It does not extend to other professional advisers such as personnel consultants and, presumably, trade union officials and other advice workers even though the advice is clearly in the nature of legal advice.[28] The difficulty with this restriction in tribunal proceedings is that because of the open nature of the forum and the lack of legal aid, applicants (in particular) are often likely to have received advice from those who are not legal professionals. If that advice-giver is merely acting as the means of communication between the applicant and a professionally qualified legal adviser, the communication will still be privileged, but if the advice comes direct from a non-qualified source, no privilege will attach.

Without prejudice communications

It is a rule of evidence that without prejudice communications between the parties should not be disclosed to a court.[29] This rule applies to tribunals.[30] In *Catterall* the public policy behind the rule was described; parties should be free to try and settle their differences without fear that anything they say in the course of

---

28 *New Victoria Hospital v Ryan* [1993] ICR 201; [1993] IRLR 202, EAT.
29 *Cutts v Head* [1984] Ch 290, CA.
30 *Independent Research Services Ltd v Catterall* [1993] ICR 1 EAT.

negotiations will be used in evidence as a sign of weakness or lack of confidence in their case. On the assumption that negotiations are 'genuine' and not a pretext to hide a threat, without prejudice correspondence – for example, describing an offer made by an employer to settle an applicant's case – will be excluded as inadmissible and cannot be orderd to be disclosed.

Usually such correspondence is headed 'without prejudice' but the presence or absence of these words is not conclusive. Material can be excluded if it forms part of a series of negotiations, some of which are properly headed 'without prejudice' and some are not.[31] In *Catterall* (above) the EAT held that an exception could be made to the rule excluding the without prejudice material only if excluding it would allow a dishonest case to be advanced.

On the other hand, just because a letter is headed 'without prejudice' does not mean to say it will be privileged; it will be the contents of the letter which matter. If these are written with a view to settlement, the communication will be privileged; if not, then the fact that it is so labelled will do nothing to create a privilege where none exists.[32]

Communications with ACAS conciliation officers

In tribunal proceedings, this 'without prejudice privilege' extends to communications between a party and an ACAS conciliation officer unless the privilege is expressly waived by the party communicating with the conciliation officer.[33]

Medical reports

Medical reports will often be confidential documents. Where, for instance, the applicant is the subject of the report in question, s/he may never have seen the report before the tribunal proceedings and may be surprised and even distressed by its contents. Such considerations, however, should not outweigh the need to order discovery and inspection to the applicant in appropriate case.[34] Safeguards may, however, be employed, such as covering up irrelevant parts of

---

31 *South Shropshire District Council v Amos* [1986] 1 WLR 1271, CA.
32 *Chocoladefabriken Lindt & Sprungli AG v Nestle Co Ltd* [1978] RPC 287, ChD.
33 ITA 1996 s18(7) and *M & W Grazebrook Ltd v Wallens* [1973] ICR 256; [1973] IRLR 139, NIRC (see chapter 15).
34 *McIvor v Southern Health & Social Services Board* [1978] 1 WLR 757; [1978] 2 All ER 625, HL.

the report or limiting disclosure to legal advisers.[35] Even where disclosure could be detrimental to a party's mental health, this consideration may be outweighed by the need to ensure that s/he is not prejudiced in presenting his/her case.[36]

Disclosure of medical reports obtained by an employer will rarely be refused in a case where the reason given for the applicant's dismissal is incapability due to ill-health.[37]

Medical Reports Act 1988

This Act gives an employee a statutory right to access to medical reports prepared for employment purposes by a medical practitioner with responsibility for the clinical care of the employee, ie, the employee's own GP or hospital doctor or consultant or the company's doctor where the employee has been under his/her care and so the report is not the result of a one-off examination.

The Act also protects the employee in the normal course of his/her employment as it places restrictions upon the obtaining of medical information by the employer from the employee's own adviser.

Waiver of privilege

The privilege which attaches to certain documents can be lost if the party who could claim it chooses to 'waive' that protection. Where this occurs, the document becomes as any other and can no longer be claimed to be 'privileged' from disclosure or production.

In most cases, the privilege will be the property of the client and not the lawyer or other adviser; consequently, only the client can waive the privilege which attaches to a particular document. A lawyer or adviser can, however, waive privilege on the client's behalf. In the case of 'without prejudice' communications, the privilege belongs to both parties to the document and it can only be waived by them jointly; it is not capable of unilateral waiver.[38]

Diplomatic privilege can only be waived by the state to whom it belongs or by the ambassador on behalf of that state.[39]

In High Court and county court proceedings, a formal list is used

---

35 *DHSS v Sloan* [1981] ICR 313, EAT.
36 *DHSS v Sloan* (No 2) (unreported) EAT 342/81.
37 *Ford Motor Co Ltd v Nawaz* [1987] ICR 434; [1987] IRLR 163, EAT.
38 *Walker v Wilsher* (1889) 23 QBD 335, CA.
39 *R v Madan* [1961] 2 QB 1, CA.

for discovery purposes which contains separate sections for privileged and non-privileged documents (High Court Form No 26, county court N265). Whilst there is no standard form of list in tribunal proceedings, caution must still be taken not to list as available for inspection those documents in respect of which privilege may be claimed (see below).

Privilege may be lost by reference to the document concerned during the course of a hearing. This may occur by the party owning the privilege giving evidence with reference to that document or by the party's representative mentioning it in the course of speeches or in questioning a witness. If it is not intended for privilege to be waived, then the party wishing to claim it should be careful not to rely on the document during the course of the proceedings.

Mistaken disclosure

When a privileged document is mistakenly included in a list of documents on discovery, the privilege is not necessarily to be taken as having been 'waived': in such circumstances the party wishing to claim privilege should seek as soon as practicable to rectify the mistake by amending the list of documents. If, however, the other party is allowed to inspect the document concerned or is even supplied with a copy, it may be far more difficult subsequently to seek to assert privilege in respect of it. In such circumstances, the party wishing to claim privilege should seek to rectify the situation as soon as possible by notifying the other side of the mistake which has occurred and identifying the document as one in respect of which privilege is claimed. Whether or not privilege will still attach to the document will depend on the circumstances of the disclosure and the conduct of the parties. If the party to whom the document has been disclosed consciously took advantage of the opponent's mistake to obtain a copy, the tribunal may be persuaded to rectify that mistake so that the privilege may be reclaimed.[40]

Partly privileged documents

A party claiming privilege in respect of a document will not be permitted to rely on parts of that document on a self-selected basis. Just as with other documents, a party is under a duty not to give partial discovery:

---

40 *Derby & Co Ltd v Weldon (No 8)* [1991] 1 WLR 73, CA.

Where a party is deploying in court material which would otherwise be privileged, the opposite party and the court must have an opportunity of satisfying themselves that what the party has chosen to release from privilege represents the whole of the material relevant to the issue in question. To allow an individual item to be plucked out of context would be to risk an injustice through its real weight or meaning being misunderstood.[41]

Where a document deals with more than just one subject-matter and privilege is claimed in respect of one distinct part, then it will be possible to disclose the other part or parts of the document without having been taken to have waived privilege in respect of the whole.[42] If the privileged part of the document is not so self-contained, however, part disclosure may be taken to be a waiver of the whole.

If there is any doubt, no part of the document should be disclosed but the guidance of the tribunal should be sought at an interlocutory stage: if the tribunal orders that part of the document concerned be edited out, there can be no doubt but that the party claiming the privilege has not thereby waived his/her right to protection from disclosure of the concealed part.

Documents from third parties

Rule 4(1)(b) only provides the tribunal with the power to order discovery as between parties. If discovery is desired from another person who is not a party to the proceedings, and who is not prepared to produce the document(s) in question voluntarily, then the tribunal is given the power by r4(2)(b), either on the application of a party or of its own motion, to order the attendance of any person at an appointed time and place (r4(2)(a), and see chapter 11) and to require that person 'to produce any document relating to the matter to be determined'.

Such an order may be required in a number of cases, eg, cases involving a transfer of an undertaking where the previous employer (the transferor) or the receiver is reluctant to release certain documents on a voluntary basis. Furthermore, as the tribunal's power is not limited merely to requiring a non-party to attend before a hearing of the tribunal, the order made can require the person concerned to produce the document before any substantive hearing

41 *Nea Karteria Maritime Co Ltd v Atlantic and Great Lakes Steamship Corp* [1981] Com LR 139, QBD per Mustill J.
42 *Great Atlantic Insurance Co v Home Insurance Co* [1981] 1 WLR 529, CA.

in the case. This may be the best means of securing sight of the document before a full hearing, giving all parties prior knowledge of its contents and thus time to prepare their respective cases properly in the light of this, without the need to adjourn a full hearing. Non-parties can only be ordered to attend and produce documents if they are present within Great Britain. In considering whether to order production of documents by someone who is not a party to the proceedings, the tribunal will apply the same tests of relevance and necessity as already outlined above. Furthermore, the person subject to such an order will also be able to rely on privilege from production in the circumstances already set out in this chapter.

Any person who fails, without reasonable excuse, to comply with an order to attend and produce documents is liable on summary conviction to a fine not exceeding level 3 on the standard scale.[43]

Oppressive requests

In considering whether or not to order discovery and inspection of documents, tribunals will also bear in mind the extent of the demand being made on the party who will have to produce the documents in question. Usually the respondent will hold most of the relevant documentation and where the evidence sought by the applicant relates (as it may in a discrimination or equal pay case) to a large number of persons or a period of many years, the respondent may well have grounds for claiming that an order for full discovery would be oppressive. In such a case, the order made may be limited to selective discovery, as in *Perera v Civil Service Commission*,[44] where the application for discovery would have involved the disclosure of documents relating to some 1,600 people.

Much will depend on the particular circumstances of the case and tribunals will be prepared to order quite wide-scale discovery where necessary to determine the issues which arise in a particular case. In *Selvarajan v Inner London Education Authority*[45] the EAT held, in a race discrimination case, that documents which had come into existence over a period of some 15 years before the RRA 1976 would be the subject of an order for discovery as they could be logically probative of subsequent discrimination.

43 ITA 1996 s7(4) and r4(6).
44 [1980] ICR 699; [1980] IRLR 233, EAT.
45 [1980] IRLR 313, EAT.

Where an application is given for selective discovery in such cases, it is always open to the tribunal to re-consider the matter subsequently and make a fuller order if appropriate. The proper course of action for the tribunal is first to isolate the issues to which discovery is relevant and then make orders for discovery which address those issues if necessary. If it subsequently turns out that the issues are broader than first appeared, or if further discovery is required to meet those issues, then this can be re-considered by the tribunal later in the proceedings, as in *Rolls Royce Motor Cars Ltd v Mair and Others*,[46] a case involving some 150 claims of unfair dismissal in a large-scale redundancy exercise over various divisions of the employing company.

It has also been held that there is no general principle whereby applicants are entitled to gain discovery of appraisal scores in a redundancy selection exercise.[47]

Equal pay and discrimination cases

In cases claiming equal pay, documentary evidence of previous wage-bargaining or of the background to a collective agreement may well be relevant and necessary to a determination of the issues between the parties, even though it requires consideration of matters which now appear to be ancient history. Discovery may be sought to assist the applicant in identifying an appropriate comparator, although there should be some evidence that a prima facie case is made out so the application can be shown to be more than a mere fishing expedition.[48]

Where an applicant claims discrimination, very often that claim will depend on documentary evidence relating to the treatment of other employees, including statistical and monitoring information. Guidance was given on the approach which should be taken in respect of discovery in such proceedings in *West Midlands Passenger Transport Executive v Singh*.[49] In that case, the Court of Appeal held that, in determining whether information sought in a discrimination case was relevant, the special features of discrimination proceedings should be borne in mind.

46 (unreported) EAT 794/92.
47 See *British Aerospace plc v Green and Others* [1995] IRLR 433, CA; a more generous view was taken in *FDR Ltd v Holloway* [1995] IRLR 400, EAT.
48 See *Clwyd County Council v Leverton* [1985] IRLR 197, EAT.
49 [1988] ICR 614; [1988] IRLR 186, CA.

a) The document(s) in question need not conclusively prove that the employer has discriminated; for the purposes of the discovery application it need only be established that the document(s) *may tend to prove* that such discrimination has taken place.

b) Direct discrimination means that the complainant has not been assessed according to individual merit but has been treated less favourably as a member of a particular group. Statistical information may establish a discernible pattern in the treatment of that particular group (eg, under-representation in certain jobs, lack of promotion) which may in turn give rise to an inference of discrimination against members of the group.

c) If a practice is being operated against a group, then, in the absence of a satisfactory explanation, it will be reasonable to infer that the complainant, as a member of that group, has been treated less favourably on the grounds of race or sex.

d) Evidence of discrimination against a group in relation to promotion may be more persuasive evidence of discrimination in the particular case than previous treatment of the applicant, which may be indicative of personal factors peculiar to the applicant.

e) As suitability of candidates can rarely be measured solely by objective means but will generally involve subjective judgements, evidence relating to the success or failure of members of a particular group may indicate that the real reason for failure is a conscious or unconscious discriminatory attitude which involves stereotyped assumptions about members of that group.

f) As employers are permitted to adduce evidence demonstrating that in practice they operate a policy of non-discrimination, the employee must be entitled to seek evidence to the contrary.

West Midlands Passenger Transport Executive v Singh involved allegations of race discrimination, but the principles set out by the Court of Appeal apply to complaints of discrimination generally.

As discovery in discrimination cases may include applications and assessments in relation to other candidates or employees, questions of confidentiality might well arise. Often these can be resolved by covering up references which name or otherwise identify the particular individual, but this should not be at the expense of obtaining the necessary information from the document, ie, relating to the sex or race and to the qualifications and experience of the person concerned.

CHECKLIST: DISCOVERY

- Before making an application to the tribunal, ask the other side for voluntary disclosure of documents: if there are likely to be equal quantities of documents on both sides, propose mutual exchange of copy documents; if the other side holds the bulk of the documentation, offer to pay the reasonable photocopying charges for the documents to be provided in full or seek inspection so that copies of the actual documents (or parts) required can be sought specifically.
- If you are aware of the existence (or likely existence) of certain documents, be specific in your request. If you are unsure as to the documentation in the other side's possession, ask more generally for disclosure of documents relevant to the issues in the case. In any event, it is often useful to add a 'catch-all' request for all relevant documents: however certain you are as to the existence of particular documents, you are unlikely to have full knowledge of all documentation in the other side's possession.
- If necessary, make the appropriate application to the industrial tribunal for disclosure of the documents sought, making the basis for the request clear and indicating that you have already sought voluntary disclosure but without success.
- If you are not satisfied with the discovery given, keep the tribunal informed, making clear your reasons for dissatisfaction.
- If an order for discovery has been made against you in your absence with which you are unhappy, apply to the tribunal as soon as possible (and certainly within the time period specified) for that order to be varied. If you feel it would assist, ask at the same time for an oral hearing on the question.
- When considering the documents you have to disclose, bear in mind the protection offered by the principles relating to confidentiality and privilege. Be careful not to waive privilege unless that is what you really want.
- If you realise that you have included a privileged document in a list sent to the other side without indicating that privilege is claimed, immediately amend that list to make the claim clear.
- If a privileged document has actually been sent to the other

side by mistake, immediately seek the return of that document, making it clear that privilege is claimed in respect of the document concerned.

- If questions of confidentiality or privilege arise in relation to *part* of a document, consider whether it is possible to reach agreement with the other side on a means of presenting that document without disclosure of the confidential or privileged part. If you do reach agreement, make it clear that discovery is being given on the basis of that agreement and that you do not waive privilege in respect of the document as a whole. If agreement cannot be reached and if in doubt as to the severability of that part of the document which you regard as privileged, do not disclose the document in part but refer the dispute to the tribunal.

- If a person who is not a party to the tribunal proceedings has relevant documents and is unwilling to give these up voluntarily, apply for an order for that person to attend and produce them.

- If at all possible, seek to 'agree' a bundle of documents for use before the tribunal. If agreement cannot be reached in relation to particular documents, put the rest into an agreed bundle and deal with the issues relating to the disputed documents at an interlocutory hearing or as a preliminary issue or at some other appropriate time at the substantive hearing.

CHAPTER 10

Interim relief

Tribunals have additional powers to intervene at an interlocutory stage in two kinds of dismissal cases, those involving trade union activities and health and safety at work. The powers are to grant interlocutory remedies pending the hearing of the case, notably to provide for the continuation of the contract of employment. This is felt to be an important safeguard to the rights of union activists and certain others and operates as a kind of injunction preserving the status quo, or at least allowing the employee to be treated as suspended rather than as dismissed.

Dismissal for union or health and safety reasons

The right to claim interim relief is confined to cases of dismissal where the principal reason is alleged to be the applicant's involvement in trade union matters or health and safety at work. Such dismissals are automatically unfair. Not all these dismissals are susceptible to an application for interim relief, however. This arises only if the principal reason for dismissal was that the applicant

- was or proposed to become a member of an independent trade union; or
- took part or proposed to take part at an appropriate time in its activities; or
- was *not* a member of any union or a particular union, or refused to join or proposed to refuse to join or remain in a union; or
- carried out or proposed to carry out activities in connection with preventing or reducing risks to health and safety at work, having been designated by the employer to do so; or

99

– performed or proposed to perform the functions of a health and safety representative or a member of a safety committee.[1]

There are other forms of automatically unfair dismissal which are not eligible for interim relief, such as that the applicant was *selected for redundancy* for one of the above reasons (TULRCA 1992 s153), or was dismissed for refusing to work in dangerous conditions (ERA 1996 s92(1)(c-e)), or was a protected shop or betting shop worker (ERA 1996 s93), or had asserted a statutory right (ERA 1996 s104).

Procedural steps

References to the statutory procedure described here are to dismissals for union involvement but the nature of the procedure applies equally to health and safety cases.

The application for interim relief is separate from the originating application claiming unfair dismissal but may be made on the same IT1 form, or on a different form at the same or a different time. It must be presented not later than seven days after the dismissal.[2] An applicant claiming infringement of union rights, rather than non-union or health and safety rights, must also present a certificate signed by an official of the relevant union authorised to give such a certificate, and the union must be independent. The official should say that:

a) the applicant was or proposed to become a member of the union at the date of dismissal; and

b) there appear to be reasonable grounds for supposing that the reason for the dismissal was the one alleged, ie, union involvement.[3]

The certificate must deal with the reasonableness of the belief and not simply assert the opinion of the union official, although it is axiomatic that the official would consider his or her beliefs to be founded on reasonable grounds.[4]

---

1 See TULRCA ss152, 161 (union involvement) and ERA 1996 ss100 and 128 (health and safety).
2 TULRCA 1992 s161, p34.
3 TULRCA 1992 s162.
4 *Bradley v Edward Ryde & Sons* [1979] ICR 488, EAT.

The hearing

Interim relief is one of the cases which will usually be heard by a chairman alone (see p5). The tribunal is required to secure a hearing and make a determination as soon as practicable. This has three effects. First, the employer is to be given copies of the application and certificate and at least seven days' notice of the hearing. Provision is made for additional parties to be joined on three days' notice (TULRCA 1992 s162). Secondly, the tribunal is not to exercise its ordinary powers to postpone the hearing unless 'it is satisfied that special circumstances justify' it. Thirdly, the tribunal is required to announce its findings at the hearing (TULRCA 1992 s163). The intention is that a decision should be made as quickly as practicable.

The central issue at the hearing is whether it appears likely that the tribunal hearing the full case will find that the applicant was unfairly dismissed for the alleged reason, ie, union involvement. This is really a balance of probabilities rather than a higher test, but it is more than a reasonable prospect of success.[5] If some other reason emerges which will also lead to a finding of unfair dismissal, the tribunal is not entitled to make an interim relief order.

Frequently, no witnesses are called but a submission is made by the applicant's representative and documents and a chronology are referred to. Since the evidence is likely to be controversial and subject to lengthy cross-examination, it is often counter-productive to call witnesses, since the main facets of the applicant's case will have been exposed. In the face of predicted long cross-examination, it is sometimes felt more useful to go straight to an expedited full tribunal hearing. Nevertheless there are no rules as to the type of evidence adduced and in many cases brief evidence from the applicant or the union official is appropriate.

Remedies

It is assumed the applicant wants reinstatement, so the tribunal must ask the respondent if it is willing to reinstate or re-engage on no less favourable terms and conditions of employment. If the respondent is willing to re-engage on different terms and conditions of employment in another job, the tribunal will decide whether any refusal by the applicant is reasonable. If the respondent refuses

---

5 *Taplin v C Shippam Ltd* [1978] ICR 1068; [1978] IRLR 450, EAT.

both, or the applicant reasonably refuses re-engagement, the tribunal must make an order for the continuation of the contract of employment.[6]

This is an order that for the purposes of the benefits of the contract of employment, seniority and pensions, and for continuity of employment under statute, the contract continues from the date of termination until determination or settlement of the case, including the hearing of any appeal.[7] The tribunal specifies the amounts and dates of payment of wages.

Between the hearing and final determination or settlement either party can apply (to any tribunal) for a revocation or variation of the order on the ground of a relevant change in circumstances.[8] These are not defined and appear to be widely drafted. The same urgent timescale is to be observed. There is no reason why the same tribunal should not deal with variations but it may be unfair for it to deal with interim relief and the full hearing, because it will already have expressed a view.[9]

The applicant may complain to a tribunal that the employer has not complied with the terms of an order for reinstatement or re-engagement and the tribunal may then order the continuation of the contract of employment *and* order compensation to be paid.[10]

6 TULRCA 1992 s163(6).
7 *Zucker v Astrid Jewels* [1978] ICR 1088; [1978] IRLR 385, EAT.
8 TULRCA 1992 s165 and *British Coal Corporation v McGinty* [1988] IRLR 7, EAT.
9 *British Coal* (above).
10 TULRCA 1992 s166.

CHAPTER 11

Interlocutory stages

Joinder

A tribunal can order that:

- a person be joined (added) or in Scotland 'sisted' as a party to proceedings (r17(1)); or
- a respondent be dismissed from being a party to proceedings (r17(2)); or
- one party represent a number of parties who have the same interests (r17(3)).

Such orders may be made either by the tribunal on its own motion or on application by a party usually to a chairman alone (p5).

The tribunal's powers are limited to the persons *against whom relief is sought*. So a tribunal cannot join a person if the relief sought cannot be ordered against that individual or organisation. In *Sandhu v Department of Education and Science*[1] an order joining the DES as respondent to a race discrimination claim was refused on the basis that it was not the applicant's employer, nor was there any evidence to show that the Department had aided the employer in any discriminatory act.

Where it is apparent to a tribunal that an individual should be joined to proceedings, but the applicant has failed to include that person in his/her application, this power enables the tribunal to resolve the problem of its own accord. It is a power which might conveniently be exercised in a case involving the transfer of an undertaking, where the applicant might not be sure who the correct legal respondent is.

1 [1978] IRLR 208, EAT.

The tribunal may require any party making an application under r17 to serve notice of that application on other parties (r13(5)), although there is no requirement that notice be served on the person whom it is sought to join. If an order for joinder is made under r17(1) without first hearing the person to be joined, the order will be treated as having been provisionally made *ex parte* and it will be open to the additional party to apply to be disjoined. The application is treated as an application for 'consequential directions' under r17(1).[2]

If the actions or advice of a third party are relevant to the issues in a claim, eg, an ACAS officer's involvement in a conciliated settlement, or an adviser's negligence in a claim made out of time, the tribunal cannot order that they be joined as parties unless relief can be ordered against them in the tribunal proceedings. But it may be able to order that they attend as witnesses (see p93).[3]

Industrial pressure from third parties

More specifically, the question of joinder of parties is raised by TULRCA 1992 ss150 and 160, which provide that where a dismissal (s160) or action short of dismissal (s150) takes place due to trade union or shop-floor pressure, an employer *or* the dismissed employee may request that the tribunal join the trade union or other persons exerting the pressure as additional respondent(s).

If such a request is made before the hearing begins, the tribunal *must* allow it; if it is made later, the tribunal may refuse it. If it is made after the tribunal has already given its determination as to the appropriate remedy, it must refuse it (ss150(2) and 160(2)). Where the request is made before the hearing, the tribunal has no choice but to order that the joinder take place: the person making the application for joinder does not even have to show a prima facie case. Once joined, however, the trade union or other individual concerned has the right to seek an adjournment, to ask for a pre-hearing review, or to make any other appropriate application under the 1993 Rules, just as if it had been a party from the outset.

---

2 *Reddington v S Straker & Sons Ltd* [1994] ICR 172, EAT.
3 *Marshall v Alexander Sloan & Co Ltd* [1981] IRLR 264, EAT and *Riley v Tesco Stores Ltd* [1980] ICR 323; [1980] IRLR 103, CA.

Race and sex discrimination cases

Other instances where it may be appropriate to join an individual to tribunal proceedings include race and sex discrimination cases where an individual employee might be held to be personally responsible for discriminatory acts for which their employer is also liable.

National Insurance Fund

Claims can be made against the Secretary of State for payments from the National Insurance Fund for redundancy or on an employer's insolvency. The Secretary of State has rights under the Rules even when not joined as a party: to receive notices of applications, to make interlocutory applications, to make representations on a pre-hearing review, to appear as if a party and to be heard at any full or interlocutory hearing.

In addition, the tribunal may join the Secretary of State as a party under the general provisions of r17.

Combined proceedings

On the application of a party or of its own motion, a tribunal may order that applications be considered together (r18(1)) where:

– some common question of law or fact arises in two or more applications; or
– the applications arise out of the same set of facts; or
– there is some other reason which makes it desirable that those cases are heard together.

This power might be exercised where there are several unfair dismissal claims arising out of a large-scale redundancy exercise, where there are common issues of law and fact; or where an applicant has made separate applications, eg, for unfair dismissal and racial discrimination, arising out of substantially the same set of facts.

An order that cases be considered together is not the same as decision that there will be a test case (see p107): the tribunal is still hearing separate applications. Any decision should deal separately with points of difference in the cases, even if that means that separate decisions are given.[4] For instance, in a redundancy resulting in a number of unfair dismissal claims, while there may be common

4 See *Paine & Moore v Grundy (Teddington) Ltd* [1981] IRLR 267, EAT.

questions relating to the selection criteria and collective consultation, *individual* application of the selection criteria and consultation might vary considerably.

Before making an order that cases be combined under r18, the tribunal must *either* give all parties concerned the opportunity at a hearing to show cause why such an order should not be made, *or* send notice to parties giving them the opportunity to show such cause (r18(2)). On the application of a party or of its own motion, the tribunal also has the power, under r18(3), to vary or set aside an order made for the combining of cases under r18(1). The tribunal must give each party the opportunity to make oral or written representations (r18(3)).

In many cases where there are multiple applications involving similar issues of fact or law, an order combining cases is in everyone's interest. It saves having to adduce evidence or to make legal submissions more than once. It can lead to a substantial saving in costs and time, particularly where large numbers of witnesses are involved.

Parties may, however, have genuine concerns about combining applications, particularly if this may prejudice one person's case. In *Dietmann and Wahlstrom v London Borough of Brent,*[5] a case arising out of the public enquiry into the death of the child Jasmine Beckford, two social workers, each claiming that she had been unfairly dismissed, argued against their cases being consolidated. Each said that her answers to the allegations against her might be used to cross-examine the other. Their appeals were rejected, as the Court of Appeal held that justice could not be said to be done if there were two separate hearings at which each applicant was exonerated by the tribunal and the blame laid at the feet of the other. The court also emphasised the discretionary nature of the tribunal's decision in ordering that cases be combined. Once the tribunal has made its decision, it will, therefore, be difficult to appeal against that exercise of its discretion.

Where cases have been combined, the tribunal can make further directions as to how it will go about hearing the different applications (r18(1)). In some cases, all the applicants' evidence will be heard together; in others the tribunal will hear each case in total, giving its reasons in one case before moving on to the next. This latter procedure may be of assistance where cases involve identical issues of law; the finding in the first case might well be decisive for the parties in other cases (and see below, 'test cases'). Ultimately the

5 [1987] IRLR 146, CA.

tribunal hearing the cases which have been combined has the right to control its procedure as it sees fit, although a directions hearing is useful to canvass such questions with the parties in advance of the hearing.

Test cases

Tribunals do not have the same powers as other courts to order that representative applications be heard as 'test' cases which would bind all others bringing claims on the same grounds. The only way of proceeding with a test case in the tribunal is to use the provision for combining proceedings under r18. For example, a number of cases can be combined and a few 'test' applications heard which are representative of all the other cases. Findings of the tribunal will be decisive in all other cases. This is particularly useful where there are numerous applicants with equal pay applications.[6]

There is no power to allow representative actions to be brought and subsequently relied upon by individuals who did not themselves bring claims within the specified time limit. This means that all potential applicants must still present their claims as individuals within the time limit. They cannot rely on claims brought by others.

While 'test' cases can be mutually advantageous for the parties in expediting matters and saving costs, it is often difficult to select lead cases which are truly representative of all classes of applications. In many multi-applicant cases arising out of the same facts or involving the same issues of law, it is not possible to carry out this exercise because the applications each raise individual issues which will need separate consideration; hence the need for individual hearings in the Ministry of Defence pregnancy discrimination claims in the early 1990s. Before ordering that cases be combined and 'test' cases selected for initial consideration, the tribunal should be satisfied that exactly similar issues arise so as to justify the same result in each case.

In selecting 'test' cases, assistance may be derived from the Supreme Court Procedure Committee's *Guide for Use in Group Actions*:[7]

> It is important that a sufficient number of lead cases should be chosen to obtain decisions on all the points required for the disposal of as many of the cases as possible. Equally, to achieve the greatest saving in interlocutory costs, the selection of the lead cases should be made as

6 See *Ashmore v British Coal Corporation* [1990] ICR 485; [1990] IRLR 283, CA.
7 May 1991, chapter 3D.

soon as possible. On the other hand, some issues may not become apparent until fairly late in the preparations for trial. A measure of flexibility will usually be appropriate in Group litigation. . . .

A decision in a test case binds all the other cases in the combined proceedings in so far as the issues are similar. Where a party to an application which has been combined seeks to pursue a tribunal case despite the test case decision, the tribunal may exercise its powers under r13(2)(e) to strike out the originating application or notice of appearance in that case.[8]

Witness orders

By r4(2) of the 1993 Rules, a tribunal, which may be a chairman sitting alone (r13(8)), may on application by any party or of its own motion order any person within Great Britain, including a party, to attend as a witness. It will specify the time and place at which the individual concerned is to attend.

If such an order is made against a person in his/her absence, whether a party or not, s/her may apply to the tribunal to vary or set aside the order by sending notice to the secretary before the time when s/he is required to attend as a witness (r 4(5)). The secretary will serve notice of the application to set aside or vary on all other parties to the proceedings.

The power given to tribunals to order a witness to attend is analogous to the power of the High Court under RSC Order 38 r14 to subpoena a person to attend before it. If a person who is subject to a tribunal witness order fails to comply with its terms, s/he is liable on summary conviction to a fine (ITA 1996 s7(4)).

The tribunal's power to order a witness to attend is discretionary in nature and it is therefore difficult to appeal against it. Since it is interlocutory, there is no power to review the order. It is, therefore, all the more important for anyone applying for a witness order to make sure that all the facts relied on are clearly set out. Similarly, an application to set aside or vary the order should be made as soon as possible, clearly setting out the grounds relied on. If necessary, an oral hearing should be requested.

The relevant considerations to be borne in mind by tribunals before deciding whether or not to make a witness order were set out by Sir John Donaldson in *Dada v Metal Box Co Ltd*:[9]

8 *Ashmore v British Coal Corporation* [1990] ICR 485; [1990] IRLR 283, CA.
9 [1974] ICR 559; [1974] IRLR 251, NIRC.

The first is that the witness prima facie can give evidence which is relevant to the issues in dispute. . . . We do not suggest that the tribunal should ask the applicant to give a full proof of his evidence but the applicant should indicate the subject-matter of his evidence and show the extent to which it is relevant. The second . . . is that it is necessary to issue a witness order. . . . [W]itnesses should always be invited to attend by the applicant before he applies for witness orders. If they agree to attend and the applicant is quite satisfied that they will attend, then it is unnecessary to issue witness orders. . . . A witness may not reply to the request for an undertaking that he will attend. In those circumstances, it may be necessary to issue such an order. He may refuse, in which case . . . a witness order is clearly needed. Again, he may equivocate . . . In such circumstances it will . . . be a matter for the judgment of the tribunal, . . . Finally, although not exclusively . . . there is the . . . the witness who says, 'Certainly I will come and give evidence, but it would be very much easier for me to come if I had a witness order requiring me to come'. That situation can arise if an employer is unwilling to release a witness. Again that would be a reason for granting a witness order.

In practice, tribunals are prepared to grant witness orders subject to any subsequent application to vary or set aside.

In most cases, a witness order should not be necessary: those witnesses who will give evidence in a party's favour are unlikely to refuse to attend, although they may prefer to do so under a witness order for the reasons outlined in the *Dada* case. A potential witness who is reluctant to attend on behalf of a particular party is unlikely to co-operate before the hearing in the drafting of a witness statement or proof of evidence. As a general rule, if one is unsure what a person may say when called to give evidence, it is unwise to call him/her. Applying for a witness order to require the attendance of someone who may be hostile to the client's case would be giving a hostage to fortune. It is far better to leave it to the other side to call a witness, so that there is the opportunity to cross-examine (see chapter 17).

In some cases, a party may have little choice but to apply for a witness order to require the attendance of a person whose evidence may or may not be favourable. For instance, in a TUPE case, the respondent-transferee may apply for a witness order requiring the receiver who carried out the dismissals of the applicant employees to attend, although that receiver may not be prepared to provide a witness statement in advance.

When calling witnesses subject to a witness order, one should bear in mind that the order may need to be amended to state a different date and time if the hearing goes part-heard before that witness's evidence is completed. When the witness has finished giving evidence, it is necessary to ask the tribunal if s/he may be 'released', so that s/he will not be in breach of the order by leaving the tribunal after having given evidence but before the expiry of the time period specified in the order.

Striking out

Scandalous, frivolous or vexatious applications

At any stage of the proceedings, a tribunal may order any originating application or notice of appearance, or anything contained within those documents, to be struck out or amended on the basis that it, or the conduct of a party, is scandalous, frivolous or vexatious (r13(2)(d) and (e)). Before exercising its power to strike out, the tribunal must either give the party against whom such an order is proposed the opportunity to show cause orally why it should not be made or send notice to that party giving him/her an opportunity to show such cause orally or in writing (r13(3)).

When considering whether the originating application or notice of appearance or a party's conduct is frivolous or vexatious, the tribunal will adopt much the same approach towards those expressions as it would towards an application for costs (see p177). 'Frivolous' and 'vexatious' include matters which constitute an abuse of process; a term which may be widely construed and is not limited to dishonest claims or defences, or to conduct which is in bad faith. In *Ashmore v British Coal Corporation*[10] Stuart-Smith LJ expressed the following view:

> A litigant has a right to have his claim litigated, provided it is not frivolous, vexatious or an abuse of the process. What may constitute such conduct must depend on all the circumstances of the case; the categories are not closed and considerations of public policy and the interests of justice may be very material.

In *Ashmore*, the originating application was struck out as an abuse of process; the applicant was one of 1,500 women canteen workers who brought equal pay claims against British Coal. The claims had been combined and 14 sample cases selected for consideration.

10 [1990] ICR 485, [1990] IRLR 283, CA.

While these were expressly stated not to be 'test' cases, all the other claims had been stayed. When the sample cases were determined against the applicants, Ms Ashmore applied to have the stay on her case lifted. British Coal's application to have her claim struck out on the ground that it was vexatious was upheld by the tribunal. It was held to be an abuse of the process to seek to re-litigate an issue which had already been fully litigated in the sample cases which were representative of all the other claims. There were no material differences between the sample cases and hers, and her union (the UDM) had been present when the lead cases had been selected, yet had made no representations against this procedure.

In an application to strike out a claim on grounds similar to those in *Ashmore*, a prima facie burden lies with the party making the application. There is an entitlement to relitigate the same issues between different parties unless it can be shown that there are special reasons (such as those applying in *Ashmore*) which would render it an abuse of process.[11]

Tribunals rarely exercise the power to strike out proceedings, even where there seems to be little left for the applicant to gain by pursuing a complaint. In *Telephone Information Services Ltd v Wilkinson*,[12] an employer had made an offer to pay to an employee bringing a claim of unfair dismissal the maximum statutory compensation which could be awarded for such a claim. The employee was not prepared, however, to withdraw the originating application and the EAT upheld the tribunal's refusal to strike it out. The employee was entitled to pursue a claim in the expectation that a *finding* of unfair dismissal might be made regardless of any extra monetary compensation.

If an applicant withdraws a claim, and the tribunal dismisses it, and the applicant then seeks to institute the same complaint within the time limit for commencing proceedings, the tribunal will strike out the second claim if it is wholly misconceived.[13] In such circumstances, however, the appropriate course of action is for the applicant to apply for a review of the tribunal's decision to dismiss the first application on withdrawal by the applicant. Where the remedy of review is still open to the applicant, the EAT has held that it *would* be appropriate to strike out the second application, as in

---

11 *Department of Education and Science v Taylor and Others* [1992] IRLR 308, QBD.
12 [1991] IRLR 148, EAT.
13 *Mulvaney v London Transport Executive* [1981] ICR 351, EAT.

Acrow (Engineers) Ltd v Hathaway,[14] a case from which the applicant withdrew on the grounds of ill-health.

The vexatious litigant

When an individual is persistently and unreasonably vexatious in making applications to the tribunal or in instituting appeals to the EAT, the EAT has the power, by way of a restriction of proceedings order, to prevent proceedings by that person being instituted or continued, either in the tribunal or EAT, unless leave is given to do so.[15]

Want of prosecution

The tribunal has the power, on the application of a respondent or of its own motion, to strike out an originating application for want of prosecution (r13(2)(f)). In exercising its discretion the tribunal will apply the same guidelines as apply in the High Court.[16] These are laid down by the House of Lords in *Birkett v James*[17] which distinguished between two types of case:

a) where there has been intentional and contumelious default by the applicant, ie, where the applicant has failed to comply with an order of the tribunal and it has been made clear that the originating application would be struck out unless the applicant complied with the order within the time allowed;

b) where there has been (i) inordinate and inexcusable delay on the part of the applicant or his/her lawyers *and* (ii) that delay will give rise to a substantial risk that it is not possible to have a fair trial of the issues in the action or is such as is likely to cause or to have caused serious prejudice to the respondent.

In the first type of case, the normal rules for striking out or debarring will be followed where a party acts in default of an order for further particulars, discovery or written answers (r4(7) and see pp76, 83 and 78 respectively).

Before the tribunal strikes out an originating application for want of prosecution, the applicant must be given the opportunity to show cause orally why such an order should not be made or notice must

---

14 [1981] ICR 510, EAT.
15 ITA 1996 s33 (see p225).
16 *Evans' Executors v Metropolitan Policy Authority* [1993] ICR 151; [1992] IRLR 570, CA.
17 [1978] AC 297 and see Arbitration Act 1950 s13A(2).

be sent giving him/her an opportunity to show such cause orally or in writing (r13(3)).

Directions hearings

A tribunal may at any time, either on the application of a party or of its own motion, give directions on any matter arising in connection with the proceedings before it (r16(1)). An application for directions should be made by written notice to the secretary, setting out the title of the case and the grounds of the application (r16(2)). Directions are frequently given following a preliminary determination under r6 or a pre-hearing review under r7.

Directions can either be given at a hearing, usually an interlocutory hearing, or merely on written application without any hearing having taken place. Any directions given *ex parte* will remain provisional until all parties have had the opportunity to make representations to the tribunal.[18]

Hearings for directions in the tribunal are analogous to pre-trial reviews in the civil courts, eg, under CCR Order 17 r10. They are often useful in ensuring that the case proceeds to a final hearing in an orderly and coherent manner and their use has been encouraged by the EAT in a number of cases.[19] Directions can be given not just as to the form of the hearing of the case (eg, the order in which the issues will be considered or the way in which combined applications will be heard), but also as to the time-table for all further interlocutory stages. As there are no automatic directions in tribunals, this can be helpful in ensuring that matters such as discovery and inspection take place in good time to allow the parties to prepare for the substantive hearing.

In *Halford v Sharples*[20] the EAT again emphasised the desirability of directions hearings in many tribunal cases and sought to make a number of suggestions for the conduct of these interlocutory hearings. Many of these suggestions now also form the subject of guidance in the 1994 Practice Direction No 1[21] (see Appendix 3.11). In summary:

18 *Reddington v S Straker & Sons Ltd* [1994] ICR 172, EAT.
19 eg, *Brooks v British Telecommunications plc* [1991] ICR 286; [1991] IRLR 4, EAT.
20 [1992] ICR 146.
21 Guidance on Judicial Procedure for the Industrial Tribunals in England and Wales (COIT, November 1994).

- hearings for directions will not be held as a matter of course or for particular jurisdictions;
- an interlocutory hearing for directions will be confined to lengthy or very complex cases;
- where there is a preliminary determination under r6 or where there has been a pre-hearing review, a directions hearing may follow on immediately.
- the hearing will not involve lay members but ideally the hearing will be conducted by the chairman who will have conduct of the case at the substantive hearing (except where this chairman has been involved in a pre-hearing review); and
- the date for the full hearing should be fixed.

To make the best use of a directions hearing in the tribunal, the parties should be represented by those who have so far had conduct of the case and/or will be presenting the case. If agreement can be reached with the other side as to the directions to be made and the interlocutory time-table to be observed, this should be put to the chairman, preferably in the form of a schedule. If no agreement can be reached, the parties should at least try to identify the issues upon which directions are required in advance of this interlocutory hearing. The parties should bring their full files to the directions hearing, and those attending should be prepared to fix a date for the substantive hearing and so should attend with a clear, and preferably agreed, time estimate and with the dates when representatives, parties and witnesses are able to attend.

CHECKLIST: INTERLOCUTORY STAGES

- Are there one or more applications involving common questions of law or fact, or is there other good reason why cases should or should not be considered together?
- If cases have been combined, what would be the best way for them to be heard?
- Can any of these issues be resolved by agreement with other interested parties?
- Would a directions hearing be useful, either to resolve these issues or to consider generally any further issues that might arise?

CHAPTER 12

Pre-hearing review

The pre-hearing review (PHR) under r7(4) is a procedure for institutionalising the threat of costs against an applicant or, less frequently, a respondent. Its purpose is to weed out whole cases, or single contentions in any given case, which 'have no reasonable prospect of success'. The tribunal may order the party to pay a deposit which may be used to defray a later award of costs.

Procedure

The procedure can be initiated by either party or by the tribunal giving notice. The tribunal must provide an opportunity for the parties to be heard and to make written and oral representations. The hearing, which is not the hearing of the originating application, may take place before a chairman sitting alone by virtue of r13(8).

The material available to the tribunal is strictly limited and the tribunal's consideration is confined to:

a) the contents of the originating application and notice of appearance;
b) any representations in writing; and
c) any oral argument (r7(1)).

Since there is no live evidence, the only way in which evidence can be submitted is by way of written representation. There is no reason why the written representation should not include either extracts from or the totality of witness statements to be used at the hearing. Legal argument can of course be addressed both in writing and orally.

If the tribunal considers that there is no reasonable prospect of success in any given contention, it must record its reasons in *summary* form. There is no obligation to provide or right to demand extended reasons (r7(6)). That document is then sent to the parties with an explanatory note.

Order to pay a deposit

Once the tribunal makes such a determination, it may make a deposit order as a condition of a party being allowed to continue with the contention or the case as a whole. The matter is still discretionary (r7(4)). But it would be difficult for a tribunal to justify a finding of no reasonable prospect without an order against a party who has the means to comply with it. The order itself is that the party must pay a deposit of up to £150 as a condition of being permitted to continue to take part in the proceedings *'relating to that matter'*. Before making the order, the tribunal must take reasonable steps to ensure that the party against whom the order is made can comply with the order, and it must take account of information received in determining the amount.

Once the order has been served, the party has 21 days in which to pay the deposit. A further period of up to 14 days' grace is allowed if representations are made within the initial 21 days. If the order is not complied with, the tribunal has no discretion and must strike out either the originating application or the notice of appearance or the relevant part of either to which the order relates. So, when an order has been made, it is a condition for continuing with the case, or with that part of the case coverd by the order, that the deposit is paid.

The deposit is refundable in full as a general rule. It is refundable on withdrawal of the originating application, since proceedings would then be at an end. The rules do not provide this but the deposit ought to be refundable as soon as the party agrees to take out the offending part of the originating application or the notice of appearance; or if at the PHR hearing the tribunal makes the determination, it could, in its discretion, decline to order the deposit to be made if the document is amended.

The deposit is also refundable at the end of the proceedings *unless* (r7(7)):

a) the tribunal hearing the originating application finds against the party on the specific matter for which s/he was ordered to pay the deposit; *and*

b) the tribunal has made an award of costs, either arising out of the matter for which the deposit was ordered or for any other reason.

Costs at the main hearing after a deposit order

If no award of costs is made at the substantive hearing, the tribunal must still go on to consider in a case where a deposit has been ordered whether to award costs against the party 'on the ground that he conducted the proceedings relating to the matter unreasonably in persisting in having the matter determined by a tribunal', (r12(7)). It must consider the reasons set out by the first tribunal when it ordered a deposit, and the second tribunal must have come to the opinion that the first tribunal's reasons were 'substantially the same' as its own reasons.

The issue of costs is in the discretion of the second tribunal and it does not follow automatically that because a deposit order has been made, and an adverse finding has been reached for substantially the same reasons at the full hearing, that costs must be awarded (r12(7)). If they are, the deposit is set off against and used to discharge any award of costs made by the tribunal, whether for the matters covered by the deposit or otherwise (r12(8)).

At the substantive hearing, no member of the tribunal who sat on the PHR may take part (r7(9)), even if no order was made. There is no reason why the second tribunal should not know and have read the reasons of the first tribunal if it made an order, but in practice the decision recording the making of the order or refusing to make one is kept in a sealed envelope on the file and not read until the end of the substantive hearing.

CHAPTER 13

Preliminary hearings

It is sometimes useful, but often counter-productive, for a preliminary hearing to take place on an issue before full consideration of all the issues in a case. If a case can be disposed of by taking one short preliminary point, it is obviously sensible to do so. But often the issues raised in a preliminary point overlap into matters more appropriate for a substantive hearing. And sometimes preliminary points of law are taken to the highest level before the facts have been determined, only to frustrate or exhaust one of the parties. Preliminary points of law were taken to the House of Lords in, for example, *Barclays Bank plc v Kapur*,[1] where it was held that failure by the bank to give pension credit for previous service in East Africa was a continuing act and the claim was not time-barred. On trial of the merits of the claim, however, the EAT and Court of Appeal overturned the tribunal's finding that the action was based on race discrimination,[2] thus rendering pointless the findings in the preliminary hearings.

It is important to distinguish three forms of proceeding: preliminary hearings on jurisdiction, the hearing of a preliminary point of law, and reference of a preliminary point to the European Court of Justice.

Preliminary hearings on jurisdiction

A tribunal can at any time 'before the hearing of an originating application', either on application by a party or of its own motion, 'hear and determine any issue relating to the entitlement' of a party

1 [1991] ICR 208, [1991] IRLR 136, HL.
2 [1995] IRLR 87, CA.

to bring or contest proceedings (r6(1)). Notice must be given to all the parties in writing and an opportunity given to advance oral argument before the tribunal. Since this does not constitute the hearing of the originating application itself, it is likely that r13(8) empowers a chairman sitting alone to determine the preliminary issue, and Practice Direction No 1 carries this into effect (see Appendix 3.9).

The scope of this rule is pre-eminently designed for issues of jurisdiction, eg, to determine whether an applicant has sufficient qualifying service to bring a claim for unfair dismissal, or whether a claim is brought within the relevant limitation period. At first sight, a dispute about whether a respondent is properly joined in a TUPE case might be one about the entitlement of a party to contest proceedings. But here it would be necessary for the tribunal to make findings of fact clearly overlapping with the task of the tribunal hearing the substantive originating application. It is for this reason that the EAT and the Court of Appeal have been keen to restrict the use of preliminary hearings in employment law, reflecting the warnings against such procedures given in *Allen v Gulf Oil Refining Ltd*.[3] In *Secretary of State for Education v Birchall*[4] Mummery J said:

> there are . . . dangers in isolating an issue from the main dispute and ordering it to be determined as a preliminary point on the basis of assumed facts. It is often quicker and cheaper to find all the facts first and then to resolve the issues.

That statement arose in a case where allegations of race discrimination, normal retirement age and fixed term contracts were all raised.

Cases dealing with jurisdiction are different from those where 'the complaint itself fails in some essential or fundamental element'.[5] In Equal Pay Act cases the defence under s1(3) that the difference in pay between men and women is due to a genuine, material factor other than sex is frequently taken as a preliminary point: and this may usefully avoid expenditure and further delays on requisitioning an independent expert.[6]

But in constructive dismissal cases, where the entitlement of an employee to bring a claim depends on him or her proving a

---

3 [1981] AC 1001, HL: see *Munir v Jang Publications Ltd* [1989] ICR 1; [1989] IRLR 224, CA; *Post Office Counters Ltd v Malik* [1991] ICR 355.
4 [1994] IRLR 630, EAT.
5 *Post Office Counters v Malik* (n3 above) per Wood J.
6 *British Coal Corporation v Smith* [1994] ICR 810; [1994] IRLR 342, CA (see p191).

dismissal (and therefore that the tribunal has jurisdiction), it is frequently counter-productive to hear evidence relating to a dismissal without consideration of all of the surrounding facts. This would make it inappropriate to hold a preliminary hearing etiher on jurisdiction or on a preliminary point of law.

Preliminary point of law

An entirely separate concept is a hearing to determine an issue of law which might either finally conclude the case or finally conclude one aspect of the case. There is no dispute on the power of the tribunal to hear the case, but it is contended that a material aspect of the claim will fail and, if so, it should be decided on its own. It *is* the hearing of the originating application but it proceeds in stages, starting with evidence and submissions on a preliminary point which, once decided, will affect the further stages in the case.[7] This is usually achieved by raising a preliminary point on assumed facts, as for example in *Pickstone v Freemans plc*[8] on the construction of the Equal Pay Act 1970. In such a case the parties should seek to agree facts in writing by exchange with each other, or alternatively call sufficient evidence to enable findings to be made, and then make submissions as to the law.

If substantial disputed evidence has to be brought, it seems that tribunals are more inclined to allow a full hearing to determine all issues. There is much to be said for allowing a tribunal to make findings on the substantive point in addition to the preliminary point, so that, if the case is pursued to appeal, the relative strength of the parties' cases on the substantive merits is known to them, and indeed to the higher court. This is why constructive dismissal claims are unsuitable for preliminary rulings, whereas a preliminary point such as the existence of a contractual term for the purposes of deductions under the wages protection legislation can readily be determined.

Reference to the European Court

By article 177 of the Treaty of Rome, a preliminary ruling can be sought from the European Court of Justice (ECJ) on the interpreta-

7 *Post Office Counters v Malik* (n3 above).
8 [1988] ICR 697; [1988] IRLR 357, HL.

tion of the Treaty and the validity and interpretation of acts of the institutions of the European Union. This will include directives and the effect of directives. Power to refer is given to any national court or tribunal, but in all cases the ruling must be sought on a preliminary point and the ruling must be 'necessary' for the tribunal to reach its decision. The ruling, in other words, must be sought before the decision of the tribunal is reached. Generally speaking it will be more convenient to leave it to the EAT or the Court of Appeal to make a reference but some landmark cases such as *Johnston v RUC*[9] have been referred directly by tribunals.

The reference will not be sent to the ECJ until the time for appealing the order has expired (r19A). By analogy with the High Court, the reference should include the questions to be decided together with a summary of the facts, an outline of the parties' cases and the relevant provisions of national law (RSC Order 114).

9 [1987] ICR 83, [1986] IRLR 263, ECJ.

CHAPTER 14

Adjournment and postponement

The tribunal has power to regulate its own procedure (r13(1)) and to extend time (r15) and it has a general power in the interests of justice to adjourn or postpone. There is also a specific power under (r12(4)) to order costs to be paid when a party has sought a postponement or an adjournment.

There is a further specific power to adjourn or postpone where by statute conciliation procedures are available, in order to give an opportunity for the case to be settled by conciliation or withdrawal (r13(7)). See p132 for the statutory provision for conciliation officers to be sent copies of the originating application.

Apart from these specific examples, the tribunal has wide powers, as was made clear in *Jacobs v Norsalta Ltd*,[1] a case where tribunal proceedings were stayed pending High Court proceedings involving complicated questions of compensation:

> ... the tribunal has a complete discretion, so long as it exercises it judicially, to postpone or adjourn any case provided there is good, reasonable ground for so doing.

An application should be made in writing and may lead to an oral hearing. The tribunal should not adjourn or postpone without giving all parties an opportunity to make representations.[2] Nor can a postponement or adjournment be granted dependent on payment of costs.[3]

---

1 [1977] ICR 189, EAT per Phillips J.
2 *Bowater plc v Charlwood* [1991] ICR 798; [1991] IRLR 340, CA.
3 *Cooper v Weatherwise (Roofing and Walling) Limited* [1993] ICR 81, EAT.

The position of the party making the application

It is relevant to bear in mind who is making the application, since there are sometimes tactical advantages associated with delay. For example, postponement of a hearing on compensation following a finding on liability against an employer would have the beneficial effect (from the employer's point of view) of delaying the running of interest from an award of compensation. Generally speaking, an employee in unfair dismissal or wrongful dismissal proceedings is more likely to be granted a stay of the tribunal proceedings than the employer.

Factors relevant to a decision

The following factors are relevant to the decision whether or not to grant an application to postpone or adjourn.

Ill-health or unavailability of parties and witnesses

In order to avoid uncertainty, an application based on the ill-health of a party or a witness should be accompanied by a doctor's certificate. Unavailability of a witness, for example by being on holiday abroad or working abroad, should also be grounds for postponing or adjourning. On the other hand, proceedings could commence to some extent without a relevant witness and then adjourn part-heard in order to accommodate the witness's availability.

A last-minute change of representation might also justify an application. Plainly the interests of justice require a party to be represented properly and the sudden change of representation might frustrate this if the new representative was unprepared. Practice Direction No 1[4] (see Appendix 3.9) makes no allowance for difficulties caused to advocates by a case being adjourned unfinished (part-heard) to another date when they are booked for another case. This common practical problem could be overcome with sympathetic and realistic exercise of discretion in re-listing cases.

---

4 Guidance on Judicial Procedure for the Industrial Tribunals in England and Wales (COIT, November 1994).

Proceedings in other cases

Sometimes a case raises a legal issue which is waiting to be determined in another case by a higher United Kingdom court, or the European Court, and this might affect the outcome of a given case. Although it might make sense and save costs to postpone a hearing which might become abortive as a result of the outcome of different proceedings in a different court, the parties and the tribunal have no control over those other proceedings. They should not be required to delay a hearing, and an application on these grounds will usually be refused.

For example, in *Financial Times v Byrne (No 2)*[5] it was argued that the hearing of a preliminary point on equal pay should be stayed pending the determination by the ECJ of *Enderby v Frenchay Health Authority.*[6] The application was rejected partly because the *Enderby* case would not determine all of the relevant issues in the *Financial Times* case; but also because the applicants in that case had no control over the *Enderby* proceedings, which might have been settled without a hearing, have been further delayed or determined without reference to the issue relevant in the *Financial Times* case.

High Court proceedings

A tribunal is more likely to stay proceedings if there is a very similar issue to be determined in the High Court (or the county court) and it is likely to bring about a final conclusion of all or major issues in the tribunal proceedings. An applicant who claims unfair dismissal and wants to reserve the right to issue procedings for wrongful dismissal should make a claim in the originating application seeking at the same time a stay of tribunal proceedings.[7] S/he should do this if the claim is worth more than the limit on contract claims in the tribunal or if s/he is seeking remedies other than damages.[8]

It is generally desirable for the same issues to be determined by the High Court rather than by a tribunal.[9] Otherwise 'the Judge

---

5 [1992] IRLR 163, EAT (leave to appeal refused by CA).
6 [1994] ICR 112; [1993] IRLR 591.
7 *Warnock v Scarborough Football Club* [1989] ICR 489, EAT.
8 See Industrial Tribunals (Extension of Jurisdiction) Orders 1994 SI No 1623 (England and Wales) and SI No 1624 (Scotland).
9 *Green v Hampshire County Council* [1979] ICR 861, ChD.

would be put in a strait jacket'.[10]

Considerations which point to waiting until after the High Court case has been decided are:

- the desirability for strict rules of evidence to be applied;[11]
- the use of strict pleadings;[12]
- the total amount of damages may be higher than a tribunal can award;
- complexity of the issues;[13]
- the availability of discovery, award of costs, better remedies and the prospect of delay.[14]

If these are not important considerations, there is no reason to postpone the tribunal.

Foreign proceedings

A postponement was granted pending the imminent issue of High Court proceedings in England coupled with the existence of other actions abroad in *JMCC Holdings Ltd v Conroy*.[15] Again, similarity of issues together with convenience of location are matters to be considered.

Criminal proceedings

In cases involving allegations of dishonesty, such as unfair dismissal for misconduct, and a concurrent prosecution in the Crown Court, it is desirable for tribunal proceedings to be stayed so as to allow complete flexibility for the applicant and his/her advisers in the criminal trial. Yet in *Bastick v James Lane (Turf Accountants) Ltd*[16] the EAT declined to interfere with a chairman's decision to refuse a postponement sought by an applicant charged with theft in circumstances leading to a claim for unfair dismissal. The chairman decided that the issues were not sufficiently similar. Of course, the issues *are* different: whether there was sufficient material before the

10 *Automatic Switching Ltd v Brunet* [1986] ICR 542, EAT per Sir R Kilner Brown.
11 *Bowater plc v Charlwood* [1991] ICR 798; [1991] IRLR 340, EAT.
12 Ibid.
13 *Jacobs v Norsalta* (n1 above).
14 Ibid.
15 [1990] ICR 179, EAT.
16 [1979] ICR 778.

employer to justify a dismissal, compared with whether the employee committed theft beyond reasonable doubt. There are however very strong policy reasons for allowing criminal proceedings to go first even if, on acquittal, hopes are raised for an applicant that s/he will automatically succeed in an unfair dismissal claim. Such would be false hopes, given the different tasks of the tribunal and the Crown Court.

In Scotland, the practice is generally to adjourn the hearing of the tribunal application until the resolution of the criminal proceedings.

Appeal

There is no obligation on a tribunal to adjourn pending an appeal, eg, on a preliminary point or a ruling on procedure against a party. Similarly, there is no obligation on a tribunal to stay a hearing on remedies pending an appeal by an employer on liability. It may be in the parties' interest to agree to stay further proceedings for the saving of costs, but in the absence of agreement, there is no reason why an applicant's case should be held up. A solution might be to agree subject to appeal that time for computing interest on any award is deemed to run from the date a compensation hearing would have taken place.

Internal procedures

The 1993 Rules contain no requirement for a party to try and exhaust internal procedures before commencing tribunal proceedings. Nevertheless, the possibility of a settlement through conciliation is always a ground for exercising discretion in favour of a stay. The hearing of an internal appeal might be just such a ground, since it is possible that a favourable result for the applicant would avoid the need to continue tribunal proceedings.

Costs on adjournment

Once the interests of justice have identified a reason for granting a stay, any resulting disadvantage to the other party can be compensated in costs. There is no requirement that the pejorative terms of r12(1), 'unreasonable' etc, should be complied with. Rather, r12(4) is entirely neutral and allows the tribunal to exercise its discretion to award costs on the application of a party for a postponement or an adjournment without the need to attribute unreasonableness to a party. Costs can be awarded in favour of or against the party applying.

CHAPTER 15

Settlement and conciliation

copy clay

General considerations

In tribunal proceedings, as in any litigation, there are often a number of advantages in settling the case before (or during) the full hearing. Settling a case means entering into an agreement with the other side, with both parties being bound by the terms of that agreement without having to have the issues in the case determined by the tribunal.

Concluding an action by this means is often advantageous for both parties because:

- agreeing to settle an action avoids the risk of losing as well as the unpleasantness of a hearing;
- the recoupment provisions[1] do not apply to settlements;
- both parties avoid the costs of fighting the case to the end (apart from legal costs, there will generally be costs in preparing for and attending the tribunal, whether in terms of taking time off work or loss of management time);
- while the remedies open to the tribunal are limited by statute, the parties may agree to include in the agreement matters which are outside the tribunal's jurisdiction, such as an agreed form of reference or a confidentiality clause.

The advantages of resolving tribunal proceedings have long been recognised by parliament and a statutory conciliation procedure is available through the offices of the Advisory, Conciliation and Arbitration Service (ACAS).

---

1 Employment Protection (Recoupment of Unemployment Benefit and Supplementary Benefit) Regulations 1977 SI No 674.

Settlements in tribunal proceedings are not, however, without risk. Anyone entering into an agreement to settle a case should only do so if s/he understands and agrees to the terms on which the case is to be compromised. The terms of the settlement form a binding contract between the parties which can be enforced in the ordinary courts. Those terms may include an agreement by the employee to waive certain legal rights arising out of the employment relationship: care should be taken not to surrender legal rights unintentionally. If it is not intended to compromise any future claims relating, eg, to accidents at work or to pension rights, then the agreement should make this clear. If a settlement includes terms relating to pension rights, then particular care should be taken to ensure that the agreement comes within the terms of the pension scheme.

Generally speaking, any attempt to contract out of an employee's statutory employment rights will be invalid.[2] Apart from the specific statutory exceptions to this rule (eg, on the failure to renew a fixed-term contract where the requirements of ERA 1996 s197 are met), an employee can only contract out of his/her right to bring tribunal proceedings in relation to statutory employment rights by:

- entering into a settlement through ACAS;
- entering into a compromise agreement after having been advised by a suitably qualified (and insured) professional adviser; or
- entering into an agreement during the course of a hearing before a tribunal which forms the basis of a tribunal's decision by consent.

These protections do not, however, apply to contract claims arising out of the employment relationship which can be brought in the tribunal. Such claims are founded on common law principles and are treated as they would be in any court; an agreement between the parties can effectively contract out of the right to pursue the complaint in question provided it meets the normal requirements for legally binding contracts at common law:

- there has been a valid offer and acceptance;
- consideration (eg, compensation) has been provided for the agreement;
- there is an intention to create legal relations between the parties; and
- a party's consent to the agreement is not rendered void by reason of duress, undue influence, misrepresentation or mistake.

2 See ERA 1996 s203, SDA 1975 s77 and RRA 1976 s72.

Compromising statutory rights

Employment rights given by statute can be taken away only by statute and the protections provided apply until all questions of liability and remedy have been determined by the tribunal. Therefore, even where the question of liability has been determined and the issue of remedy has been adjourned to another day, an agreement between the parties will be void unless it conforms with one of the methods of compromising a claim provided by statute.[3]

There are, however, ways in which an employer can circumvent these protective measures, even in relation to the employee's statutory rights. Those acting for employees should not be surprised by the use of such tactical devices (particularly as part of a termination package) which give employers some guarantee against future claims without having to face the obstacles presented by the statutory means of settlement.

If an agreement is concluded with the employee which does not purport to exclude the employee's right to go to a tribunal but does provide (for example) for the payment of a sum of money by way of an agreed settlement of all claims (including statutory claims) for compensation, the employee's subsequent application to a tribunal may enable the employer to argue that the original agreement has been breached by the employee. This would not stop the employee continuing with the claim to the tribunal but may render it inadvisable to do so: s/he may lose the entitlement to receive the money promised under the original agreement. To give the employer greater certainty, this form of agreement may expressly provide that payment of the money is conditional on no legal proceedings (including tribunal proceedings) being commenced in relation to the (eg) dismissal, or for the money (or at least part of it) to be paid only after the relevant time-limits for making a claim have expired. This does not breach the statutory provisions against contracting out, as it does not purport to stop the employee going to the tribunal but merely states that s/he will have to seek compensation via the tribunal and not under the terms of the agreement, if s/he chooses to do so.

In any event, if an employee did still proceed with a claim in the tribunal after accepting such a payment it is likely that this sum would be deducted from any compensatory award if s/he succeeded

---

3 *Courage Take Home Trade Ltd v Keys* [1986] ICR 874; [1986] IRLR 427, EAT.

in a complaint. The question for the tribunal will be whether it would be just and equitable to deduct the sum paid; clearly if, for example, an employer has sought to put undue pressure on the employee to contract out of his/her rights, it is difficult to see how that employer could contend that it would not be just and equitable to make any further award.[4] Furthermore, even if the employer agrees to pay a sum equal to the statutory maximum, there is no guarantee that a further sum will not be awarded. The compensatory award is calculated by assessing the employee's loss from the date of the dismissal, less sums received from the employer and by way of mitigation. It is only after this calculation that the statutory ceiling is applied. If the employee's overall loss is very high, the ex gratia payment by the employer may do little to offset the compensatory award.

Sums paid by the employer voluntarily may also be taken to reduce any liability in respect of a redundancy payment or basic award, but only if it can be established that the payment made was clearly meant to represent settlement of this liability.[5] This will depend on the particular circumstances of each case. If a payment is intended to cover any liability for redundancy entitlement or for a basic award in an unfair dismissal claim, this should be made clear. An employer who makes a payment without expressly stating what that money is intended to cover risks having to make a further payment to cover a basic award in any subsequent tribunal proceedings.[6]

Alternatively, where an employer has already conceded liability (for example, by admitting that the dismissal was unfair) and has made an open offer to pay the maximum sum the tribunal could award to an employee who succeeds in his/her claim, pursuing an application to the tribunal may result in an award of costs being made against the employee concerned. Without a concession as to liability, however, a tribunal should not award costs against an employee simply because an open offer has been made of the maximum award possible.[7] (See chapter 19 on costs.) Thus, while such offers do not purport to restrict the employee's right to bring tribunal proceedings, pursuing a claim is rendered pointless and puts the employee at risk of costs.

4 *Courage Take Home Trade Ltd v Keys* [1986] ICR 874 at 881 per Popplewell J; [1986] IRLR 427, EAT.
5 *Chelsea Football Club and Athletic Co Ltd v Heath* [1981] ICR 323; [1981] IRLR 73, EAT.
6 *Boorman v Allmakes Ltd* [1995] IRLR 553, CA.
7 *Telephone Information Services v Wilkinson* [1991] IRLR 148, EAT.

ACAS

The Advisory, Conciliation and Arbitration Service (ACAS) was established under the Employment Protection Act 1975, expressly to promote the improvement of industrial relations (see now TULRCA 1992 s209). The Secretary of State appoints the members of ACAS after consulting both employers' and workers' organisations (TULRCA 1992 s248). ACAS is organised into regional offices, a list of the addresses of which is set out at Appendix 4.

The primary function of ACAS is to conciliate in trade disputes and the majority of its work falls outside the terms of this book. ACAS does, however, have express duties in individual employment disputes and plays an important role in conciliation in tribunal cases.

The role of ACAS in tribunal claims

Conciliation officers may (and must if asked to do so by a party to a complaint) attempt to conciliate any complaints which could form the basis of a claim to a tribunal. They will only get involved in such cases *before* the presentation of a claim, however, if expressly asked to do so by one of the prospective parties (ITA 1996 s18). ACAS cannot be used as a 'rubber-stamp' for agreements entered into between employers and employees.

The July 1990 ACAS Practice Direction sets out three conditions which must be met before ACAS will agree to be involved in any conciliation process:

a) the employee must have been dismissed, or received notice of dismissal (or ACAS has to be satisfied that the employee believes him/herself to have been constructively dismissed);
b) the employee's employment rights must have been infringed; and
c) the parties must not have agreed all the terms of the settlement, ie, there must remain some role for the services of ACAS.

Once a claim has been presented to the relevant OIT, a conciliation officer is appointed by ACAS for all claims of:

– unfair dismissal;
– unlawful sexual discrimination or breach of an equality clause under the Equal Pay Act;
– unlawful racial discrimination;
– unlawful deduction of wages;
– infringement of rights listed under TULRCA 1992 s290; and

– unlawful discrimination under the Disability Discrimination Act 1995.

Where a claim is presented to a tribunal and any of the above provisions applies, the secretary of the tribunals will send copies of all documents and notices relating to that claim to the conciliation officer concerned (r20(7)).

The conciliation officer appointed to a claim presented to the tribunal under these provisions is under a duty to endeavour to promote a settlement between the parties before its determination by the tribunal (r17(2)), either:

– on a request to do so by the parties; or
– where, in the absence of such a request, the conciliation officer considers there are reasonable prospects of settling the claim.

In most cases, the conciliation officer will contact the parties as a matter of course. If no such contact has been made, a party can find out which conciliation officer has been appointed to the case by contacting the relevant ACAS office (see Appendix 4).

In unfair dismissal cases, and cases of sex, race or disability discrimination, where the complainant has *ceased* to be employed by the employer, the conciliation officer has a specific duty to promote the reinstatement or re-engagement of a dismissed employee (ITA 1996 s18(4)). This obligation will only arise, however, if appropriate in the circumstances of any particular case; the officer is not under an absolute duty to promote reinstatement or re-engagement if it would clearly be futile to do so.[8]

The conciliation officer's duty does not end when a case goes to hearing but continues until the determination of all questions of liability and remedy. Clearly the services of a conciliation officer may be of great assistance where liability has been determined but the question of compensation has been left open for a further hearing, even if attempts at conciliation were previously to no avail.

If the services of the conciliation officer are utilised, it is worth bearing in mind the following:

– the conciliation officer is independent and does not have the same relationship with a party as, eg, a lawyer or adviser;
– the conciliation officer is not an arbiter of tribunal cases and is not there to judge the merits of the case or to try to review the evidence;

8 *Moore v Duport Furniture Products Ltd* [1982] ICR 84; [1982] IRLR 31, HL.

- the conciliation officer will also be talking to the other side and will pass on information given, although s/he could not be called to give evidence about a matter raised during negotiations if that was properly the subject of privilege and the communicator had not given permission;
- any settlement reached with the help of a conciliation officer is still an agreement between the parties: the conciliation officer is not there to impose terms on the parties or even to recommend a particular settlement.

The effect of an agreement through ACAS

Before the presentation of a claim or at any point after the commencement of claim of unfair dismissal, an agreement through the conciliation officer to forego the right to pursue a claim to the tribunal will be upheld in so far as it relates to the rights set out under ITA 1996 s18(1)(d). This will not, however, preclude the applicant from bringing a claim under (for example) SDA 1975 or RRA 1976 or under European law *unless* the agreement *specifically* prohibits all such possible claims. An agreement 'in full and final settlement of all claims' will not suffice.[9] In other words, to ensure that the agreement does dispose of all possible employment claims, it should expressly be stated to be in settlement of all claims, whether under ERA, TULRCA, SDA, RRA, DDA or EU law.

Otherwise, the powers of conciliation officers in assisting in the settlement of tribunal claims have generally been liberally construed and the courts have demonstrated a reluctance to interfere with the actions of conciliation officers providing they have been carried out in good faith.[10]

Conciliation officers usually record agreements on Form COT3 (see Appendix 2), although this form does not have to be used for the parties to be bound by the agreement. Indeed, terms agreed in this latter way may still be binding on the parties even though they have not been reduced to writing at all.[11] Provided the conciliation officer has 'taken action' under ITA 1996 s18, the contract will be binding unless it is expressed to be part of the agreement that it should be recorded in a particular document.

---

9 *Livingstone v Hepworth Refractories plc* [1992] ICR 287; [1992] IRLR 63, EAT.

10 *Hennessy v Craigmyle & Co Ltd and ACAS* [1986] ICR 461; [1986] IRLR 300, CA.

11 *Gilbert v Kembridge Fibres Ltd* [1984] ICR 188; [1984] IRLR 52, EAT.

Once a settlement has been achieved through a conciliation officer, it will be extremely difficult to challenge it later. It would probably require evidence that the conciliation officer acted in bad faith or adopted unfair methods in seeking to achieve a settlement before the agreement could be set aside.[12]

Any agreement entered into through the conciliation officer on behalf of a party by his/her adviser or representative will be binding on that party provided the adviser or representative concerned has been held out as having authority to act on the applicant's behalf and no notice has been given to the contrary: the adviser or representative has ostensible authority to act as the party's agent for these purposes. If, in fact, that authority has not been given, the party concerned will have an action in the normal courts against the adviser or representative but will still be bound by the agreement apparently entered into on his/her behalf.[13] This principle applies to all types of adviser or representative, not just to qualified lawyers: in the *Freeman* case the adviser was a CAB worker. Anyone acting for a party should make sure that s/he does have express authority to enter into a particular agreement, checking that the client has seen the terms of the agreement and/or approved the wording of the settlement before it is finalised.

Compromise agreements and contracts

Another means by which parties (or potential parties) to tribunal claims can effectively agree to 'contract out' of their statutory employment rights is by entering into a compromise agreement or contract under ERA 1996 s203(3) and (4), SDA 1975 s77, RRA 1976 s72, TULRCA 1992 s288 or DDA 1995 s9(2). The term 'compromise agreement' is used in relation to all claims under ERA 1996. For those under SDA 1975, RRA 1976, TULRCA 1992 and DDA 1995 the appropriate term is 'compromise contract': there is no substantive difference between the two. A compromise agreement is narrowly defined and must comply with the strict requirements laid down if it is to be effective. As one of the requirements is that the employee has received independent legal advice from a qualified lawyer before entering into the agreement, some applicants will inevitably fall back on to the services of ACAS.

The compromise agreement procedure was really intended to

12 *Slack v Greenham (Plant Hire) Ltd* [1983] ICR 617; [1983] IRLR 271, EAT.
13 *Freeman v Sovereign Chicken Ltd* [1991] ICR 853; [1991] IRLR 408, EAT.

assist those parties who knew precisely where they stood and wanted to enter into a binding agreement without subsequent claims in the tribunal. In such cases ACAS had taken the view that it should not be used merely as a rubber stamp where agreement had already been reached and issued a Practice Direction in July 1990 to this effect.

To provide for cases which did not fall within the ACAS conditions, the compromise agreement exception to the prohibition on contracting out was provided by TURERA 1993 s39, which amended the previous statutory position.

Compromise agreements or contracts may relate to potential claims under ERA 1996, SDA 1975, RRA 1976, TULRCA 1992 and DDA 1995 and may be made in order to prevent any proceedings being instituted or may relate to cases where proceedings have already been instituted. While there is some debate whether potential unfair dismissal claims are covered, the correct view appears to be that they are: certainly this seems to have been the intention of parliament at the time of introducing the procedure.

Requirements of an effective compromise agreement

The conditions relating to such agreements are as follows:

a) the agreement must be in writing;
b) the agreement must relate to the specific complaint;
c) the employee must have received independent legal advice from a qualified lawyer on the terms and effect of the proposed agreement and in particular its effect on his/her ability to pursue his/her rights before a tribunal;
d) there must be in force, when the adviser gives the advice, a policy of insurance covering the risk of a claim by the employee in respect of loss arising in consequence of taking the advice;
e) the agreement must identify the adviser; and
f) the agreement must state that the conditions regulating compromise agreements under the relevant Act are satisfied.

'Independent', in relation to legal advice given to the employee, means that it is given by a lawyer who is not acting in the matter for the employer or an associated employer. 'Qualified lawyer' means:

a) in England and Wales, a barrister, whether in practice or employed to give legal advice, or a solicitor who holds a practising certificate;

b) in Scotland, an advocate, whether in practice as such or employed to give legal advice, or a solicitor who holds a practising certificate.

The requirement that the lawyer must be covered by a 'policy of insurance' has led to unforeseen difficulties. It appears that this probably requires more than the professional indemnity insurance which all solicitors are obliged to have under the Solicitors' Rules. The government has undertaken to introduce an amendment to overcome this difficulty so that the cover can be provided by the Solicitors' Indemnity Fund (see ppxxxviii and 284).

The requirement that the agreement or contract must relate to a specific complaint means that this form of settlement cannot rule out all possible future claims and cannot exclude potential claims on the off chance that these might be raised at some point in the future. There is, therefore, no way of avoiding the difficulties which arose in *Livingstone v Hepworth Refractories plc*[14] (see p134). Where the employee has raised a number of grievances in an originating application or in a letter before action, however, there seems no reason why one compromise agreement cannot deal with all those specific complaints raised which the parties have now agreed to settle, although each such complaint should be dealt with separately within the agreement and it should be clear that terms have been agreed by way of settlement under each head.

If a compromise agreement or contract is entered into which meets these requirements, then the claims specified in it will have been effectively compromised and will even override statutory rights.

Decisions by consent

Many agreements between parties take place at the door of the tribunal. While this means that costs will already have been expended and tribunal time will be wasted, it is an inevitable aspect of litigation: very often parties will not have assessed the relative strengths of their cases until late in the day or just before the hearing, when they know (for example) which witnesses the other side intends to call. There is also something about the prospect of walking into a court or tribunal which seems to focus the mind and encourage parties to be more favourably disposed to the idea of a settlement of the case.

14 [1992] ICR 287; [1992] IRLR 63, EAT.

One way of disposing of the tribunal proceedings at that stage is for the applicant simply to withdraw the complaint. The tribunal may then make an order dismissing the claim on the applicant's withdrawal under r13(2)(a). If the respondent subsequently reneges on the agreement, the applicant will not, however, be able to reinstate the tribunal claim but will have to seek a remedy for breach of contract (breach of the agreement) in the county court. Even where the relevant time limit in respect of the claim in question has not expired, a subsequent claim brought by the employee in these circumstances may be struck out as frivolous or vexatious.[15] In such circumstances, it may be possible to apply to the tribunal to review its decision, on the ground that the interests of justice require a review (r11(1)(e)), or to commence fresh proceedings where the circumstances of the case could justify this approach[16] and where a review has been refused.

Alternatively, where parties to a tribunal case have come to an agreement, the tribunal has the power to make a decision in the terms of that agreement (r13(2)(b)). A tribunal 'decision' is defined as including a declaration, an order, a recommendation or award or a determination (reg 2).

A decision 'by consent' can be expressed directly in the terms agreed between the parties, ie, that the respondent is ordered to pay the applicant a certain sum of money. This order will be recorded as a decision of the tribunal and will be enforceable in the county court. A decision in this form, however, has a number of disadvantages: it can only include matters within the tribunal's jurisdiction – if a tribunal would not normally have the power to make an order in the terms sought, then the fact that the parties have agreed to it will not change the situation. Furthermore, if the agreement is for the payment of money from the respondent to the applicant and this is recorded as a decision of the tribunal, the recoupment provisions[17] apply, ie, money received by an employee in unemployment benefit, jobseekers' allowance or income support may be recouped from the sum agreed to be paid in the tribunal proceedings.

To avoid these problems, parties can instead ask the tribunal to make a decision merely to stay or adjourn the proceedings on terms scheduled to the tribunal's order. This decision can use the form of order used in civil courts generally called the 'Tomlin Order': ie, that all further proceedings in the case be stayed upon the terms

15 *Acrow (Engineers) Ltd v Hathaway* [1981] ICR 510.
16 *Mulvaney v London Transport Executive* [1981] ICR 351, EAT.
17 See n1 above (p128).

scheduled to the order save for the purpose of carrying such terms into effect, with liberty to apply for that purpose. The form of words approved in civil courts generally is set out in a *Practice Note*.[18] As the terms of the agreement are not actually part of the tribunal's decision but are merely scheduled to it, they can include matters which are outside the tribunal's jurisdiction (such as the terms of a reference, a confidentiality clause etc) and payments of money will not attract the attention of the recoupment provisions.

If the proceedings are stayed or adjourned with liberty to apply, where an employer defaults on the agreement the employee can chose to re-instate the proceedings by applying to lift the stay or to seek an order from the tribunal or the county court in the terms of the agreement (although the tribunal would only be able to make such an order in so far as the terms were within its powers). If there is no provision for liberty to apply, the employee would be restricted to re-instating the proceedings, by lifting the stay, or pursuing a claim for breach of the agreement in the county court.

The right to re-instate proceedings in the tribunal can be extremely important for employees. Not only does it re-instate the threat of the hearing against the employer, with the costs and publicity implications that that entails; it also means that where the employer has been found to be insolvent, the employee can still pursue a claim for a basic award or redundancy payment which can then be recovered from the Secretary of State under the provisions relating to the protection of employees on an employer's insolvency.

Where a party is represented in tribunal proceedings and the representative (whether a lawyer, adviser or lay representative) agrees to a decision being made 'by consent', it will be assumed that the party concerned has *in fact* consented, even if the representative acted without taking proper instructions. The party's remedy, if any, lies against the representative.[19] Those acting for parties in the settlement of a case by these means should adopt the same cautious approach as when entering into an agreement through a conciliation officer or by any other means: it is the representative's duty to make sure that the individual is properly advised on the terms and effect of the agreement and that s/he does in fact consent to that compromise of the claim.

---

18 [1927] WN 290, HC; see White Book para 4616 and Green Book pp327 and 331 (and see Appendix 2 p285).
19 *Times Newspapers Ltd v Fitt* [1981] ICR 637, EAT.

CHECKLIST: SETTLEMENT AND CONCILIATION

For employees:
- If an offer of settlement has been made, how does it compare to the value of the claim as it is likely to be assessed by a tribunal?
- Are there advantages in compromising the claim rather than going ahead with the hearing (ie, the provision of a reference or the avoidance of the recoupment provisions)?
- Could acceptance of the offer mean that rights other than those pursued in the tribunal proceedings might be lost (eg, a personal injury claim; pension rights etc)?
- If considering entering into a compromise agreement, do so only on taking **independent** advice.
- Does the wording and form of the settlement achieve the things important to you (eg, will it avoid the recoupment provisions? Will it ensure that the agreed reference will be provided without subsequent contradiction?)
- Before accepting any offer: if in doubt, get advice.

For employers:
- Is the employee willing and able (ie, indpendently advised by a qualified, insured lawyer) to enter into a binding compromise agreement or contract? If so, can an agreement be reached which would avoid the risk of subsequent proceedings?
- If the employee is unwilling or unable to enter into any agreement but there is a risk of subsequent tribunal proceedings, consider making an offer which includes a concession of liability, without prejudice save as to costs.
- If any payment is to be made to the employee, consider whether it should be made in open correspondence or 'without prejudice'.
- If a payment is made to the employee, make it clear what that payment is intended to cover: if it includes an amount in respect of a possible basic award, this should be expressly stated.
- If tribunal proceedings are contemplated or have been commenced, consider utilising the services of ACAS and entering into an agreement through a conciliation officer, recorded on Form COT3.
- If an agreement is intended to cover *all* possible claims,

make this clear by expressly referring to the claims that are envisaged by the terms of the compromise.

For advisers:

- Is your client in a sufficiently well-informed position to assess the pros and cons of settlement properly?
- If advising the employee, do you meet the definition of a qualified independent legal adviser for the purposes of entering into a compromise contract or agreement?
- Has an ACAS conciliation officer been involved in seeking to reach a compromise of the claim?
- If an agreement has been reached, does your client understand the full implications of the terms of the agreement?
- Keep a record of any agreement reached, signed by your client and those acting for the other party.
- Pay attention to time limits (for payment of money etc) set out in the agreement and consider restoring the claim in the tribunal if these are not met.
- If the recoupment provisions apply to your client, is the settlement recorded in such a way as to avoid recoupment?

Preparing for the hearing

Notice of the hearing

Notice must be given at least 14 days before the hearing unless the parties agree with the tribunal office to a shorter period (r5(2)). The notice of hearing includes guidance to the parties on witnesses and documents (see p144). The notes accompanying the notice of hearing include advice on attendance, making representations in writing, disposal of the case against a respondent who has not entered a notice of appearance, the possibility of the case not getting on, witness statements (see p144), and a note to employers to be prepared to deal with the issue of re-instatement and expenses.

Listing

The tribunal office will make arrangements for the listing of the case according to the practice operated in that particular region. The length of time the case is likely to take to present and for the tribunal to reach a decision needs to be carefully evaluated and reasons given. It is wise to be cautious, and give ample time; it is better for the hearing to end before the scheduled day than for it to adjourn part-heard, with all parties coming back weeks or even months later.

It is neccessary to check the availability of all witnesses and any representative, and then send the tribunal the estimate of length and dates to avoid.

Preliminary points of law

142   An application to seek a preliminary hearing should already have

been made by now but if not, it should be made forthwith (see p118).

Chairman alone?

If either party wants the case to be heard by either a chairman sitting alone, or by a full tribunal, and there is a discretion given to the tribunal to decide this (see p5 for when this arises), the preference should be made known to the tribunal, with reasons.

Hearing in public

The hearing of an originating application must be in public unless a government minister directs otherwise (or the tribunal so decides on grounds of national security (r8(2) and (3)). If there are allegations of a sexual offence or sexual misconduct, orders protecting the identity of those involved can be sought at this stage. This is discussed in chapter 17 (pp151–152).

Written representations

Written representations can be made to the tribunal. They should be sent seven days before the hearing with copies to other parties but the tribunal has power to consider them even if they have been submitted within seven days of the hearing (rr8(5) and 13(2)(c)).

Skeleton arguments

In practice the tribunal will welcome the presentation of written arguments in skeleton form, as is the growing practice in courts. A short summary of the issues in opening, or a skeleton argument and draft findings of fact presented in closing, are usually accepted gratefully. They save time and release the tribunal from making detailed notes on oral submissions. There is no need to send them in advance to the tribunal or the other side unless there is an agreement to do so.

Agreed facts

Some cases are heard without any live evidence being called because there is no dispute on the facts. TUPE cases and wages protection claims might usefully centre on issues of law alone. So it might be worthwhile to draft a statement and send it to the other side to see if agreement is possible.

Witness statements

Each party should decide which witnesses it is likely to call and take a detailed statement from them.

Evidence from non-expert witnesses is increasingly called for in the form of written statements (see p164). The notes to accompany the notice of hearing in England and Wales include the following (see p380):

> The length of the hearing and the consequent expense may be reduced if you prepare written statements for yourself and your witnesses. Such statements may help you and your witnesses to include all the matters that you consider important. You may then apply at the hearing for the evidence you wish your witness to give to be read by him or her from the statement. It will be for the tribunal to decide whether the witness can do so after hearing what you and the other party have to say about it. If the written statement is read, the witness may be questioned by the other party, and the tribunal.

The statement should therefore be in a form which can be disclosed in full to the other side and to the tribunal. There is no requirement to exchange or send it in advance. Witness statements are rarely used in Northern Ireland and never in Scotland.

A party should also consider whether an expert is needed, eg, on job evaluation in an equal pay case. Evidence given by an expert in the form of an opinion in the county court and the High Court must be provided in advance of the trial.[1] There is no specific requirement for this at a tribunal but if an expert witness is produced without prior notice or an indication of the nature of his/ her evidence, an application for adjournment is likely to be granted and costs could be awarded against the party producing the expert evidence. It is obviously unsatisfactory for one party to be unprepared for the evidence of an expert. Without advance access to its own expert, the other side is unable properly to evaluate, cross-examine and challenge any opinion given.

---

1 RSC Order 38 rr36–44; CCR Order 20 rr27, 28.

Documents

Parties are encouraged to agree what documents are going to be put to the tribunal. In unfair dismissal cases the employer will usually open the case and the preparation of the index and paginated bundles should be up to its representative in the first place. Both sides should have a clear idea of the relevant material and the best way to present it. Usually this will be in chronological order, but there may be separate issues, or separate originating applications which justify discrete bundles or sections.

If an application for the costs to be paid by the losing side may be made, perhaps on the ground of being put to unnecessary preparation, a separate bundle should be prepared for this purpose to use at the end of the hearing (see p182).

Authorities to be referred to

It is neccessary to consider what law is relevant to the case. A list of cases to be referred to should be handed in to the clerk at the tribunal on the hearing day, and exchanged with the other side before that. It is helpful to the tribunal and to one's own submissions if a bundle of photocopies is provided for each tribunal member so that they and the advocate can highlight the relevant passages.

The EAT does not follow the practice of the Court of Appeal in requiring cases to be cited in the ICR if there is a choice of law report; IRLR and other reports can be used. Tribunals are flexible. To maintain uniformity, and to be ready if the case goes to appeal, it is sensible to cite ICR, or at least use IRLR or ICR consistently.

The tribunal chairman (but not the wing members) will have access to the legislation, so if it is necessary to refer to several statutes and European directives, it will help the case to have these photocopied too.

Warning witnesses to attend

A representative on the record is responsible for ensuring that the client is warned of the hearing date and that notice of the hearing is given to witnesses. A witness should be sent the final version of his/her statement and asked to sign it. There is nothing wrong in all witnesses seeing each others' statements, and indeed it saves time if a witness can comment in his/her own statement on evidence in other statements, especially if both people were at the same meeting or saw the same events. This is not encouraged in Scotland, where witnesses do not know other witnesses' testimony.

CHAPTER 17

The hearing

This chapter sets out the principal features of a tribunal hearing with references to the law relating to procedure, and advice on the best practice in conducting a hearing.

Administration

Arrangements at the tribunal

All tribunal hearing centres have a reception check-in to enable parties and witnesses to register. It is important for all who are likely to be called as witnesses to register either personally or through their representative. This is because the list is then seen by the tribunal and members can quickly see whether their knowledge of any witness might cause them to be excused from hearing the case.

In most hearing centres there are separate rooms for parties and witnesses for each side of the case, ie, applicants and respondents. This appears to be the only civil forum where separation is deemed necessary – the civil courts do not have separated waiting areas.

In some hearing centres there are conference rooms available free of charge on a first come, first served basis.

In some hearing centres rooms are made available for members of the tribunal adjacent to the hearing rooms. This enables the members to enter and withdraw while the parties are in the room. In other centres, no facilities are available and so the tribunal is already seated on the bench when the parties are ushered in by the tribunal clerk. Whenever possible, it is useful for clients and witnesses to see the tribunal room's layout before the hearing starts in order to feel comfortable.

While waiting for the case to come on, applicants are frequently asked if they are claiming social security benefits and if so, to give the name of the office where they are registered. This is in case an award of compensation is made and recoupment of benefits provisions apply. At the same time the tribunal clerk will take a note of the full name and job title or position of each witness and establish whether the witness is to swear an oath and if so, upon which holy text, or whether the witness will affirm.

Listing

Parties are warned in the advance notes sent to them that the case may not start on time. This is because the policy of the tribunals is to overbook so that on any given day there will be a number of 'floaters' which will be slotted in as and when any of the cases are settled or disposed of. These floaters are not attached to any particular tribunal and will go to the first one which becomes available. If there is no reasonable prospect of the floater being reached, parties will be advised by the tribunal clerk. Another date will be fixed.

From time to time, a major mistake occurs in listing, eg, a party is not sent a notice of hearing, or a chairman fails to appear. In such circumstances it is possible to make a claim against the Department of Trade and Industry, which administers tribunals, although there is no guarantee that such claims will be met.

Documents

Copies of documents which will be referred to should be handed in to the tribunal clerk. This enables the tribunal to have a more detailed look at the documents in the few minutes available before the hearing. In practice, tribunals do not see any documents in advance of the day of the hearing. On the day, a small bundle is prepared of the tribunal documents, ie, originating application, notice of appearance, relevant correspondence with the tribunal, orders made and directions given, but this is all that will be available to the tribunal unless the parties themselves provide a more detailed bundle. It is advantageous to hand in bundles of documents at once so the tribunal can start reading and get a picture of the case.

Witness statements are in a different category and are dealt with at p144.

Authorities to be referred to

A list of cases to be referred to or a bundle of photocopies of the reports should be handed in to the clerk and exchanged with the other side. It is helpful to the tribunal and to one's own submissions if a bundle of photocopies is provided for each tribunal member. Otherwise only the chairman will be found a copy by the tribunal clerk, making it invidious for the lay members.

Procedure

By r9, tribunals are enjoined to avoid formality and are not bound by rules of evidence in the same way as courts are. They must make inquiries of advocates and witnesses so as to clarify the issues and handle the proceedings justly. Subject to the rules of procedure which govern particular aspects of the tribunal's powers, 'a tribunal may regulate its own procedure', (r13(1)).

Despite the encouragement of informality, tribunals are usually conducted very formally. The requirement that tribunals should make inquiries, introduced in 1993, entitles the tribunal to be more inquisitorial and directive than the courts: indeed a tribunal has the power to call a witness itself (r4(2)(a)). Almost all the rules of procedure may be activated by the tribunal of its own motion, whether or not any party makes an application. This combination of informality and inquiry provides the legal justification for tribunals to take a far more interventionist line than was common practice before 1994.

Chairman and members

The cases where a chairman can sit without lay members are set out on p5.

Challenge to composition of tribunal

Given the local composition of tribunals, it is inevitable from time to time that members will know parties or witnesses in a case they are about to hear. Any direct interest in the case would automatically exclude a member from sitting.[1] That constitutes bias in the technical

---

1 *R v Gough* [1993] AC 646, HL.

sense of having a pecuniary or proprietary interest in the outcome of proceedings. But objection can be made to the composition of the tribunal on far less tangible grounds, since it is important to avoid any possibility of a challenge during or after a tribunal hearing.

The members should be selected at random from the panels of people drawn from both sides of emploment relations. In cases of race discrimination, effect is given to an assurance given during debates on the Race Relations Act 1976 that there should be at least one member with special knowledge or experience of race relations in the employment field. A separate list of persons so qualified is kept by the tribunals. The absence in a race discrimination case of such a person will not invalidate the proceedings but administrative arrangements are generally made to ensure such a person sits.[2] A similar assurance was not given in debates on the Sex Discrimination Act, but in practice administrative arrangements are usually made to ensure that members of both sexes sit on cases of sex discrimination and equal pay.

The most appropriate time to make an objection about the composition of the tribunal is before the hearing starts, while it remains a potential problem and before it becomes an actual problem. In *Halford v Sharples*[3] a member had 'specialist' knowledge of personnel practices in police forces and was specifically chosen to sit on a claim of sex discrimination brought by a senior officer. The EAT decided the tribunal should be selected at random and not by reference to any specialist experience. The proper test is:

> Could the reasonable and disinterested observer present at the hearing ... reasonably take the view ... that the continued presence of the member was undesirable in that a party could reasonably feel that injustice might occur during the hearing? (Wood J)

And in *University College of Swansea v Cornelius*[4] a tribunal decision was overturned because one of the members was the mother-in-law of a person who had sat on an internal appeal.

If a list of potential witnesses has been handed in at the outset, the tribunal can consider whether any person on the list is known to any member. The proper approach is for the chairman to draw this to the attention of the parties and invite comments. Generally

2 *Habib v Elkington & Co Ltd* [1981] ICR 435; [1981] IRLR 344, EAT.
3 [1992] ICR 146, EAT.
4 [1988] ICR 735.

speaking, any objection which is not 'irresponsible, frivolous or wholly without content'[5] will be acted on. If no objection is made once the possible conflict is pointed out, the case can go on; if objection is made, the member should stand down.

Absence of a member

If a conflict arises before or during the course of the hearing and a member stands down, or becomes indisposed, the hearing cannot continue without him/her without consent of all parties (reg 7(3)). If consent is given, a decision can be made by a member and a chairman together and if they disagree the chairman has a casting vote (r10(1)). It is therefore imperative to weigh carefully the advantages of making an objection, since it may abort the proceedings. It is useful to know which panel (TUC or CBI) the member comes from. The longest case ever before a tribunal was heard by a chairman and one member following the death of the other – the claims of unfair dismissal on the grounds of trade union activity raised by dockworker shop stewards lasted for 197 days, the member dying after seven days.[6]

Consent need not be obtained from a person who is debarred from participating.

Hearing in public

The hearing of an originating application must be in public (r8(2)). But it can be in private if a minister so directs on the grounds of national security (r8(2) and ITA 1996 s10(1)). The tribunal has discretion, however, to hear certain evidence in private (r8(3)), but this applies only in respect of specific evidence and not speeches and other evidence or aspects of the case. The grounds are that public disclosure of evidence would:

a) be against the interests of national security;
b) involve breach of a statutory provision;
c) involve disclosure of information given to the witness in confidence;
d) cause substantial injury to any undertaking, excluding matters relating to the effect on collective bargaining.

---

5 *Halford v Sharples* at p171.
6 *Port of London Authority v Payne* [1994] ICR 555, [1994] IRLR 9, CA.

A decision as to whether a hearing should be held in private must be made by the full tribunal[7] and there is no right for the application itself to be heard in private.

Interlocutory applications are not required to be heard in public and in practice are heard by a chairman alone in chambers.[8] This is because a 'hearing', which must be in public under reg 2(1), does not include the making of 'any other interlocutory order or any other decision on an interlocutory matter than striking out an originating application or notice of appearance' (reg 2(2)).

In England and Wales and Northern Ireland, witnesses are generally permitted to sit in the tribunal room before giving evidence. In Scotland those who may be called to give evidence remain outside the tribunal until they are called.

Allegations of sexual offences and sexual misconduct

Provisions introduced by TURERA 1993 s40 (now ITA 1996 s11) allow tribunals to restrict reporting of cases involving sexual misconduct. Sexual misconduct means:

> the commission of a sexual offence, sexual harassment or other adverse conduct (of whatever nature) related to sex, and conduct is related to sex whether the relationship with sex lies in the character of the conduct or in its having reference to the sex or sexual orientation of the person at whom the conduct is directed (ITA 1996 s11(6)).

In such a case (and in cases under DDA 1995 involving evidence of a personal nature, under r14(1A)) the tribunal, having given the opportunity to the parties to advance oral arguments, can decide to make a restricted reporting order (r14(3)). The order specifies the person who may not be identified in reports of the case. The ban remains in force until the decision of the tribunal is promulgated unless it is revoked earlier.

The rules require a notice to be affixed to the door of the tribunal and to the list of cases on the notice board at the tribunal office. The effect of such a notice is to provide a warning to all journalists in the hearing centre. Breach of a restricted reporting order exposes people who publish the identity of a person to a fine (ITA 1996 s11(2)). For newspapers and other media, liability rests on the proprietor and the editor, and in respect of broadcast programmes, the company providing the service and anybody fulfilling functions corresponding to an editor. A person publishing the

7 *Milne v Waldren* [1980] ICR 138, EAT.
8 *Jones v Enham Industries* [1983] ICR 580n.

identity in any other form is also liable. Ignorance and lack of suspicion of the existence of an order is a defence (s11(3)).

In addition to a restricted reporting order, tribunals must take certain steps where a case involves a sexual *offence*. This is defined as offences specified in the Criminal Procedure (Scotland) Act 1995 s274(2) and the Sexual Offences (Amendment) Acts 1976 and 1992 in England (ITA 1996 s11(6)).

Where there are allegations of the commission of a sexual offence, the tribunal office must omit from the register, or delete from it, and any document recording the proceedings available to the public, any material which might 'lead members of the public to identify any person affected by or making such an allegation' (r13(6)). The (possibly unintended) effect of this is to restrain publication of identifying material until the decision is promulgated and then to permit publication of names which must, on the other hand, be omitted from or deleted from the official record.

Representation at the tribunal

There is no restriction on the kind of person who may represent a party at the proceedings and so representation by counsel, solicitor, trade union official, employer's association, voluntary worker, friend or anyone at all is permitted.

Any party may give evidence, call witnesses, question witnesses and address the tribunal (r9(2)). In addition, the Secretary of State can be treated as a party in proceedings which may involve payment out of the National Insurance Fund (r8(6)).

A respondent who fails to comply with an order for further particulars, discovery or written answers to questions may have its notice of appearance struck out and 'where appropriate' be debarred from defending altogether (r4(7)). A respondent who has not entered an appearance at all cannot take part in the proceedings except to the extent that it is necessary for the purposes of an application for further particulars, an extension of time and an application for review (r3(2)).

If a party which has been given notice of the hearing fails to attend, the tribunal has a wide range of powers. For an applicant, the case may be dismissed, the application may be disposed of or the hearing may be adjourned. But if the application is to be dismissed or disposed of, the tribunal must consider the originating application, notice of appearance, any written representations and any answers provided in accordance with the question and answer procedure under r4(3) (r9(3)). In practice, some tribunal offices make inquiries to ensure that the applicant has had proper notice of the hearing by making phone calls, eg, to his/her home and his/her employers. A tribunal is likely to allow some leeway to an applicant, and may take another case whilst waiting for the applicant to arrive. It will be reluctant to determine or dismiss the case in the absence of any explanation from the applicant, but it certainly has the power to do so. In such a situation an award of costs might be appropriate under r12 (see p176).

Written representations

Written representations can be made to the tribunal. They should be sent seven days before the hearing with copies to other parties, but the tribunal has power to consider them even if they have been submitted within seven days of the hearing (rr8(5) and 13(2)(c)). In practice the tribunal will welcome the presentation of written arguments in skeleton form, as is the growing practice in courts. A short summary of the issues in opening, or a skeleton argument and draft findings of fact presented in closing, are usually accepted gratefully. They save time and release the tribunal from making detailed notes on oral submissions.

The real purpose of the rule allowing for written submissions is not clear: they do not replace oral evidence, especially as the tribunal has power to call witnesses and ask questions (r4(2)). In pre-hearing reviews, however, written representations are crucial (see chapter 12).

Adjournment or postponement

The circumstances in which an adjournment or postponement is ordered are dealt with in chapter 14. The tribunal has a very wide discretion and in addition has a discretion specifically in relation to costs (r12(2) and (5)).

The issue to be determined

In most cases the issue to be determined will be clear: unfair dismissal, unlawful deduction, sex discrimination etc. But in unfair dismissal cases, for example, tribunals frequently prefer to take evidence and make a decision on liability before dealing with remedies. It is important at the outset that the tribunal should announce, having considered representations, what issue it is about to determine. If liability is to be determined at a split hearing, it should also be made clear by the tribunal whether or not evidence is to be heard relating to liability for contributory fault or other conduct under ERA 1996 ss122(2) and 123(6).[9]

It would be contrary to the rules of natural justice for a tribunal which had announced it was to deal with only one issue to make findings on more than one without giving the parties an opportunity to make representations and call further evidence. If an announcement has not been made at the outset, it is appropriate at the conclusion of, say, the evidence-in-chief of the main witness for the employer to raise the issue as to whether evidence should be called relating to mitigation, remedies, reinstatement and so on.

As a matter of practice it is convenient for remedies to be dealt with after a finding on liability, but it is important to ensure that a date is fixed for the resumed hearing on remedies, should the tribunal make a finding on liability. It is also convenient for all issues of liability, ie, liability and contributory conduct, to be dealt with at a single hearing, since the evidence will be more or less the same, and it will enable the parties to make headway on negotiating a settlement following a successful result for the applicant on liability once it is known whether, and if so to what extent, the applicant contributed to the dismissal.

In Scotland, tribunals tend to try to avoid split hearings on liability and remedies.

Separate hearings are usually convenient for testing the material factor defence in *equal pay* claims.

In *constructive dismissal* cases, it is usually unhelpful to separate the issue of breach of contract from unfair dismissal (see p119). Again, the evidence is likely to be coterminous so that the applicant will be producing evidence to show that the employer behaved so badly that there was a breach of contract, and the employer will produce material either denying the facts said to constitute a breach of contract or seeking to show it behaved fairly.

In these circumstances, not much is to be gained by splitting the legal issues from the factual issues under ERA 1996 s95(1) and s98(4). Most tribunals hearing an application to separate these considerations will hear all the evidence and make determinations on

9 See *Iggesund Converters Ltd v Lewis* [1984] ICR 544; [1984] IRLR 431, EAT.

dismissal, ie, repudiation under s95, reason for dismissal under s98(1) and reasonableness of the dismissal under s98(4). If the tribunal finds there was no dismissal, it is useful (for any future appeal) to invite the tribunal before the end of the hearing to make decisions on the alternative hypothesis that if there *was* a dismissal, it was fair or alternatively unfair.

Late amendment, new allegations, late disclosure

Disputes about documents should be resolved at the outset of the hearing; as should any last minute amendments to the originating application, notice of appearance and answers given pursuant to written requests. Concessions should also be made at this stage. Of course, amendments and concessions can be made during the course of proceedings. They are usually made orally, and if necessary can be reduced into writing at the end of the day.

Who goes first?

The running order should depend on where the onus of proof lies. As a rule of thumb, first in, last out operates so that the party who has to prove any particular issue goes first and finishes last. Once the onus of proof falls on a party, that party has not only the duty but the right to go first.[10] In unfair dismissal cases the onus of proof lies initially on the employer: to show the reason for dismissal and that it falls within the categories of fair dismissal in ERA 1996 s98(1) and (2). The practical effect is that the employer goes first.

If the dismissal is not admitted, the onus of proof is on the employee. This assertion will be made either in the notice of appearance or at the outset of the hearing. If the employer disputes that there has been a constructive dismissal and claims the employee resigned or retired, the onus of proof is on the employee. The onus is on the employer where there is a challenge to the jurisdiction of the tribunal, eg, because the applicant is said not to have the two years' continuous service entitling him/her to bring a claim of unfair dismissal. This practice has been approved by the EAT in *Post Office Counters Ltd v Heavey*.[11] But since the tribunal is free to

10 *Gill v Harold Andrews Sheepbridge Ltd* [1974] ICR 294, [1974] IRLR 109, NIRC.
11 [1990] ICR 1; [1989] IRLR 513.

adopt its own procedure, subject to the rules it can decide to ask the employee to go first.[12]

Certain practical factors affect the way in which tribunals make this decision. If the applicant is unrepresented and is making allegations of unfair dismissal in a general way, it is often useful for the applicant to go first, not least because the concept of 'putting your case' is difficult to master, if it means ensuring that every part of the case is put first to an employer's witnesses. If the employer is represented by a solicitor or counsel, the tribunal often invites the lawyer to outline briefly the facts and legal issues before inviting the applicant to give evidence.

Although almost all unfair dismissal cases where the dismissal is admitted show the employer's evidence going first, there is logically no reason why this should be the case when a dismissal for a particular reason is accepted by the applicant. For example, the applicant claims she was dismissed, the reason given is dishonesty and the applicant accepts that that was the reason but that the facts do not disclose dishonesty or do not give grounds for a dismissal in the circumstances. Here the employer has discharged the onus of proving the reason and a potentially fair reason and therefore, there being no onus of proof under ERA 1996 s98(4), it is more logical to allow the applicant to make her allegations first and then to hear the evidence relating to the employer's explanation.

In both discrimination and dismissal cases there is a very real advantage to the applicant in going first which should be seized if at all possible. In lengthy dismissal cases where the respondent opens, the first the tribunal hears from the applicant is after several days of evidence given by managers painting a very negative picture of his/her behaviour. In discrimination cases, the applicant naturally wishes to establish at the outset the wrong done to her. If the tribunal allows an opening speech to be made (see p158), this is the ideal opportunity for a statement to be made. And of course the press is more likely to be in attendance at the start of a hearing than halfway through.

In claims for redundancy payments there is a presumption that a dismissal is on account of redundancy (ERA 1996 s163(2)). So an employer who claims the reason for dismissal was not redundancy would go first, the onus being on the employer to prove this.

In claims combining unfair dismissal and discrimination, it is submitted that as between the duty of the employer to show a

---

12 *Hawker Siddeley Power Engineering Ltd v Rump* [1979] IRLR 425, EAT.

reason for a dismissal and the right of an applicant to open a discrimination case, priority should be given to the applicant's right so that s/he would open all aspects of the discrimination and dismissal cases.

In equal pay cases where a material factor defence is raised under Equal Pay Act 1970 s1(3), the onus is on the employer. But the applicant is still required to show an employment relationship and establish the basic facts against which (it is contended by the employer) a material factor defence exists to a claim for equal pay. Again, on a purely practical basis, the applicant should be allowed to open her case and call evidence. Although the focus of attention will quickly shift to the employer's material factor defence, at least the applicant will have established elementary components in her claim and the tribunal will have heard from her. At least one major equal pay case went to the Court of Appeal, back to the tribunal, then was referred to an independent expert, and it was more than five years before any woman gave evidence.[13]

The opening speech

There is a right to make an opening speech only in appeals against training levies, prohibition, improvement and non-discrimination notices.[14] Otherwise there is no formal right. Rule 9(2) entitles a party 'to address the tribunal' but this does not require the address to be made at the start of the case. Further, r9(2) is *subject* to r9(1), which gives the tribunal a wide discretion as to the handling of the proceedings. In Scotland, opening speeches are never made, except for appeals (above). In England, Wales and Northern Ireland, at least a brief opening is usually permitted. If there are several applicants, each should be given the same right to open, as should multiple respondents if they open. If a respondent employer opens a case, the applicant employee coming second does not in practice make an opening speech.

The purpose of an opening speech is to make a brief impression on the tribunal and to give a summary of the principal issues of law and of where disputes of fact will lie, together with a statement of what the person opening the case will achieve. An outline of the evidence to be called and the names of witnesses is often given but is not necessary. As a matter of practicality, it is important to direct

---

13 *Bromley v H & J Quick Ltd* [1988] ICR 623; [1988] IRLR 249, CA.
14 see Schs 3–5 to 1993 Regulations.

the tribunal to the relevant statutes (not quite so necessary in respect of ERA 1996 s98) and the names and at least the headnotes of relevant authorities which should be borne in mind by the tribunal during the hearing.

It is not necessary to explore the bundles of documents. These will have to be examined by the relevant witnesses in any event – for example a letter written by the manager dismissing the applicant will be examined by the writer and the recipient when they give their evidence. A brief introduction to the issues of law and fact to be decided will generally be welcomed by the tribunal, but its patience will be tried if all the documents are read at the outset. The law should be described neutrally but there is nothing wrong in making tendentious statements on one's case at this stage.

Conduct of the hearing

Within the scope of the tribunal's duty under r9(1) to avoid formality and conduct the proceedings 'in such manner as it considers most appropriate for the clarification of the issues ... and the just handling of the proceedings', the tribunal has a very wide discretion. The amendment in the 1993 Rules placing a duty on tribunals to 'make such enquiries of persons appearing before it and witnesses as it considers appropriate' clearly envisages a more interventionist role by tribunals than had been the case previously. The following issues may well arise in a hearing.

Natural justice

The conduct of the hearing is subject to the rules of procedure (but not the civil law of evidence) and the rules of natural justice. These are that each side should be given the opportunity to present its case through evidence and argument and to cross-examine each other's witnesses. A decision should not be made on any issue about which a party has not been given the opportunity to present evidence and address arguments.[15] As Lord Bridge said in *Lloyd v McMahon*:[16]

> ... the so-called rules of natural justice are not engraved on tablets of stone. [W]hat the requirements of fairness demand when any body, domestic, administrative or judicial, has to make a decision which will affect the rights of individuals depends on the character of the decision-

15 *Laurie v Holloway* [1994] ICR 32, EAT.
16 [1987] AC 625 at 702.

making body, the kind of decision it has to make and the statutory or other framework in which it operates . . .

And in *Wiseman v Borneman*[17] Lord Reid said:

> Natural justice requires that the procedure before any tribunal which is acting judicially should be fair in all the circumstances, and I would be sorry to see this fundamental general principle degenerate into a series of hard and fast rules.

Formality

In *Aberdeen Steak Houses v Ibrahim*[18] the EAT laid down its own summary of what was required of tribunals under the rules of natural justice:

> Over the years a number of cases have given guidance on the appropriate procedure and on rules of evidence . . .
>
> a) Decisions bearing upon the party who should present his case first: *Gill v Harold Andrews Sheepbridge Ltd* [1974] ICR 294 and *Oxford v DHSS* [1977] ICR 884.
>
> b) It is for the party and not the tribunal to decide the order in which he calls his witnesses: *Barnes v BPC (Business Forms) Ltd* [1975] ICR 390.
>
> c) It is the duty of the parties to ensure that all relevant evidence is put before the tribunal and that it is not for the tribunal themselves to do this: *Craig v British Railways (Scottish Region)* (1973) 8 ITR 636 and *Derby City Council v Marshall* [1979] ICR 731.
>
> d) A tribunal should not allow a party to be taken by surprise by an allegation of dishonesty made at the last minute, but should adjourn and give directions: *Hotson v Wisbech Conservative Club* [1984] ICR 859.
>
> e) Where a party specifically states that he will not be calling evidence, he will normally be bound by his statement: *Stokes v Hampstead Wine Co Ltd* [1979] IRLR 298.
>
> f) Tribunals cannot refuse to admit evidence which is admissible and probative of one or more issues: *Rosedale Mouldings Ltd v Sibley* [1980] ICR 816.

Nevertheless in the same case the tribunal eschewed informality pursuant to r9(3) and said:

> It is possible for informality to go too far and it is important for parties appearing before any judicial body and for their legal advisers in preparing for trial to know the rules normally to be applied during the hearing. It is important there should be consistency . . . Total informality

17 [1971] AC 297 at 308.
18 [1988] ICR 550 at 557 per Wood J; [1988] IRLR 420.

and absence of generally recognised rules of procedure and evidence can be counter-productive.

The application of these dicta would ensure that tribunals do behave quite formally.

Admissibility of evidence

Estoppel

Estoppel is a rule of evidence which prevents cases, or issues in cases, being litigated twice. It operates as a defence and can be raised in tribunal proceedings.[19] An issue decided by a tribunal between the same parties will prevent either of the parties re-opening the issue in, for example, subsequent tribunal proceedings or parallel county court or High Court proceedings.[20]

The rule can prevent the re-opening of a single issue or a whole cause of action. But the original decision must have been within the competence of the original tribunal and have been essential for the decision in that case. Otherwise the decsion will be *obiter dicta*, not binding on subsequent tribunals and courts.

Hearsay

A statement made by a person who is not a witness in proceedings, adduced for the purpose of establishing the truth of what that person said, is hearsay and would be admissible in a court to the extent permitted by the Civil Evidence Act 1995. Tribunals may and frequently do take hearsay evidence. It is quite proper, albeit tactically injudicious, to object to it being heard at the time, and to lay down a marker so that in a closing speech the tribunal can be asked to pay less attention to that evidence because it was not subject to cross-examination.

Quite often the issue before a tribunal is not the truth, but what was known to an employer at the time a decision to dismiss was made. So in *Coral Squash Clubs Ltd v Matthews*[21] it was held that it was quite proper and indeed necessary for hearsay evidence to be adduced before the tribunal about information given to the employer. It did not matter whether the information was correct or not; the central question was what material was available before the

---

19 *Munir v Jang Publications Ltd* [1989] ICR 1; [1989] IRLR 224, CA.
20 *Green v Hampshire County Council* [1979] ICR 861 and *O'Laoire v Jackel International Ltd* [1990] ICR 197; [1991] IRLR 70, CA.
21 [1979] ICR 607; [1979] IRLR 390, EAT.

employer decided to dismiss. Clearly, if the information is unsatisfactory and requires further investigation, it will often be unreasonable for the employer to dismiss on that basis.

The short point about hearsay evidence is that anyone who has relevant evidence must be brought to the tribunal as a witness. The more important their evidence, the more necessary it is for them to be there. If they are going to give evidence, hearsay evidence from another witness is unnecessary. If they are not going to give evidence, hearsay evidence is of limited weight. Objection at the moment of its being given is often counter-productive, but the point should be made when addressing the tribunal in a closing speech.

Material before and after the relevant event

As a general rule, events after the relevant date are immaterial, eg, after the date of dismissal in an unfair dismissal case.[22] In such a case the central question is the information available to the employer at the time of the dismissal.

In cases of discrimination, particularly where the applicant still works for the employer, events before and after the event giving rise to the claim may be introduced in evidence 'if logically probative of a relevant fact'. In *Chattopadhyay v Headmaster of Holloway School*,[23] for the purpose of proving racial discrimination, evidence was admissible of hostility to the applicant both before the relevant event and after it.

If what is alleged is a series of discriminatory acts, then of course all evidence within the relevant time period will be admissible.

Without prejudice communications

These should not be introduced in the procedings in evidence-in-chief or cross-examination; see p89.

Credibility and collateral matters

As Wood J said in *Aberdeen Steak Houses Ltd v Ibrahim*:[24]

> When in cross-examination questions go to credit only, the party cross-examining should be bound by the answers of the witness.

This means strictly that it is not possible to call evidence to contradict evidence given by a witness going to the witness's credibility. It is part of a rule which prevents the admission of collateral

---

22 *Devis Ltd v Atkins* [1977] ICR 662; [1977] IRLR 314, HL.
23 [1982] ICR 132; [1981] IRLR 487, EAT.
24 [1988] ICR 550.

evidence as to character or disposition indicating (largely to create an aura of prejudice) that the witness is inclined on previous occasions to have done wrong and therefore is likely to have done so on the occasion in question.

In *Snowball v Gardner Merchant Ltd*[25] an applicant complaining of persistent sex discrimination was cross-examined as to her propensity to talk to fellow employees freely about sexual matters. She denied this and it was anticipated that evidence would be called by the employers to show that she was lying. The EAT upheld the admissibility of this evidence. The applicant argued that her attitude was in any event irrelevant to the question of whether she had been sexually harassed, but the EAT held that such evidence was relevant to any injury or detriment she may have claimed. It was therefore admitted even though indirectly it went to her credit (as was its purpose).

The general rule, more likely to be enforced in the light of the 1993 rule changes relating to the non-disclosure of the identity of those affected by allegations of sexual misconduct (p152), is that evidence given in cross-examination relating to credit is binding on those doing the cross-examining, and no new evidence may be brought to contradict it. Furthermore, evidence of an alleged propensity to sexual permissiveness is not relevant, and is therefore collateral, to the central issue of liability for sexual harassment.

It follows that, contrary to cases in criminal courts, evidence as to character is seldom going to be admissible.

Sworn evidence

Tribunals are given power to administer oaths by r9(4). In practice an oath or affirmation is invariably taken from witnesses. Similarly, in cases where interpreters are used, they are required to take an oath or affirmation that they will interpret truthfully and faithfully what the witness says. The usual practice in the absence of a clerk is for the chairman to administer the oath or affirmation. A supply of holy books is available in all tribunals, and staff have been instructed to pay particular attention to the respectful preservation and handling of them.

25 [1987] ICR 719; [1987] IRLR 397, EAT.

Notes of evidence

There is no statutory requirement for the chairman or other members to take notes. However, it has been held that a clear note should be taken of the relevant evidence by the chairman which should be made available if directed by the EAT in an appeal alleging, for example, perversity.[26] The Tribunals and Inquiries Act 1992 s10, which regulates tribunals, requires the relevant tribunal to give reasons, and this is specifically required by r10(3).

Witness statements

Evidence from non-expert witnesses is increasingly called for in the form of written statements: see the note at p144. This almost corresponds to the production of witness statements by exchange in the High Court and the county court.[27] The practice in the tribunals is to encourage parties to exchange witness statements but there is no power to insist on it.

The witness statement itself is not evidence until it is adduced by the relevant witness. Practice varies from region to region but it is usual for a witness to read his/her own statement. S/he may be asked supplementary questions by the representative of the party for whom s/he is giving evidence. This is most likely when this party's case is presented second, since the witness may need to deal with any conflicts which have emerged in the case thus far.

Witness statements are a very powerful tool. Given proper attention, a witness's evidence can be honed to perfection by skilled advisers. Since they are not exchanged in advance, it is difficult to cross-examine immediately on every line in the statement. Examination-in-chief in the traditional way gives more time to absorb the material and prepare cross-examination in addition to that prepared in advance. Nevertheless, this is now common practice where parties are represented at a tribunal. Sometimes the procedure is shortened even further – if there are no other people appearing before the tribunal apart from the parties and their witnesses, the tribunal itself may retire to read the witness statements.

A witness statement is usually read aloud by the witness. The tribunal has no power to direct in advance that evidence is to be exchanged, unless the parties consent. At the hearing it is unlikely to direct that the witness statement alone should stand as evidence-

---

26 *Houston v Lightwater Farms Ltd* [1990] ICR 502; [1990] IRLR 469, EAT.
27 See RSC Order 38 r2A(1) and (2), CCR Order 20 r12A.

in-chief. This is particularly so in respect of evidence given on behalf of the party coming second, since a witness in that position will usually need to deal with the evidence given by the witnesses for the first party by way of supplementary questions and answers.

Live evidence given by a person who has not presented a written statement cannot be excluded on that ground alone, and it will be a breach of the rules of natural justice to refuse it to be heard.

Witnesses who provide a written statement for lawyers and other representatives should carefully read the statement, making alterations and corrections as appropriate, and sign it if correct. One advantage of written statements is that the parties can see where the conflict lies if, before the hearing, there has been an exchange of statements.

The sequence of evidence

Evidence-in-chief

On the assumption that the employer is opening the case, evidence-in-chief from the primary witness will be called first. If a witness statement exists, it should be read. Questions may be asked in non-leading form. The best answers are monosyllabic or one-liners. It is important that the witness gives evidence in relation to all matters about which s/he has any information. In particular, s/he should be asked about all documents in the bundle for which s/he is responsible, ie, those that s/he has written, or, for example, if s/he is the personnel manager, documents relevant to the personnel function – procedure agreements, disciplinary codes and so on. S/he should also be asked about letters which s/he has received so that s/he can say what s/he did when s/he received them and what reaction s/he had to them. All relevant matters must be spoken to.[28]

Leading questions must not be asked without the tribunal's permission.

Cross-examination

The (usually elusive) goal of cross-examination is extraction of an admission on one of the main issues in favour of the party cross-examining. Such admissions are quite rare and admissions as to motives may be of limited value. Even an admission that the employer did not behave fairly or reasonably is not conclusive of the issue; the tribunal will still have to make up its own mind

---

28 *Aberdeen Steak Houses v Ibrahim* [1988] ICR 550; [1988] IRLR 420, EAT.

irrespective of admissions made by witnesses for one of the parties. That in a sense is a question of opinion. Admissions as to facts will however be important.

The more prosaic purpose of cross-examination is to ensure that all points of the applicant's case have been put to the respondent. The applicant cannot raise evidence about matters which s/he has not given the respondent witnesses an opportunity to comment on. If s/he does, it is likely to invoke an application to recall one of the respondent's witnesses which will have the attendant disadvantage of reinforcing that witness's testimony by leaving in the mind of the tribunal the enduring image of him/her.

Cross-examination consists of asking leading questions and is not restricted to material which has been adduced in chief. Questioning can be on any matter relevant to the issues to be decided. Any document about which the witness has some relevant input can also be put in cross-examination.

Questions by the tribunal

The most appropriate time for this to occur is immediately following cross-examination, but practices vary. For example, some tribunals ask questions throughout the hearing, some remain silent until after re-examination. The advantage in having the tribunal ask questions immediately following cross-examination is that it cuts down on the number of opportunities given to the representatives to ask further questions and therefore saves time. If questions are asked at this stage, the tribunal ought, in accordance with the rules of natural justice, to allow an opportunity to cross-examine on any new matter arising out of questions by the tribunal.

Re-examination

This ought to be strictly confined to matters which have been raised in cross-examination and in questions by the tribunal. If a document has been raised in cross-examination, the whole of the document can be the subject of re-examination. As before, questions must be in non-leading form. If you have forgotten to put a point, it is better to own up, seek leave from the tribunal, and offer the other side an opportunity to cross-examine on it.

Rulings during the course of the hearing

Depending on the degree of intervention by the chairman, tribunals make rulings from time to time or throughout a hearing. Parties are encouraged to move on in their questioning and to give more attention to certain points, and they 'need not be troubled by' a particular point. A chairman might openly reflect on what appear to the tribunal to be the essentials of the case. Most of this is done as directions without being the subject of a formal ruling. However, three situations may call for a ruling in the course of the hearing.

Admissibility of evidence

If there is a dispute on the admissibility of evidence, with arguments addressed by both sides, the chairman should be asked to give a ruling. The ruling may be accompanied by reasons at the time or by an undertaking that the reasons will form part of the reasons for the substantive decision.

Half-time submission of no case to answer

After the presentation of the whole of one side's evidence and the closing of its case, it is sometimes possible to make a submission that there is no case to answer. The EAT has approved this practice for both simple unfair dismissal cases and for constructive dismissals.[29] The device is particularly appropriate where there is a burden of proof and the party with the burden has a very weak case, or where an essential component for liability is missing. Such submissions are, however, rare.

The party making the submission is not required by the tribunal to make an election as is the rule in criminal cases. In other words, the party does not have to choose between a submission and calling no evidence. If the submission fails, evidence can still be called. The only danger to representatives is that the submission should not include a statement that no evidence will be called. This happened in *Stokes v Hampstead Wine Co Ltd*[30] and so when the submission was rejected, the tribunal refused to allow the party to call any evidence. There is thus no *formal* risk to the case except the inherent danger that in making the submission you draw attention to a weakness or missing component in the other side's case, which may be put right on cross-examination of your own witnesses.

It is dangerous to call no evidence if the submission has been rejected. The tribunal will have made clear that it needs further persuasion and probably more evidence before it makes a decision in the respondent's favour on the merits.

29 *George A Palmer Ltd v Beeby* [1978] ICR 196; *Walker v Josiah Wedgewood & Sons Ltd* [1978] ICR 744; [1978] IRLR 105.
30 [1979] IRLR 298, EAT.

Because of the tripartite character of the tribunal, it is less likely than a court or a chairman sitting alone to accept such a submission. Tribunals generally prefer to have both sides give their evidence. This is particularly so when the party going first is unrepresented and the party going second is.

In *Coral Squash Clubs Ltd v Matthews*[31] Slynn J said:

> ... this Appeal tribunal has never said that the industrial tribunal cannot stop a hearing at the end of the case of the party whose evidence and submissions come first. It clearly is a power which must be exercised with caution; but if the tribunal is satisfied that the party upon whom the onus lies and who goes first has clearly failed either in law or in fact to establish what he set out to establish, then ... the tribunal is entitled to decide the case at that stage.

A middle road which often emerges is encouragement by the tribunal to the parties to 'consider their positions' and try and settle. This practice, if done subtly and without expressing a firm view, is encouraged by the EAT as a means of shortening cases. For example, having heard the employer's witnesses about the circumstances of a dismissal and the absence of a proper procedure to deal with it, there may be little the applicant needs to add for a finding of unfair dismissal to be made, at least on procedural grounds. If the tribunal takes the provisional view that the employer's case is hopeless when it is closed, there is no reason to give them the chance to improve their case by exposing the applicant to cross examination.

Unfairness during the hearing

The conduct of the hearing by the chairman or the interventions by members can be the subject of a complaint of bias, apparent bias or unfairness. Bias in its strict sense, and prior knowledge of members either of the subject matter or of the witnesses, are grounds for complaint at the start (see p149). The proper objective test to apply to the conduct of a hearing is whether there is a real danger of bias.[32]

Complaints of bias should be raised by way of appeal – parties are not expected to raise such matters during the course of the hearing.[33] In *Simper* an application was made criticising the chairman's biased comments at the end of the applicant's cross-examination and before an adjourned hearing. In fact the case was

---

31 [1979] ICR 607; [1979] IRLR 390, EAT.

32 *Greenaway Harrison Ltd v Wiles* [1994] IRLR 380, EAT.

33 *Peter Simper & Co Ltd v Cooke* [1986] IRLR 19, EAT per Peter Gibson J.

remitted to a fresh tribunal, but it was stressed that the proper course is to wait until the case is concluded:

> Save in extraordinary circumstances, it cannot be right for a litigant, unhappy with what he believes to be the indications from the tribunal as to how the case is progressing, to apply, in the middle of the case, for a re-hearing before another tribunal.

This is because it is undesirable for the tribunal to have to adjudicate on its own bias.

Although the test in complaints of bias is an objective one, Lord Goff has said:

> . . . having ascertained the relevant circumstances, the Court should ask itself whether, having regard to those circumstances, there was a real danger of bias on the part of the relevant member of the tribunal in question, in the sense that he might unfairly regard, or have unfairly regarded, with favour, or disfavour, the case of a party to the issue under consideration by him.[34]

If the conduct of the tribunal does become unacceptable, it is worth bearing in mind the EAT Practice Direction of April 1996[35] which provides (para 9) that full particulars of any complaint must be given in the Notice of Appeal, and affidavits must be sworn by the complainant or relevant witnesses and advisers. These will all be sent to the chairman for appropriate comments.

This means that a party will need to be ready to justify fully any allegation made. In practice, complaints are rare and successful complaints even rarer.

On the other hand, complaints about the conduct of the hearing which do not fall into the categories of bias or apparent bias should be raised forthwith. So, a complaint that a member is not paying attention or has fallen asleep should be raised at once.[36]

Recall of witnesses

If new material emerges during the evidence of the party giving evidence second, it is right to allow the recall of evidence by witnesses whose case was presented first. But it would not be right to allow a represented party to make an allegation in cross-

---

34 *R v Gough* [1993] AC 646 at 670, HL.
35 See p382.
36 *Red Bank Manufacturing Co Ltd v Meadows* [1992] ICR 204; [1992] IRLR 209, EAT.

examination which could have been dealt with in evidence-in-chief by his/her own witness, in order to have a second bite at the cherry. For example, in an unfair dismissal case with the employer giving evidence first, allegations relating to contributory fault must be made during that evidence and should not be put for the first time in cross-examination of the applicant.

Given the requirement to attempt informality, most tribunals would allow an application to recall the witness either because of the mistake by an advocate or an unrepresented party in not addressing the issue properly first time around, or because the interests of justice require it. It should be borne in mind that as a matter of weight, little would be attached to the recall of a witness to deal with a matter which could have been dealt with by evidence-in-chief; it rather gives the impression of second thoughts or a last-ditch attempt to win the case.

Closing speeches

According to the rule of 'last in, first out', which is usually followed in English tribunals, the party giving evidence second goes first with closing speeches. In Scotland, closing speeches generally follow the order in which the evidence in the case was led. This will be the party's first opportunity to address the tribunal and is the manifestation of the right to do so contained in r9(2). In a well-conducted case, any authorities either party relies on will have been notified to each other and to the tribunal at the outset, and may have been described briefly by the representative opening the case. A representative is obliged to deal with all authorities relevant to the case, whether helpful or unhelpful to the case, and in particular s/he must not wait for the other side to cite an authority first and hope to be given the opportunity to reply to it. The closing speech summarises the main points of the evidence. Where there is a conflict, the tribunal should be invited to make findings of fact in accordance with the evidence as the representative sees it and submissions made on the law. On some points the tribunal may interrupt and give a right to reply once it has heard the way the other side puts it. It will do this where, during the course of the hearing, the argument may have become much more difficult for the other side to oppose.

A closing speech for the party which has the burden of proof comes last. Since this party will at least briefly have opened on the central issues of law, it is not so necessary to deal in detail with all the authorities. It is quite proper to ask the other side when reading passages from an authority to read passages in addition to those already read so as to draw the tribunal's attention to parts of the case on which it is intended to rely, and avoid repetition when making the closing speech. Otherwise it is best to keep quiet.

At this stage it is permissible for the tribunal to indicate its likely finding on any particular point. It does so by 'not calling on' the representative to deal with any particular point. In other words, it is convinced of the facts and the legal arguments relating to a particular point in that side's favour, and having given the other side an opportunity to deal with it, it is unnecessary to ask for the point to be elaborated further. If a representative is stopped in his/her tracks in this way, it will be a breach of the rules of natural justice for the tribunal to find against his/her client on that point.

The other side is not normally entitled to say anything after the party going first has made a closing speech. Occasionally, where new points of law or new cases are referred to in the closing speech, the other side has a right to reply but it does require a careful application and a sympathetic tribunal. If the other side has been informed of the cases on which it is intended to rely, the fact that they are raised for the first time in the closing speech does not entitle the other side to come back in reply and have the last word. It should have dealt with them in its own closing speech.

CHAPTER 18

The decision

The decision of the tribunal must have formal characteristics. It includes a declaration, an order, a recommendation, an award, and sometimes a determination as to who is entitled to bring or contest proceedings, but does not include interlocutory orders or decisions on interlocutory matters (reg 2(2); see p208). It also includes a direction under the Health and Safety at Work Act 1974 where an appeal has been lodged (reg 2(4)) and a direction following appeals under SDA 1975 and RRA 1976 (reg 2(5)).

The decision is entered on the register, which is open for public inspection (reg 9). Any parts of the decision or of the reasons which identify people involved in an allegation of a sexual offence must be omitted from the register (r13(6)), as must the reasons in a case where there has been a national security direction or the tribunal has for other reasons sat in private (r10(6)).

The decision must be signed by the chairman or, if s/he is unable to do so because of incapacity, it must be signed by the other members. The decision of the tribunal can be by a majority but if only two people constitute the tribunal, the chairman has a casting vote (r10(1) and (12)).

The tribunal must give reasons for its decision, which can either be in summary or extended form (r10(3)). The decision and the reasons need not be given at the same time. The requirement is for tribunals to give reasons in summary form (r10(4)) except where the rules require them to be in extended form. This is in relation to proceedings:

a) of sex or race discrimination or equal pay;
b) in which a request has been made orally at the hearing;
172 c) in which a request is made in writing at any time before

summary reasons have been sent or within 21 days of the date on which they were sent; or

d) where the tribunal considers 'that reasons given in summary form would not sufficiently explain the grounds for its decision'.

According to r10(2) the decision can be given orally at the end of a hearing or reserved (ie, kept secret until promulgated in writing) or a decision can be given with reasons to follow.

What is important is for the chairman to explain precisely the form in which the reasons are or are to be given. In simple cases, the chairman explains in general terms the reasons for the decision and says that the definitive form will appear as summary reasons in due course. If extended reasons are given orally, they should be recorded on tape at the time, as no other reasons in writing can be adduced without a caveat.[1] The caveat is that the official reasons will be those promulgated in writing in due course.

The Practice Direction No 1 of November 1994 (see p375) encourages reasons to be given orally and recorded on tape, in extended and summary form at the same time. The summary form is transcribed and becomes the reasons sent to parties. If parties request extended-form reasons, the earlier part of the tape is transcribed and promulgated.

If a party has lost, or looks likely to lose, it is worth asking at the hearing for reasons to be given in extended form. An appeal to the EAT may only be made accompanied by reasons in extended form. On the other hand, there is no reason why a successful party should make life easier for the other side by seeking full reasons in writing. For this reason, the chairman will show some resistance to a request by the successful party for extended reasons.

A mistake in the chairman's reasons relating to a fact such as a date or the name of a person should be pointed out and (tactfully) invite a correction. Leaving errors on the record is undesirable and encourages false hopes of an appeal.

If both parties agree in writing on the terms of a decision, the tribunal can make a decision in those terms (r13(2)(b)). This power is not affected by provisions relating to compromise agreements (see chapter 15), since under this provision the case is disposed of by the tribunal rather than by the parties. Decisions by consent are dealt with on p137.

In an equal value case, the report of an independent expert must be attached to the reasons (1993 Regulations Sch 2 r10(4A)).

---

1 *Trollope & Colls v Sharpe* EAT/812/92.

The content and depth of the reasons vary from tribunal to tribunal. In summary form, they rarely extend beyond two pages. The adequacy of the reasons can be considered on appeal to the EAT, since extended reasons must be attached to the appeal. The reasons should:

> . . . contain an outline of the story which has given rise to the complaint and a summary of the tribunal's basic factual conclusions and a statement of the reasons which have led them to reach the conclusion which they do on those basic facts. The parties are entitled to be told why they have won or lost. There should be sufficient account of the facts and of the reasoning to enable the EAT . . . to see whether any question of law arises; and it is highly desirable that the decision of an industrial tribunal should give guidance both to employers and trade unions as to practices which should or should not be adopted.[2]

When making findings of fact where evidence is disputed, tribunals are not required to give detailed pros and cons for accepting or rejecting any witness's evidence. It is the conclusion (rather than the detailed reasoning) which must be ascertainable.[3] On disputed issues, the reasons should specify the conclusion drawn by the tribunal, and where inferences are relied on the primary facts giving rise to the inference should be set out.[4] Sir John Donaldson in *Martin v MBS Fastenings (Glynwed) Distribution Ltd*[5] said: 'So far as the findings of fact are concerned, it is helpful to the parties to give some explanation for them but it is not obligatory.'

Once a decision has been made and registered, it can be changed to correct clerical mistakes and accidental slips and omissions only (r10(9)). Otherwise a *review* under r11 is required. Before registration, the tribunal has limited powers. If it has announced no oral decision, it clearly has power to recall the parties to hear additional evidence and additional arguments. After it has announced an oral decision with or without reasons, its powers are much more limited. In *Hanks v Ace High Productions Ltd*[6] it was held that the power did not extend to hearing further arguments 'when already a clear decision has been reached'; and yet in that very case the tribunal, which *did* allow further argument, had its decision upheld. There is

---

2   *Meek v City of Birmingham District Council* [1987] IRLR 250, CA at 251 per Bingham LJ.

3   *Levy v Marrable & Co Ltd* [1984] ICR 583, EAT.

4   *British Gas plc v Sharma* [1991] ICR 19; [1991] IRLR 101, EAT.

5   [1983] ICR 511; [1983] IRLR 198.

6   [1978] ICR 1155; [1979] IRLR 32, EAT.

a conflict of authorities on the power to recall a case after a decision and/or reasons have been given.

On the one hand, it is arguable that a decision is not a decision until it is signed in the chairman's hand (r10(2)) but this rule expressly includes oral decisions, and tribunals have been overruled for giving a decision and reasons orally and changing them in writing.[7] This was because the decision was changed, rather than because it was doubted that there is power in a tribunal so to do. Obviously the EAT and the Court of Appeal are more likely to intervene when a decision has been changed, and that is the only case they are likely to be dealing with. The better view is that the tribunal is not discharged from its duty as soon as it announces its oral decision but remains seised of the case until promulgation of the decsion and reasons. However, if it wishes to reconsider its decision, it must give the parties an opportunity to be heard.

7 *Arthur Guinness Son & Co (Great Britain) Ltd v Green* [1989] ICR 241; [1989] IRLR 288, EAT; *Lamont v Fry's Metals Ltd* [1985] ICR 566; [1985] IRLR 470, CA.

CHAPTER 19

Costs

The costs of bringing a case to a tribunal should have been considered at an early stage (see p22).

Unlike in cases in the High Court and most cases in the county court, a party cannot normally expect to be awarded costs if s/he wins, nor will s/he generally have to pay the other side's costs if s/he loses. This fact can encourage parties to seek to keep costs down and to take a 'commercial view' in tribunal proceedings. It is also in keeping with the aims of ensuring that tribunals are not expensive to use and remain the forum of the parties and not their lawyers.

The reality is, however, that many parties will use lawyers or other advisers to assist them in their tribunal case and will incur costs in so doing. At all times it should be borne in mind that those costs will probably not be recoverable. Advisers should be careful to consider whether there is some way of meeting the costs of legal or other professional representation, eg, by use of the legal aid green form scheme (advice only, not representation), by recourse to a trade union or other professional body or trade association, by using the assistance of bodies such as the CRE or the EOC, or by applying for assistance under the increasingly common provisions for legal costs in many home and vehicle insurance policies.

A threat to apply for costs can be a powerful weapon in tribunal proceedings. It is quite common for employers to use this as a means of discouraging the continuation of a claim by an applicant. Applicants and their advisers should not, however, be disheartened: costs orders are still relatively infrequent and, if made, generally concern small amounts. Furthermore, claims are just as often defended by respondents in a frivolous, vexatious or unreasonable manner and there is no reason in principle why the threat of a costs order should not be made against the employer as much as the employee.

When costs can be awarded

There are four circumstances in which specific provision is made for costs orders. They are:

– unreasonable (etc) conduct
– failure to accede or reply to request for reinstatement
– conduct leading to adjournment or postponement of a hearing (see p126)
– following determination of a pre-hearing review (see p117).

Unreasonable conduct

Tribunals have no power to order costs or witness allowances except in limited circumstances. In general the power will only arise where:

> . . . in the opinion of the tribunal, a party has in bringing or conducting the proceedings acted frivolously, vexatiously, abusively, disruptively or otherwise unreasonably . . . .

The previous rule relating to costs (1985 Rules r11(1)) included the words 'a tribunal shall not normally make an award in respect of the costs or expenses incurred by a party to the proceedings but . . .'. These words are omitted from the 1993 Rules, but this is not a difference of any significance: tribunals have no power to award costs or witness allowances except in the circumstances set out in r12.

'Frivolously'

Guidance on the meaning of this term was given in *ET Marler Ltd v Robertson*,[1] where it was indicated that conduct would be frivolous if:

> the employee knows that there is no substance in his claim and that it is bound to fail, or if the claim is on the face of it so manifestly misconceived that it can have no prospect of success. . . .

It has also been held that 'frivolously' might cover those cases where a party ought to have known s/he had no prospect of success, as in *Cartiers Superfoods Ltd v Laws*.[2] This view met with some approval in the *Marler* case, with the caveat that it cannot be said that a party 'ought' to have known that which it has taken the

1 [1974] ICR 72, NIRC.
2 [1978] IRLR 315, EAT.

tribunal some time to find out, through fully testing the evidence available – per Sir Hugh Griffths at p77. The EAT in Scotland in *Lothian Health Board v Johnstone*[3] also sounded a cautionary note in considering the *Cartiers* case, warning that it does not lay down any general proposition and must be considered in the light of its particular facts.

'Vexatiously'

This term was also considered in the *Marler* case, where it was held that:

> [i]f an employee brings a hopeless case not with any expectation of recovering compensation but out of spite to harass his employers or for some other improper motive, he acts vexatiously, and likewise abuses the procedure.

'Abusively, disruptively'

These terms were added by the 1993 Rules to be applied where a party has been abusive during the course of a tribunal hearing or has sought to disrupt it.

'Otherwise unreasonably'

This expression is wider than the expressions which precede it in the rule. Its separate categorisation suggests that 'otherwise unreasonably' is not to be read as merely another way of saying 'frivolously' or 'vexatiously' but refers to conduct of a different kind. Tribunal decisions on costs, however, indicate that this kind of distinction is not a precise science, with many orders based on 'unreasonable conduct' which could also be considered as 'frivolous' or 'vexatious' within the *Marler* guidelines. In *Stein v Associated Dairies Ltd*,[4] costs were awarded because of the applicant's unreasonable behaviour in pursuing a claim where he ought to have known that he had no prospect of succeeding, knowing that another employee dismissed for the same offence on the same day had failed in his unfair dismissal claim.

Costs against respondents

Costs orders on this ground against respondents are less likely to be made than against applicants. In *Cartiers Superfoods Ltd v Laws* (above) it was stated that 'great care' should be exercised by tribunals before making an award against a respondent as 'obviously, a respondent must be entitled to defend proceedings brought against him'.

However, the right to defend proceedings does not mean that the defence can be conducted unreasonably, and a respondent guilty of such conduct is just as liable to have an order for costs made against him/her as an applicant in similar circumstances.

An award of costs cannot, however, be made against a respondent in respect of the conduct leading to the dismissal or other act complained of. It is the behaviour of the respondent *qua* respondent that is relevant, ie, how the employer reacts to the applicant's claim rather than its conduct prior to any complaint being made.[5]

Reinstatement, re-engagement, pregnancy and the right to return to work

A further specific power to award costs and expenses is provided by r12(5). This rule is applicable to complaints of unfair dismissal where:

a) the applicant has expressed a wish to be reinstated or re-engaged and has communicated that wish to the respondent at least seven days before the hearing of the complaint; or

b) the proceedings arise out of the respondent's failure to permit the applicant to return to work after an absence due to pregnancy or confinement.

The tribunal *must* make an order of costs if the proceedings have to be postponed or adjourned due to the respondent's failure, without special reason, to adduce reasonable evidence as to the availability of the job from which the applicant was dismissed or which she held before her absence, or of comparable or suitable employment, as appropriate.

The power does not depend on the respondent having behaved in the ways provided for by r12(1). The tribunal must make an order in the circumstances set out in r12(5), unless 'special reasons' are made out to excuse the respondent's failure to adduce the evidence required.

5 *Davidson v John Calder (Publishers) Ltd and Calder Educational Trust Ltd* [1985] ICR 143; [1985] IRLR 97, EAT.

Relevant considerations for a costs order

The tribunal will consider whether the conduct complained of falls under one or more of the heads set out in r12(1) and then what (if any) costs have been occurred as a result of that conduct. A party may have conducted proceedings quite disgracefully, but if this has not led to any additional costs being incurred, a tribunal is unlikely to make any order for costs to be paid.

Whilst rr12(1)(a) and (b) are not expressly limited to costs *caused by* the specified conduct, the award of costs is compensatory, not punitive, in its nature.[6] Costs will not be awarded unless it can be shown that they were incurred as a result of the behaviour complained of.

The tribunal will also take into account the ability to pay of the party against whom it is minded to make a costs order. In *Wiggin Alloys Ltd v Jenkins*[7] a tribunal refused to award costs against an applicant who was in prison and was unlikely to be able to meet an order for costs in the foreseeable future. On the other hand, the fact that a party is wholly without funds does not always mean that no order will be made.[8] It remains a matter for the tribunal's discretion in each case. It may make an award but order that it should not be enforced without further application.[9]

In considering a party's ability to pay, the tribunal should consider only the means of that party and not the means of a body such as a trade union, the EOC or the CRE which has supported him/her in the proceedings.[10]

In-house lawyers and other representatives

The legal costs incurred in tribunal litigation by in-house lawyers are as much recoverable as are the costs incurred by employing independent solicitors.[11]

---

6 *Davidson v John Calder (Publishers) Ltd and Calder Educational Trust Ltd* (above).
7 [1981] IRLR 275.
8 *Wiggin Alloys* (above n7).
9 *Nial v Baxters (Butchers) Ltd* (1985) *Times* 9 February, EAT.
10 *Carr v Allen-Bradley Electronics Ltd* [1980] ICR 603; [1980] IRLR 263, EAT.
11 *Wiggin Alloys* (above n7).

Volunteer representatives

More difficult to recover, however, are costs in respect of representation by volunteers or by other representatives or advisers who appear at no direct cost to the party they represent: union or CAB advisers, law centre or FRU representatives, and lawyers whose costs are met by an insurance policy. The difficulty in such cases is establishing that any costs have been incurred by the party using these services. On the other hand, there seems to be no reason in principle why the basic cost incurred by the representing body should not be recoverable in the same way as the costs of in-house lawyers. Ultimately the party using the services of that representative is likely to have to pay something towards the cost (whether directly by means of some claw-back provision or indirectly through trade union subscription or insurance policy premiums) and the difficulty in quantifying this sum should not prevent an order for costs being made in appropriate circumstances.

Wasted costs

Costs may only be ordered in favour of a party or against a party: there is no scope for a costs order against lawyers who have wasted costs by their conduct of the proceedings as there is in the courts, since the Courts and Legal Services Act 1990 s4 (amending Supreme Court Act 1981 s51, see RSC Order 62 r2) does not apply to tribunals.

Contingency fees

Costs will not be ordered if the obligation of the applicant to pay his/her adviser arises only if the tribunal should make an finding on liability or an order for costs in his/her favour. This is an unlawful contingency arrangement; further, the tribunal cannot order a respondent to pay an applicant in respect of sums which the applicant is not liable to pay to his/her adviser.[12]

Equal value claims

Similar rules apply to equal value claims, where the costs include the investigations carried out by the independent expert in preparing the report (1993 Regs Sch 2 r12).

12 *British Waterways Board v Norman* (1994) 26 HLR 233, DC.

When the application should be made

The Rules do not provide any specific time within which an application for costs should be made. In *Johnson t/a Richard Andrew Ladies Hairstylists v Baxter*[13] the EAT stated that an application for costs should be made within a reasonable time, that is to say, if the tribunal does not reserve its decision, the application should be made forthwith; where the decision is reserved, then it should be made in advance of the decision (at the end of the substantive hearing) if at all possible so as to avoid an additional hearing on costs alone. In practice, this decision may be difficult to assess, and sensitive to make, since the result of the case and the reasons are not known at that stage. Yet the application should still be made on the footing that the tribunal will make a favourable finding and the tribunal invited to deal with it in its reserved decision.

As the power to make a costs order is discretionary, any delay in the making of the application will be a relevant consideration for the tribunal, particularly when it might have caused prejudice to the party against whom the order is sought. In *Lothian Health Board v Johnstone*[14] the Scottish EAT indicated that any application for costs should by made as soon as possible – in that case only two members of the original tribunal were able to hear the application for costs made some seven months after the original decision.

How to make the application

Many applications for costs in tribunals fail because of inadequate preparation. If, in advance of the hearing, it is likely that such an application will need to be made, it is important to ensure that all relevant documentation, including correspondence and evidence in relation to the costs claimed, is put together in an easily readable form – a separate *costs bundle* if necessary.

The costs bundle will include correspondence relied on, such as pre-hearing warnings as to the frivolous or vexatious nature of the complaint or grounds of resistance and early attempts to put the other side on notice as to an application for costs. The bundle may also include letters written 'without prejudice save as to costs' (see p89) or which might show the unreasonable conduct of the party

13 [1984] ICR 675; [1985] IRLR 96.
14 [1981] IRLR 321.

against whom the order is sought. Ideally, a separate schedule will also be made available to the tribunal, setting out the costs incurred at the different stages of the proceedings (see below).

Amounts to be awarded

The tribunal may order the party against whom the award is made to pay:

a) the costs of another party to that party; and/or

b) the allowances payable by the Department to any party or witness for attendance at the tribunal, which includes a party's expenses: r12(1) and an independent expert (Sch 2 r8A(10E)).

In other words, the tribunal has power both to compensate another party in respect of costs incurred and to protect the public purse.

An order for costs can be made in one of three ways under r12(3), ie, that one party must pay to the other:

a) a specified sum not exceeding £500;

b) a sum which has been agreed between the parties; or

c) the whole or a specified part of the costs to be taxed.

In many cases, the costs involved will be less than £500 and so the tribunal will itself be able to carry out the assessment of how much should be paid. If a party wants the tribunal to make this order, it should be prepared to submit details when making the application. It should set out in the form of a schedule the costs incurred at each stage, including both solicitor and counsel costs if appropriate. If there has been no time to prepare a schedule, a party should still be in a position to advance some figures and evidence relating to costs so that the tribunal can carry out the assessment. It is always good practice for the case file to be available at the hearing with an up-dated print-out of the bill of costs included. If counsel has been instructed, the tribunal may wish to see the brief fee marked on the back-sheet to the instructions or be told what fee has been agreed. Anyone who wants an order for costs must be in a position to give the tribunal the material it needs.

If the costs are greater than £500, and no agreement can be reached, the tribunal will merely order an award for the whole or some proportion of the costs incurred but will not specify any amount. The bill of costs claimed will then be subject to 'taxation', which the tribunal will order to be on the appropriate county court scale depending on the nature of the claim (r12(6)).

'Taxation' is the process by which the bill of costs claimed by a party is considered by a district judge (or deputy district judge) of the county court.[15] The court orders to be paid only what has been reasonably incurred. In other words, if the party in whose favour the award is made has run up legal costs which were unnecessary, or has paid over the odds, it will not be entitled to recover these from the other party. It is only entitled to such costs as it can establish were reasonably incurred. The only exception to this will be where the tribunal orders that the costs should be taxed on an 'indemnity basis', in which case it will be for the party against whom the order has been made to establish that those costs were unreasonably incurred.

The additional burden of submitting a bill of costs to taxation can encourage a party in whose favour an award has been made to try to agree a sum with the other side. Alternatively, there is nothing to prevent a party which applies for costs asking for a sum limited to £500 so that this can be specified in the tribunal's order. Obviously, this would only be attractive if costs were not significantly greater than £500.

Allowances

The allowances paid by the Secretary of State to parties and witnesses attending the tribunal (regardless of the outcome) cover loss of wages, travel costs and other expenses. They will rarely fully compensate a person for any loss of wages, and fixed scales are set out under each head (ITA 1996 s5(3)). They do not extend to the costs of professional representatives.

In the circumstances set out by r12, it is open to the tribunal to order that these are repaid to the Secretary of State by a party against whom an order for costs has been made. In practice, tribunals rarely make such an order.

---

15 CCR Order 38 r2.

CHAPTER 20

Equal pay claims

The procedures for claiming equal pay differ from other tribunal actions and merit a chapter of their own. Section references in this chapter are to the Equal Pay Act 1970 unless otherwise indicated.

Equal pay claims may be brought (by women or men) on three grounds under the Equal Pay Act 1970 and the Treaty of Rome:

a) the applicant claims she is employed on 'like work' with her comparator (Equal Pay Act 1970 s1(2)(a));
b) the applicant claims she is employed on work 'rated as equivalent' to that of her chosen comparator under a job evaluation study (JES) (s1(2)(b));
c) the applicant claims she is employed on work which is different but of equal value to that of the comparator (s1(2)(c)).

European law

An applicant may claim equal pay for the same work, or for work done on a job classified as equal, or for work which is of equal value, but nevertheless find that the Equal Pay Act 1970 gives her no effective remedy. Article 119 of the Treaty of Rome and Directive 75/117/EEC (the Equal Pay Directive), which has been held to facilitate article 119 (see *Jenkins* below), can be relied on in the tribunal.[1]

Article 119 can be relied on directly only if it is clear and can be operated to give equal pay without recourse to national implementing measures necessary to define discrimination.[2] In *Pickstone v*

---

1 *Secretary of State for Scotland and Greater Glasgow Health Board v Wright and Hannah* [1991] IRLR 187, EAT.
2 *Worringham v Lloyds Bank* [1981] ICR 558, ECJ at 589; [1981] IRLR 178.

Freemans plc[3] the Court of Appeal held that article 119 could be relied on directly in an equal value case where the discrimnation is obvious on a direct comparison of the two types of work.[4] Because equal value claims are not so obvious, and require some form of expert or at least experienced evaluator, it must still be doubted if article 119 may be directly enforced in many claims.[5]

No enforcement procedure is specified in the Treaty or the Directive, so the UK's own procedures governing tribunals are operated.[6]

Procedures under the Equal Pay Act

Like work claims

The basis of a *like work* claim is that a woman is doing work which is the same as, or is of a broadly similar nature to, that of a man. The procedure is designed to lead to a declaration that the woman's contract contains an equality clause, so that *any* term of her contract which is or becomes less favourable than his is a breach of contract. The procedure involved in bringing cases based on like work and on a JES is generally the same as that for other types of tribunal claims described in this book.

In *equal value* cases (considered later in the chapter), different (and more complex) rules apply, varying the procedure in a number of respects. These are known as the Complementary Rules of Procedure (Sch 2 to the 1993 Regulations) and are made under reg 8(2).

A comparable male worker

The applicant in each type of case has to show that a man is doing this work

a)   in the same establishment for the same employer; *or*

b)   at a different establishment in Great Britain for the same employer where common terms and conditions of employment are observed.[7]

---

3   [1987] ICR 867; [1987] IRLR 218, CA (affirmed on different grounds [1988] ICR 697; [1988] IRLR 357, HL).

4   Ibid ICR per Purchas LJ at 895 and Nicholls LJ at 880.

5   See the view of Lord Oliver in [1988] ICR 697 at 723, strictly obiter and the only speech containing a reference to this problem.

6   *Pickstone v Freemans plc* (above) and *Livingstone v Hepworth Refractories plc* [1992] ICR 287; [1992] IRLR 63, EAT.

7   Equal Pay Act 1970 s1(6) and *British Coal Corporation v Smith* [1994] ICR 810; [1994] IRLR 342, CA.

For practical purposes the applicant must cite a male comparator at an early stage, although the choice of comparator is hers alone.[8] So it has been held that she need not prove the comparator is representative of a particular group of employee.[9] Difficulties may arise if a wholly anomalous comparator is chosen, since the respondent is likely to justify a material factor other than the difference of sex as the reason for the different pay under s1(3). This defence was argued unsuccessfully in *McPherson v Rathgael Centre for Children and Young People*,[10] where it was held that even a 'gross but understandable error' (comparator paid higher by mistake and employer refused to reduce his pay when mistake discovered) did not justify unequal pay.

The combined effect of the Equal Pay Act 1970 and article 119 allows claims to be made with a comparator who is not working simultaneously with the applicant, for example, when she is appointed to replace him but on a lower salary.[11] It is also strongly arguable that if there is *no* male comparator in sight but it can be shown that a male would have been paid at a higher rate for the same work, the Equal Pay Act 1970 will not apply but a claim can be based on article 119.[12]

Restricting inter-establishment claims to Great Britain and not the whole of the United Kingdom is probably open to a successful challenge that the Treaty of Rome and the Equal Pay Directive are not properly implemented in the United Kingdom because of the sub-division of the member state. Comparison is prevented with establishments in Northern Ireland, even though Northern Ireland has its own equivalent legislation.

Burden of proof

This is on the applicant, although each element of the defence of a genuine material factor under s1(3) is for the employer to prove.[13] The employer must also prove the existence of a JES under s2A(2). Further, it seems that the employer is under a duty to show that any

---

8 *Ainsworth v Glass Tubes and Components Ltd* [1977] ICR 347; [1977] IRLR 74, EAT.

9 *Thomas v NCB* [1987] ICR 757; [1987] IRLR 451, EAT.

10 [1991] IRLR 206, NI CA.

11 *Macarthys Ltd v Smith (No 2)* [1980] ICR 672; [1980] IRLR 209, CA.

12 *Hammersmith and Queen Charlotte's Special Health Authority v Cato* [1988] ICR 132; [1987] IRLR 483, EAT.

13 *Financial Times v Byrne* [1992] IRLR 163, EAT.

pay structure or policy is not discriminatory when it is not transparent (that is, so as to enable a woman to see how her pay and others' is made up),[14] or has the effect of placing women on average below men.[15]

Procedure

Claims for equal pay for like work under s1(2)(a) and article 119 of the Treaty of Rome 1957 are made to a tribunal in accordance with the 1993 Rules. The Treaty and the Equal Pay Directive, which facilitates implementation of the Treaty (see *Jenkins v Kingsgate Ltd*)[16] are directly enforceable in the tribunal in respect of like work.[17] In this case the tribunal will apply its normal rules of procedure including those relating to time limits.[18]

Claims based on a job evaluation study

A JES is relevant under the EqPA 1970 in two different situations (as noted by Dillon LJ in *Bromley v H & J Quick Ltd*):[19]

- it can form the basis of a claim for equality based on s1(2)(b);
- it can defeat a claim for equal value without reference to an independent expert.

The applicant's claim for equal pay

If the applicant and the comparator are not doing like work, the applicant can say under s1(5) that:

a) there has been a JES;
b) it was made using an evaluation of the demand of the job on the job-holder under headings such as effort, skill and decision (ie, decision-making);
c) it compared her job and the comparator's;
d) it rated the work as equivalent, *or* would have if the system had not given different values for men and women under the same headings; and
e) she has not been given equal pay.

---

14 *Danfoss* case [1991] ICR 74; [1989] IRLR 532, ECJ.
15 *Enderby v Frenchay Health Authority* [1994] ICR 112, [1993] IRLR 591, ECJ.
16 [1981] ICR 592 at 614; [1981] IRLR 228, ECJ.
17 *Pickstone v Freemans plc* (above).
18 *Livingstone v Hepworth Refractories plc* (above) and see p26.
19 [1988] ICR 623 at 627; [1988] IRLR 249, CA.

By definition the work of each will be different. A JES which meets the test in (b) is properly described as 'analytical', since it compares the components of different jobs by analysing the special features demanded in each job, by reference to several factors common to all the jobs evaluated.

A JES will not meet the test in (d) if gender bias has entered into the scheme, or its application. The Court of Appeal has approved the use of the booklet *Job Evaluation Schemes Free of Sex-Bias* (EOC, 1993) on the need to avoid such bias.[20]

It is to be assumed that any JES which did rate the jobs as equivalent would also pave the way for equal pay. The point, however, is that for practical purposes the task facing an applicant is to establish that a JES which rated her *below* her comparator was defective because *either*

– it was not sufficiently rigorous to qualify as analytical; *or*
– it was biased towards men's characteristics in the selection of factors, or in its practical application.

The respondent's defence based on a JES

An applicant has the right to have her claim considered under the equal value provisions unless her claim is clearly hopeless (s2A(1)). As a specific illustration, s2A(2) declares conclusively ('there shall be taken') that a claim is unreasonable if a non-sexist, truly analytical JES has already concluded that her job is of less value than that of her comparator.

When there is a JES, the procedural steps in dealing with a claim for equal pay for work of equal value, which is not based on s1(2)(b) but on s1(2)(c), are:

a) the applicant claims equality;
b) the respondent claims there has been a JES;
c) the JES was made using an evaluation of the demand of the job on the job-holder under headings such as effort, skill and decision (ie, decision-making);
d) there are no reasonable grounds for saying the JES was based on a system which discriminated (either directly or indirectly) on the grounds of sex (s2A(2)(b) and 2A(3));
e) the JES compared her job and the comparator's;
f) the JES did not rate the work as equivalent.

---

20 See *Bromley* (above) at 622, and see also *Aldridge v BT* [1989] ICR 790; [1990] IRLR 10, EAT.

This might even be a JES carried out *after* the commencement of the tribunal proceedings.[21] But there is no reason why an equal value claim should be held up to await the carrying out of a JES by an employer after proceedings have been commenced.[22] Any JES relied on in this way must, of course, be analytical (see above), ie, it must consider the demands of the jobs under various (non-sex-related) headings such as effort, skill, decision-making.[23]

An employer seeking to rely upon a JES to show that the claim is hopeless will bear the burden of proving that the JES meets the requirements of the Equal Pay Act 1970.[24] In the absence of a JES, the burden of showing that the claim is or is not hopeless is a neutral one.[25] But when a JES is put forward, the practical effect is that applicant has to adduce evidence to attack it as being non-analytical or sex-biased.

There is a corresponding duty under the Equal Pay Directive (75/117/EEC) article 1 to exclude sex-based criteria from 'job classification schemes' and to ensure there is no discrimination in the drawing up of the criteria. The Directive does not enlarge the obligations under article 119 of the Treaty of Rome, but merely clarifies them, facilitates the practical application of the principle of equal pay and specifies the conditions necessary for a valid JES.[26]

A JES which indirectly discriminated against, and led to lower pay for, women would be in breach of article 119 of the Treaty and of the Directive.[27] The EqPA 1970 deals expressly with studies which discriminate on the grounds of sex and this can be taken to include indirect discrimination as defined by SDA 1975 s1(1)(b).

Equal value claims

The right to bring a complaint based on work of equal value was introduced after the ECJ found in *Commission of the European Communities v United Kingdom*[28] that the UK government had

---

21 *Dibro Ltd v Hore* [1990] ICR 370; [1990] IRLR 120, EAT.

22 *Avon County Council v Foxhall and Others* (unreported) EAT 113/89.

23 See Equal Pay Act 1970 s1(5) and *Bromley v H & J Quick Ltd* (n19 above).

24 *Bromley v H & J Quick Ltd* (above).

25 *Dennehy v Sealink UK Ltd* [1987] IRLR 120, EAT.

26 *Jenkins v Kingsgate Ltd* [1981] ICR 592 at 614; [1981] IRLR 228, ECJ.

27 *Bilka-Kaufhaus v Weber von Hartz* [1987] ICR 110 at 125; [1986] IRLR 317, ECJ.

28 [1982] ICR 578; [1982] IRLR 333.

failed to fulfil its obligations under European law. Special rules of procedure applicable to such claims were subsequently introduced by the Industrial Tribunals (Rules of Procedure) (Equal Value Amendment) Regulations 1983 and are now to be found as the Complementary Rules of Procedure in Sch 2 to the 1993 Regulations (set out at appendix 3.5).

Practical experience of these claims indicates that, far from empowering workers to bring equal value complaints, the procedures introduced are open to abuse and often delay removal of the inequality. Cases can take many years to complete – four years for Julie Hayward[29] and seven years for Sybil Bromley.[30] All too often applicants are put off by delay, cost and legal complexity and the procedure does not tackle the very real problems of inequality in pay.

In *Aldridge v British Telecommunications plc*[31] Wood J said:

> The present restrictions on procedure imposed by the Rules give rise to delays which are properly described as scandalous and ... amount to a denial of justice to women seeking remedy through the judicial process.

The situation has changed little and similar criticisms were again made by Wood J in the EAT in *British Coal Corporation v Smith*.[32] The Equal Opportunities Commission made a formal complaint in 1993 to the European Commission about the UK government's failure to provide proper procedures for delivery of effective remedies. In 1996 new rules on time limits were introduced (Sch 2 r8A).

Procedural steps

It is hoped that the approach taken in relation to the procedural steps in equal value cases in this chapter may assist those involved in such claims and may encourage parties to use the procedure in keeping with the aims of the European Treaty and Directive.

Step 1 Completion of IT1/IT3
Follow normal procedure (see p45).

---

29 [1988] ICR 464; [1988] IRLR 257, HL.
30 [1988] ICR 623; [1988] IRLR 249, settled in 1993.
31 [1989] ICR 790; [1990] IRLR 10, EAT.
32 [1993] ICR 529, [1993] IRLR 308 and [1996] IRLR 404.

Step 2 Interlocutory stages

a) *Pre-hearing review* (Sch 2 r7) and *application to strike out* etc
   (Sch 2 r13(2)(d)). These are unlikely to be used in the light of the
   specific provision in step 4 below.

b) *Requests for further particulars* of IT1/IT3, and for written
   answers to questions: as in other tribunal claims (see p77).

c) *Discovery*: employers are often reluctant to make full discovery
   in discrimination cases, claiming confidentiality. But in *Nassé v
   Science Research Council*[33] the House of Lords held that the
   necessary information to support a claim of discrimination is
   almost always in the possession of the employer, who can be
   ordered to disclose documents. An employer can refuse only
   when there is some overriding public interest in maintaining the
   confidentiality of documents.[34] But an employer who may be
   able to claim the public interest is against disclosure of certain
   classes of document in its possession will not succeed on that
   ground in withholding *all* documents.[35] Note the additional
   power of the tribunal under Sch 2 r4(2A) to order discovery and
   information at the request of an independent expert (IE) appointed in the case (see below).

d) *Preliminary hearing*: issues of jurisdiction; applications for further particulars, discovery etc.

e) *Directions hearing*: often set up at an early stage in equal pay
   cases to get a clearer idea of the issues between the parties.
   These include considering

   - whether the claim can more conveniently be processed as a
     'like work' or JES case;
   - whether to consider together a number of similar claims
     against an employer, and whether there are *by agreement* any
     test or sample cases. This rule (Sch 2 r18(1)) is the nearest
     thing to consolidation, a power which is not in the Rules;
   - whether the applicant's claim that her work is of equal value
     may be put forward as an alternative should she fail to
     establish a like work claim. Here the equal value claim is
     heard after the other claim has been dismissed.

f) *Conciliation:* ACAS is sent copies of equal pay claims and is
   under a duty to promote the settlement of the dispute if so

---

33 [1979] ICR 921; [1979] IRLR 465, HL.
34 *Halford v Sharples and Others* [1992] ICR 583, CA.
35 *Commissioner of Metropolitan Police v Locker* [1993] ICR 440, EAT.

requested or if there is a reasonable prospect of achieving a settlement (SDA 1975 s64(1)).

Step 3 Invitation to adjourn

Under the Rules, the first obligation on the tribunal is to invite the parties, before hearing them on the claim itself, to apply for an adjournment for the purpose of seeking a settlement of the claim (Sch 2 r13(6A)). The adjournment must be by consent of all parties. The compromise of discrimination and equal pay claims is seen as a desirable objective and the Rules relating to equal value claims reflect this perception by making specific provision for the consideration of settlement at this early stage in the procedure. There is specific provision for this in SDA 1975 s64(1). The duty to consider adjourning matters to permit settlement discussions in equal value cases is in addition to the tribunal's (or a chairman's) general discretionary power to order that proceedings be adjourned (under Sch 2 r13(7)).

Step 4 The initial hearing

Assuming that the parties do not wish to adjourn to consider a settlement of the claim or that, having adjourned, settlement negotiations have broken down, the tribunal proceeds to an initial hearing at which the following matters can be raised:

a) Whether there are *no reasonable grounds for determining that the work is of equal value*. This applies only to equal value claims. It is designed to stop wholly unrealistic comparisons, eg, of a typist with the managing director. It means that the claim is hopeless.[36] If the employer attacks in this way, the tribunal has no choice but must determine this question at an initial hearing before going on to appoint an expert (see below).[37]

One reason for holding a claim to be hopeless at this stage is that the relevant jobs have already been given different values in a JES which did not itself discriminate on grounds of sex (EqPA 1970 s2A(1)(b) below).

In 1994 the EOC presented its view to the government that this provision (s2A(1)(a)) should be repealed.

b) Whether there is a *genuine material factor* (GMF) defence. If asked to consider a GMF defence at this stage, the tribunal can

---

36 See *Bromley v H & J Quick Ltd* [1988] ICR 623 at 637; [1988] IRLR 249, CA and EqPA s2A(1)(a).
37 *Sheffield Metropolitan District Council v Siberry* [1989] ICR 208.

do so, but does not have to. If it finds the GMF defence is made out, the tribunal must dismiss the claim. It is generally in the employer's interest to raise the GMF defence at this stage. By the 1994 amendments it was intended that the GMF defence may be raised once only and not again at step 7. This is certainly the import of the explanatory note to the Regulations, but it is not clear that the amended regulation carries that purpose into effect.[38] It is assumed in this chapter that the legislative purpose of a once-only argument and evidence is upheld, except for transitional cases where the tribunal had already begun to hear the GMF defence before 1 April 1994 (reg 8).

The GMF defence is available to the employer under EqPA 1970 s1(3). It is open to any party to apply to the tribunal at the initial hearing of an equal value claim to consider this question (although it is unlikely that applicants would wish to do so!) (r9(2E)). A tribunal does not have to accede to the request at this stage, but if it does so and concludes that the defence is made out, then it must forthwith dismiss the claim.[39] On the other hand, if the tribunal does not hear the defence at this stage, the respondent can still raise it after the independent expert's report has been received (r9(2E) as amended): see step 7 below.

An employer not wishing the tribunal to consider the question of a GMF defence at this stage (although it is hard to see why any employer would take this view) would still be well-advised to raise the point at as early a stage as possible (preferably in the notice of appearance). If an employer indicates at this stage that it does not intend to rely on any GMF defence, it may be barred from raising it subsequently.[40]

Step 5 Commissioning a report from an independent expert

If a claim is not dismissed at the initial hearing, the tribunal is entitled to commission an IE to prepare a report on whether the applicant's work is of equal value to that of her chosen comparator(s). At this stage, if the applicant's case appears to be extremely strong and/or the issues clear-cut, the tribunal can

---

38 Industrial Tribunals (Constitution and Rules of Procedure) Regulations 1994 SI 1994 No 536 reg 6, amending Sch 2 r9(2E) of the 1993 Rules.

39 *Reed Packaging Ltd v Boozer and Everhurst* [1988] ICR 391; [1988] IRLR 333, EAT.

40 *Hayward v Cammell Laird Shipbuilders Ltd* [1985] ICR 71; [1984] IRLR 463, IT.

simply rely on its own expertise and judgment to determine the case.[41]

The independent expert   The IE is a member of a panel designated as suitably qualified and independent by ACAS, although s/he cannot be a member or employee of ACAS (EqPA 1970 s2A(4)). Since 1990, members of the IE panel have adopted a self-denying ordinance for their non-statutory practices and will not accept instructions to advise, give evidence or represent anyone in a case where it is likely that an IE will be required to report.

The requirement   The tribunal will set out a written requirement for the expert's report, which will include details of the parties and of the relevant workplace, will set out 'the question' to be determined and will identify the comparator(s). Copies of the requirement will be supplied to the parties (Sch 2 r8A(2)).

The report   The requirement stipulates that in compiling the report the expert must:

– take no account of the difference of sex and at all times act fairly;
– take into account all information supplied and any representations made which are relevant to the question to be determined;
– send a written summary of information supplied and representations made to each of the parties and invite comment on that material; and only then,
– compile a report, which should reproduce the summary and contain an account of the representations made as well as setting out any conclusions reached and the reasons for those conclusions (Sch 2 r8A(3)).

The IE evaluates the relevant jobs to be compared in relation to the demands made on the holders of those jobs under headings such as effort, skill, decision-making, etc (r8A). These are the same suggested headings used in EqPA s1(5) to determine whether a JES is valid. An evaluation of jobs according to headings such as these is known as 'analytical'.[42] The purpose is to make an objective comparison of the factors demanded by each job, and it is usual for there to be between four and eight, including (say) working conditions, supervision and responsibility.

41 EqPA 1970 s2A(1)(a) as amended by the Sex Discrimination and Equal Pay (Miscellaneous Amendments) Regulations 1996 SI No 438 and Sch 2 r8A(1).
42 See Dillon LJ in *Bromley v H & J Quick Ltd* [1988] ICR 623 at 633.

It is not for the expert to take into account any GMF which may be raised by the employer, except to the limited extent that any defence may affect the demands of the job.

The parties' right to receive the summary and to make representations to the expert on this material provides the only opportunity to challenge the facts upon which the expert will rely in making his/her report.

Provision of information   The tribunal has the power, on application by the IE, to order any person (other than an ACAS officer appointed to assist conciliation of the case) to furnish in writing relevant information and/or to provide documents (Sch 2 r4(2A)). This is a wide and unique power, since it enables the tribunal to make an order at the request of an IE, and addressed to persons other than parties. The order can require documents to be produced *and* information to be 'furnished', ie, created, put in writing and handed over (Sch 2 r 4(2A)).

The tribunal has no specific power under EqPA 1970 or the 1993 Rules to order an employer to allow the IE access to the workplace, although a respondent has been ordered to allow the applicant's expert access to the workplace,[43] under the general power to regulate proceedings in equal value cases (r9(1)). This seems to be an entirely sensible use of this general power and one which is in keeping with the spirit and intent of European law; a domestic tribunal should not be deterred in its consideration of questions of equal value by the obstructive tactics of one of the parties.

Adjournment   While the IE is preparing the report, the proceedings will be adjourned (r8A(6)). The delays at this stage of the procedure have been the subject of much criticism by, for example, the Equal Opportunities Commission. The 1993 Rules attempt to prevent undue delays: 14 days after the expert has been notified of the requirement to prepare a report, s/he must give the tribunal a 'projected date' for the presentation of the report, or say why such a projection cannot be given (r8A(8)) and give regular progress reports (r8A(9)), and the IE must say if there is any reason, eg, the obstructiveness of a party, for the delay. The tribunal can order costs (r8A(4)). Failure to maintain progress gives the tribunal the right after hearing the parties to revoke the requirement, ie, to dismiss and appoint another IE (Sch 2 r8A(10)).

43 *Whitmore and Others v Frayling Furniture* (unreported) 1985 COIT 1680/204.

Realistically, reports by IEs will often take months, particularly where a number of applicants and/or comparators are involved. The tribunal is unlikely to delay matters further by instructing a different expert unless there are very good grounds for so doing.

Step 6 *Receipt of the report*

The IE sends the completed report to the tribunal, which in turn sends a copy to each of the parties.

The tribunal then proceeds to fix a date for the hearing of the case to be resumed not less than 14 days after the date on which the report was sent to the parties (Sch 2 r 8A(11)).

After receiving the expert's report, the tribunal may at any time require that expert (or another expert from the ACAS panel) to explain any matter contained within that report. Such a requirement must be made by the tribunal in the same way as the request for the original report was made and the parties must again be given the opportunity to make any relevant representations and should be sent a copy of the expert's reply (Sch 2 r8A(15)–(17)).

Step 7 *The resumed hearing*

Either party may apply to the tribunal at this stage to exclude the expert's report if:

- the expert has not complied with the rules relating to the preparation, contents and presentation of the report; or
- the conclusion arrived at in the report could not reasonably have been reached; or
- for some other material reason, other than disagreement with the conclusion that the applicant's work is or is not of equal value or with the reasons for such a conclusion, the report is unsatisfactory (Sch 2 r8A(13)).

In considering whether to exclude the report (on its own decision or on an application), the tribunal should consider any representations made by the parties and may permit evidence from the parties or the expert to be adduced (Sch 2 r8A(14)).

In practice, tribunals are reluctant to exclude the expert's report at this stage and will not do so solely on the basis of a challenge to the methodology or a criticism that factors involving substantial sex bias have been deployed in the evaluation.[44]

---

44 See, eg, the Equal Opportunities Commission's *Job Evaluation Schemes free of Sex Bias.*

This is, however, the last opportunity a party has to challenge the factual basis of the expert's report unless the report is inconclusive. Once a report has been admitted, no challenge can be made to the facts on which it has been based.[45]

If the tribunal determines that the expert's report should not be admitted, it must then require another report to be commissioned and the procedure will re-commence. In these circumstances no further account will be taken of the first expert's report (Sch 2 r8A(13) and (18)).

Admission of the report and expert evidence   The IE's report will be admitted as evidence at the resumed hearing (Sch 2 r8A(12)). The report is, however, merely evidence to be taken into account by the tribunal in determining the issue of equal value; it is not conclusive, it does not change the burden of proof and the tribunal is entitled to reach a different conclusion without necessarily being considered perverse.[46]

A tribunal may (and should, if a party so requests) require the expert to attend the resumed hearing to give evidence and be cross-examined by the parties on the contents, conclusions and reasoning of the report (Sch 2 r 9(2A)). It is not unique in tribunal proceedings for a witness to be called by the tribunal: it has the power to do so under Sch 2 r4(2). In equal value proceedings the forensic consequence is that one party will seek to uphold the IE's report, yet there is no rule of evidence preventing *leading* questions being asked for that purpose. In practical terms, one can cross-examine a favourable expert.

At this resumed hearing, either party may apply to call one expert witness each and this witness will then be available for cross-examination and re-examination in the normal way (Sch 2 r9(2B)). A tribunal cannot order that a party be interviewed by the other party's expert.[47] There is no rule of evidence requiring prior disclosure to the IE or to the other party of each side's own expert's report. However, reference to the obvious reasons for such a practice in RSC Order 38 rr36–37 might persuade the tribunal to order disclosure.

Other than in the provision for expert evidence, the conduct of the resumed hearing will be similar to that for tribunals generally,

45 *Hayward v Cammell Laird Shipbuilders Ltd* [1985] ICR 71; [1984] IRLR 463, IT.
46 *Tennants Textile Colours Ltd v Todd* [1989] IRLR 3, NI CA.
47 *Lloyds Bank plc v Fox* [1989] ICR 80; [1989] IRLR 103.

although no evidence of fact can be called by the parties unless the IE has been unable to reach a conclusion or the evidence goes to support or challenge a GMF defence which has been raised by the employer.

Tactical advice for applicants

If a GMF defence has been raised by the employer, the better view is that evidence on this cannot be adduced for the second time after the independent expert's report has been considered (see p194). Obviously, if the tribunal first finds that the equal value application has no reasonable prospects under EqPA 1970 s2A(1), the issue of a GMF defence will not arise.

It is generally convenient for the tribunal to consider these issues separately, making its findings on the question of equal value before hearing any evidence on the GMF defence. The tribunal should not allow parties to use this opportunity, however, as a means by which the proceedings can be further delayed; there is no reason why both sides should not be fully prepared for a hearing on the GMF defence immediately after the tribunal's findings on the question whether there are reasonable grounds to send the case to an IE and, after the IE's report, that the jobs are of equal value.

The purpose of this initial hearing is to weed out claims which clearly have no chance of succeeding or where the differences are explicable by reference to some genuine material factor which is discernible at this early stage. The use of the independent expert part of the procedure (see step 5 above) is expensive and time-consuming and the initial hearing is utilised as a way of short-circuiting this element where possible. Practical experience demonstrates clear misuse of this initial stage; it is often used to delay proceedings and discourage applicants.

If the employer does use this procedure, the applicant must be ready to produce evidence of the relative value of the two jobs so as to convince the tribunal that the case is not hopeless. In many cases she will already have commissioned her own report from an expert (not disclosed to the employer) which says the jobs are of equal value. In cases involving multiple applicants or comparators, this is an important preparatory step. The report and the expert can then be produced at the initial hearing to defeat the attack that the case is hopeless. At this stage the analysis need not be as rigorous as that to be undertaken by the IE in accordance with the Act. But the applicant's expert will need to address the issue whether the comparison is likely to be reasonable when a proper job evaluation exercise is undertaken.

In addition, the applicant's expert should have considered any grounds for the GMF defence which might be taken into account in the IE's job evaluation exercise. Some defences will be based on reasons which are outside the experts' evaluation, such as separate collective bargaining arrangements, or the personal history of the comparator. It may still be possible, however, for the applicant's expert to give advice on the more general issues.

Other grounds advanced may have a bearing on the evaluation and should be discussed. For example, in *Financial Times v Byrne (No 2)*[48] the employer was set to argue that the male comparator got higher pay because he worked in unpleasant conditions. This would be evaluated, and weight given to it, so the applicant should know in advance of embarking on the claim whether such a factor could account for the jobs not being of equal value. Once such a factor formed part of the evaluation, it could not be used again as a GMF defence, as it would be double-counted.

48 [1992] IRLR 163, EAT.

CHAPTER 21

Review

Scope

Underlying all proceedings of a judicial nature is the principle that there should be finality in litigation. This consideration of public policy also lays down the general rule that tribunal decisions cannot be re-opened or re-litigated. Exceptions are provided in limited circumstances: when the tribunal has made an error of law the decision can be *appealed* to the EAT (see chapter 23), and when specific grounds exist, there is a power to *review* a tribunal's decision.

A tribunal's power of review is unusual in judicial proceedings and has been said to provide

> ... a useful corrective, designed to prevent any injustice being suffered as a result of the very considerable relaxation of the rules of evidence and procedure which, in the interests of informality and an absence of legalism, is encouraged at industrial tribunal hearings.[1]

This does not mean that the power is to be called upon by any party aggrieved at a tribunal decision seeking a re-hearing of the case: the power is 'not intended to provide parties with the opportunity of a re-hearing at which the same evidence can be rehearsed with different emphasis, or further evidence adduced which was available before'.[2]

---

1 Per Waite J in *Carryfast Ltd v Dawkins* (unreported) EAT 290/83.
2 *Stevenson v Golden Wonder Ltd* [1977] IRLR 474, EAT.

Clerical mistakes

Purely clerical mistakes or errors arising from an accidental slip or omission in any decision of a tribunal, or statement of reasons, or of compensation (r10(2) and (3)), may be corrected at any time by the tribunal chairman by certificate (r10(9)). Where the chairman is unable to sign the certificate as required, eg, due to death or incapacity, the other members of a tribunal will sign the certificate and certify that the chairman was unable to do so (r10(12)).

This power may be exercised at any time and is generally referred to as 'the slip rule'. It is limited to clerical slips and arithmetical mistakes, such as a reference to a limited company respondent as a 'plc', and should not be confused with the power of review.

In practice, any slips are corrected and initialled by the chairman in manuscript on the original decision, which is then sent together with the certificate of correction to the secretary so that the entry in the register can be altered (r10(10)). If the document was previously omitted from the register in circumstances where the tribunal sat in private, any corrected document will be sent to the parties by the secretary of tribunals (r10(12)).

The power to review

A tribunal can review its decision in the following circumstances (r11(1)):

a) the decision was wrongly made as a result of an error on the part of the tribunal staff;

b) a party did not receive notice of the proceedings leading to the decision;

c) the decision was made in the absence of a party;

d) new evidence has become available since the conclusion of the hearing, providing that its existence could not have been reasonably known of or foreseen at the time of the hearing; or

e) the interests of justice require such a review.

Error by staff

'Tribunal staff' do not include the chairman or other members of the tribunal. In practice, it is rare for a review to be based on this ground, as most errors on the part of the administrative staff of tribunals would either be capable of correction under the slip rule or would more appropriately be considered under r11(1)(b) or (c), ie, failure to give proper notice of the proceedings or reaching a decision in the absence of a party.

Furthermore, the mere fact that a member of the tribunal staff has made an error will not be sufficient for a party to succeed on an application for review on this ground: the power to review on this basis only arises when a decision was *wrongly made as a result of* the error concerned.

No notice of proceedings

Under r5(1) the Secretary is obliged to send all parties a notice of hearing at least 14 days before the date fixed for that hearing. By r20(3) this notice is authorised to be sent by post. The provisions of the Interpretation Act 1978 s7, relating to service of documents by post, have been held to apply to tribunal proceedings,[3] except where 'presentation' is required (see p34). Section 7 provides:

> Where an Act authorises or requires any document to be sent by post ... then, unless the contrary intention appears, the service is deemed to be effected by properly addressing, prepaying, and posting a letter containing the document, and unless the contrary is proved, to have been effected at the time at which the letter would be delivered in the ordinary course of post.

This presumption that the notice has been effectively served by committing it to the post is difficult to rebut. Nor would it be sufficient for a party to claim that the document must have been intercepted after delivery by some third party or been lost within some complicated corporate structure: parties are presumed to have made adequate arrangements for the receipt of their mail during the course of tribunal proceedings. In the case of a limited company, service at the company's registered address will be deemed to have been effected, even if no reply has been received.[4]

Where no notice of appearance has been entered, for whatever reason, this is the only ground upon which the respondent concerned may apply for a review (r3(2)(c)).

---

3 *Migwain Ltd (in Liquidation) v TGWU* [1979] ICR 597, EAT and *T and D Transport (Portsmouth) Ltd v Linburn* [1987] ICR 696, EAT.
4 *Migwain* (above).

Absence of a party

This ground does not open the way for a party to choose not to attend a hearing and subsequently apply for a review of the decision on the ground of non-attendance. A party who makes the conscious choice not to appear at a tribunal hearing must take the consequences.[5]

A party wishing to apply for a review of a tribunal decision on this ground must demonstrate a good and genuine reason for the original absence, such as some unforeseen illness or accident. In *Morris v Griffiths*[6] the EAT felt that a respondent employer's explanation as to how he fell ill on the way to the tribunal hearing did give grounds for allowing a review.

Where the application is made under this head, much will depend upon the view taken by the tribunal as to the credit-worthiness of the party concerned; so where the question arises whether the reason given is 'genuine', an oral hearing of the application for review is required: see *Morris v Griffiths* (above), where the employer applying for a review in writing was disbelieved by the tribunal chairman considering the documentation, but was felt to be honest on his oral presentation before the EAT, which allowed his appeal and ordered a re-hearing of the substantive complaint.

New evidence

This must have arisen since the conclusion of the hearing to which the decision relates, provided that its existence could not have been reasonably known of or foreseen at the time of the hearing. A party wishing to apply for a review under this head must show:

a) some reasonable explanation for not having produced the evidence before the tribunal, ie, the new evidence was not available before the conclusion of the original hearing and its existence could not reasonably have been known of or foreseen at that time;

b) the new evidence is credible (although it may still be open to contradiction); and

c) the new evidence would or might have some effect on the original tribunal decision.[7]

5 *Fforde v Black* (unreported) EAT 68/80.
6 [1977] ICR 153.
7 See *Bagga v Heavy Electricals (India) Ltd* [1972] ICR 118, NIRC.

These conditions are those applied by the civil courts generally on appeal and it has been stressed by the EAT that merely because tribunals have less formal procedures than the High Court, it does not mean that applications to admit fresh evidence are likely to be favourably entertained as a matter of course.[8] The conditions have been strictly applied by tribunals. In *Flint v Eastern Electricity Board*,[9] the tribunal did not review its decision by considering new medical evidence which could have been adduced by the employee at the original hearing, although there was clearly much sympathy for the employee and the evidence was acknowledged to be genuine and to be relevant to the tribunal's decision.

A party may be unfairly confronted by evidence at the original tribunal hearing, eg, if after the respondent's case the applicant gives evidence on matters which s/he has failed to put to the respondent, the respondent should apply for an adjournment at that stage to allow time to consider whether there might be evidence in rebuttal. It would be wrong to wait until after the tribunal decision and then seek to adduce evidence in rebuttal by way of review.[10] But if the party taken by surprise is unrepresented, and the tribunal fails to drew attention to the possibility of an adjournment, an application for review under r11(1)(d) may succeed.[11]

Even if the evidence was not previously available and could not reasonably have been foreseen, the application will fail unless it can be shown that the new evidence is both relevant and probative and is likely to have an important influence upon the result of the case. In *Wileman v Minilec Engineering Ltd*[12] it was held that the applicant's subsequent behaviour in posing for a national newspaper, in what was described as a flimsy costume, did not meet the test of relevance and was unlikely to have any influence in determining her complaint of sexual harassment.

In other cases, however, evidence of matters which have taken place subsequent to the tribunal decision have been held to be admissible under this rule. In *Help the Aged Housing Association (Scotland) Ltd v Vidler*[13] evidence of the applicant's subsequent employment was held to be admissible and led to a reduction in the

8 *Borden (UK) Ltd v Potter* [1986] ICR 647, EAT.
9 [1975] ICR 395; [1975] IRLR 277, QBD.
10 *Douglas Water Miners Welfare Society Club v Grieve* (unreported) EAT 487/84.
11 *Grieves v Coldshield Windows Ltd* (unreported) EAT 218/82.
12 [1988] ICR 318; [1988] IRLR 144, EAT.
13 [1977] IRLR 104, EAT.

compensation previously awarded; and in *Ladup Ltd v Barnes*[14] the EAT held that it was unjust not to allow a review where there has been a subsequent conviction in relation to the very matter for which the employee had been dismissed where the tribunal had previously held that there had been no contributory fault. However, in *Yorkshire Engineering and Welding Co Ltd v Burnham*[15] the NIRC held that a change in circumstances of a less substantial nature was not sufficient to give rise to a ground for a review of the previous award of compensation. Further, generally speaking, evidence which simply goes to the credibility of a witness will not be admitted unless it can be shown to be central to the main issue(s) of the case (see pp162–163).

When applying for a review under r11(1)(d), details should be given of the new evidence which is sought to be adduced, as well as stating the reasons why it was not produced before the first hearing.[16]

Interests of justice

Whilst this residual ground gives a wide discretion to tribunals, the discretion must be exercised judicially and with regard to the interests of *all* parties, and to the public interest requirement of finality in litigation.[17] It has further been stressed that the power to grant a review on this ground should be exercised cautiously.[18]

It is not merely an alternative to the other grounds for review and a party will rarely succeed on this basis when the reasons for making the application have already been rejected under another head; there needs to be 'some special additional circumstance ... or mitigating factor' (*Flint* (above)), which leads to the conclusion that justice does in fact require a review. In *General Council of British Shipping v Deria*[19] the EAT put the test even higher, as requiring 'exceptional circumstances' which relate not to wider matters such as the unusual nature of the case or the public importance attached to it, but to factors relating to the case itself. In *Deria*, the tribunal had allowed the application for a review of the original decision (based on grounds of new evidence and the interests of justice), as

---

14 [1982] ICR 107; [1982] IRLR 7, EAT.
15 [1974] ICR 77; [1973] IRLR 316, NIRC.
16 *Vauxhall Motors Ltd v Henry* [1978] ITR 332, EAT.
17 *Flint* (above).
18 *Lindsay v Ironsides Ray & Vials* [1994] ICR 384, EAT.
19 [1985] ICR 198, EAT.

the case involved 'an issue of widespread public importance and related to a technical loophole in the Race Relations Act', matters which outweighed the public interest requirement of finality in litigation. On appeal, the EAT reversed the tribunal's decision, holding that the approach taken had been wrong in principle.

Cases which fall under 'interests of justice' alone have been divided into two categories: (1) those involving some procedural mishap, and (2) those where the tribunal's decision has been undermined by events occurring shortly thereafter.

(1) Procedural mishaps

These include the following:

a) where a party has not been given a fair opportunity to address the tribunal on a point of substance, eg, on the questions of remedy or mitigation of loss;[20]
b) where a point going to the tribunal's jurisdiction to hear the case was not raised before the original hearing;[21]
c) where the originating application was withdrawn at the original hearing due in part to a mistaken view of the law on the part of the tribunal chairman and in part to a failure to disclose all relevant documents.[22]

Some procedural mishaps might involve the tribunal also correcting an error of law when reviewing the previous decision; this is not, however, a bar to the carrying out of the review in such cases, even where the error of law is a major or substantial one; see *Trimble* (n20 above), where Browne-Wilkinson J stated that it was irrelevant whether the tribunal's error was minor or major, provided the erroneous decision had been reached after some procedural mishap. An application for review may even be the correct approach where a simple mistake has led to the tribunal failing to consider a question of jurisdiction, as in *British Midland Airways Ltd v Lewis* (n21 above).

(2) Subsequent events

Subsequent events which might give rise to grounds for applying for a review of the original decision in the interests of justice include the following:

20 *Trimble v Supertravel Ltd* [1982] ICR 440; [1982] IRLR 451, EAT.
21 *British Midland Airways Ltd v Lewis* [1978] ICR 782, EAT.
22 *Harber v North London Polytechnic* [1990] IRLR 198, CA.

a) where the compensatory award was made on forecasts as to earnings which subsequently are found to have been falsified by the applicant, as in *Yorkshire Engineering and Welding Co Ltd v Burnham* (n15 above) – although in that case the application for a review failed;

b) where a compensatory award has been made in full with no deduction for contributory fault, when a subsequent criminal conviction has been secured in relation to the matters of misconduct to which the dismissal related: see *Ladup v Barnes* (p206 above).

A *decision*

The power to review only relates to a *decision* of the tribunal. A decision is defined by reg 2(2) as including:

> a declaration, an order, including an order striking out any originating application or notice of appearance made under r4(7) or 13(2), a recommendation or an award of the tribunal and a determination under r6 but does not include any other interlocutory order or any other decision on an interlocutory matter.

There is no power, therefore, to review an interlocutory order of the tribunal such as an order relating to further particulars, discovery, or joinder. In the case of an interlocutory order the appropriate course of action for an aggrieved party is either to appeal to the EAT, if there is some error of law in the order (although most interlocutory orders will involve a pure exercise of discretion on the part of the tribunal), or to apply to the tribunal for further directions.[23] In particular, if an interlocutory order is originally made after considering representations from only one party, the order is provisional and may be reconsidered by the tribunal on an application for further direction from another party.[24]

If an originating application has been dismissed or struck out as a result of some error which gives rise to a ground for review, the applicant should apply for a review and not issue a further originating application, even if still in time to do so. The issue of a further originating application in such circumstances has been held to be vexatious,[25] and may be struck out on that ground under r13(2)(d).

No distinction is made between oral and written decisions, and

23 *Nikitas v Metropolitan Borough of Solihull* [1986] ICR 291, EAT.
24 *Reddington v Straker & Sons Ltd* [1994] ICR 172, EAT.
25 *Acrow (Engineers) Ltd v Hathaway* [1981] ICR 510, EAT.

decisions in extended or summary form: the power to review applies to them all.

The number of applications

The tribunal can consider reviewing a particular decision more than once, although it is unclear as to whether a second consideration of the question of a review must be on new grounds. In *Raybright TV Services Ltd v Smith*[26] the NIRC held that, in exceptional circumstances, a second application for a review, made on the same grounds as an earlier application, was permissible. However, in *Stevensons (Dyers) Ltd v Brennan*[27] it was held that a party could not make the same application for a review more than once. At the time of both decisions the power of review was linked by rule to the county court power to order a new trial, in respect of which only one application is permissible. No such link now exists, which may undermine the judgment in *Stevensons*. On the other hand, any second application would have to be heard by a differently constituted tribunal in any event (the first would be *functus officio*) and it may be predicted that most tribunals would be extremely reluctant to allow a party further attempts at the evidence without any new grounds.

Application of party or on tribunal's own motion

A review can be considered either on the application of a party or of the tribunal's own motion.

Tribunal

It is only the tribunal which made the decision which may review it of its own motion: r11(2). It must then follow the procedure laid down under r11(3), ie, it must, within 14 days after the date on which the decision was sent to the parties (although the tribunal may extend time for *itself* under r15(1)), send notice to each of the parties explaining in summary form the grounds on which, and reasons why, it is proposed to review the decision and giving them an opportunity to show cause why there should not be a review.

---

26 [1973] ICR 640, NIRC.
27 [1974] ICR 194, NIRC.

Parties

If one of the parties wishes to apply for a review, the application can either be made orally at the hearing, or in writing to the secretary (or regional secretary for the particular tribunal) within 14 days after the date on which the decision was sent to the parties (although time may be extended under r15(1)). On a written application to the secretary, the party should set out in full the grounds on which the application is made (r11(4)).

As a matter of practice, an application for a review should set out not only the grounds for seeking a review but also the grounds for contending that the decision of which a review is sought is wrong, so as to demonstrate that the application is not merely a matter of academic technicality.[28]

An application for review made by one of the parties may be refused by the president or by the chairman of the tribunal which decided the case or by a regional chairman, if s/he considers that the application has no reasonable prospect of success (r11(5)). Before an application is refused on this basis, however, the party applying for the review should be given the opportunity to give further reasons in writing as to the grounds upon which the application is made.[29] In practice, when full grounds are set out, tribunals hold an oral hearing to decide whether there should be a review. If the applicant is successful at this hearing in showing that there is a prima facie case for a review, the tribunal will generally proceed into the full review hearing.

If a party seeks to review a decision under either r11(1)(b) or (c), ie, that s/he did not receive notice of the proceedings or that the decision was made in his/her absence, it has been held that it would be inappropriate for the question of whether the application has reasonable prospects of success to be considered by a chairman alone, but rather should be considered by the full tribunal.[30] There appears to be no statutory basis for this restriction on the rule.

Hearing the application

If the application for a review made by a party is not refused as having no reasonable prospects of success (whether that refusal is on the papers or after an oral hearing), the review itself is then

28 *P J Drakard & Sons Ltd v Wilton* [1977] ICR 642, EAT.
29 *P J Drakard* (above).
30 *Hancock v Middleton* [1982] ICR 416, EAT.

heard by the tribunal which decided the case unless (a) it is not practicable for it to be heard by that tribunal, or (b) the original decision was made by a chairman acting alone under r13(8). In either case, the review will then be heard by a tribunal appointed by the president or a regional chairman (r11(6)).

Even if the original decision was made by a chairman sitting alone, therefore, the review will be carried out by a full tribunal (r11(6)(b)). Furthermore, r13(8)(c) expressly excludes the power to review a decision reached by a full tribunal from the list of instances in which a chairman can act alone (see p5).

The exceptions under r11(6)(a) and (b) apply only to a review on the application of a party. If the review takes place of the tribunal's own motion, only the fully constituted original tribunal can carry out the review (r11(2)).

The procedure at the hearing of the review will depend on the grounds on which the application is made; some explanation of the reason for applying for a review will be required and evidence may need to be called. For instance, in an application under r11(1)(c), once it has been established that the ground for the application has been made out, ie, the decision was made in that party's absence, evidence which would have been adduced at the original hearing will need to be called to demonstrate that the original decision was wrong. In an application under r11(1)(d) where new evidence has become available, before the tribunal goes on to consider its effect, evidence may first need to be given to establish why the existence of the evidence in question could not reasonably have been known or foreseen at the time of the previous decision, before the tribunal allows the evidence itself to be adduced.

Where evidence is called, any party resisting the application for review will have the opportunity to test that evidence, by way of cross-examination or by calling further evidence in rebuttal. The review hearing also gives both parties the opportunity to make oral submissions.

Review and appeal

The hearing of an application for a review can continue even if the decision is also under appeal to the EAT. If the chairman of the tribunal deciding the question of review considers it undesirable to adjudicate upon the application pending the hearing of the appeal, the correct procedure is for the chairman to consult with the registrar of the EAT on the most appropriate course to follow.[31] In practice, the grounds of appeal and the grounds for review may differ in nature and there may be no difficulty in allowing the two procedures to run in tandem. The delays in EAT listing make it likely that the application for review will be considered before the appeal. Where the grounds do overlap, the chairman may be reluctant to proceed with any consideration of the merits of the review application, preferring the matter to be considered first by the EAT.

The distinction between grounds suitable for appeal and grounds suitable for review were considered by the EAT in *Trimble v Supertravel Ltd*,[32] where Browne-Wilkinson J stated:

> We do not think it is appropriate for an industrial tribunal to review their decision simply becasue it is said there was an error of law on its face. If the matter had been ventilated and properly argued, then errors of law of that kind fall to be corrected by this appeal tribunal. If, on the other hand, due to an oversight or to some procedural occurrence one or other party can with substance say that he has not had a fair opportunity to present his argument on a point of substance, then that is a procedural shortcoming in the proceedings before the tribunal which, in our view, can correctly be dealt with by a review . . . however important the point of law or fact may be. In essence, the review procedure enables errors occurring in the course of the proceedings to be corrected but would not normally be appropriate when the proceedings had given both parties a fair opportunity to present their case and the decision had been reached in the light of all relevant argument.

As the tribunal has the power to review its decision of its own motion, a further complication may arise where a party has entered an appeal against the decision. Although the tribunal obviously considers the case to be suitable for a review, if the grounds overlap with those which form the basis of the appeal, the *Blackpole Furniture* case (n31 above) would seem to provide authority for the proposition that the tribunal should still consult with the registrar of the EAT before proceeding with the question of review.

Where new evidence has become available, the appropriate course is for the party seeking to adduce this evidence to apply for a review under r11(1)(d) rather than seeking to do so on appeal. Indeed, where an appeal has been pursued in order to try to adduce the new evidence, costs have been awarded against the unsuccessful appellant for bringing an unnecessary appeal when the proper course is to

---

31 *Blackpole Furniture Ltd v Sullivan* [1978] ICR 558, EAT.
32 [1982] ICR 440; [1982] IRLR 451.

apply for a review; see *Green & Symons Ltd v Shickell and Another*[33] and *William P Harrower Ltd v Hogg*.[34]

Revocation or variation of the original decision

On reviewing its decision, a tribunal may confirm its original decision or may vary or revoke it. If the original decision is revoked, the tribunal will order the case to be re-heard, either before the same or a differently constituted tribunal (see r11(7)).

The power to vary a decision includes the power to replace the previous decision completely if appropriate:

> [T]he tribunal can . . . decide that at the original hearing the decision it came to was wrong, and the right answer is so obvious that it can go straight to that right answer. . . .[35]

Furthermore, the subsequent decision may replace the original completely, even though the application for review was directed only at one aspect of the decision:

> . . . a litigant who asks a tribunal to review its decision cannot pick and choose between which parts of the decision he wishes to have reviewed. If an application is made for a review and is acceded to, then the tribunal is free to review the whole of its decision.[36]

In such cases, however, the tribunal is bound to give the parties proper warning of the potentially wider consequences than envisaged by the application for review, and to allow them adequate opportunity to be heard fully on all points potentially in issue. In *Estorffe* (n36 above) the case was remitted to allow the parties opportunity to be heard on issues again 'at large' before the tribunal, although this was not initially envisaged in the review application.

CHECKLIST: REVIEW OF DECISIONS

- Is there a 'decision' in respect of which an application for review might be made?
- If there is no 'decision' but only an interlocutory order, is it possible to seek further directions from the tribunal which might lead to a reconsideration of the order or should an appeal be pursued?

---

33 (Unreported) EAT 528/83.
34 (Unreported) EAT 215/78.
35 *Stonehill Furniture Ltd v Phillippo* [1983] ICR 556, EAT.
36 *Estorffe v Smith* [1973] ITR 627, NIRC.

- Does the party's dissatisfaction with the original decision properly fall to be considered under the limited grounds upon which an application for review can be considered?
- If the grievance relates to a technical error in the decision, might this properly be corrected by use of the 'slip rule'?
- Is an application for review the proper course, or would an appeal be the more appropriate procedure?
- If an application for a review is made at the same time as an appeal is in progress, should the review continue or be stayed pending the outcome of the appeal?
- Is an application for review still in time or will the tribunal need also to be asked to consider extending time under r15(1)? If the latter, what is the reason for the late application?
- In making the review application, detailed grounds should be presented in writing setting out both the specific ground on which the application is made and demonstrating why the original decision needs to be reviewed in the light of these grounds.
- Where the application is made under r11(1)(a), (b) or (c), sufficient detail should be given to demonstrate that the application is not merely technical in nature.
- Where the application is made under r11(1)(d), a full description of the new evidence should be provided, demonstrating how it is relevant and probative and likely to have an important effect on the original decision.
- The application should ask for the opportunity to be heard on the question of whether or not there should be a review as well as at any actual review.
- If the review is allowed and the tribunal indicates that it is likely to revoke the original decision, consider whether representations should be made as to whether the re-hearing should be before the same or a differently constituted tribunal.

CHAPTER 22

Enforcement

Enforcement of awards by tribunals differs according to the nature of the award and the person in whose favour an award is made.

Non-monetary awards

Failure to comply with certain orders of a tribunal may lead to enforcement procedures in front of the tribunal itself. For example, non-compliance with a reinstatement or re-engagement order under ERA 1996 s113 will be subject to enforcement by the automatic award by the tribunal of a higher sum by way of compensation (ERA 1996 s117). A similar provision applies to awards for failure to comply with an order following a finding of dismissal for trade union reasons under TULRCA 1992 s166. A declaration by a tribunal of an individual's right not to be excluded or expelled unlawfully from a union can be enforced by an application for compensation to the tribunal or, if the individual has not been admitted or re-admitted to the union, by an application direct to the EAT to assess compensation (TULRCA s176).

Monetary awards

In order to obtain enforcement of an award, the decision must be registered at the county court in England or the sheriff court in Scotland (ITA 1996 s15(1) and (2)). By this method the enforcement machinery of the county court is brought into play for the purposes of a tribunal award of 'any sum payable in pursuance of a decision'. The procedure is to apply on affidavit ex parte, verifying the   215 amount of the sum due and producing a copy of the decision registered at the Central Office, ie, a copy of the decision promulgated (CCR Order 25 r12). A specific form (Form N322) is required.

This machinery is not available for non-monetary awards, even those parts of awards for reinstatement which include back pay. Imaginative exploitation of the reinstatement provisions following unfair dismissal was blocked in *O'Laoire v Jackel International Ltd*.[1] The upper limit on compensation awards is raised to enable a tribunal to award more by a reinstatement order than it could had it not ordered a reinstatement (ERA 1996 s124(3)). But the award remains essentially a non-monetary award, ie, an order for reinstatement under ERA 1996 s113 rather than an award of compensation under s118. The former is not, therefore, amenable to enforcement in the county court.

Once the application for enforcement has been heard (usually by a district judge) in the county court, the sum is recoverable as though it were an order of the county court. In Scotland it can be enforced 'in like manner as an extract registered decree arbitral bearing a warrant for execution' issued by the sheriff court (ITA 1996 s15(2)). In effect, this means enforcement must be effected by execution against goods, a charging order, bankruptcy proceedings, garnishee proceedings, an administration order or attachment of earnings orders.

Interest

There are two provisions dealing with interest. Under the Industrial Tribunals (Interest) Order 1991 SI No 479 interest becomes payable on tribunal awards 42 days after the date of the decision. The interest rate is that specified in relation to the Judgments Act 1838 (8% in 1996). So from the end of the time limit for an appeal, interest runs at the specific rate. It is therefore important to ensure that the tribunal does wherever possible make an award, rather than adjourning the matter for the parties to attempt to settle.

A slightly modified provision applies in relation to claims under the legislation on sex and race discrimination and equal pay. Here the date from which interest begins to accrue is the date of the decision (reg 10(a)), but if the award of the tribunal is paid by the

---

1 [1990] ICR 197; [1990] IRLR 70, CA.

respondent within 14 days of the decision, no award of interest is made.

An entirely separate provision made for interest under the sex and race discrimination legislation gives the tribunal a power (it does not automatically arise) to award interest on monetary awards. Interest runs in respect of an award for injury to feelings from the date of the discriminatory act for the whole of the period up to the date of the decision. For other monetary awards in a discrimination case interest runs for the whole of the period at half of the rate: for more detail see Sex Discrimination and Equal Pay (Remedies) Regulations 1993 SI No 2798 and Race Relations (Interest on Awards) Regulations 1994 SI No 1748.

Rights after death

Certain employment provisions may be enforced on behalf of an employee who has died before or after the commencement of proceedings, ie, ERA 1996 Parts I (so far as it relates to itemised pay statements), III, V, VI (ss50–57 and 61–63), VII, VIII, IX (ss92 and 93) and X to XII, dealing with most employment protection rights including unfair dismissal and redundancy pay (see ERA 1996 s207). Enforcement of orders made on behalf of the personal representatives of a dead employee is regulated by the Industrial Tribunals Awards (Enforcement in Cases of Death) Regulations 1976 SI No 663. This provides for awards to be made in favour of the estate of an employee who has died. It is not necessary for the personal representative to obtain letters of administration or probate or (in Scotland) confirmation.

Insolvent employers

Commencement and maintenance of proceedings against insolvent respondents is dealt with at p19. Some debts due are recoverable from the Secretary of State under ERA 1996 ss167 (redundancy pay) and 182 (some other payments). Otherwise, employees rank as preferential creditors to the extent of certain elements of back pay and holidays (up to a total of £800) and collect debts according to their priority in a winding-up.

CHAPTER 23

Appeals

This chapter deals in summary terms with the scope to appeal from a tribunal to the Employment Appeal Tribunal. The Employment Appeal Tribunal Rules 1993 SI No 2854 (EAT Rules) and a Practice Direction (PD)[1] regulate the EAT's procedure. In Northern Ireland, appeal lies to the Northern Ireland Court of Appeal, in practice by way of case stated.[2]

Constitution

The EAT's powers derive from ITA 1996 s20. It is almost exclusively an appellate tribunal. There are however exceptions. It can hear:

a) Claims for compensation by members unjustifiably disciplined or expelled from a trade union, and individuals unlawfully excluded from membership of a union (TULRCA 1992 ss67(2) and 176(2)). In each case the reference to the EAT follows a declaration in the individual's favour by a tribunal and a failure by the union to rectify the unlawful conduct.

b) Appeals on questions of law from decisions of the certification officer relating to the application of union funds for political objects (TULRCA s95) and amalgamations and transfer of engagements (TULRCA s104).

c) Appeals on questions of law *or fact* from decisions of the certification officer relating to the certification and listing of a trade union (TULRCA ss3 and 4).

Ironically, appeals from tribunals to the EAT are an exception to

---

1 29 March 1996: see p382.

2 Industrial Training (NI) Order 1984 article 31 and RSC (NI) 1980 Order 61.

the principal statutory rule, which is that appeals lie to the High Court under the Tribunals and Inquiries Act 1992 s11 and Sch 1 and RSC Order 55 r4. Only a handful of cases have been heard in this manner since the EAT was founded in 1976, mainly concerning compensation for public servants on loss or diminution of emoluments. Otherwise, appeals from tribunals under all the employment protection and discrimination legislation go to the EAT.

The President of the EAT is nominated by the Lord Chancellor (ITA 1996 s22). In practice he has held office for between three and six years. Other judges, who must include one from the Court of Session, are nominated to a panel. They include judges of the High Court and circuit judges appointed under powers under the Administration of Justice Act 1985 s9.

The lay members of the EAT are appointed by the Queen on the recommendation of the Lord Chancellor and the Secretary of State and they must have 'special knowledge or experience of industrial relations, either as representatives of employers or representatives of workers'. There is no formal system of advertisement or nomination by representative bodies, and there is no training. In practice, most members are retired trade union national officials and serving or retired directors of corporations or service organisations.

Appeals must be heard by a judge and one member from each side of industry, and occasionally by a judge and two members from each side (ITA 1996 s28(2)). Parties may consent to a hearing with one member absent (ITA 1996 s28(3)). On appeals from decisions made by a tribunal chairman sitting alone (see p5), the appeal is heard by a judge alone (ITA 1996 s28(4)).

The EAT is a superior court of record (ITA 1996 s20(3)), which means it can punish for contempt and compel attendance of witnesses. Contempt of a tribunal can be dealt with by a reference by the tribunal to the Divisional Court (RSC Order 52 r1), since the tribunal is at the same time an 'inferior court'. But it seems the reference cannot be made to the EAT even if it is chaired by a judge of the Queen's Bench Division.

The EAT is bound by the doctrine of precedent, so it must follow judgments of the Court of Appeal. It is not bound by judgments of the divisions of the High Court. It is not bound by a decision of the Court of Session (unless it is hearing a Scottish appeal), although the latter's construction of a statute is highly persuasive. The EAT sits in London and Edinburgh but can sit anywhere in England, Wales and Scotland and its decisions are binding on tribunals throughout Great Britain. Its decisions are not binding on tribunals in Northern Ireland but they are customarily followed. The EAT will normally follow a decision of another division of the EAT, whether sitting in England, Wales or Scotland, and where there are two decisions of different divisions of the EAT, and the second has considered all the arguments and not followed the first, the EAT will follow the second unless it is convinced that it was certainly wrong.[3]

There are unrestricted rights of audience before the EAT:

> Any person may appear . . . in person or be represented by Counsel or by a solicitor or by a representative of a trade union or an employer's association or by any other person . . .[4]

Legal aid is available for advice and representation at the EAT (Civil Legal Aid (General) Regulations 1989 SI No 339 reg 149).

Questions of law

With one exception (determination of the certification officer – see above) an appeal to the EAT lies only on a question of law (ITA 1996 s21 and TULRCA 1992 s291(2)). The EAT is jealous of its jurisdiction restricted to questions of law. When it strays outside that jurisdiction, the Court of Appeal and the Court of Session have trenchantly criticised it.[5]

Error of law

This is described as misdirection, misapplication or misunderstanding of the law.[6] If a tribunal fails to ask the right legal question or misconstrues a statute or fails to answer the correct statutory question, there is an error of law.

Perversity

In order to run a case based on perversity, it is generally necessary to have the chairman's notes so that a complete record of proceed-

---

3 *Colchester Estates (Cardiff) v Carlton Industries plc* [1986] Ch 80 (although this doctrine of *stare decisis* has been doubted in its application to an appellate court such as the EAT in the *obiter* comment of Beldam LJ in *Tracey and Others v Crosville Wales Ltd* (1995) 31 July CA (unreported)).
4 ITA 1995 s28.
5 *Hereford and Worcester County Council v Neale* [1986] ICR 471; [1986] IRLR 168, CA.
6 *British Telecommunications plc v Sheridan* [1990] IRLR 27, CA.

ings before the tribunal, as well as the documents, are all available to the EAT.[7] The EAT then has some material upon which it can decide that no reasonable tribunal properly considering this evidence and directing itself according to the law *could* have reached the decision which it did. Full particulars must be given (PD para 2).

This is a more stringent test than a complaint that the tribunal made a decision contrary to the weight of evidence or did not adequately consider an aspect of the evidence. In these latter cases, the tribunal is the sole judge and arbiter of the facts, the inferences and the weight to be given to the evidence, and the EAT ought not to intervene.[8]

No evidence

The absence of evidence is a specific ground of appeal, although it might well fall within the category of perversity (see *Sheridan* (n6 above)). It is an error of law for a tribunal to make a decision for which there is no evidence in support. However, provided there is *some* evidence dealing with the subject-matter, the tribunal decision ought not to be interfered with. If evidence on the particular subject has been given and challenged, the tribunal is entitled to accept or reject that evidence. If the evidence is unchallenged, the tribunal ought to accept it, and if it makes a decision contrary to it, the decision will fall into the 'no evidence' category.

Wrongful exercise of discretion

This could form a ground within perversity but it is mentioned here because the test is much more stringent against appeals. The wrong exercise of a discretion will rarely be capable of successful challenge.[9] This includes taking into account a factor which it was improper to take into account, failing to take account of a proper factor and the exercise of a discretion 'so far beyond what any reasonable tribunal or Chairman could have decided . . .'

---

7 *Piggott Brothers & Co Ltd v Jackson* [1992] ICR 85; [1991] IRLR 309, CA.
8 *Hollister v National Farmers Union* [1979] ICR 542; [1979] IRLR 238, CA.
9 *Bastick v James Lane Turf Accountants Ltd* [1979] ICR 778, EAT and *Carter v Credit Change Ltd* [1979] ICR 908; [1979] IRLR 361, CA.

Bias

Bias or apparent bias is a ground for setting aside a decision of a tribunal (see pp150 and 168). The Practice Direction para 9 requires a specific complaint to be made with full and sufficient particulars in the notice of appeal and an opportunity is given for allegations to be put on affidavit and referred to the tribunal criticised. A successful allegation of bias or apparent bias is an error of law because it is a breach of the rules of natural justice.

Academic appeals

The EAT, like other courts and appellate jurisdictions, will not hear academic or hypothetical cases.[10] There must be a live issue between the parties which requires decision by the EAT. If the employer has been found liable for unfair dismissal, has already paid compensation in full and said in correspondence it would not seek to recover anything from the employee, there is no live issue.[11] A respondent wishing to appeal must make the payments subject to the appeal. Of course, there is nothing to stop an employer who succeeds in the EAT waiving the right to recover compensation already paid.

The scope of an appeal relates to the decision rather than the reasons for it. It follows that if there is a favourable decision, although the reasons given for it are objectionable, there is no appeal.[12] A successful party is effectively stopped from challenging the reasons or the findings unless the other side appeals, in which case the other party can cross-appeal.

Time limits

A notice of appeal must be lodged with the EAT substantially in accordance with the precedent set out in forms at the back of the EAT Rules. These are fairly simple and require the nature of the claim and the grounds on which criticism is made of the tribunal to be set out. The appeal must be served with a copy of the extended written reasons for the decision 'within . . . 42 days from the date on which extended written reasons . . . were sent to the appellant'

10 *Sun Life Assurance v Jervis* [1944] AC 111, HL, and see the editorial to *Supreme Court Practice 1995* 59/1/000.
11 *IMI Yorkshire Imperial Ltd v Olender* [1982] ICR 69, EAT.
12 *Harrod v Ministry of Defence* [1981] ICR 8, EAT.

(EAT Rules r3). It follows from the rules on counting time (chapter 4 above) that if the date on the extended reasons is a Wednesday you have until the close of play on Wednesday six weeks later to serve the notice on the EAT. Since extended reasons must accompany the notice, you effectively have only 21 days following summary reasons to apply for extended reasons in order to mount an appeal.[13]

An application for an extension of time can be made (PD para 4(b)) and the rules set out in *Marshall v Harland & Wolff Ltd*[14] will be applied to determine whether there is any justifiable excuse, what the length of the delay is and the degree of prejudice caused to the other party. The EAT has a discretion to extend time under EAT Rules r37. It should be borne in mind that it exercises its powers sparingly and on the same principles as the Court of Appeal. It is more reluctant to extend time for entering an appeal than for complying with an interlocutory order, since the appellant has already had one chance to have a trial of the merits.[15]

No time scale is prescribed for the service of a respondent's answer and notice of cross-appeal by the rules but the Registrar, on service of a notice of appeal on a respondent, sets out the relevant time scale, which is usually 14 days. An application to extend this period is usually granted without a hearing.

Preliminary matters

Interlocutory applications

By EAT Rules r20, the registrar considers interlocutory applications, must 'have regard to the just and economical disposal of the application' and may decide the matter him/herself or put it to a judge, who may decide it or put the matter to a full appeal tribunal.

An appeal lies from the registrar to a judge, who may decide it or refer it to a full appeal tribunal (EAT Rules r21). Notice of appeal must be given within five days of the decision appealed from.

---

13 *William Hill Organisation Ltd v Gavas* [1990] IRLR 488, CA.
14 [1972] ICR 97; [1972] IRLR 90.
15 *Costellow v Somerset County Council* [1993] 1 WLR 256; [1993] 1 All ER 952, CA, applied in *Fire Brigades Union v Knowles* (unreported) EAT 123/94.

Lack of jurisdiction

As a matter of practice, the registrar decides whether or not an appeal ought to be rejected for lack of jurisdiction. In this case, an appeal is not registered and a letter is sent by the registrar. If the appellant is unhappy with the result, the matter is then referred to a judge.

No arguable point of law

The 1981 PD has been superseded on this point by a procedure for preliminary hearings. A case is listed for hearing by a full EAT. Usually several are listed on the same day to take place before the hearing of substantive appeals. The hearing is ex parte, although the potential respondent occasionally appears and may at the discretion of the EAT be heard. The purpose of the hearing is for the appellant to show cause why the appeal should not be rejected. If an arguable point is raised, and in practice this means impressing at least one of the three members of the EAT, the hearing will cease and the matter will be listed for hearing before a full EAT on another date. If the appeal shows no arguable case, judgment will be given rejecting the appeal and this is a substantive judgment of the EAT.

Directions

Chairmen's notes

The EAT can give directions (EAT Rules r24) on its own motion or on the application of a party. Characteristically these would deal with issues likely to be raised, duration, amendment of pleadings, consolidation and documentation (EAT Rules r24(5)). An application for the preparation by the chairman of his/her notes of evidence should be made as soon as possible, and preferably in the notice of appeal. Running a case of perversity without the chairman's notes is likely to be impossible.[16]

The EAT is increasingly reluctant to order the production of the chairman's note of evidence and will not do so merely to allow the appellant to conduct a fishing expedition. In Scotland, the chairman's note will not be supplied to parties for an appeal unless they show cause. In England a specific application must be made, citing the issues and the witnesses to which the notes are relevant (PD para 7).

16 *Hampson v Department of Education and Science* [1988] ICR 278, [1988] IRLR 87, EAT and *Piggott Brothers & Co Ltd v Jackson* (n7 above).

An agreed note by the parties may be sufficient (PD para 10). If there is disagreement, the chairman's note prevails.[17] A specific challenge to the accuracy of the chairman's notes must be made in accordance with a procedure set out in *Dexine Rubber Co Ltd v Alker*,[18] ie, submission of a competing note to the chairman with an opportunity for the chairman to agree or disagree; if the chairman's note is not accepted by the party criticising it, but is accepted by the other side, the matter can be taken no further.

Restriction orders

A party can be debarred from proceeding if the time limit for presenting a respondent's answer has passed and also if the party fails to comply with any direction (EAT Rules r26). There is also a specific provision in ITA 1996 s33 precluding vexatious litigants from instituting or continuing proceedings. An opportunity must be given before an order is made for the party to make representations. The effect of a restriction order is that leave is required for the continuation of any further proceedings. The application is made to the EAT by the Attorney General or the Lord Advocate.

Witnesses

It is very rare for the EAT to hear live evidence. It has power to require attendance (EAT Rules r27).

The hearing

The case will be listed before the full EAT. Parties are usually consulted about appropriate dates. Cases are given fixed dates and do not run over from one day to the next unless they are booked for more than one day. Parties are required to notify the EAT should the time estimate originally given change. Certain cases are put on the 'fast-track', ie, those which involve other applicants or new legislation or appeals from interlocutory decisions (PD para 12).

There is a requirement for skeleton arguments and a chronology to be prepared in advance in England (PD para 8). The EAT seeks to encourage skeleton or outline arguments and professional representatives without such an argument are usually given short

17 *Houston v Lightwater Farms Ltd* [1990] ICR 502; [1990] IRLR 469, EAT.
18 [1977] ICR 434, EAT.

shrift. They should be served on the EAT and exchanged with the other parties 14 days before the hearing. On a practical note, this enables the argument to be sent with the relevant papers to the members of the EAT so they may read them before the hearing. There is clearly an advantage to an advocate in having a written skeleton argument served in good time.

A list of authorities should also be sent no later than the day before the hearing. The EAT encourages parties to cite from the same law report, ie, ICR *or* IRLR for the same case (PD para 15). Copies are available for all three members of the EAT, but it is very useful for the members and for the advocate presenting a case for photocopies to be made of the relevant authorities so the members can mark their own versions as the argument unfolds. Each member is supplied with a copy of the relevant legislation, usually Butterworth's *Employment Law Handbook*.

The EAT prepares an index of the main documents and the decision of the tribunal appealed against. It selects documents it considers relevant and parties should make sure that any other relevant documents are included. Parties must make up their own bundles according to the EAT index, but often bundles used in the tribunal can be photocopied and re-used without repagination. As a rule of thumb, all documents available to the tribunal below should be made available to the EAT, although there are many occasions when the scope of the appeal is much narrower and all the documents are not required. The EAT has power to admit new material but in practice it rarely does.

Hearings are in public at a dedicated building, Audit House, Victoria Embankment, London or Melville Crescent, Edinburgh, although the EAT occasionally sits in Crown Court buildings elsewhere. A restricted reporting order can be made on the same lines as can be made by a tribunal (see EAT Rules r23) in cases involving sexual misconduct. Similarly, where a sexual offence is alleged, identifying material must be omitted from the register of the EAT.

New points of law

In general, the EAT will not allow points to be taken on appeal which have not been raised at the tribunal. This is a harsh rule, particularly where parties are represented, for example, by non-lawyers at a tribunal and by lawyers on appeal, where new points legitimately can be thought of and taken. The reason for the EAT's reluctance is that it would be unable to decide the appeal finally without remitting the case to the tribunal to hear more evidence.[19] On a point of pure construction, which is simply a matter of law, the EAT can and should hear additional arguments and it then can make up its own mind on the construction without the necessity for additional evidence.

The EAT will also hear new points which affect the jurisdiction of the tribunal.[20] In other words, where the ground of attack affects the jurisdiction of the tribunal to have heard the case in the first place, the EAT will allow argument on it and arguably is required, even if the point is not raised by the parties, to raise it itself. However, the broad scope of this exception is limited by dicta in *Russell v Elmdon Freight Terminal Ltd*,[21] which allowed the EAT a discretion to weigh the interests of justice in allowing a new point to be raised.

New evidence

An appeal can be made on the ground that new evidence has become available since the tribunal hearing. As Sir John Donaldson said:

> Such evidence will be admitted only if some reasonable explanation can be produced for its not having been put before the tribunal ... and if the new evidence is credible and if it would or might have had a decisive effect upon the decision.[22]

These rules are essentially those for appeals to the Court of Appeal set out in *Ladd v Marshall*.[23]

Judgment

Judgment is usually given orally immediately following the argument and a retirement of the three members to consider it. It is tape-recorded and a written revised judgment is made available. Unlike

19 *Kumchyk v Derby County Council* [1978] ICR 1116, EAT.
20 *House v Emmerson Electric Industrial Controls* [1980] ICR 795, EAT.
21 [1989] ICR 629, EAT.
22 *Bagga v Heavy Chemicals (India) Ltd* [1972] ICR 118, NIRC.
23 [1954] 1 WLR 1489; see *Wileman v Minilec Engineering Ltd* [1988] ICR 318; [1988] IRLR 144, EAT.

tribunals, the judgment of the EAT takes effect from the time it is given rather than the time it is published. If the EAT does not give a judgment on the day, it reserves its judgment and hands it down either in written form on a day fixed later or given orally by the judge. Sometimes a different judge hands down the judgment of the previous EAT. Majority decisions can be made; the wing members can incorporate their own words in the judgment given by the presiding judge or it can be given indirectly by the judge as part of the judgment.

Costs

The EAT has power to award costs (EAT Rules r4) where 'proceedings were unnecessary, improper or vexatious or . . . there has been unreasonable delay or other unreasonable conduct in bringing or conducting the proceedings'. Only a party (and not, for example, a party's trade union or employers' association) can be ordered to pay. The EAT can assess the costs or expenses itself, or can order costs to be paid by agreement or to be taxed if there is no agreement. An appeal lies from the taxing officer (in the EAT or in the Supreme Court) to a judge of the EAT.

The order

The EAT can make a reference to the European Court of Justice, although in practice it is reluctant to do so before giving leave to appeal to the Court of Appeal. See also p120.

It can make any order the tribunal below could have made. It can remit the case once it has allowed an appeal for re-hearing by the same or a different tribunal. It can substitute its own decision for that of the tribunal and will do so provided that no new evidence is required to be admitted and the EAT can tell what the tribunal decision would have been had it, for example, applied the law correctly to the material it had. If there is any doubt, the EAT should remit.[24]

---

24 *O'Kelly v Trusthouse Forte plc* [1983] ICR 728; [1983] IRLR 369, CA.

Settlement

The EAT follows the rules of the Court of Appeal if the parties want to settle an appeal or reach a consent order. In principle it will not routinely allow appeals by consent but must first be assured of the grounds for setting aside a decision of an inferior tribunal.[25] In practice appeals are disposed of by consent where the parties agree in writing. Sometimes, however, it is suggested one of the parties should attend and explain the basis of the order sought, especially if settlement occurs shortly before the hearing date.[26]

Review and appeal

An appeal from the EAT lies to the Court of Appeal or Court of Session, but only with leave. An application for leave should be made at the EAT at the conclusion of the judgment if possible. The time for appealing to the Court of Appeal or to the Court of Session is four weeks from the date on which the EAT order was 'sealed or otherwise perfected'. It is essential in England and Wales and desirable in Scotland for an application to be made to the EAT for leave to appeal higher.

The EAT has power to review its own decision (EAT Rules r33) where:

a) it was wrongly made as a result of an error on the part of the EAT;
b) proper notice was not given to a party; or
c) the interests of justice require it.

The EAT can review of its own motion or on application made within 14 days of the decision.

---

25 *J Sainsbury plc v Moger* [1994] ICR 800, EAT.
26 *British Publishing Co Ltd v Fraser* [1987] ICR 517, EAT.

Appendices

Tribunal forms

The following forms are included in Appendix 1:

1.1 Originating application (IT1)   234
1.2 Acknowledgement of originating application (IT5)   240
1.3 Notice of originating application sent to respondent (IT2)   241
1.4 Notice of appearance (IT3)   242
1.5 Suggested dates for hearing (IT4D2)   244
1.6 Notice of hearing (IT4)   245
1.7 Notice of hearing: entitlement to bring or contest proceedings   247
1.8 Notice of an industrial tribunal preliminary hearing   248
1.9 Notice of pre-hearing review   249
1.10 Notice of pre-hearing review (respondent's contentions)   250
1.11 Respondent employer's claim in contract (IT1(c))   251
1.12 Acknowledgement of employer's claim (IT5(c))   252
1.13 Notice of employer's claim in contract sent to applicant (IT2(c))   253
1.14 Notice of appearance by applicant to employer's claim in contract (IT3(c))   254
1.15 Notes on tribunal decisions (IT9)   255
1.16 Questionnaire: sex and race discrimination   259

1.1   Originating application (IT1)

Application to an Industrial Tribunal in England and Wales
for proceedings in Scotland use IT1(Scot)

Guidance Notes

If you think you have a case for an Industrial Tribunal:

- Read booklet ITL1(E&W). It tells you about:

  what types of complaint they can consider;

  the Industrial Tribunal procedure;

  which booklet describes your complaint more fully.

- Read the booklet which describes your complaint. It tells you about:

  who to contact if you need advice or representation;

  qualifying periods - how long you have to work for an employer before you can apply to an Industrial Tribunal.

  time limits - you must send us your application form within the time allowed for your complaint.

You can get the booklets free from any Employment Service Office.

If we do not receive your application with the time-limit stipulated for your type of complaint, we may not be able to deal with it. If you are in doubt, please contact the Advisory Conciliation and Arbitration Service (ACAS) (Booklet ITL1 E/W gives addresses and telephone numbers) or contact your local Employment Service Office.

If you need advice or help to complete your application, you can seek help from for example, your Trade Union or local Citizens Advice Bureau.

You can present the case yourself or have a representative to act for you . If you name a representative, all further communications will be sent to them and not to you. Please arrange for them to keep you informed of the progress of the case.

If your complaint concerns equal pay or sex discrimination you may wish to contact the Equal Opportunities Commission for advice about representation. If your complaint concerns race discrimination you may wish to contact the Commission for Racial Equality.

If you are disabled and need any special arrangements when visiting an Industrial Tribunal, please inform the staff at the office dealing with your case who will do all they can to help you.

If you have a question about the Industrial Tribunal procedure and cannot find the answer in the booklets, please ring the Industrial Tribunal Enquiry line on 0345 959775. (All calls are charged at local rate).

Please answer all the questions on the application that apply to your complaint.

When you have completed the form detach and retain these notes and send the application form to the relevant Tribunal office.

Applications can be faxed, delivered by hand or posted. If you fax your application do not post a copy as well. If you post the application take a copy for your records.

Guidance on where to send your application is on page 3

Where To Send Your Application

- You will need to know the post code area for the place you were employed or where the action you are complaining about took place.
- Refer to the chart below and send it to the tribunal office listed against that code e.g PE10,11 or 12 should go to Nottingham Office. (The full address of each office is on the reverse of these notes).
- Sending your application to the wrong office may cause delay. If you are in doubt where to send it call the Industrial Tribunal Enquiry line on 0345 959775.

Post Code Area	Tribunal Office	Post Code Area	Tribunal Office	Post Code Area	Tribunal Office	Post Code Area	Tribunal Office
AL	BEDFORD	GU1-10	LONDON SOUTH	PE1-6	LEICESTER	SW1	LONDON SOUTH
B	BIRMINGHAM	GU11-14	SOUTHAMPTON	PE7	BURY ST EDS	SW2-20	LONDON NORTH
BA1-16	BRISTOL	GU15-16	LONDON SOUTH	PE8	BEDFORD	SY1-22	SHREWSBURY
BA20-22	EXETER	GU17	READING	PE9	LEICESTER	SY23-25	CARDIFF
BB	MANCHESTER	GU18-25	LONDON SOUTH	PE10-12	NOTTINGHAM	TA1-5	EXETER
BD	LEEDS	GU26-35	SOUTHAMPTON	PE13-19	BURY ST EDS	TA6-9	BRISTOL
BH	SOUTHAMPTON	HA	LONDON NORTH	PE20-25	NOTTINGHAM	TA10-24	EXETER
BL	MANCHESTER	HD	LEEDS	PE30-38	BURY ST EDS	TD ****	NEWCASTLE
BN	SOUTHAMPTON	HG	LEEDS	PL	EXETER	TF	SHREWSBURY
BR	ASHFORD	HP1-5	LONDON NORTH	PO	SOUTHAMPTON	TN1-4	ASHFORD
BS	BRISTOL	HP6-22	READING	PR1-7	MANCHESTER	TN5-7	LONDON SOUTH
CA	NEWCASTLE	HP23	LONDON NORTH	PR8-9	LIVERPOOL	TN8-18	ASHFORD
CB	BURY ST EDS	HP27	READING	RG1-13	READING	TN19-22	SOUTHAMPTON
CF	CARDIFF	HR	CARDIFF	RG14-15	SOUTHAMPTON	TN23-31	ASHFORD
CH1-3	LIVERPOOL	HU	LEEDS	RG16-20	LONDON SOUTH	TN32-33	SOUTHAMPTON
CH4-8	SHREWSBURY	HX	LEEDS	RG21-28	SOUTHAMPTON	TN34-38	ASHFORD
CM	STRATFORD	IG	STRATFORD	RG29-45	READING	TN39-40	SOUTHAMPTON
CO	BURY ST EDS	IP	BURY ST EDS	RH1-14	LONDON SOUTH	TQ	EXETER
CR	LONDON SOUTH	KT	LONDON SOUTH	RH15-17	SOUTHAMPTON	TR	EXETER
CT	ASHFORD	L	LIVERPOOL	RH18-20	LONDON SOUTH	TS	NEWCASTLE
CV	BIRMINGHAM	LA1-6	MANCHESTER	RM	STRATFORD	TW	LONDON SOUTH
CW1-5	SHREWSBURY	LA7-23	NEWCASTLE	S1-62	SHEFFIELD	UB	LONDON NORTH
CW6-10	LIVERPOOL	LD	CARDIFF	S63-64	LEEDS	W	LONDON NORTH
CW11-12	SHREWSBURY	LE	LEICESTER	S65-66	SHEFFIELD	WA1-2	LIVERPOOL
DA	ASHFORD	LL	SHREWSBURY	S70-75	LEEDS	WA3	MANCHESTER
DE1-7	NOTTINGHAM	LN	NOTTINGHAM	S80-81	SHEFFIELD	WA4-13	LIVERPOOL
DE11-15	LEICESTER	LS	LEEDS	SA	CARDIFF	WA14-16	MANCHESTER
DE21-75	NOTTINGHAM	LU	BEDFORD	SE	LONDON SOUTH	WC	LONDON NORTH
DH	NEWCASTLE	M	MANCHESTER	SG1-7	BEDFORD	WD	LONDON NORTH
DL	NEWCASTLE	ME	ASHFORD	SG8-14	BURY ST EDS	WF	LEEDS
DN1-20	LEEDS	MK	BEDFORD	SG15-19	BEDFORD	WN1-7	MANCHESTER
DN21	NOTTINGHAM	N	LONDON NORTH	SK	MANCHESTER	WN8	LIVERPOOL
DN22	SHEFFIELD	NE	NEWCASTLE	SL	READING	WR	BIRMINGHAM
DN31-40	LEEDS	NG	NOTTINGHAM	SM	LONDON SOUTH	WS	BIRMINGHAM
DT1-5	SOUTHAMPTON	NN1-13	BEDFORD	SN1-6	BRISTOL	WV	BIRMINGHAM
DT6-8	EXETER	NN14-18	LEICESTER	SN7	READING	YO1-18	LEEDS
DT9-11	SOUTHAMPTON	NN29	BEDFORD	SN8-16	BRISTOL	YO21-22	NEWCASTLE
DY	BIRMINGHAM	NP	CARDIFF	SO	SOUTHAMPTON	YO25	LEEDS
E	STRATFORD	NR	BURY ST EDS	SP	SOUTHAMPTON	**** TD POST CODE	
EC	STRATFORD	NW	LONDON NORTH	SR	NEWCASTLE	AREA - ENGLISH	
EN	STRATFORD	OL1-13	MANCHESTER	SS	STRATFORD	LOCATIONS ONLY -	
EX	EXETER	OL14	LEEDS	ST1-13	SHREWSBURY	SCOTLAND HAS ITS	
FY	MANCHESTER	OL15-16	MANCHESTER	ST14	LEICESTER	OWN TRIBUNALS	
GL	BRISTOL	OX	READING	ST15-21	BIRMINGHAM		

Industrial Tribunal Offices In England And Wales

ASHFORD - TUFTON HOUSE TUFTON STREET ASHFORD TN23 1RJ — (FAX: 01233 624423)

BEDFORD - 8-10 HOWARD STREET BEDFORD MK40 3HS — (FAX: 01234 352315)

BIRMINGHAM - PHOENIX HOUSE, 1-3 NEWHALL STREET, BIRMINGHAM B3 3NH — (FAX: 0121 2366029)

BURY ST EDMUNDS - 100 SOUTHGATE STREET BURY ST EDMUNDS IP33 2AQ — (FAX: 01284 706064)

BRISTOL - THE CRESCENT CENTRE, TEMPLE BACK, BRISTOL BS1 6EZ — (FAX: 0117 925 3452)

CARDIFF - CARADOG HOUSE, 1-6 ST ANDREWS PLACE, CARDIFF CF1 3BE — (FAX: 01222 225906)

EXETER - RENSLADE HOUSE, BONHAY ROAD, EXETER EX4 3BX — (FAX: 01392 430063)

LEEDS- ALBION TOWER, 11 ALBION STREET, LEEDS LS1 5ES — (FAX: 01132 428843)

LEICESTER - 5A NEW WALK, LEICESTER, LE1 6TE — (FAX: 01162 517602)

LIVERPOOL - UNION COURT , COOK STREET, LIVERPOOL L2 4UJ — (FAX: 0151 2311484)

LONDON NORTH - 19-29 WOBURN PLACE LONDON WC1 OLU — (FAX: 0171 2738686)

LONDON SOUTH - 101 LONDON ROAD, WEST CROYDON CRO 2RF — (FAX: 0181 6499470)

MANCHESTER - ALEXANDRA HOUSE, 14-22 THE PARSONAGE, MANCHESTER M3 2JS — (FAX: 0161 8320249)

NEWCASTLE - QUAYSIDE HOUSE, 110 QUAYSIDE, NEWCASTLE UPON TYNE NE1 3DX — (FAX: 0191 2221680)

NOTTINGHAM - 3RD FLOOR, BYRON HOUSE, 2A MAID MARION WAY, NOTTINGHAM NG1 6HS — (FAX: 01159 507612)

READING - 5TH FLOOR, 30-31 FRIAR STREET, READING RG1 1DY — (FAX: 01734 568066)

SHEFFIELD - 14 EAST PARADE, SHEFFIELD S1 2ET — (FAX: 01142 762551)

SHREWSBURY - PROSPECT HOUSE, BELLE VUE ROAD, SHREWSBURY SY3 7NR — (FAX: 01743 244186)

SOUTHAMPTON - 3RD FLOOR, DUKES KEEP, MARSH LANE, SOUTHAMPTON SO14 3EX — (FAX: 01703 635506)

STRATFORD - 44 THE BROADWAY, STRATFORD E15 1XH — (FAX: 0181 2210398)

INDUSTRIAL TRIBUNALS
ENGLAND and WALES

Received by Industrial Tribunals	FOR OFFICE USE
	Case Number
	Code
	Initials ___ ROIT

Application to an Industrial Tribunal

- This form has to be photocopied. If possible please use BLACK INK and CAPITAL letters.
- Where there are tick boxes, please tick the one that applies.

1 Please give the type of complaint you want the tribunal to decide (for example: unfair dismissal, equal pay). A full list is given in booklet ITL1. If you have more than one complaint list them all.

2 Please give your details.

Mr ☐ Mrs ☐ Miss ☐ Ms ☐

Surname

First names

Date of birth

Address

Postcode

Telephone

Daytime Telephone

Please give an address to which we should send documents if different from above

Postcode

3 If a representative is acting for you please give details.

Name

Address

Postcode

Telephone

Reference

4 Please give the dates of your employment.

From ___ To ___

5 Please give the name and address of the employer, other organisation or person against whom this complaint is being brought.

Name of employer, organisation or person

Address

Postcode

Telephone

Please give the place where you worked or applied to work, if different from above.

Address

Postcode

6 Please say what job you did for the employer (or what job you applied for). If this does not apply, please say what your connection was with the employer.

IT1 (E/W)

3

7 Please give the number of normal basic hours worked each week.

Hours per week

9 If your complaint is *not* about dismissal, please give the date when the action you are complaining about took place

8 Please give your earning details.

Basic wage/salary £ : p, per

Average take home pay £ : p, per

Other bonuses /benefits £ : p, per

10 Unfair dismissal applicants only.
Please indicate what you are seeking at this stage, if you win your case.

☐ **Reinstatement:** to carry on working in your old job as before. (An order for reinstatement normally includes an award of compensation for loss of earnings.)

☐ **Re-engagement:** to start another job or new contract with your old employer: (An order for re-engagement normally includes an award of compensation for loss of earnings.)

☐ **Compensation only:** to get an award of money

11 Please give details of your complaint.
If there is not enough space for your answer, please continue on a separate sheet and attach it to this form.

12 Please sign and date this form , then send it to the address given on page 2

Signed

Date

IT1 (E/W) 4

1.2   Acknowledgment of originating application sent to applicant (IT5)

THE INDUSTRIAL TRIBUNALS
19 - 29 Woburn Place, London, WC1H 0LU.

Telephone 0171 273
FAX 0171 273 8686

Case Number

Applicant   Respondent

v

ACKNOWLEDGEMENT OF APPLICATION

1. The application has been received at this office, which will now deal with the case. Please quote the case number shown above in all correspondence.

2. The application has been Registered and a copy has been sent to the Respondent, whose response, if any, will be copied to you.

3. At least 14 days notice will be given of the hearing of the case unless the parties agree to less.

4. If you do not already have a copy of the booklet "Industrial Tribunals Procedure" (ITL1 E&W) you should ensure you obtain one from an Employment Service Office.

To   Signed

                                                            for Regional Secretary of the Tribunals

                                                            Dated

Form IT5 E&W - 1/95

1.3 Notice of originating application sent to respondent (IT2)

THE INDUSTRIAL TRIBUNALS
19 - 29 Woburn Place, London, WC1H 0LU.

Telephone 0171 273
FAX 0171 273 8686

Case Number

Applicant   Respondent

v

NOTICE OF ORIGINATING APPLICATION

1. The Industrial Tribunal has registered a complaint made against you by   Please
quote the case number shown above in all future correspondence.

2. I enclose a copy of:

    (i) Originating Application to an Industrial Tribunal;

    (ii) Explanatory booklet ITL1 (E&W);

    (iii) A Notice of Appearance form (IT3).

3. Under the Rules of Procedure you are required to enter an appearance within 14 days of
receiving the application. This may be done by completing and returning the enlosed form IT3.

4. If you do not enter an appearance you will not be entitled to defend the proceedings. However
you will be sent a copy of the Tribunal's decision.

5. You can conduct your case yourself or appoint a representative to act for you. If you name a
representative all further communications will be sent to that representative and not to you. Help in
completing your Notice of Appearance may be available from your employers' association or other
professional adviser.

6. If you are disabled and need any special arrangement when visiting an Industrial Tribunal please
inform the staff at the office dealing with this case who will do all they can to help.

To   Signed

                                for Regional Secretary of the Tribunals

                                Dated

Form IT2 E&W - 1/95

1.4   Notice of appearance (IT3)

THE INDUSTRIAL TRIBUNALS
NOTICE OF APPEARANCE BY RESPONDENT

In the application of

Case Number
(please quote in all correspondence)

* This form has to be photocopied, if possible please use Black Ink and Capital letters
* If there is not enough space for your answer, please continue on a separate sheet and attach it to this form

1. Full name and address of the Respondent:	3. Do you intend to resist the application? (Tick appropriate box)
	YES ☐ NO ☐
	4. Was the applicant dismissed? (Tick appropriate box)
	YES ☐ NO ☐
	Please give reason below
	Reason for dismissal:
	5. Are the dates of employment given by the applicant correct? (Tick appropriate box)
Post Code:	YES ☐ NO ☐
Telephone number:	please give correct dates below
2. If you require documents and notices to be sent to a representative or any other address in the United Kingdom please give details:	Began on
	Ended on
	6. Are the details given by the applicant about wages/salary, take home or other bonuses correct? (Tick appropriate box)
	YES ☐ NO ☐
	Please give correct details below
	Basic Wages/Salary £ per
	Average Take Home Pay £ per
	Other Bonuses/Benefits £ per
	PLEASE TURN OVER
	for office use only
	Date of receipt Initials
Post Code:	
Reference:	
Telephone number:	

Form IT3 E&W - 1/95

7. Give particulars of the grounds on which you intend to resist the application.

8. Please sign and date the form.

Signed   Dated

DATA PROTECTION ACT 1984
We may put some of the information you give on this form on to a computer. This helps us to monitor progress and produce statistics. We may also give information to:
* the other party in the case
* other parts of the Employment Department Group and organisations such as ACAS (Advisory Conciliation and Arbitration Service), the Equal Opportunities Commission or the Commission for Racial Equality.

Please post or fax this form to : The Regional Secretary 44 Broadway, Stratford, London, E15 1XH.

* IF YOU FAX THE FORM, DO NOT POST A COPY AS WELL
* IF YOU POST THE FORM, TAKE A COPY FOR YOUR RECORDS

Form IT3 E&W - 1/95

1.5   Suggested dates for hearing (IT4D2)

3rd Floor, Dukes Keep, Marsh Lane, Southampton SO14 3EX

Telephone   01703 639555
Fax   01703 635506

Case Number

THE INDUSTRIAL TRIBUNALS

Applicant   Respondent

-v-

This case will be listed during

(IF YOU HAVE A REPRESENTATIVE, PASS THIS FORM TO THEM)

If I do not hear from you by   , a date for hearing will be fixed and you will be informed of the time and place. Once a date has been fixed, a postponement will be allowed <u>only in exceptional circumstances</u> and requests must be made in writing, stating the full grounds.

_____

for Regional Secretary to the Tribunals

Date _____

(PLEASE TICK RELEVANT BOX) Applicant   ☐   Respondent   ☐

Delete those dates on which you CANNOT attend

1	2	3	4	5	6	7	8	9	10	11	12
13	14	15	16	17	18	19	20	21	22	23	24
25	26	27	28	29	30	31					

1	2	3	4	5	6	7	8	9	10	11	12
13	14	15	16	17	18	19	20	21	22	23	24
25	26	27	28	29	30	31					

The case will be listed for one day unless there are circumstances which make you think that this case will take longer. if so, please indicate your estimate of the number of days required and give your reasons, so that appropriate arrangements can be made.

_____

_____

HOW MANY WITNESSES DO YOU EXPECT TO CALL ? _____
(Witnesses : see Booklet ITL1)

DATE _____ NAME IN BLOCK CAPITALS _____
Form IT4D2 11/94

1.6 Notice of hearing (IT4)

NOTICE OF AN INDUSTRIAL TRIBUNAL HEARING

Case Number: 12345/95/LN/C

Applicant:
Mr A Smith

Respondent(s):
Jones & Co Ltd

This application is to be heard at an industrial tribunal at:
Regional Office of the Industrial Tribunals, London (North)
19–29 Woburn Place
London WC1H 0LU

Direct line 0171 273 8597
Switchboard 0171 273 3000
Fax 0171 273 8686

on Tuesday 2 January 1996 at 10.00 am. The application will be called on for hearing at that time or as soon as a tribunal becomes available to take it. *Please attend by 10.00 am and allow 1 day for the hearing unless otherwise stated.*

Attendance
You may choose whether to attend or to put your case in writing instead. However, if the facts of your case are in dispute, the Tribunal may find it difficult to decide what is the truth without hearing witnesses from both sides. If you do decide to put your case in writing, you must send a copy to the Tribunal, and a copy to the other party, 7 days or more before the hearing.

You may present your own case, or ask somebody else to do it for you.

If you do not decide to come or to be represented at the hearing, please write to tell us immediately.

If an applicant (or someone else acting for the applicant) is due to attend a hearing but fails to appear, the Tribunal may dismiss the application in his/her absence; or similarly the Tribunal may make an order against a respondent in his/her absence; or order either party to pay costs on the ground that in bringing, resisting or conducting the proceedings he/she has acted frivolously, vexatiously or otherwise unreasonably.

Note to representatives
It is up to you to inform the person you represent of the date, time and place of the hearing. If you are a professional adviser, would you please prepare a bundle containing all the papers you intend to rely on at the hearing, arranged in the right order and numbered consecutively. If possible, there should be an agreed bundle.

To the Applicant (Ref)
Mr A Smith
[address]

Copies to:
Conciliation Officer, ACAS

To the Respondent (Ref)
Jones & Co Ltd
c/o Black White & Co, Solicitors
[address]

Signed. . . . .
for the Regional Secretary of the Tribunals

Date: 11 December 1995

Please see further notes on the reverse of this letter.

Papers

If you intend to refer to any papers in support of your case at the hearing, it would help if you would send a list to the other party and to me, well in advance of the hearing. The other party may then ask to see or have a copy of any such papers. Please try to co-operate with each other on this. It can help us all by avoiding delays at the hearing.

It is very important that both parties bring to the hearing any papers that may be needed. For example, a letter of appointment, contract of employment, working rule agreement, pay slips, income tax forms, wages book, details of benefits and contributions under any pension or superannuation scheme. It will help if you bring to the hearing:

  – your own set of papers;
  – one copy for the use of all witnesses (not a copy for each);
  – a copy for the other party (unless you have already sent them);
  – three copies for the members of the Tribunal.

Note to employers

On a complaint of unfair dismissal (or failing to permit a woman to return to work after pregnancy), the Tribunal may consider ordering reinstatement or re-engagement. You should, therefore, be prepared to give evidence as to:

  – the availability of the job which the applicant held or of similar jobs;
  – whether you would take the applicant back, either in old job, or in a similar one.

Note to Applicants and Respodents

If you are disabled, and are concerned about toilet arrangements or entry/exit facilities to the Tribunal, please contact the Tribunal Office at the address shown at the top of the front of this form.

Notes:

1.7 Notice of hearing: entitlement to bring or contest proceedings

Case Number: 11111/11/LN/A

Applicant:
Mr F G Applicant

Respondent(s):
Responders Ltd

DETERMINATION OF ISSUE RELATING TO THE ENTITLEMENT OF A PARTY TO BRING OR CONTEST PROCEEDINGS

The preliminary issue(s) in this case relate to the entitlement of a party to bring or contest the proceedings. The issue will be determined by a Chairman alone under rules 6 and 13(8) of the Industrial Tribunals Rules of Procedure 1993.

The hearing to determine the issue will take place at:
Regional Office of the Industrial Tribunals, London (North)
19–29 Woburn Place
London WC1H 0LU

Direct line 0171 273 8597
Switchboard 0171 273 3000
Fax 0171 273 8686

on 11 November 199_ at 09.45 am, or as soon thereafter as the Chairman can deal with it. Parties are entitled to submit representations in writing and to advance oral argument before the Chairman. **The Tribunal will give any pre-hearing directions at the above hearing.**

Attendance
You may present your own case, or ask somebody else to do it for you. If you do not decide to come or to be represented at the hearing, please write to tell me immediately.

Note to representatives
It is up to you to inform the person you represent of the date, time and place of the hearing. If you are a professional adviser, would you please prepare a bundle containing all the papers you intend to rely on at the hearing, arranged in the right order and numbered consecutively. If possible, there should be an agreed bundle.

To the Applicant (Ref)
F G Applicant
[address]

Copies to:

Conciliation Officer

To the Respondent (Ref)
Responders Ltd
c/o Black White & Co, Solicitors
[address]

IT4 (PH + CHA)

Signed. . . . .
for the Regional Secretary of the Tribunals

Date:
Please see further notes on the reverse of this letter. [not reproduced]

1.8   Notice of an industrial tribunal preliminary hearing

PRELIMINARY HEARING   Case Number: 11111/11/LN/A

Applicant: **Respondent:**
Mr F G Applicant   Responders Ltd

This application is to be heard at an industrial tribunal at:
  Regional Office of the Industrial Tribunals, London (North)
  19–29 Woburn Place
  London WC1H 0LU   Direct line 0171 273 8111
                                             Switchboard 0171 273 3000
                                                      Fax 0171 278 5068

on 11 November 199_ at 09.45 am. The application will be called on for hearing at that time or as soon as a tribunal becomes available to take it. Please attend by 10.00 am and allow 1 day for the hearing unless otherwise stated.

Attendance
You may choose whether to attend or to put your case in writing instead. However, if the facts of your case are in dispute, the Tribunal may find it difficult to decide what is the truth without hearing witnesses from both sides. If you do decide to put your case in writing, you must send a copy to the Tribunal, and a copy to the other party, 7 days or more before the hearing.

The Tribunal will give any pre-hearing directions at the above hearing.

You may present your own case, or ask somebody else to do it for you.

If you do not decide to come or to be represented at the hearing, please write to tell us immediately.

If an applicant (or someone else acting for the applicant) is due to attend a hearing but fails to appear, the Tribunal may dismiss the application in his/her absence; or similarly the Tribunal may make an order against a respondent in his/her absence; or order either party to pay costs on the ground that in bringing, resisting or conducting the proceedings he/she has acted frivolously, vexatiously or otherwise unreasonably.

Note to representatives
It is up to you to inform the person you represent of the date, time and place of the hearing. If you are a professional adviser, would you please prepare a bundle containing all the papers you intend to rely on at the hearing, arranged in the right order and numbered consecutively. If possible, there should be an agreed bundle.

To the Applicant (Ref)   Copies to:
F G Applicant
[address]   Conciliation Officer

To the Respondent (Ref)   Signed. . . . .
Responders Ltd   for the Regional Secretary of Tribunals
c/o Black White & Co, Solicitors
[address]   Date:
                                        Please see further notes on the reverse of
IT4 (1993)   *this letter.* [*not reproduced*]

1.9 Notice of pre-hearing review into applicant's contentions

Regional Office of the Industrial Tribunals, London (North)
19–29 Woburn Place
London WC1H 0LU

Direct line 0171 273 8111
Switchboard 0171 273 3000
Fax 0171 278 5068

Case No: 11111/11/LN/A

NOTICE OF PRE-HEARING REVIEW
in the case of

Applicant: **Respondent(s):**
Mr F G Applicant   Responders Ltd

Notice is hereby given that under rule 7 of the Industrial Tribunal Rules of Procedure 1993 a Tribunal will hold a pre-hearing review at **19–29 Woburn Place, London WC1R 0LU, on 11 November 199_ at 09.45 am.**

1 The parties are entitled to attend and be heard at this pre-hearing review and to submit representations in writing. A party may bring a representative if he/she so wishes. Attendance should be at the above time and place.

2 No oral evidence will be taken. The Tribunal will only consider the contents of the originating application and notice of appearance, any written representations and any oral argument on behalf of a party.

3 If the Tribunal considers that the originating application or any particular contention of the applicant appears to have no reasonable prospect of success, it may indicate that, in its opinion, if the application is not withdrawn or the contention is persisted in up to or at the hearing, the applicant may at the hearing be ordered to pay costs under the provisions of rule 12 of the above Rules of Procedure.

4 If at the pre-hearing review the Tribunal gives an indication of its opinion under rule 7, written notice to that effect will be sent to the parties.

5 **The tribunal will give any pre-hearing directions at the above hearing.**

Fax 0171 278 5068

To the Applicant (Ref)   Copies to:
F G Applicant
[address]   Conciliation Officer

To the Respondent (Ref)   Signed. . . . .
Responders Ltd   for the Regional Secretary of Tribunals
c/o Black White & Co, Solicitors
[address]   Date:

Please see further notes on the reverse of this letter. [not reproduced]

Note: Representatives who receive this notice must inform the party they represent of the date, time and place of hearing. The party will not be notified direct.

1.10   Notice of pre-hearing review into respondent's contentions

Regional Office of the Industrial Tribunals, London (North)
19–29 Woburn Place
London WC1H 0LU

Direct line 0171 273 8111
Switchboard 0171 273 3000
Fax 0171 278 5068

Case No: 11111/11/LN/A

NOTICE OF PRE-HEARING REVIEW
in the case of

Applicant:
Mr F G Applicant

Respondent(s):
Responders Ltd

Notice is hereby given that under rule 7 of the Industrial Tribunal Rules of Procedure 1993 a Tribunal will hold a pre-hearing review at **19-29 Woburn Place, London WC1R 0LU, on 11 November 199_ at 09.45 am.**

1 The parties (other than a respondent who has not entered an appearance) are entitled to attend and to be heard at this pre-hearing assessment and to submit respresentations in writing. A party may bring a representative if he/she so wishes. Attendance should be at the above time and place.

2 No oral evidence will be taken. The Tribunal will only consider the contents of the originating application and notice of appearance, any written representations and any oral argument by or on behalf of a party.

3 If the Tribunal considers that the contention(s) of the respondent that
   [statement of contentions]
   has/have no reasonable prospect of success it may indicate that in its opinion if the contenion(s) is/are persisted in up to or at the hearing of the originating application, the respondent may at the hearing be ordered to pay costs under the provisions of rule 12 of the above Rules of Procedure.

4 If at the pre-hearing review the Tribunal gives an indication of its opinion under rule 7, written notice to that effect will be sent to the parties.

5 **The tribunal will give any pre-hearing directions at the above hearing.**

Fax 0171 278 5068

To the Applicant (Ref)
F G Applicant
[address]

To the Respondent (Ref)
Responders Ltd
c/o Black White & Co, Solicitors
[address]

Copies to:

Conciliation Officer

Signed.......................
for the Regional Secretary of Tribunals

Date:

Please see further notes on the reverse of this letter. [not reproduced]

Note: Representatives who receive this notice must inform the party they represent of the date, time and place of hearing. The party will not be notified direct.

1.11 Respondent employer's claim in contract (IT1(c))

INDUSTRIAL TRIBUNALS	Received at Tribunals		Employers claim Reference number	
			ROIT	

Employer's Claim relating to application number [——] by [——]

*This form has to be photocopied. If possible, please use BLACK INK and CAPITAL letters
*Where there are tick boxes, please tick the one that applies

1. Please give details of the person or organisation making the employer's claim

Name of Organisation or person	
Address	
	Postcode
Telephone	

Please give an address to which document should be sent if different from above

	Postcode

2. If a representative is acting for you, please give details

Name	
Address	
	Postcode
Telephone	
Reference:	

3. Please give details of Employer's Claim. If there is not enough space for your answer please continue overleaf

1.12 Acknowledgment of employer's claim (IT5(c))

INDUSTRIAL TRIBUNALS	Employer's claim number (please quote in all correspondence)

ACKNOWLEDGEMENT OF EMPLOYER'S CLAIM

To Employer claimant	From:

Employer claimant   v   Respondent to Employer claim

*Your employer's claim relating to applications number   by
has been received at this office. It has been entered in the register and given the reference number
shown above.

*A copy of your claim form has been sent to the respondent to the employer's claim and any reply
will be copied to you.

*The original claim by the applicant and the employer's claim will be heard together. You will be
given at least 14 days' notice in writing of when the case to be heard by the tribunal.

*A copy of your employer's claim has been sent to the Advisory Conciliation and Arbitration Services
(ACAS). The services of a Conciliation Officer are available free to the parties. ACAS is a separate
organisation and is not part of the Industrial Tribunals.

* If you think it may be possible to settle this case through conciliation, you can contact ACAS
yourself and ask to speak to a Conciliation Officer. The address and telephone number of your
nearest office can be found in the ITL1 booklet.

Signed: . . . .
for Secretary of the Tribunals

Name in capitals: . . . .   Date: . . . .

IT5(c) Nov.1994

1.13   Notice of employer's claim in contract sent to applicant (IT2(c))

INDUSTRIAL TRIBUNALS	Case Number:

NOTICE OF EMPLOYER'S CLAIM

To Respondent to employer's claim	From:
	The Industrial Tribunals Ground Floor, The Crescent Centre Temple Back BRISTOL BS1 6EZ

Employer claimant   v   Respondent to Employer Claim

*I enclose a copy of an originating application in respect of an employer's claim naming you as the respondent

*Under the rules, if you wish to defend the claim you must enter an appearance, either by completing and returning the enclosed form IT3(c), or by sending a letter giving the same information.

*If you do not do either within 14 days, you will not be entitled to defend the claim (except to apply for an extension of time to enter an appearance). If you do not defend the claim, a decision may be given against you.

*The processing of this application will be regulated by the Rules of Procedure, which are explained in the booklet ITL1. If you do not already have a copy, I can supply one on request.

*Both the applicant and the respondent may appear and be heard in person or be represented by anyone they choose.

*A copy of the employer's claim form has been sent to the Advisory Conciliation and Arbitration Service (ACAS); both parties may contact ACAS if they wish.

Signed: . . . .
for Secretary of the Tribunals

Name in capitals: . . . .   Date: . . . .

IT2(c) Nov.94

1.14   Notice of appearance by applicant to employer's claim in contract (IT3(c))

INDUSTRIAL TRIBUNALS	Received at Tribunals		Employer's claim reference number	
			ROIT	

Notice of Appearance in response to an employer's claim number   by

*This form has to be photocopied, please use **BLACK INK** and **CAPITAL LETTERS**
*Where there are tick boxes, please tick the one that applies

1. Please give your details

Name:
Address:

                       Postcode

Telephone:
Please give an address to which documents should be sent if different from above

                       Postcode

2. If a representative is acting for you, please give details
Name:
Address:

                       Postcode

Telephone:

Reference:

3. If you intend to resist the Employer's Claim please give details below. If there is not enough space for your answer please continue overleaf

1.15   Notes on tribunal decisions (IT9)

REGIONAL OFFICE OF THE INDUSTRIAL TRIBUNALS

1.—Please read these notes carefully. There are time limits for seeking review of a decision or appealing against it; these limits are described in paragraphs 14 and 19 below.

2.—The decision of the Industrial Tribunal is set out in the attached document. These notes are for guidance only and are not a comprehensive statement of law. They are intended to assist persons concerned with the decision to understand how certain requirements of the decison should be carried out and what may be done if it is considered that the decision is wrong.

Reasons in full or summary form

3.—The reasons for the decision state whether they are in full or in summary form. If the reasons for your decision are given in summary form, you may request that the tribunal give extended written reasons. If you are going to appeal against the decision, you will need extended reasons (see paragraph 19 below). The request for extended reasons must be made in writing within 21 days of the date on which the decison was sent to you. This date can be found stamped on the decision document. Your request should be sent to the Regional Secretary at the Regional Office of the Industrial Tribunals.

Payment of awards

4.—A sum of money awarded by an Industrial Tribunal is payable without further notice by the party against whom the award is made direct to the party entitled to receive it except when benefits have been paid during a period of unemployment. In such cases the whole or part of these benefits may be recovered by the Department of Employment from the award before it is paid. In that event the appropriate notice is given in an annex attached to the tribunal's decision. The respondent may be obliged by law to make some deduction from gross wages or salary in respect of income tax and/or national insurance.

5.—Enforcement of awards by Industrial Tribunals is a matter for the County Court, under the provisions of the Employment Protection (Consolidation) Act 1978 Schedule 9 paragraph 7(1). If a sum of money awarded by an Industrial Tribunal is not paid when due, a request that enforcement action should be taken may be made by the person entitled to receive it to the nearest County Court. (The address of the County Court may be obtained from the public library, Citizens Advice Bureau or Legal Aid office). The Court staff will need to be shown (a) the decision of the tribunal and (b) any recoupment notice that may have been served by the Department of Employment in respect of unemployment or supplementary benefit or income support received. They will explain the methods of enforcement that are available. Extended written reasons for the decision are not necessary in relation to enforcement proceedings.

6.—A certified copy of the tribunal decision for production at the County Court may, if required, be obtained without charge upon application to the Regional Secretary at the Regional Office of Industrial Tribunals.

7.—If there is any difficulty in obtaining payment of an award in redundancy or maternity payment cases, or where the employer is insolvent, the advice of the Department of Employment should first be obtained.

8.—If a tribunal has made an order that a respondent should take certain actions, e.g. to reinstate or re-engage the applicant, and he fails to do so, the applicant should notify the Regional Secretary of the Tribunals.

Changing the decision

9.—The Industrial Tribunals are independent judicial bodies and their decisions may be changed only (a) if the tribunal decides, at the request of one of the parties before it, to review its own decision and to change it; or (b) upon the direction of a superior court or tribunal, normally following an appeal by one of the parties to whom the decision applies. The circumstances in which an application for a review, or an appeal, may be made are set out below.

10.—Except as described in paragraph 9 above, no person or body has any power to change the decision of an Industrial Tribunal or to set it aside and order a new hearing.

11.—Particular attention should be paid to the time limits referred to in these notes. It should not be assumed that any time limit will be extended, although in exceptional circumstances application may be made to the Industrial Tribunal, or Appeal Tribunal as the case may be, to consider an extension of time.

Review of tribunal's decision

12.—In certain limited circumstances the Industrial Tribunal may be asked to review and, if appropriate, change or revoke its own decision. The provisions relating to such a review are set out in Rule 11 of the Industrial Tribunals (Constitution and Rules of Procedure) Regulations 1993 (SI 1993 No 2687). These Regulations are obtainable from HM Stationery Office Bookshops or through booksellers.

13.—The grounds upon which a tribunal has power to review its decision are that:
   a) the decision was wrongly made as a result of an error on the part of the tribunal staff; or
   b) a party did not receive notice of the proceedings leading to the decision; or
   c) the decision was made in the absence of a party or person entitled to be heard; or
   d) new evidence has become available since the conclusion of the hearing to which the decision related provided that its existence could not have been reasonably known of or foreseen; or
   e) the interests of justice require such a review.

14.—If you wish to apply for a review you should do so in writing to the Regional Secretary of the Tribunals at the Regional Office before the end of the period of 14 days after the date on which the decision was sent to you. This date can be found stamped on the decision document. Your letter should set out the grounds for your application. In the case of an application under paragraph 13(d) a full statement of the evidence which it is sought to introduce should be supplied.

15.—A tribunal will not agree to review its decision merely because you disagree with it. There must be valid grounds for a review. A Chairman of Industrial Tribunals has power to refuse an application for a review if, in his opinion, it has no reasonable prospect of success.

Appeal against tribunal decision

16.—An appeal against a tribunal decision may (with one exception), only be made upon a point of law; that is to say, if it is considered that the tribunal has made a mistake in the application of the law relating to the issues before it. It has been held that a decision which is inconsistent with the evidence, or has been taken in the absence of evidence of matters upon which it is based, may be wrong in law. However (with the one exception mentioned below) the tribunal is the sole judge of the facts and no issue of law arises if the tribunal simply misunderstood or misapplied the facts.

17.—The exception referred to relates to cases in which the issue before the Industrial Tribunal is that of exclusion or expulsion from a trade union and arises under Section 4 of the Employment Act 1980. In such cases an appeal may be made on an issue of fact or law.

18.—Notice of appeal should be in, or substantially in accordance with, the official appeal form. Appeal forms may be obtained from the Registrar, the Employment Appeal Tribunal, Audit House, 58 Victoria Embankment, London EC4Y 0DS, to whom any questions relating to the time for appeal (see paragraph 19 below) should be addressed.

19.—The notice of appeal should be accompanied by a copy of the Industrial Tribunal decision and a copy of the extended written reasons for it. If you have received a decision giving only summary reasons you should request extended reasons (see paragraph 3 of this Note). The notice of appeal must be served on the Employment Appeal Tribunal within 42 days of the date on which the extended written reasons for the decision which is the subject of the appeal, were sent to you. This date is shown on the last page of the document containing the extended written reasons. An application for review (see paragraphs 12–15 above) does not alter the time for the notice of appeal which continues to run. Action to appeal may be taken while awaiting the result of an application for review.

20.—When an appeal has been made, the Employment Appeal Tribunal may wish to examine documents or other exhibits produced in evidence before the Industrial Tribunal. Such exhibits will normally have been returned to the parties at the close of the Industrial Tribunal hearing or subsequently. They should be retained by the parties for production, if required, at any appeal.

Legal advice and legal aid

21.—Preliminary legal advice about review and appeals may be obtained, under the [Legal Aid Act 1988], from any solicitor who has joined the Legal Advice and Assistance Scheme. Lists of such solicitors are held by Citizens Advice Bureaux.

22.—Such advice may be given without charge if the person applying for it qualifies for assistance. Whether such assistance can be given will depend upon financial circumstances; the solicitor concerned will advise about whether assistance can be given.

23.—More extensive legal services, including legal representation before the Employment Appeal Tribunal, may be available. These may be given under the [Civil
Legal Aid (General) Regulations 1989] (as amended) without charge or at a
reduced charge. Whether such assistance can be given will also depend upon
financial circumstances. Information about how to apply for assistance under
this scheme may be obtained from the addresses given in the attached list
entitled "Legal Aid".

NOTE: The Review procedure described in para 12 of these notes is not applicable
to a Decision of the tribunal upon an appeal under an Industrial Training Levy
order.

1.16 Questionnaire: sex and race discrimination

THE SEX DISCRIMINATION ACT 1975 SECTION 74(1)(a)

QUESTIONNAIRE OF PERSON AGGRIEVED (THE COMPLAINANT)

Name of person to be questioned (the respondent)	To ....
Address	of ....
	....
Name of complainant	1. I ....
Address	of ....
	....
	consider that you may have discriminated against me contrary to the Sex Discrimination Act 1975.
Give date, approximate time, place and factual description of the treatment received and of the circumstances leading up to the treatment (see paragraph 9 of the guidance)	2. On
Complete if you wish to give reasons, otherwise delete the word "because" (see paragraphs 10 and 11 of the guidance)	3. I consider that this treatment may have been unlawful because

SD 74(a)

Note: a questionnaire in similar form applies for race discrimination.

This is the first of
your questions to the
respondent. You are
advised not to alter it

4. Do you agree that the statement in paragraph 2 is an accurate description of
what happened? If not in what respect do you disagree or what is your version of
what happened?

This is the second of
your questions to the
respondent. You are
advised not to alter it

5. Do you accept that your treatment of me was unlawful discrimination by you against
me?
If not

    a   why not?

    b   for what reason did I receive the treatment accorded to me?

    c   how far did my sex or marital status affect your treatment of me?

Enter here any other
questions you wish to
ask (see paragraphs
12—14 of the guidance)

6.

*Delete as appropriate
If you delete the first
alternative, insert the
address to which you
want the reply to be
sent

7. My address for any reply you may wish to give to the questions raised above is
*that set out in paragraph 1 above/the following address

See paragraph 15
of the guidance

Signature of complainant...

Date...

NB *By virtue of section 74 of the Act, this questionnaire and any reply are (subject to the provisions of the section)
admissible in proceedings under the Act and a court or tribunal may draw any such inference as is just and
equitable from a failure without reasonable excuse to reply within a reasonable period, or from an evasive or
equivocal reply, including an inference that the person questioned has discriminated unlawfully.*

THE SEX DISCRIMINATION ACT 1975 SECTION 74(1)(b)

REPLY BY RESPONDENT

Name of complainant	To ....
Address	of ....
	....
Name of respondent	1. I ....
Address	of ....
	....
Complete as appropriate	hereby acknowledge receipt of the questionnaire signed by you and dated
	....which was served on me on (date)..
*Delete as appropriate	2. I *agree/disagree that the statement in paragraph 2 of the questionnaire is an accurate description of what happened.
If you agree that the statement in paragraph 2 of the questionnaire is accurate, delete this sentence. If you disagree complete this sentence (see paragraphs 21 and 22 of the guidance)	I disagree with the statement in paragraph 2 of the questionnaire in that
*Delete as appropriate	3. I *accept/dispute that my treatment of you was unlawful discrimination by me against you.
If you accept the complainant's assertion of unlawful discrimination in paragraph 3 of the questionnaire delete the sentences at a, b, and c. Unless completed a sentence should be deleted (see paragraphs 23 and 24 of the guidance)	a My reasons for so disputing are

SD 74(b)

b   The reason why you received the treatment accorded to you is

c   Your sex or marital status affected my treatment of you to the following extent:—

Replies to questions in paragraph 6 of the questionnaire should be entered here

4.

*Delete the whole of this sentence if you have answered all the questions in the questionnaire. If you have not answered all the questions, delete "unable" or "unwilling" as appropriate and give your reasons for not answering.

5.   I have deleted (in whole or in part) the paragraph(s) numbered...
above, since I am **unable/unwilling** to reply to the relevant questions of the
questionnaire for the following reasons:—

See paragraph 25 of the guidance

Signature of respondent...

Date..

THE SEX DISCRIMINATION ACT 1975 SECTION 74(1)(b)

REPLY BY RESPONDENT

Name of complainant	To ....
Address	of ....
	....
Name of respondent	1. I ....
Address	of ....
	....

Complete as appropriate

hereby acknowledge receipt of the questionnaire signed by you and dated

....which was served on me on (date)...

*Delete as appropriate

2. I *agree/disagree that the statement in paragraph 2 of the questionnaire is an accurate description of what happened.

If you agree that the statement in paragraph 2 of the questionnaire is accurate, delete this sentence. If you disagree complete this sentence (see paragraphs 21 and 22 of the guidance)

I disagree with the statement in paragraph 2 of the questionnaire in that

*Delete as appropriate

3. I *accept/dispute that my treatment of you was unlawful discrimination by me against you.

If you accept the complainant's assertion of unlawful discrimination in paragraph 3 of the questionnaire delete the sentences at a, b, and c. Unless completed a sentence should be deleted (see paragraphs 23 and 24 of the guidance)

a My reasons for so disputing are

SD 74(b)

b   The reason why you received the treatment accorded to you is

c   Your sex or marital status affected my treatment of you to the following extent:—

Replies to questions in
paragraph 6 of the
questionnaire should be
entered here

4.

Delete the whole of
this sentence if you
have answered all the
questions in the
questionnaire. If you
have not answered all
the questions, delete
"unable" or "unwilling"
as appropriate and
give your reasons for
not answering.

5.   I have deleted (in whole or in part) the paragraph(s) numbered...
above, since I am **unable/unwilling** to reply to the relevant questions of the
questionnaire for the following reasons:—

See paragraph 25 of
the guidance

Signature of respondent..

Date..

Precedents

A. ORIGINATING APPLICATIONS

Marginal references are to the boxes or para nos in forms IT1 (p234), IT3 (p242) and IT5(c) (p252) (see Appendix 1).

Case I: Written particulars: *Originating application*

1.—Determination under s11 Employment Rights Act 1996, as to the particulars of the applicant's terms and conditions of employment.

11.—(1) The applicant has been employed by the respondent for more than two months (having commenced her employment on [date]). She has yet to receive a written statement of her employment particulars.

(2) The applicant therefore seeks a determination by the tribunal as to the particulars of her employment as required by s1 Employment Rights Act 1996.

Case II: Action short of dismissal: *Originating application*

1.—Action short of dismissal.

11.—(1) The applicant is a member and Branch Officer of the [title]: an independent trade union, and is an employee of the respondent.

(2) On [relevant date/s], as the union Branch Officer, the applicant successfully represented a number of union members in pay negotiations with her employer. Management had agreed that the applicant should be able to represent her members during the negotiations.

(3) After the conclusion of the pay negotiations, the applicant found that she was no longer offered overtime opportunities, although these were available to other employees of the same grade as her. On [date] it was indicated to the applicant by [identify informant] that this was due to her stance during the pay negotiations.

(4) The applicant therefore believes that the respondent has taken action against her as an individual for the purpose of deterring her from, or penalising her for, participating in the activities of an independent trade union at an appropriate time. The applicant seeks a declaration to this effect and compensation.

Case III: Unfair dismissal (capability/competence): *Originating application*

1.—Unfair dismissal.

11.—(1) The applicant was employed by the respondent as a [position] from [date] to [date]. The respondent is a company which carries out the business of [identify] and employs some [state number] people.

  (2) On [date] the applicant was promoted against her wishes to a senior position. She was given no training in her new duties.

  (3) On [date] the applicant was told by [identify by name and position] that the respondent was not satisfied with her performance. She asked for training in her new duties and for more time. She also said that she would be happy to return to her old position. None of these suggestions was agreed. On [date] the applicant was told that she was dismissed and was not required to work out her contractual notice period of one month.

  (4) There were no further discussions with the applicant and she was not given the opportunity to appeal against the decision to dismiss her. In the circumstances the applicant believes that she was unfairly dismissed and claims compensation.

Unfair dismissal (capability/competence): *Notice of appearance* alleging insufficient continuity, alternatively contending dismissal was fair

7.—(1) It is admitted that the applicant commenced employment with the respondent on [date] as a [position]. It is further admitted that the respondent carries on business as [identify] and is a small company employing only [number] staff. It is denied that the applicant's employment terminated on [date]. The applicant was dismissed with immediate effect on [date] and was paid one week's wages in lieu of notice. In the circumstances the applicant did not have two years' continuous service with the respondent as at the date of her dismissal and she has no right to bring this complaint to the industrial tribunal.

  (2) Without prejudice to the respondent's primary case, the respondent contends that the dismissal of the applicant was by reason of her poor performance and was in all the circumstances (including the size and administrative resources of the respondent) fair.

  (3) It is denied that the applicant was promoted to a new position: she was merely asked to take up the responsibilities for which she had originally been appointed after an extended probationary period. During that probationary period, the applicant had received training whilst she worked with her predecessor in post. She was offered further training opportunities in the form of external courses on [dates] but refused to attend.

  (4) It is admitted that on [date] that the respondent told the applicant that it was not satisfied with her performance. She was given a final warning as to her poor performance by [identify] but this was the last in series of warnings given to the applicant both orally and in writing on [dates].

  (5) It is further denied that the applicant asked for further training. It is accepted that she asked to go back to her previous duties but this was not possible as these did not represent all the duties for the post to which she had been appointed. The respondent simply could not afford to continue to employ someone in the position of [applicant's position] who did not

carry out all the duties of that post. Ultimately the respondent felt it had no choice but to dismiss the applicant. The decision to dismiss the applicant was taken by [identify] who occupies the most senior post in the company. The applicant had no contractual right of appeal and in the circumstances there was no-one senior to whom she could have appealed.

Case IV: Unfair dismissal (capability/ill-health): *Originating application*

1.—Unfair dismissal.

11.—(1) The applicant was employed as a secretary by the respondent, a large company which carries on business as [identify] and employs some [state number] people. She was so employed for [number] years, from [date] to [date].

(2) On [date], the applicant began to suffer pains in her wrists and on [date] she went sick due to repetitive strain injury ('RSI') caused by her work. She was off work for six months, during which time she produced regular certificates from her GP. The applicant also underwent operative treatment for her injury and (at her own expense) undertook a re-training course to enable her to resume keyboard work without injury in the future.

(3) On [date] the applicant wrote to the respondent indicating that she would soon be ready to return to work. She received a letter in reply [date] stating that the respondent did not feel able to keep her job open any longer and that she was dismissed with immediate effect.

(4) The applicant appealed against this decision and her appeal was heard on [date]. The manager [identify] who took the decision to dismiss her also sat on the appeal panel, despite the applicant's objection. The applicant pointed out that she could return to work but [the manager] did not believe her, although he made no contact with her GP. The decision to dismiss her was upheld.

(5) In the circumstances the applicant considers her dismissal was unfair and seeks an order for re-instatement or re-engagement as well as compensation.

Unfair dismissal (capability/ill-health): *Notice of appearance* alleging application not presented in time, alternatively contending dismissal was fair

7.—(1) Paragraph 1 of the originating application is admitted save that the applicant's employment was terminated on [date], not [date], which was the date of the subsequent appeal. In the circumstances it is the respondent's contention that the applicant's claim was presented more than three months after the effective date of termination and that the tribunal has no jurisdiction to hear this complaint.

(2) Without prejudice to the above, the respondent contends that in any event the dismissal of the applicant was by reason of her incapability due to ill-health and was fair in all the circumstances.

(3) For the purpose of these tribunal proceedings only, it is admitted that the applicant was off work suffering from RSI from [date]. During that time she was examined by the respondent's doctor who confirmed that she was unfit for work. The applicant was also visited on a number of occasions

[dates] by the respondent's personnel officer [identify] who suggested various alternative employment positions within the company but these were all rejected by the applicant. By [date] the respondent was experiencing extreme difficulties as a result of the applicant's absence. A further examination was undertaken by the respondent's doctor who stated his opinion that the applicant should still not return to work, notwithstanding the operative treatment and retraining she had undertaken. The respondent therefore felt it had no choice but to dismiss the applicant and notified her of its decision by letter of [date], her employment terminating on [date].

(4) The applicant appealed against this decision and her appeal was held on [date]. She was represented by her trade union officer. It is not true that the manager who took the original decision was on the appeal panel – he was present only as a witness. The appeal was a complete re-hearing of all the issues but ultimately the applicant was unsuccessful and the decision to dismiss was upheld.

Case V: Unfair dismissal (misconduct)/breach of contract/unlawful deduction of wages: *Originating application*

1.—(1) Unfair dismissal and/or (2) Breach of contract: damages in lieu of notice and/or (3) Unlawful deduction of wages.

11.—(1) The applicant was employed as a [position] by the respondent which operates in the [identify] business and is a large employer with some [state number] staff. She commenced her employment on [date] and was so employed until [date] on the following terms and conditions:

a) She would receive £[amount] per week basic pay (as provided at para [ ] of her letter of appointment of [date]).

b) She would be given a company car for private as well as business use; at the time of her dismissal the applicant enjoyed the use of a [identify] car.

c) She would be entitled to receive notice of the termination of her employment. There being no express provision for the period of that notice; the applicant was entitled to receive reasonable notice which she contends [in all the circumstances/by reason of custom and practice/by reference to the statutory minimum] to have been [period].

(2) On [date] the applicant was informed by [identify by name and position] that she was to be suspended from her employment without pay whilst an investigation into her conduct was carried out. She was given no details of any allegations against her.

(3) On [date], the applicant was called back into work with no prior notice and attended a meeting with [identify by name and position]. She was not allowed to be represented nor was she given any further details of the allegations against her nor the opportunity to put her case. She was told that she was to be dismissed with immediate effect. The applicant sought to appeal against her dismissal and on [date], [identify person] of the respondent wrote to her stating that the decision had been reviewed but would be upheld and the appeal was therefore dismissed.

(4) In the circumstances, the applicant believes that she was unfairly dismissed.

(5) The applicant further contends that the respondent made unlawful deductions from her wages during the period of her unpaid suspension, such deduction amounting to £[amount].

(6) The applicant also complains of the respondent's breach of contract in failing to give her the [period] notice to which she was entitled, by reason of which she claims damages in lieu of notice.

Particulars of Damages Claimed

Pay in lieu of notice (£[ ] per week × [period])	£[amount]
Loss of use of car (valued according to AA Schedule at £[amount] per week × [period])	£[amount]
Total	£[amount]

Unfair dismissal (misconduct)/Breach of contract/Unlawful deduction of wages: *Notice of appearance and employer's contract claim*

7.—(1) Save that the respondent contends that a reasonable period of notice in the applicant's case would amount to [period] and save that her employment was also subject to the terms set out below, paragraph (1) of the originating application is admitted.

(2) The applicant's employment was also subject to the following terms and conditions:

a) That should she be suspended by reason of misconduct relating to dishonesty, that period of suspension would be without pay (as accepted by the applicant in writing as an addendum to the letter of appointment).

b) That should she be found to have committed an act of gross misconduct, the respondent would be entitled to terminate her employment summarily and without any payment in lieu of notice (a term implied into the applicant's contract of employment).

c) That on the termination of her employment with the respondent, the applicant would return any of the respondent's property forthwith, including the [make] motor car.

(3) On [date], evidence came to the respondent's attention that the applicant had [general account of allegation, eg, falsified her expenses claims in the sum of [amount]]. This allegation was put to the applicant orally by [identify] on [date]. In the absence of any satisfactory response, the applicant was suspended without pay, in accordance with the terms of her contract, whilst an investigation was carried out.

(4) At the end of the investigation, the applicant was invited to a disciplinary hearing on [date], chaired by [identify]. The applicant was asked if she would prefer the hearing to be on a later date but she stated that she wanted it held as soon as possible. She attended the hearing with a solicitor but was told that this was not appropriate nor allowed under the disciplinary procedure, which specifies representation by a work colleague. The respondent offered to adjourn the hearing while she found alternative representation but she refused this offer. The allegations and the outcome

of the investigation were put to the applicant but she was unable to give any satisfactory response. In the circumstances, the decision to dismiss her by reason of gross misconduct was taken by [identify].

(5) The applicant appealed against this decision under the disciplinary procedure and [identify] carried out a full review of the decision. As there was no new evidence, or explanation submitted by the applicant, it was felt that a further hearing was not necessary and the decision to dismiss was upheld.

(6) In all the circumstances of the case, the respondent believes that the dismissal of the applicant by reason of her misconduct was fair.

(7) The respondent further contends that there has been no unlawful deduction of wages as the period of unpaid suspension was pursuant to a relevant provision of the applicant's contract and/or was previously consented to by the applicant.

(8) As the respondent was entitled summarily to terminate the applicant's employment for gross misconduct, it is further denied that there has been any breach of contract by reason of the failure to give the applicant notice of dismissal.

(9) In the alternative, if the respondent is found to be liable to the applicant for any breach of contract, the respondent counterclaims as follows.

Particulars of Employer's Contract Claim

a) Since the date of her dismissal, the applicant has retained in her possession the [make] motor car belonging to the respondednt and has refused to return this to the respondent.

b) By reason of this breach of contract by the applicant, the respondent has suffered loss in the sum of £[amount].

Breach of contract and employer's contract claim: *Applicant's notice of appearance to employer's claim*

3.—(1) The applicant denies, if the same is alleged by the respondent, that her employment was subject to any express or implied term that she was under an obligation to take the respondent's vehicle back to its premises.

(2) In fact, as soon as the respondent told the applicant that she had been summarily dismissed and would receive no further wages and had no further entitlement to use of the car, the applicant returned the car keys to the respondent and has made it clear that the car could be collected from her home at any time. The respondent has chosen not to collect the vehicle which remains at the applicant's premises. The applicant has not had use of the car since her dismissal.

(3) In the circumstances, it is denied that the respondent has suffered any loss by reason of the applicant's conduct as claimed or at all.

Case VI: Unfair dismissal/redundancy payment: *Originating application*

1.—(1) Unfair dismissal and/or (2) Redundancy payment.

11.—(1) The applicant was employed as a [position] by the respondent, a large company in the business of [identify] which employs some [number] people. The applicant was so employed from [date] to [date].

(2) On [date] the respondent announced a redundancy programme which would lead to some [number] dismissals. The applicant was given no details as to the type or grade of employee likely to face redundancy nor as to the way in which the selection process was to take place. No further information was provided until [date] when the applicant received a letter from [identify] giving her notice that she was going to be dismissed by reason of redundancy.

(3) The applicant's employment was terminated on [date], with no further consultation and without any opportunity to appeal against the decision. Further, the respondent has refused to pay the applicant a redundancy payment.

(4) The applicant therefore claims a statutory redundancy payment. Further and/or in the alternative, the applicant believes she was unfairly dismissed.

Unfair dismissal/redundancy payment: *Notice of appearance* denying applicant was an employee/contending dismissal was fair

7.—(1) The respondent carries on business as [identify], and employs a small number of staff with few administrative resources.

(2) In meeting the requirements of its business the respondent engages a number of freelance workers on contracts for services. The applicant was so engaged by the respondent to work on a number of projects from [date] to [date]. The applicant was never an employee of the respondent but remained self-employed and carried on a business on her own account: she had no staff contract and was free to take on work from other companies, including competitors of the respondent. Further, she carried out her work for the respondent in her own time, from her own premises and using her own equipment. She was self-employed for tax purposes. In the circumstances, the applicant has no entitlement to complain of unfair dismissal and/or to claim a statutory redundancy payment.

(3) Without prejudice to the above, the respondent in any event contends that, in all the circumstances (including its size and administrative resources), the dismissal of the applicant was fair.

(4) On [date], the respondent received notification that it had lost a number of contracts, including that upon which the applicant had worked. It therefore notified all those freelance workers affected that once their current work was finished, the respondent would not be able to offer them any more work. As soon as it became apparent that the applicant was working on the last project available for her, on [date] the respondent wrote notifying her that the relationship between them would come to an end on [date].

(5) In the circumstances, there was no process of selection as only those working on the particular projects which came to an end were affected. Furthermore, those concerned were kept fully informed at all times as to the situation facing the respondent and were aware of the absence of any alternative work available. The applicant never made any complaint about the situation prior to her application to this tribunal nor did she ask to be afforded an opportunity to appeal against the decision.

Case VII: Redundancy payment: *Originating application*

1.—Redundancy payment.

11.—(1) The applicant was continuously employed by the respondent from [date] to [date]. At the time of her dismissal she was aged [age] years.

(2) On [date], the applicant was dismissed by the respondent by reason of redundancy and a payment was made to her of £[amount] which purported to satisfy the applicant's entitlement to a statutory redundancy payment.

(3) In fact, by reason of her [number] years service, the applicant was entitled to a statutory redundancy payment of £[amount].

(4) The applicant seeks a determination as to her right to receive a statutory redundancy payment and as to the amount of the payment to which she is entitled.

Redundancy payment: *Notice of appearance* **admitting entitlement but denying amount**

7.—(1) The respondent accepts its obligation to pay the applicant a redundancy payment pursuant to statute on the termination of her employment on [date] by reason of redundancy.

(2) The respondent, however, contends that it has satisfied its obligation so to do by paying the applicant the sum of £[amount], calculated on the following basis:
[set out calculation]

(3) The respondent contends that the applicant's period of continuous employment commenced only on [date]. Whilst it is accepted that the applicant previously worked for the respondent from [date], that employment ended on [date] and there was therefore a break in continuity from [date] to [date].

Case VIII: Constructive unfair dismissal: *Originating application*

1.—Constructive unfair dismissal.

11.—(1) The applicant was employed by the respondent as a [position] from [date] to [date]. During her employment she worked four days per week on a weekly shift rota.

(2) On [date], the respondent announced a change to the terms and conditions of all employees in the applicant's position. With effect from [date] it was stated that they would have to work a five-day shift rota.

(3) The applicant complained about this change and sought to invoke the grievance procedure. The respondent, however, refused to discuss the matter further or to consider making an exception in the applicant's case.

(4) The applicant considered that the proposals amounted to an anticipatory breach of the express terms of her contract of employment and/or that the respondent's behaviour amounted to a breach of the implied term to maintain trust and confidence. She considered that she could therefore no longer remain in the respondent's employment and accordingly left on [date], confirming her reasons for so doing by letter of [date].

(5) In the circumstances, the applicant considers that she has been constructively unfairly dismissed.

Constructive unfair dismissal: *Notice of appearance* denying dismissal/alleging dismissal fair, for some other substantial reason in alternative

7.—(1) Paragraph 1 of the originating application is admitted. The applicant's written terms and conditions of employment confirmed, however, that whilst she would initially be working a four-day rota, the times and shift patterns of her employment could be changed by the respondent at any time.

(2) It is also admitted that on [date] the respondent announced that it would be changing its shift system to a five-day rota. The respondent explained at the time that this was due to changes in technology which meant that it had to adjust its working practices if it was to make full use of the equipment it had introduced and thereby remain competitive.

(3) The respondent conducted a number of meetings with the employees affected and listened to the concerns raised. It revised some of its plans in the light of those concerns, which included extending the date for implementation of the new rota to give employees more time to adjust to the arrangements. By [date] all employees concerned had agreed to work the new arrangement but for the applicant. The respondent did not feel it could treat the applicant differently to all other staff and confirmed that she too would be subject to the new rota. It is accepted that the applicant resigned from the respondent's employment on [date], stating by letter of [date] that she considered herself to have been constructively dismissed.

(4) The respondent denies that it acted in breach of contract. It was entitled to alter the applicant's shift and rota arrangements and sought to do so in a reasonable manner, giving the applicant plenty of warning of the new arrangements and spending some time consulting with all employees so affected. In the circumstances, it is also denied that the respondent's conduct amounted to a breach of its implied obligation to maintain trust and confidence.

(5) If, contrary to the respondent's case, the applicant is found to have been dismissed, the respondent contends in the alternative that the dismissal was for some other substantial reason, namely a business re-organisation necessitating a change to the rota, and was fair in all the circumstances, including its size and administrative resources.

Case IX: Unfair dismissal (transfer of undertaking): *Originating application*

1.—Unfair dismissal.

11.—(1) The applicant was employed as a [position] from [date] to [date] by [identify transferor] which carried on the business of [identify]. The applicant was employed in that part of the undertaking which supplied [identify service] at/to [identify premises].

(2) On [date], it was announced that the [transferor] had lost the contract to supply services at [premises] and notices of redundancy were issued to the applicant and the other staff employed in that part of the undertaking.

(3) On [date] the applicant learned that the respondent had taken over the contract to supply services at [premises] and had started to do so after a gap of only [period]. The respondent re-employed some 75% of the staff who had previously worked for [transferor] at [premises] including [managerial staff if relevant].

(4) In the circumstances, the applicant believes that there was a relevant transfer to the respondent of that part of the [transferor's] undertaking which involved the supply of [service] to [premises] and in which the applicant had previously been employed. Further the applicant believes that her dismissal was by reason of the transfer and was accordingly unfair.

Unfair dismissal (transfer of undertaking): *Notice of appearance* denying transfer/denying dismissal by reason of transfer/alleging economic technical or organisational reason

7.—(1) The respondent makes no admissions as to the applicant's employment by [transferor].

(2) It is denied that there was a relevant transfer of an undertaking or part thereof from [transferor] to the respondent.

(3) If, contrary to the above, there is found to have been a relevant transfer, it is denied that the applicant was dismissed by reason of that transfer. The respondent understands that the applicant was dismissed on the ending of the [transferor's] contract to provide [service] at [premises]. At that stage, no tenders had been invited for a future contract nor was it necessarily envisaged that tendering would take place. The respondent therefore denies that the applicant was dismissed by reason of the transfer.

(4) In the further alternative, if the applicant is found to have been dismissed by reason of a relevant transfer, the respondent contends that the same was due to an economic, technical or organisational reason and was, in all the circumstances, fair.

(5) On taking the provision of [service] at [premises] the respondent deployed its existing organisational structure which included a greater use of [equipment/machines] than had previously been operated by [transferor]. The respondent therefore had no need to employ staff as [applicant's position] for economic, technical and organisational reasons. Further, the respondent is a small company employing only [number] people and has few administrative resources. In the circumstances in which it took over a contract after the applicant's dismissal, the respondent believes that its actions fall within the range of responses of a reasonable employer and that the dismissal was fair.

Case X: Sex discrimination (direct: sexual harassment/victimisation): *Originating application*

1.—Sex discrimination: (1) direct sex discrimination contrary to s1 SDA 1975 and (2) victimisation contrary to s4 SDA 1975.

11.—(1) The applicant was employed by the respondent as a [position] from [date] and remains so employed at the date of this application.

(2) On or about [date] a new employee [identify] was appointed to the applicant's department as [position].

(3) From [date] he began to harass the applicant, subjecting her to unwanted humiliating and distressing comments and assaults of a sexual nature. In particular:

[give details of incidents complained of: particularising all allegations relied on, specifying dates and times so far as possible and indicating the sense of injury to feelings suffered by the applicant on each occasion]

(4) On [date] the applicant complained to her line manager [identify] about these matters, giving details of the incidents set out above, but was told that she would have to learn how to deal with these things herself and that nothing would be done by the respondent.

(5) On [date], the applicant was told to start working in another department, where she has less opportunity to earn commission and bonus. When she asked why this decision had been made, she was told that she clearly could not get on with the people in her old department.

(6) In the circumstances the applicant claims that she has been the subject of unlawful sex discrimination and further that she was victimised when she sought to raise a complaint of discrimination. The applicant seeks:

a) a declaration;

b) compensation and interest thereon;

c) a recommendation that she be re-engaged in her former department.

Sex discrimination (direct: sexual harassment/victimisation): *Notice of appearance* denying vicarious liability/arguing took all reasonably practicable steps to avoid/disputing facts/contending applicant motivated by bad faith

7.—(1) It is admitted that the applicant was employed by the respondent as a [position] from [date], and was initially so employed in [identify] department. It is further admitted that on or about [date], a new employee, [identify] commenced working in the same department as [position].

(2) The respondent accepts that there was a personality clash between the [new employee] and the applicant and that both made complaints to their line manager [identify] on or about [dates]. It is denied that the applicant made allegations of unlawful sex descrimination on this occasion.

(3) The respondent does not believe the allegations made in the originating application to be true but contends in any event that it took such steps as were reasonably practicable to prevent [identify new employee] acting in the manner described during the course of his employment. In particular, the respondent will rely on the fact that it operates a policy against sexual harassment in the workplace and ensures that all new employees undergo equal opportunities training (including familiarisation with the policy on harassment) before commencing their jobs. This training was undertaken by [new employee] on [date/s].

(4) Further or alternatively, the respondent contends that the behaviour complained of could not in any event be said to have been carried out in the course of [new employee's] employment and therefore denies vicarious liability for the same.

(5) In respect of the allegations against [new employee] made by the applicant on [date], the respondent investigated them on [date/s] and came to the conclusion that they were untrue and had been made by the applicant in bad faith. On the other hand, the investigation into the allegations made by [new employee] suggested that his allegations were true. In the circumstances the respondent did not feel matters were sufficiently serious to

subject the applicant to disciplinary proceedings but decided it was best for her to carry out her work in a different department. This was accordingly done on [date]. It is denied that this necessarily entails a reduced opportunity for the applicant to earn commission and bonus.

(6) If, which is denied, the respondent's decision to move the applicant is found to have been in response to a complaint about matters which could amount to unlawful discrimination, the respondent contends that the applicant made complaints which were false and which were not made in good faith and that, in the circumstances, she is not entitled to complain of victimisation.

Case XI: Race discrimination (indirect): *Originating application*

1.—Indirect race discrimination.

11.—(1) The applicant is of [race] origin and is a qualified [occupation]. The applicant's qualifications were obtained from [institution, country].

(2) On [date], the respondent, which carries on business as [identify], advertised for additional [positions]. The applicant answered the advertisement and applied for a position as [identify] by letter of [date].

(3) The respondent replied to the applicant's letter on [date], informing her that she had not been appointed as she did not have the additional qualification as a [qualification].

(4) The applicant could not comply with the requirement or condition that she have this additional qualification and thereby suffered a detriment.

(5) The qualification identified is only available from [institution, country]. The proportion of [identify pool, ie, by reference to occupation] of [applicant's racial origin] who can comply with this requirement or condition is considerably smaller than the number of [identify pool for comparison by reference to occupation and race] who can comply with it.

(6) The applicant therefore seeks:
   a) a declaration;
   b) compensation and interest thereon;
   c) a recommendation that the respondent take action to remove the said requirement or condition.

Race discrimination (indirect): *Notice of appearance* disputing proportionality and putting forward defence of justification

7.—(1) The respondent does not know of, but accepts, the applicant's racial origin but can confirm that she applied for an advertised position as a [post] with the respondent on [date]. The respondent also accepts that the applicant was notified that she was unsuccessful on [date] due to the fact that she did not hold the qualification of [identify].

(2) The requirement that the post-holder should have this qualification was applied to all candidates regardless of their race or ethnic origin. It is denied that this has a significant discriminatory effect on persons of any particular racial or ethnic group including the applicant's.

(3) Further the requirement is one which is necessary in order for that person to have the appropriate specialised skills and training to carry out the

duties of the post. If, which is denied, the requirement is found to have a discriminatory effect, it is contended that its necessity for the post and thus for the respondent's business is such as to justify its imposition.

Case XII: Equal pay: *Originating application*

1.—Equal pay under the Equal Pay Act 1970 and/or Article 119 of the EEC Treaty and/or the Equal Pay Directive 75/117.

11.—(1) The applicant is a woman employed by the respondent as a [occupation]. The respondent is [identify business] [and as such is a state authority, in respect of which the Equal Pay Directive 75/117 has direct effect].

(2) In carrying out her duties for the respondent, the applicant is employed on like work to [name comparator], a male [identify post/department etc] who has been so employed since [date]. Alternatively, the applicant is employed on work of equal value to [name comparator].

(3) The applicant's pay is determined by [refer to relevant contractual provision] of her contract of employment at a rate of £[identify rate]. That clause is less favourable than the comparable clause in [comparator]'s contract of employment which provides for his rate of pay to be £[identify rate in consistent manner, ie, per hour/week/etc].

(4) The applicant therefore claims:

a) A declaration that the term of her contract relating to pay be treated as modified so as to be not less favourable than the clause relating to pay in the contract of [comparator].

b) Damages: being the arrears of pay from [date] to the date of the determination herein at the rate of £[difference in pay] per week.

c) Interest.

Equal pay: *Notice of appearance* raising genuine material factor defence

7.—(1) The respondent admits the applicant is employed by it as a [occupation] and has been so employed since [date]. The respondent also accepts that it carries on business as [identify] [but denies that it does so as an emanation of the state and/or that the Equal Pay Directive 75/117 can be relied upon as having direct effect against it].

(2) The respondent further denies that the applicant is employed on like work to that carried out by [comparator] and/or that her work is of equal value to his.

(3) The respondent accepts the respective rates of pay cited by the applicant in her originating application but contends that any difference in rate of pay is attributable to the different nature of the work carried out and the different value given to the duties of the applicant and her comparator.

(4) If the applicant is found to be employed on like work/work of equal value to that of [comparator], the respondent alternatively contends that the whole of the difference in rate of pay is attributable to a genuine material factor other than sex, namely [specify genuine material factor relied upon, eg, the red-circling of comparator's pay when he was moved from one post to his current post].

B. INTERLOCUTORY REQUESTS AND RESPONSES

I: Request for further particulars of originating application (Case A III, p266)

REQUEST FOR FURTHER PARTICULARS OF THE
ORIGINATING APPLICATION

Under paragraph 11(2)

OF: '. . . the applicant was promoted against her wishes to a more senior position. She was given no training in her new duties.'

REQUESTS:

1.—State what was the new position to which the applicant says she was promoted, giving details as to the ways in which the applicant contends it was 'senior'.
2.—Give full particulars of the 'new duties' to which the applicant refers.

Under paragraph 11(3)

OF: '. . . She asked for training in her new duties and for more time. She also said that she would be happy to return to her old position.'

REQUESTS:

3.—Please state what training the applicant sought, from whom and when. If the applicant's alleged request was made in writing, identify the document(s) relied upon and provide copies of the same. If made orally, give details of each conversation, including the time, date and occasion of each and the gist of the words used.
4.—Give like details in respect of the request to return to 'her old position'.
5.—State now, to what duties does the applicant mean to refer by the term 'her old position'?

Under paragraph 11(4)

OF: '. . . In the circumstances the applicant believes that she was unfairly dismissed and claims compensation.'

REQUESTS:

6.—Give full details of the compensation claimed by the applicant, demonstrating how the same is calculated and particularising all steps taken by the applicant to mitigate any loss claimed.

The respondent requests that the further particulars sought are supplied within 14 days of the date of this letter. If not so supplied the respondent will apply to the tribunal for an order, pursuant to r4(1)(a) of the Industrial Tribunal Rules of Procedure 1993, that the applicant reply to these requests.
[signed]

Replies to request for further particulars of the originating application

FURTHER PARTICULARS OF THE ORIGINATING APPLICATION:
PURSUANT TO REQUEST/ORDER DATED [DATE]
Under paragraph 12(2)
OF: '. . . [repeat as per Request] . . .'

REQUESTS:
[repeat as per Request] . . .

ANSWERS
1.—[identify title/grade of new position]. The applicant contends that this was
   senior to her previous position as [identify] in that [set out reasons relied
   upon].
2.—The post of [identify senior post] required the applicant to undertake new
   duties in that she [set out new duties relied upon].

Under paragraph 11(3)
OF: '. . . [repeat as per Request] . . .'

REQUESTS:
[repeat as per Request] . . .

ANSWERS:
3.—[refer to specific course if appropriate or give general details, eg: 'sufficient
   training to enable the applicant to carry out her new duties'.] This was sought
   [orally/in writing . . . give details as appropriate].
4.—[give details as appropriate].
5.—[refer to previous post].

Under paragraph 11(4)
OF: '. . . [repeat as per Request] . . .'

REQUESTS:
[repeat as per Request]

ANSWERS:
6.—The applicant claims a basic award and compensation for her loss of earnings
   from the date of her dismissal to the date of the hearing and thereafter for such
   period as the tribunal considers reasonable. The respondent is not entitled to
   seek further particulars of loss and of the applicant's attempts to mitigate
   that loss at this stage.

II: Request for written answers to questions

REQUEST FOR WRITTEN ANSWERS

With reference to the assertion at paragraph 7(5) of the notice of appearance:

1.—Is it not the case that [identify] holds a position within the respondent senior to [identify manager who took decision to dismiss]?

2.—Is it not the case that in the past the right to appeal against the decision to dismiss has been afforded to the respondent's employees?

3.—If the answer to 2 is in the negative, when in the past two years has an employee been dismissed by the respondent without being afforded the right of appeal?

The applicant requests that the above questions are answered in writing within 14 days of the date of this letter. If not so answered, the applicant will apply to the tribunal for an order for the same, pursuant to r4(3) of the Industrial Tribunal Rules of Procedure 1993.

[signed]

Written answers

WRITTEN ANSWERS: PURSUANT TO REQUEST/ORDER DATED [DATE]

The respondent answers as follows:

1.—In response to the question [set out question] . . . the respondent states that this is not the case . . . [complete as appropriate].

[give other answers in similar form]

[Signed]

III: Request for discovery and inspection of documents

[Address]

[Date]

Re: [industrial tribunal case name and number]

REQUEST FOR DISCOVERY AND INSPECTION OF DOCUMENTS

The applicant requests discovery and inspection of the following documents:

1.—The applicant's personnel file.

2.—All notes and/or memoranda relating to the decision to dismiss the applicant including notes of meetings and/or conversations relevant to that decision.

3.—[Identify such other documents as are believed to be in the respondent's possession which are relevant to the issues to be determined.]

4.—All other documents relevant to the issues to be determined by the tribunal.

The applicant asks that discovery of the above documents is provided within 14 days of the date of this letter and inspection within 7 days thereafter. As an alternative to inspection the applicant will pay reasonable photocopying and postage charges for the relevant documents. If discovery is not so provided, the applicant will request an order for the same from the tribunal, pursuant to r4(1)(b) of the Industrial Tribunal Rules of Procedure 1993.

[signed]

Response to request for discovery of documents

With reference to the request dated [date], the respondent gives discovery as follows:

1. The respondent has the applicant's personnel file in its possession and will provide the applicant/her representative with a reasonable opportunity to inspect the same.
2. The respondent confirms that it has no documents under this category of the request and no such documents have ever been in its possession.
3. [answer as appropriate]
4. The respondent confirms that save for communications between it and its legal advisers, it has no other documents in its possession relevant to the issues to be determined by the tribunal in this case.

[signed]

C. SETTLEMENT AND CONCILIATION

The following represent suggested forms of words and general terms. Where it is sought to use a document as a means of avoiding an IT claim, however, particular care should be taken to mould the terms to the individual circumstances of the case. It is essential to check each aspect of the document you wish to utilise to ensure that it properly serves the purpose to which you intend to put it.

I: Letter before action containing offer of settlement (constructive unfair dismissal – Case A VIII, p272)

WITHOUT PREJUDICE

[Date]

[Potential respondent, address]

Letter before action: Ms A N Applicant

Dear Sirs,

We act for Ms A N Applicant, who was employed by yourselves as [position] from [date] until she was forced to resign, terminating her employment on [date].

During her employment she worked four days per week on a weekly shift rota. She informs us that on [date] you unilaterally announced a change to the terms and conditions of employment of all employees in our client's position: it was stated that with effect from [date] they would have to work a five-day shift rota.

Our client complained about this change and sought to invoke the grievance procedure. However, your personnel manager, Mr V Hardman, refused to discuss the matter further or to consider making an exception in her case. As it was quite impossible for her to work a five-day week due to personal and family commitments, she could no longer remain in your employment under the newly imposed conditions. She accordingly had no alternative but to tender her resignation on [date], confirming her reasons for so doing in a letter of [date]. She left on [date].

Your action in seeking to impose unilaterally this major change to our client's work pattern was in clear breach of an express term (clause 7) of her contract of employment. She accordingly intends to pursue a claim before an industrial tribunal for constructive unfair dismissal.

However, if, within fourteen days of this letter, you undertake in writing to re-instate our client in her old position on terms and conditions no less favourable than before (and specifically including a four-day working week), to pay her the wages lost during her period of enforced unemployment and to meet our reasonable costs in this matter, she is prepared to forego her right to claim.

This offer is made without prejudice, but should such an undertaking not be forthcoming, our client will have no alternative but to proceed with her claim. Should the tribunal order re-instatement or re-engagement and award her compensation equal to or greater than her loss of wages, she reserves the right to raise this offer of settlement in relation to costs before the tribunal.

Yours faithfully,

II: Termination agreement

ACAS COT 3: SAMPLE 1

ADVISORY CONCILIATION AND ARBITRATION SERVICE

Tribunal case number

....

AGREEMENT IN RESPECT OF AN APPLICATION MADE TO THE TRIBUNAL

	Applicant	Respondent
Name	....	....
Address	....	....
	....	....

Settlement reached as a result of a conciliation action.
We the undersigned have agreed:
That

Applicant
Respondent
COT3

ACAS COT 3: SAMPLE 2

ADVISORY CONCILIATION AND ARBITRATION SERVICE

Tribunal case number

....

AGREEMENT FOLLOWING CONCILIATION ON A CLAIM MADE BY AN APPLICANT TO ACAS (NO APPLICATION MADE TO TRIBUNAL AT TIME OF AGREEMENT) THAT ACTION HAD BEEN TAKEN BY THE RESPONDENT IN RESPECT OF WHICH A COMPLAINT OF [UNFAIR DISMISSAL] COULD BE MADE TO AN INDUSTRIAL TRIBUNAL

	Applicant	Respondent
Name	....	....
Address	....	....
	....	....

Settlement reached as a result of a conciliation action.
We the undersigned have agreed:
That
Applicant .... Date...........................
Respondent .... Date...........................
COT3

III: Compromise agreement/contract

AN AGREEMENT to refrain from instituting or continuing with proceedings before an industrial tribunal made pursuant to the provisions of section 203(2) Employment Rights Act 1996.

This [agreement/contract*] is made between:

.... ('the employee')

of ....

and

.... ('the employer')

of ....

1. The employer will pay to the employee the sum of £[   ] and will provide her with a reference, in the form attached to this agreement and no other, within [   ] days of the date of this agreement and the employee agrees to accept this sum and this reference in full and final setlement of any claim of unfair dismissal arising out of the termination of her employment by the employer on [   ].
2. The employer further agrees to pay to the employee the sum of £[   ] within [   ] days of the date of this agreement and the employee agrees to accept this sum in full and final settlement of any claim under the Employment Rights Act 1996 in respect of deductions from her wages which took place between [   ] and [   ].
3. The employee further agrees to accept the payments and reference specified under 1 and 2 above in full and final settlement of all common law claims she might have relating to her employment with the employer, [save in respect of any claim for damages for personal injury].
4. The employee acknowledges that, before entering into this agreement, she received independent legal advice from [   ], a qualified lawyer who carries a policy of insurance, as to the terms and effect of this agreement and in particular as to its effect in relation to her rights to bring/continue claims of unfair dismissal and of unlawful deduction of wages in the industrial tribunal.
5. The conditions regulating compromise agreements under the Employment Rights Act 1996 are satisfied in relation to this agreement.

Signed: .... (employee) [date]

Signed: .... (employer) [date]

Statement by adviser to employee

I, [name, firm, address], confirm that I am a [barrister] [solictor of the Supreme Court currently in possession of a practising certificate from the Law Society] [advocate] and that I have advised the employee as to the terms of this agreement, in particular as to its effect in relation to rights to [bring] [continue] claims in the industrial tribunal.

Signed: ....

Dated: ....

*Complete as appropriate.

IV: Consent (Tomlin) orders

1. Decision

Settlement having been agreed between the parties in accordance with the terms set out in the Schedule hereto, by consent, this Originating Application is withdrawn upon compliance by the respondents with the terms of settlement on or before ......
.... 199....... Liberty to apply on or before ....
199...... and if no application is made by this date, this Originating Application is dismissed on withdrawal by the applicant.
Schedule

2. Decision

Settlement having been agreed between the parties in accordance with the terms endorsed on Counsel's Brief, by consent, this Originating Application is dismissed on withdrawal by the applicant.

3. Decision

Settlement having been agreed between the parties in accordance with the terms endorsed on Counsel's Brief, by consent, this Originating Application is withdrawn upon compliance by the respondents with the terms of settlement on or before ......
.... 199...... Liberty to apply on or before ....
199...... and if no application is made by this date, this Originating Application is dismissed on withdrawal by the applicant.

Note: In the last two forms above it may be appropriate in some cases to change the words 'endorsed on Counsel's Brief' to 'endorsed in the sealed envelope annexed to this decision'.

D. POST-DECISION: REVIEWS AND APPEALS

I: Application to industrial tribunal for review of decision

[date]
To The Assistant Secretary of the Tribunals
[address of ROIT]

Dear Sir/Madam,

Re: [industrial tribunal case title and number]

The [applicant/respondent] applies for a review of the decision by the industrial tribunal sitting at [location] on [date] that [set out summary of that decision] under r11(1) of the Industrial Tribunal Rules of Procedure 1993 on the grounds that:

[set out grounds for application for review, eg,

The decision was wrongly made as a result of an error on the part of the staff of the tribunal in that [eg, the decision orders the respondent to pay compensation in the sum of £1,000.00 when the tribunal's calculation at paragraph [number] of the decision demonstrates that this should be £11,000.00. Alternatively this might be an accidental slip capable of correction under r10(9)].

The decision was made in the absence of the respondent [give reasons for absence, eg, who received no notification of the hearing] and who wished to contest issues relating to liability and compensation.

New evidence has become available to the applicant since the conclusion of the hearing, the existence of which she could not reasonably have known or foreseen before the hearing, namely [give details of the evidence, eg, document reference/ identity or witness and substance of evidence] which would have a material bearing on the question of [identify question considered by the tribunal to which the evidence would relate], namely [indicate how reliance is placed on that evidence].

The interests of justice require such a review as [set out grounds, eg, the tribunal's decision on compensation was made without giving the [applicant/ respondent] an opportunity to adduce evidence and address the tribunal on the question whether it was just and equitable for a full award to be made to the applicant in the light of facts discovered after her dismissal relating to [give details, indicating the evidence the respondent wished to adduce and the points upon which it would have sought to have addressed the tribunal].]

[Signed]

II: Notice of appeal to Employment Appeal Tribunal from decision by industrial tribunal

IN THE EMPLOYMENT APPEAL TRIBUNAL   *EAT/   /*
BETWEEN:

[NAME OF APPELLANT]

Appellant

and

[NAME OF RESPONDENT TO APPEAL]

Respondent

NOTICE OF APPEAL

TO:
The Registrar,
Employment Appeal Tribunal,
Audit House, 58 Victoria Embankment,
London EC4Y 0DS

[or insert address for EAT in Scotland]

1. The appellant is [name] of [address].
2. Any communication relating to this appeal may be sent to the appellant at [name, address and telephone number of representative or identify other address etc for service].
3. The appellant appeals from the decision of the industrial tribunal sitting at [location of tribunal] on [date/s of hearing] that the [summary of tribunal's decision, ie, appellant's complaint of unfair dismissal be dismissed].
4. The only party/ies to the proceedings before the industrial tribunal other than the appellant was/were [give name/s and address/es of all other parties before the tribunal or the name/s and address/es of any representative on the record].
5. A copy of the industrial tribunal's decision and of the extended reasons for that decision is attached to this notice.
6. The grounds upon which this appeal are brought are that:

[set out grounds: eg

   6.1 In concluding that [give details by reference to decision] the tribunal acted perversely in that there was no evidence of [give details] to support such a conclusion.

   6.2 The tribunal's conclusion that [give details by reference to decision] was perverse in the light of the previous findings that [give details of contradictory findings by reference to decision].

   6.3 The tribunal failed to give any reasons for its finding that [give details].

   6.4 The tribunal erred in law in construing [relevant statutory provision] as meaning [give details] when the correct approach is [set out correct construction]].

Signed:
Date:

III: Respondent's answer to notice of appeal and cross-appeal to Employment Appeal Tribunal from decision of industrial tribunal

[Heading as for II above]

RESPONDENT'S ANSWER AND CROSS-APPEAL

1.   The respondent is [name] of [address].

2.   Any communication relating to this appeal may be sent to the respondent at [name, address and telephone number of representative or identify other address etc for service].

3.   The respondent intends to resist the appeal of [name and address of appellant]. The grounds upon which the respondent will rely are [the grounds relied upon by the industrial tribunal for making the decision appealed from] [and] [the following grounds:]

[set out grounds for resisting appeal, eg,

   3.1 The tribunal's finding that [give details by reference to decision] was supported by the evidence that [give details of evidence relied upon].

   3.2 In relation to the tribunal's conclusion that [give details], even if the tribunal did not set out its full reasons for reaching this conclusion, these are implicit [give details by reference to decision] and/or are unnecessary given the tribunal's finding that [give details] and further the tribunal correctly construed [relevant statutory provision].

4.   The respondent cross-appeals from [refer to part of tribunal decision appealed from].

5.   The respondent's grounds of appeal are that:

[set out grounds of cross-appeal]

Signed
Dated

IV Appeal to the Court of Appeal of Northern Ireland by way of case stated

IN THE BELFAST INDUSTRIAL TRIBUNAL   *Case No.*
BETWEEN:

[NAME OF APELLANT]

Appellant

and

[NAME OF RESPONDENT TO APPEAL]

Respondent

APPLICATION TO STATE A CASE

To the Secretary of the Tribunals
Office of the Tribunals
Long Bridge House
20–24 Waring Street
Belfast BT1 2EB

Whereas the Appellant is dissatisfied with the decision of the Belfast industrial tribunal sitting on [date/s] as being wrong in law,

Application is hereby made pursuant to Order 61 of the Rules of the Supreme Court (Northern Ireland) 1980 that a case may be stated for the opinion of the Northern Ireland Court of Appeal.

1. By originating application of [date], the respondent claimed [set out claim]. A copy of that originating application is annexed hereto marked 'A'.
2. On [date], the appellant entered a notice of appearance in response to the claim, denying that [set out grounds of resistance]. A copy of that notice of appearance is annexed herto marked 'B'.
   [set out any other relevant history of the application]
3. The respondent's application was heard by the Belfast industrial tribunal on [date/s] when the appellant contended that [summary of appellant's arguments before the tribunal].
4. By [unanimous/majority] decision registered and issued to the parties on [date], the Belfast industrial tribunal held that: [set out summary of tribunal's findings]. A copy of the tribunal's decision and the reasons for that decision is annexed hereto marked 'C'.
5. The appellant now requires the industrial tribunal to state and sign a case on the following questions of law for the opinion of the Court of Appeal of Northern Ireland:
   [set out questions, eg:
   5.1 Whether the industrial tribunal erred in law holding that ... [set out question of law, referring to relevant part of tribunal decision as appropriate].
   5.2 Could any reasonable tribunal on the evidence adduced and the facts found, and when properly directing itself in law, have reached the decision arrived at by this tribunal?

[signed]
[dated]

Statutes, regulations and directions

3.1 Industrial Tribunals Act 1996

Part I—Industrial tribunals

Introductory

Industrial tribunals

1.—(1) The Secretary of State may by regulations make provision for the establishment of tribunals to be known as industrial tribunals.

(2) Regulations made wholly or partly under section 128(1) of the Employment Protection (Consolidation) Act 1978 and in force immediately before this Act comes into force shall, so far as made under that provision, continue to have effect (until revoked) as if made under subsection (1); and the tribunals established in pursuance of such regulations shall continue to be known as industrial tribunals.

Jurisdiction

Enactments conferring jurisdiction on industrial tribunals

2.—Industrial tribunals shall exercise the jurisdiction conferred on them by or by virtue of this Act or any other Act, whether passed before or after this Act.

Power to confer further jurisdiction on industrial tribunals

3.—(1) The appropriate Minister may by order provide that proceedings in respect of—

a) any claim to which this section applies, or

b) any claim to which this section applies and which is of a description specified in the order,

may, subject to such exceptions (if any) as may be so specified, be brought before an industrial tribunal.

(2) Subject to subsection (3), this section applies to—

a) a claim for damages for breach of a contract of employment or other contract connected with employment,

b) a claim for a sum due under such a contract, and

c) a claim for the recovery of a sum in pursuance of any enactment relating to the terms or performance of such a contract, if the claim is such that a court in England and Wales or Scotland would under the law for the time being in force have jurisdiction to hear and determine an action in respect of the claim.

(3) This section does not apply to a claim for damages, or for a sum due, in respect of personal injuries.

(4) Any jurisdiction conferred on an industrial tribunal by virtue of this section in respect of any claim is exercisable concurrently with any court in England and Wales or in Scotland which has jurisdiction to hear and determine an action in respect of the claim.

(5) In this section—

'appropriate Minister', as respects a claim in respect of which an action could be heard and determined by a court in England and Wales, means the Lord Chancellor and, as respects a claim in respect of which an action could be heard and determined by a court in Scotland, means the Lord Advocate, and

'personal injuries' includes any disease and any impairment of a person's physical or mental condition.

(6) In this section a reference to breach of a contract includes a reference to breach of—

    a) a term implied in a contract by or under any enactment or otherwise,

    b) a term of a contract as modified by or under any enactment or otherwise, and

    c) a term which, although not contained in a contract, is incorporated in the contract by another term of the contract.

Membership etc.

Composition of a tribunal

4.—(1) Subject to the following provisions of this section, proceedings before an industrial tribunal shall be heard by—

    a) the person who, in accordance with regulations made under section 1(1), is the chairman, and

    a) two other members, or (with the consent of the parties) one other member, selected as the other members (or member) in accordance with regulations so made.

(2) Subject to subsection (5), the proceedings specified in subsection (3) shall be heard by the person mentioned in subsection (1)(a) alone.

(3) The proceedings referred to in subsection (2) are—

    a) proceedings on an application under section 161, 165 or 166 of the Trade Union and Labour Relations (Consolidation) Act 1992,

    b) proceedings on a complaint under section 126 of the Pension Schemes Act 1993,

    c) proceedings on a complaint under section 23 or 188 of the Employment Rights Act 1996 or on an application under section 128, 131 or 132 of that Act,

    d) proceedings in respect of which an industrial tribunal has jurisdiction by virtue of section 3 of this Act,

    e) proceedings in which the parties have given their written consent to the proceedings being heard in accordance with subsection (2) (whether or not they have subsequently withdrawn it),

f) proceedings in which the person bringing the proceedings has given written notice withdrawing the case, and

g) proceedings in which the person (or, where more than one, each of the persons) against whom the proceedings are brought does not, or has ceased to, contest the case.

(4) The Secretary of State may by order amend the provisions of subsection (3).

(5) Proceedings specified in subsection (3) shall be heard in accordance with subsection (1) if a person who, in accordance with regulations made under section 1(1), may be the chairman of an industrial tribunal, having regard to—

a) whether there is a likelihood of a dispute arising on the facts which makes it desirable for the proceedings to be heard in accordance with subsection (1),

b) whether there is a likelihood of an issue of law arising which would make it desirable for the proceedings to be heard in accordance with subsection (2),

c) any views of any of the parties as to whether or not the proceedings ought to be heard in accordance with either of those subsections, and

d) whether there are other proceedings which might be heard concurrently but which are not proceedings specified in subsection (3),

decides at any stage of the proceedings that the proceedings are to be heard in accordance with subsection (1).

(6) Where (in accordance with the following provisions of this Part) the Secretary of State makes industrial tribunal procedure regulations, the regulations may provide that, in such circumstances as the regulations may specify, any act required or authorised by the regulations to be done by an industrial tribunal may be done by the person mentioned in subsection (1)(a) alone.

(7) Where a Minister of the Crown so directs in relation to any proceedings on grounds of national security—

a) the proceedings shall be heard and determined, and

b) any act required or authorised by industrial tribunal procedure regulations to be done by an industrial tribunal in relation to the proceedings shall be done,

by the President of the Industrial Tribunals (England and Wales) appointed in accordance with regulations made under section 1(1), or by the President of the Industrial Tribunals (Scotland) so appointed, alone.

Remuneration, fees and allowances

5.—(1) The Secretary of State may pay to—

a) the President of the Industrial Tribunals (England and Wales),

b) the President of the Industrial Tribunals (Scotland), and

c) any person who is a member on a full-time basis of a panel of chairmen of tribunals which is appointed in accordance with regulations made under section 1(1),

such remuneration as he may with the consent of the Treasury determine.

(2) The Secretary of State may pay to—

a) members of industrial tribunals,

b) any assessors appointed for the purposes of proceedings before industrial tribunals, and

c) any persons required for the purposes of section 2A(1)(b) of the Equal Pay Act 1970 to prepare reports,

such fees and allowances as he may with the consent of the Treasury determine.

(3) The Secretary of State may pay to any other persons such allowances as he may with the consent of the Treasury determine for the purposes of, or in connection with, their attendance at industrial tribunals.

Procedure

Conduct of hearings

6.—(1) A person may appear before an industrial tribunal in person or be represented by—

a) counsel or a solicitor,

b) a representative of a trade union or an employers' association, or

c) any other person whom he desires to represent him.

(2) The Arbitration Act 1950 does not apply to any proceedings before an industrial tribunal.

Industrial tribunal procedure regulations

7.—(1) The Secretary of State may by regulations ("industrial tribunal procedure regulations") make such provision as appears to him to be necessary or expedient with respect to proceedings before industrial tribunals.

(2) Proceedings before industrial tribunals shall be instituted in accordance with industrial tribunal procedure regulations.

(3) Industrial tribunal procedure regulations may, in particular, include provision—

a) for determining by which tribunal any proceedings are to be determined,

b) for enabling an industrial tribunal to hear and determine proceedings brought by virtue of section 3 concurrently with proceedings brought before the tribunal otherwise than by virtue of that section,

c) for treating the Secretary of State (either generally or in such circumstances as may be prescribed by the regulations) as a party to any proceedings before an industrial tribunal (where he would not otherwise be a party to them) and entitling him to appear and to be heard accordingly,

d) for requiring persons to attend to give evidence and produce documents and for authorising the administration of oaths to witnesses,

e) for enabling an industrial tribunal, on the application of any party to the proceedings before it or of its own motion, to order—

i) in England and Wales, such discovery or inspection of documents, or the furnishing of such further particulars, as might be ordered by a county court on application by a party to proceedings before it, or

ii) in Scotland, such recovery or inspection of documents as might be ordered by a sheriff,

f) for prescribing the procedure to be followed in any proceedings before an industrial tribunal, including provision—

i) as to the persons entitled to appear and to be heard on behalf of parties to such proceedings, and

     ii) for enabling an industrial tribunal to review its decisions, and revoke or vary its orders and awards, in such circumstances as may be determined in accordance with the regulations,

  g) for the appointment of one or more assessors for the purposes of any proceedings before an industrial tribunal, where the proceedings are brought under an enactment which provides for one or more assessors to be appointed,

  h) for authorising an industrial tribunal to require persons to furnish information and produce documents to a person required for the purposes of section 2A(1)(b) of the Equal Pay Act 1970 to prepare a report, and

  j) for the registration and proof of decisions, orders and awards of industrial tribunals.

(4) A person who without reasonable excuse fails to comply with—

  a) any requirement imposed by virtue of subsection (3)(d) or (h), or

  b) any requirement with respect to the discovery, recovery or inspection of documents imposed by virtue of subsection (3)(e),

is guilty of an offence and liable on summary conviction to a fine not exceeding level 3 on the standard scale.

(5) Subject to any regulations under section 11(1)(a), industrial tribunal procedure regulations may include provision authorising or requiring an industrial tribunal, in circumstances specified in the regulations, to send notice or a copy of—

  a) any document specified in the regulations which relates to any proceedings before the tribunal, or

  b) any decision, order or award of the tribunal,

to any government department or other person or body so specified.

(6) Where in accordance with industrial tribunal procedure regulations an industrial tribunal determines in the same proceedings—

  a) a complaint presented under section 111 of the Employment Rights Act 1996, and

  b) a question referred under section 163 of that Act,

subsection (2) of that section has no effect for the purposes of the proceedings in so far as they relate to the complaint under section 111.

Procedure in contract cases

8.—(1) Where in proceedings brought by virtue of section 3 an industrial tribunal finds that the whole or part of a sum claimed in the proceedings is due, the tribunal shall order the respondent to the proceedings to pay the amount which it finds due.

(2) An order under section 3 may provide that an industrial tribunal shall not in proceedings in respect of a claim, or a number of claims relating to the same contract, order the payment of an amount exceeding such sum as may be specified in the order as the maximum amount which an industrial tribunal may order to be paid in relation to a claim or in relation to a contract.

(3) An order under section 3 may include provisions—

  a) as to the manner in which and time within which proceedings are to be brought by virtue of that section, and

  b) modifying any other enactment.

(4) An order under that section may make different provision in relation to proceedings in respect of different descriptions of claims.

Pre-hearing reviews and preliminary matters

9.—(1) Industrial tribunal procedure regulations may include provision—

 a) for authorising the carrying-out by an industrial tribunal of a preliminary consideration of any proceedings before it (a "pre-hearing review"), and

 b) for enabling such powers to be exercised in connection with a pre-hearing review as may be prescribed by the regulations.

(2) Such regulations may in particular include provision—

 a) for authorising any tribunal carrying out a pre-hearing review under the regulations to make, in circumstances specified in the regulations, an order requiring a party to the proceedings in question, if he wishes to continue to participate in those proceedings, to pay a deposit of an amount not exceeding £150, and

 b) for prescribing—

  i) the manner in which the amount of any such deposit is to be determined in any particular case,

  ii) the consequences of non-payment of any such deposit, and

  iii) the circumstances in which any such deposit, or any part of it, may be refunded to the party who paid it or be paid over to another party to the proceedings.

(3) The Secretary of State may from time to time by order substitute for the sum specified in subsection (2)(a) such other sum as is specified in the order.

(4) Industrial tribunal procedure regulations may also include provision for authorising an industrial tribunal to hear and determine any issue relating to the entitlement of any party to proceedings to bring or contest the proceedings in advance of the hearing and determination of the proceedings by that or any other industrial tribunal.

National security etc.

10.—(1) A Minister of the Crown may on grounds of national security direct an industrial tribunal to sit in private when hearing or determining any proceedings specified in the direction.

(2) Industrial tribunal procedure regulations may enable an industrial tribunal to sit in private for the purpose of—

 a) hearing evidence which in the opinion of the tribunal relates to matters of such a nature that it would be against the interests of national security to allow the evidence to be given in public, or

 b) hearing evidence from any person which in the opinion of the tribunal is likely to consist of—

  i) information which he could not disclose without contravening a prohibition imposed by or by virtue of any enactment,

  ii) information which has been communicated to him in confidence or which he has otherwise obtained in consequence of the confidence reposed in him by another person, or

  iii) information the disclosure of which would, for reasons other than its effect on negotiations with respect to any of the matters mentioned in section 178(2) of the Trade Union and Labour Relations (Consolidation) Act 1992 cause substantial injury to any undertaking of his or in which he works.

(3) The reference in subsection (2)(b)(iii) to any undertaking of a person or in which he works shall be construed—

a) in relation to a person in Crown employment, as a reference to the national interest,

b) in relation to a person who is a relevant member of the House of Lords staff, as a reference to the national interest or (if the case so requires) the interests of the House of Lords, and

c) in relation to a person who is a relevant member of the House of Commons staff, as a reference to the national interest or (if the case so requires) the interests of the House of Commons.

(4) If on a complaint under—

a) section 146 of the Trade Union and Labour Relations (Consolidation) Act 1992, or

b) section 111 of the Employment Rights Act 1996,

it is shown that the action complained of was taken for the purpose of safeguarding national security, the industrial tribunal shall dismiss the complaint.

(5) Except where the complaint is that a dismissal is unfair by virtue of—

a) section 99(1) to (3), 100 or 103 of the Employment Rights Act 1996, or

b) subsection (1) of section 105 of that Act by reason of the application of subsection (2), (3) or (6) of that section,

a certificate purporting to be signed by or on behalf of a Minister of the Crown and certifying that the action specified in the certificate was taken for the purpose of safeguarding national security is for the purposes of subsection (4) above conclusive evidence of that fact.

(6) The reference in subsection (5) to "dismissal" shall be construed—

a) in relation to a person in Crown employment, as a reference to the termination of Crown employment, and

b) in relation to a person who is a relevant member of the House of Commons staff, as a reference to the termination of his employment as such.

Restriction of publicity in cases involving sexual misconduct

11.—(1) Industrial tribunal procedure regulations may include provision—

a) for cases involving allegations of the commission of sexual offences, for securing that the registration or other making available of documents or decisions shall be so effected as to prevent the identification of any person affected by or making the allegation, and

b) for cases involving allegations of sexual misconduct, enabling an industrial tribunal, on the application of any party to proceedings before it or of its own motion, to make a restricted reporting order having effect (if not revoked earlier) until the promulgation of the decision of the tribunal.

(2) If any identifying matter is published or included in a relevant programme in contravention of a restricted reporting order—

a) in the case of publication in a newspaper or periodical, any proprietor, any editor and any publisher of the newspaper or periodical,

b) in the case of publication in any form, the person publishing the matter, and

c) in the case of matter included in a relevant programme—

i) any body corporate engaged in providing the service in which the programme is included, and

ii) any person having functions in relation to the programme corresponding to those of an editor of a newspaper,

shall be guilty of an offence and liable on summary conviction to a fine not exceeding level 5 on the standard scale.

(3) Where a person is charged with an offence under subsection (2) it is a defence to prove that at the time of the alleged offence he was not aware, and neither suspected nor had reason to suspect, that the publication or programme in question was of, or included, the matter in question.

(4) Where an offence under subsection (2) committed by a body corporate is proved to have been committed with the consent or connivance of, or to be attributable to any neglect on the part of—

a) a director, manager, secretary or other similar officer of the body corporate, or

b) a person purporting to act in any such capacity,

he as well as the body corporate is guilty of the offence and liable to be proceeded against and punished accordingly.

(5) In relation to a body corporate whose affairs are managed by its members "director", in subsection (4), means a member of the body corporate.

(6) In this section—

"identifying matter", in relation to a person, means any matter likely to lead members of the public to identify him as a person affected by, or as the person making, the allegation,

"relevant programme" has the same meaning as in the Sexual Offences (Amendment) Act 1992,

"restricted reporting order" means an order—

a) made in exercise of a power conferred by regulations made by virtue of this section, and

b) prohibiting the publication in Great Britain of identifying matter in a written publication available to the public or its inclusion in a relevant programme for reception in Great Britain,

"sexual misconduct" means the commission of a sexual offence, sexual harassment or other adverse conduct (of whatever nature) related to sex, and conduct is related to sex whether the relationship with sex lies in the character of the conduct or in its having reference to the sex or sexual orientation of the person at whom the conduct is directed,

"sexual offence" means any offence to which section 4 of the Sexual Offences (Amendment) Act 1976, the Sexual Offences (Amendment) Act 1992 or section 274(2) of the Criminal Procedure (Scotland) Act 1995 applies (offences under the Sexual Offences Act 1956, Part I of the Criminal Law (Consolidation) (Scotland) Act 1995 and certain other enactments), and

"written publication" has the same meaning as in the Sexual Offences (Amendment) Act 1992.

Restriction of publicity in disability cases

12.—(1) This section applies to proceedings on a complaint under section 8 of the Disability Discrimination Act 1995 in which evidence of a personal nature is likely to be heard by the industrial tribunal hearing the complaint.

(2) Industrial tribunal procedure regulations may include provision in relation to proceedings to which this section applies for—

    a) enabling an industrial tribunal, on the application of the complainant or of its own motion, to make a restricted reporting order having effect (if not revoked earlier) until the promulgation of the decision of the tribunal, and

    b) where a restricted reporting order is made in relation to a complaint which is being dealt with by the tribunal together with any other proceedings, enabling the tribunal to direct that the order is to apply also in relation to those other proceedings or such part of them as the tribunal may direct.

(3) If any identifying matter is published or included in a relevant programme in contravention of a restricted reporting order—

    a) in the case of publication in a newspaper or periodical, any proprietor, any editor and any publisher of the newspaper or periodical,

    b) in the case of publication in any other form, the person publishing the matter, and

    c) in the case of matter included in a relevant programme—

        i) any body corporate engaged in providing the service in which the programme is included, and

        ii) any person having functions in relation to the programme corresponding to those of an editor of a newspaper,

shall be guilty of an offence and liable on summary conviction to a fine not exceeding level 5 on the standard scale.

(4) Where a person is charged with an offence under subsection (3), it is a defence to prove that at the time of the alleged offence he was not aware, and neither suspected nor had reason to suspect, that the publication or programme in question was of, or included, the matter in question.

(5) Where an offence under subsection (3) committed by a body corporate is proved to have been committed with the consent or connivance of, or to be attributable to any neglect on the part of—

    a) a director, manager, secretary or other similar officer of the body corporate, or

    b) a person purporting to act in any such capacity,

he as well as the body corporate is guilty of the offence and liable to be proceeded against and punished accordingly.

(6) In relation to a body corporate whose affairs are managed by its members "director", in subsection (5), means a member of the body corporate.

(7) In this section—

"evidence of a personal nature" means any evidence of a medical, or other intimate, nature which might reasonably be assumed to be likely to cause significant embarrassment to the complainant if reported,

"identifying matter" means any matter likely to lead members of the public to identify the complainant or such other persons (if any) as may be be named in the order, "promulgation" has such meaning as may be prescribed by regulations made by virtue of this section,

"relevant programme" means a programme included in a programme service, within the meaning of the Broadcasting Act 1990,

"restricted reporting order" means an order—

    a) made in exercise of a power conferred by regulations made by virtue of this section, and

    b) prohibiting the publication in Great Britain of identifying matter in a written publication available to the public or its inclusion in a relevant programme for reception in Great Britain, and

"written publication" includes a film, a sound track and any other record in permanent form but does not include an indictment or other document prepared for use in particular legal proceedings.

Costs and expenses

13.—(1) Industrial tribunal procedure regulations may include provision—

    a) for the award of costs or expenses, including any allowances payable under section 5(2)(c) or (3), and

    b) for taxing or otherwise settling any such costs or expenses (and, in particular in England and Wales, for enabling such costs to be taxed in a county court).

(2) In relation to proceedings under section 111 of the Employment Rights Act 1996—

    a) where the employee has expressed a wish to be reinstated or re-engaged which has been communicated to the employer at least seven days before the hearing of the complaint, or

    b) where the proceedings arise out of the employer's failure to permit the employee to return to work after an absence due to pregnancy or childbirth,

industrial tribunal procedure regulations shall include provision for requiring the employer to pay the costs or expenses of any postponement or adjournment of the hearing caused by his failure, without a special reason, to adduce reasonable evidence as to the availability of the job from which the complainant was dismissed, or which she held before her absence, or of comparable or suitable employment.

Interest

14.—(1) The Secretary of State may by order made with the approval of the Treasury provide that sums payable in pursuance of decisions of industrial tribunals shall carry interest at such rate and between such times as may be prescribed by the order.

(2) Any interest due by virtue of such an order shall be recoverable as a sum payable in pursuance of the decision.

(3) The power conferred by subsection (1) includes power—

    a) to specify cases or circumstances in which interest is not payable,

    b) to provide that interest is payable only on sums exceeding a specified amount or falling between specified amounts,

    c) to make provision for the manner in which and the periods by reference to which interest is to be calculated and paid,

    d) to provide that any enactment—
        i) does or does not apply in relation to interest payable by virtue of subsection (1), or
        ii) applies to it with such modifications as may be specified in the order,
    e) to make provision for cases where sums are payable in pursuance of decisions or awards made on appeal from industrial tribunals,
    f) to make such incidental or supplemental provision as the Secretary of State considers necessary.

(4) In particular, an order under subsection (1) may provide that the rate of interest shall be the rate specified in section 17 of the Judgments Act 1838 as that enactment has effect from time to time.

Enforcement

15.—(1) Any sum payable in pursuance of a decision of an industrial tribunal in England and Wales which has been registered in accordance with industrial tribunal procedure regulations shall, if a county court so orders, be recoverable by execution issued from the county court or otherwise as if it were payable under an order of that court.

(2) Any order for the payment of any sum made by an industrial tribunal in Scotland (or any copy of such an order certified by the Secretary of the Tribunals) may be enforced as if it were an extract registered decree arbitral bearing a warrant for execution issued by the sherriff court of any sheriffdom in Scotland.

(3) In this section a reference to a decision or order of an industrial tribunal—
    a) does not include a decision or order which, on being reviewed, has been revoked by the tribunal, and
    b) in relation to a decision or order which on being reviewed, has been varied by the tribunal, shall be construed as a reference to the decision or order as so varied.

Recoupment of social security benefits

Power to provide for recoupment of benefits

16.—(1) This section applies to payments which are subject of proceedings before industrial tribunals and which are—
    a) payments of wages or compensation for loss of wages,
    b) payments by employers to employees under sections 146 to 151, sections 168 to 173 or section 192 of the Trade Union and Labour Relations (Consolidation) Act 1992,
    c) payments by employers to employees under—
        i) Part III, V, VI or VII,
        ii) section 93, or
        iii) Part X,
    of the Employment Rights Act 1996, or
    d) payments by employers to employees of a nature similar to, or for a purpose corresponding to the purpose of, payments within paragraph (b) or (c), and to

payments of remuneration under a protective award under section 189 of the Trade Union and Labour Relations (Consolidation) Act 1992.

(2) The Secretary of State may by regulations make with respect to payments to which this section applies provision for any or all of the purposes specified in subsection (3).

(3) The purposes referred to in subsection (2) are—

a) enabling the Secretary of State to recover from an employer, by way of total or partial recoupment of jobseeker's allowance or income support—

   i) a sum not exceeding the amount of the prescribed element of the monetary award, or

   ii) in the case of a protective award, the amount of the remuneration,

b) requiring or authorising an industrial tribunal to order the payment of such a sum, by way of total or partial recoupment of either benefit, to the Secretary of State instead of to an employee, and

c) requiring an industrial tribunal to order the payment to an employee of only the excess of the prescribed element of the monetary award over the amount of any jobseeker's allowance or income support shown to the tribunal to have been paid to the employee and enabling the Secretary of State to recover from the employer, by way of total or partial recoupment of the benefit, a sum not exceeding that amount.

(4) Regulations under this section may be framed—

a) so as to apply to all payments to which this section applies or to one or more classes of those payments, and

b) so as to apply to both jobseeker's allowance and income support, or to only jobseeker's allowance or income support.

(5) Regulations under this section may—

a) confer powers and impose duties on industrial tribunals or adjudication officers or other persons,

b) impose on an employer to whom a monetary award or protective award relates a duty—

   i) to furnish particulars connected with the award, and

   ii) to suspend payments in pursuance of the award during any period prescribed by the regulations,

c) provide for an employer who pays a sum to the Secretary of State in pursuance of this section to be relieved from any liability to pay the sum to another person,

d) confer on an employee a right of appeal to a social security appeal tribunal against any decision of an adjudication officer as to the total or partial recoupment of an income-based jobseeker's allowance or of income support in pursuance of the regulations, and

e) provide for the proof in proceedings before industrial tribunals (whether by certificate or in any other manner) of any amount of jobseeker's allowance or income support paid to an employee.

(6) Regulations under this section may make different provisions for different cases.

Recoupment: further provisions

17.—(1) Where in pursuance of any regulations under section 16 a sum has been recovered by or paid to the Secretary of State by way of total or partial recoupment of jobseeker's allowance or income support—

a) no sum shall be recoverable under Part III or V of the Social Security Administration Act 1992, and

b) no abatement, payment or reduction shall be made by reference to the jobseeker's allowance or income support recouped.

(2) Any amount found to have been duly recovered by or paid to the Secretary of State in pursuance of regulations under section 16 by way of total or partial recoupment of jobseeker's allowance shall be paid into National Insurance Fund.

(3) In section 15—

"monetary award" means the amount which is awarded, or ordered to be paid, to the employee by the tribunal or would be so awarded or ordered apart from any provision of regulations under that section, and

"the prescribed element", in relation to any monetary award, means so much of that award as is attributable to such matters as may be prescribed by regulations under that section.

(4) In section 16 'income-based jobseeker's allowance' has the same meaning as in the Jobseekers Act 1995.

Conciliation

Conciliation

18.—(1) This section applies in the case of industrial tribunal proceedings and claims which could be the subject of industrial tribunal proceedings—

a) under—
   i) section 2(1) of the Equal Pay Act 1970,
   ii) section 63 of the Sex Discrimination Act 1975, or
   iii) section 54 of the Race Relations Act 1976,

b) arising out of a contravention, or alleged contravention, of section 64, 68, 137, 138, 146, 168, 169, 170, 174, 188 or 190 of the Trade Union and Labour Relations (Consolidation) Act 1992,

c) under section 8 of the Disability Discrimination Act 1995,

d) arising out of a contravention, or alleged contravention, of section 8, 13, 15, 18(1), 21(1), 28 or 92, or of Part V, VI, VII or X, of the Employment Rights Act 1996,

e) which are proceedings in respect of which an industrial tribunal has jurisdiction by virtue of section 3 of this Act, or

f) arising out of a contravention, or alleged contravention, of a provision specified by an order under subsection (8)(b) as a provision to which this paragraph applies.

(2) Where an application has been presented to an industrial tribunal, and a copy of it has been sent to a conciliation officer, it is the duty of the conciliation officer—

a) if he is requested to do so by the person by whom and the person against whom the proceedings are brought, or

b) if, in the absence of any such request, the conciliation officer considers that he could act under this subsection with a reasonable prospect of success,

to endeavour to promote a settlement of the proceedings without their being determined by an industrial tribunal.

(3) Where at any time—

    a) a person claims that action has been taken in respect of which proceedings could be brought by him before an industrial tribunal, but

    b) before any application relating to that action has been presented by him a request is made to a conciliation officer (whether by that person or by the person against whom the proceedings could be instituted) to make his services available to them,

the conciliation officer shall act in accordance with subsection (2) as if an application had been presented to an industrial tribunal.

(4) Where a person who has presented a complaint to an industrial tribunal under section 111 of the Employment Rights Act 1996 has ceased to be employed by the employer against whom the complaint was made, the conciliation officer shall (for the purpose of promoting a settlement of the complaint in accordance with subsection (2)) in particular—

    a) seek to promote the reinstatement or re-engagement of the complainant by the employer, or by a successor of the employer or by an associated employer, on terms appearing to the conciliation officer to be equitable, or

    b) where the complainant does not wish to be reinstated or re-engaged, or where reinstatement or re-engagement is not practicable, and the parties desire the conciliation officer to act, seek to promote agreement between them as to a sum by way of compensation to be paid by the employer to the complainant.

(5) Where at any time—

    a) a person claims that action has been taken in respect of which a complaint could be presented by him to an industrial tribunal under section 111 of the Employment Rights Act 1996, but

    b) before any complaint relating to that action has been presented by him a request is made to a conciliation officer (whether by that person or by the employer) to make his services available to them,

the conciliation officer shall act in accordance with subsection (4) as if a complaint had been presented to an industrial tribunal under section 111.

(6) In proceeding under this section a conciliation officer shall, where appropriate, have regard to the desirability of encouraging the use of other procedures available for the settlement of grievances.

(7) Anything communicated to a conciliation officer in connection with the performance of his functions under this section shall not be admissible in evidence in any proceedings before an industrial tribunal, except with the consent of the person who communicated it to that officer.

(8) The Secretary of State may by order—

    a) direct that further provisions of the Employment Rights Act 1996 be added to the list in subsection (1)(d), or

    b) specify a provision of any other Act as a provision to which subsection (1)(f) applies.

Conciliation procedure

19.—Industrial tribunal procedure regulations shall include in relation to industrial tribunal proceedings in the case of which any enactment makes provision for conciliation—

a) provisions requiring a copy of the application by which the proceedings are instituted, and a copy of any notice relating to it which is lodged by or on behalf of the person against whom the proceedings are brought, to be sent to a conciliation officer,

b) provisions securing that the applicant and the person against whom the proceedings are brought are notified that the services of a conciliation officer are available to them, and

c) provisions postponing the hearing of any such proceedings for such period as may be determined in accordance with the regulations for the purpose of giving an opportunity for the proceedings to be settled by way of conciliation and withdrawn.

Part II—The Employment Appeal Tribunal

Introductory

The Appeal Tribunal

20.—(1) The Employment Appeal Tribunal ("the Appeal Tribunal") shall continue in existence.

(2) The Appeal Tribunal shall have a central office in London but may sit at any time and in any place in Great Britain.

(3) The Appeal Tribunal shall be a superior court of record and shall have an official seal which shall be judicially noticed.

Jurisdiction

Jurisdiction of Appeal Tribunal

21.—(1) An appeal lies to the Appeal Tribunal on any question of law arising from any decision of, or arising in any proceedings before, an industrial tribunal under or by virtue of—

a) the Equal Pay Act 1970,

b) the Sex Discrimination Act 1975,

c) the Race Relations Act 1976,

d) the Trade Union and Labour Relations (Consolidation) Act 1992,

e) the Disability Discrimination Act 1995, or

f) the Employment Rights Act 1996.

(2) No appeal shall lie except to the Appeal Tribunal from any decision of an industrial tribunal under or by virtue of the Acts listed in subsection (1).

(3) Subsection (1) does not affect any provision contained in, or made under, any Act which provides for an appeal to lie to the Appeal Tribunal (whether from an industrial tribunal, the Certification Officer or any other person or body) otherwise than on a question to which that subsection applies.

Membership etc.

Membership of Appeal Tribunal

22.—(1) The Appeal Tribunal shall consist of—

a) such number of judges as may be nominated from time to time by the Lord Chancellor from the judges (other than the Lord Chancellor) of the High Court and the Court of Appeal,

b) at least one judge of the Court of Session nominated from time to time by the Lord President of the Court of Session, and

c) such number of other members as may be appointed from time to time by Her Majesty on the joint recommendation of the Lord Chancellor and the Secretary of State ("appointed members").

(2) The appointed members shall be persons who appear to the Lord Chancellor and the Secretary of State to have special knowledge or experience of industrial relations either—

a) as representatives of employers, or

b) as representatives of workers (within the meaning of the Trade Union and Labour Relations (Consolidation) Act 1992).

(3) The Lord Chancellor shall, after consultation with the Lord President of the Court of Session, appoint one of the judges nominated under subsection (1) to be President of the Appeal Tribunal.

(4) No judge shall be nominated a member of the Appeal Tribunal except with his consent.

Temporary membership

23.—(1) At any time when—

a) the office of President of the Appeal Tribunal is vacant, or

b) the person holding that office is temporarily absent or otherwise unable to act as the President of the Appeal Tribunal,

the Lord Chancellor may nominate another judge nominated under section 22(1)(a) to act temporarily in his place.

(2) At any time when a judge of the Appeal Tribunal nominated under paragraph (a) or (b) of subsection (1) of section 22 is temporarily absent or otherwise unable to act as a member of the Appeal Tribunal—

a) in the case of a judge nominated under paragraph (a) of that subsection, the Lord Chancellor may nominate another judge who is qualified to be nominated under that paragraph to act temporarily in his place, and

b) in the case of a judge nominated under paragraph (b) of that subsection, the Lord President of the Court of Session may nominate another judge who is qualified to be nominated under that paragraph to act temporarily in his place.

(3) At any time when an appointed member of the Appeal Tribunal is temporarily absent or otherwise unable to act as a member of the Appeal Tribunal, the Lord Chancellor and the Secretary of State may jointly appoint a person appearing to them to have the qualifications for appointment as an appointed member to act temporarily in his place.

(4) A person nominated or appointed to act temporarily in place of the President or any other member of the Appeal Tribunal, when so acting, has all the functions of the person in whose place he acts.

(5) No judge shall be nominated to act temporarily as a member of the Appeal Tribunal except with his consent.

Temporary additional judicial membership

24.—(1) At any time when it appears to the Lord Chancellor that it is expedient to do so in order to facilitate in England and Wales the disposal of business in the Appeal Tribunal, he may appoint a qualified person to be a temporary additional judge of the Appeal Tribunal during such period or on such occasions as the Lord Chancellor thinks fit.

(2) In subsection (1) "qualified person" means a person who—
   a) is qualified for appointment as a judge of the High Court under section 10 of the Supreme Court Act 1981, or
   b) has held office as a judge of the High Court or the Court of Appeal.

(3) A person appointed to be a temporary additional judge of the Appeal Tribunal has all the functions of a judge nominated under section 22(1)(a).

Tenure of appointed members

25.—(1) Subject to subsections (2) to (4), an appointed member shall hold and vacate office in accordance with the terms of his appointment.

(2) An appointed member—
   a) may at any time resign his membership by notice in writing addressed to the Lord Chancellor and the Secretary of State, and
   b) shall vacate his office on the day on which he attains the age of seventy.

(3) Subsection (2)(b) is subject to section 26(4) to (6) of the Judicial Pensions and Retirement Act 1993 (Lord Chancellor's power to authorise continuance of office up to the age of seventy-five).

(4) If the Lord Chancellor, after consultation with the Secretary of State, is satisfied that an appointed member—
   a) has been absent from sittings of the Appeal Tribunal for a period longer than six consecutive months without the permission of the President of the Appeal Tribunal,
   b) has become bankrupt or made an arrangement with his creditors, or has had his estate sequestrated or made a trust deed for behoof of his creditors or a composition contract,
   c) is incapacitated by physical or mental illness, or
   d) is otherwise unable or unfit to discharge the functions of a member,
   the Lord Chancellor may declare his office as a member to be vacant and shall notify the declaration in such manner as the Lord Chancellor thinks fit; and when the Lord Chancellor does so, the office becomes vacant.

Staff

26.—The Secretary of State may appoint such officers and servants of the Appeal Tribunal as he may determine, subject to the approval of the Minister for the Civil Service as to numbers and terms and conditions of service.

Remuneration, pensions and allowances

27.—(1) The Secretary of State shall pay—
   a) the appointed members,
   b) any person to act temporarily in the place of an appointed member, and
   c) the officers and servants of the Appeal Tribunal,

such remuneration and such travelling and other allowances as he may, with the relevant approval, determine; and for this purpose the relevant approval is that of the Treasury in the case of persons within paragraph (a) or (b) and the Minister for the Civil Service in the case of persons within paragraph (c).

(2) A person appointed to be a temporary additional judge of the Appeal Tribunal shall be paid such remuneration and allowances as the Lord Chancellor may, with the approval of the Treasury, determine.

(3) If the Secretary of State determines, with the approval of the Treasury, that this subsection applies in the case of an appointed member, the Secretary of State shall—

    a) pay such pension, allowance or gratuity to or in respect of that person on his retirement or death, or

    b) make to the member such payments towards the provision of a pension, allowance or gratuity for his retirement or death,

as the Secretary of State may, with the approval of the Treasury, determine.

(4) Where—

    a) a person ceases to be an appointed member otherwise than on his retirement or death, and

    b) it appears to the Secretary of State that there are special circumstances which make it right for him to receive compensation,

the Secretary of State may make to him a payment of such amount as the Secretary of State may, with the approval of the Treasury, determine.

Composition of Appeal Tribunal

28.—(1) The Appeal Tribunal may sit, in accordance with directions given by the President of the Appeal Tribunal, either as a single tribunal or in two or more divisions concurrently.

(2) Subject to subsections (3) to (5), proceedings before the Appeal Tribunal shall be heard by a judge and either two or four appointed members, so that in either case there is an equal number—

    a) of persons whose knowledge or experience of industrial relations is as representatives of employers, and

    b) of persons whose knowledge or experience of industrial relations is as representatives of workers.

(3) With the consent of the parties, proceedings before the Appeal Tribunal may be heard by a judge and one appointed member or by a judge and three appointed members.

(4) Proceedings on an appeal on a question arising from any decision of, or arising in any proceedings before, an industrial tribunal consisting of the person mentioned in section 4(1)(a) alone shall be heard by a judge alone unless a judge directs that the proceedings shall be heard in accordance with subsections (2) and (3).

(5) Where a Minister of the Crown so directs in relation to any proceedings on grounds of national security, the proceedings shall be heard by the President of the Appeal Tribunal alone.

Procedure

Conduct of hearings

29.—(1) A person may appear before the Appeal Tribunal in person or be represented by—

  a) counsel or a solicitor,

  b) a representative of a trade union or an employers' association, or

  b) any other person whom he desires to represent him.

  (2) The Appeal Tribunal has in relation to—

  a) the attendance and examination of witnesses,

  b) the production and inspection of documents, and

  c) all other matters incidental to its jurisdiction,

  the same powers, rights, privileges and authority (in England and Wales) as the High Court and (in Scotland) as the Court of Session.

Appeal Tribunal procedure rules

30.—(1) The Lord Chancellor, after consultation with the Lord President of the Court of Session, shall make rules ("Appeal Tribunal procedure rules") with respect to proceedings before the Appeal Tribunal.

  (2) Appeal Tribunal procedure rules may, in particular, include provision—

  a) with respect to the manner in which, and the time within which, an appeal may be brought,

  b) with respect to the manner in which any application to the Appeal Tribunal may be made,

  c) for requiring persons to attend to give evidence and produce documents and for authorising the administration of oaths to witnesses,

  d) for requiring or enabling the Appeal Tribunal to sit in private in circumstances in which an industrial tribunal is required or empowered to sit in private by virtue of section 10 of this Act,

  e) for the registration and proof of any award made on an application to the Appeal Tribunal under section 67 or 176 of the Trade Union and Labour Relations (Consolidation) Act 1992, and

  f) for interlocutory matters arising on any appeal or application to the Appeal Tribunal to be dealt with otherwise than in accordance with section 28(2) to (5) of this Act.

  (3) Subject to Appeal Tribunal procedure rules, the Appeal Tribunal has power to regulate its own procedure.

Restriction of publicity in cases involving sexual misconduct

31.—(1) Appeal Tribunal procedure rules may, as respects proceedings to which this section applies, include provision—

  a) for cases involving allegations of the commission of sexual offences, for securing that the registration or other making available of documents or decisions shall be so effected as to prevent the identification of any person affected by or making the allegation, and

  b) for cases involving allegations of sexual misconduct, enabling the Appeal Tribunal, on the application of any party to the proceedings before it or of its own motion, to make a restricted reporting order having effect (if not revoked earlier) until the promulgation of the decision of the Appeal Tribunal.

(2) This section applies to—

    a) proceedings on an appeal against a decision of an industrial tribunal to make, or not to make, a restricted reporting order, and

    b) proceedings on an appeal against any interlocutory decision of an industrial tribunal in proceedings in which the industrial tribunal has made a restricted reporting order which it has not revoked.

(3) If any identifying matter is published or included in a relevant programme in contravention of a restricted reporting order—

    a) in the case of publication in a newspaper or periodical, any proprietor, any editor and any publisher of the newspaper or periodical,

    b) in the case of publication in any other form, the person publishing the matter, and

    c) in the case of matter included in a relevant programme—

        i) any body corporate engaged in providing the service in which the programme is included, and

        ii) any person having functions in relation to the programme corresponding to those of an editor of a newspaper,

shall be guilty of an offence and liable on summary conviction to a fine not exceeding level 5 on the standard scale.

(4) Where a person is charged with an offence under subsection (3) it is a defence to prove that at the time of the alleged offence he was not aware, and neither suspected nor had reason to suspect, that the publication or programme in question was of, or included, the matter in question.

(5) Where an offence under subsection (3) committed by a body corporate is proved to have been committed with the consent or connivance of, or to be attributable to any neglect on the part of—

    a) a director, manager, secretary or other similar officer of the body corporate, or

    b) a person purporting to act in any such capacity,

he as well as the body corporate is guilty of the offence and liable to be proceeded against and punished accordingly.

(6) In relation to a body corporate whose affairs are managed by its members "director", in subsection (5), means a member of the body corporate.

(7) "Restricted reporting order" means—

    a) in subsections (1) and (3), an order—

        i) made in exercise of a power conferred by rules made by virtue of this section

        ii) prohibiting the publication in Great Britain of identifying matter in a written publication available to the public or its inclusion in a relevant programme for reception in Great Britain, and

    b) in subsection (2), an order which is a restricted reporting order for the purposes of section 11.

(8) In this section—

"identifying matter", in relation to a person, means any matter likely to lead members of the public to identify him as a person affected by, or as the person making, the allegation,

"relevant programme" has the same meaning as in the Sexual Offences (Amendment) Act 1992,

"sexual misconduct" means the commission of a sexual offence, sexual harassment or other adverse conduct (of whatever nature) related to sex, and conduct is related to sex whether the relationship with sex lies in the character of the conduct or in its having reference to the sex or sexual orientation of the person at whom the conduct is directed,

"sexual offence" means any offence to which section section 4 of the Sexual Offences (Amendment) Act 1976, the Sexual Offences (Amendment) Act 1992 or section 274(2) of the Criminal Procedure (Scotland) Act 1995, applies (offences under the Sexual Offences Act 1956, Part I of the Criminal Law (Consolidation) (Scotland) Act 1995 and certain other enactments), and

"written publication" has the same meaning as in the Sexual Offences (Amendment) Act 1992.

Restriction of publicity in disability cases

32.—(1) This section applies to proceedings—

    a) on an appeal against a decision of an industrial tribunal to make, or not to make, a restricted reporting order, or

    b) on an appeal against any interlocutory decision of an industrial tribunal in proceedings in which the industrial tribunal has made a restricted reporting order which it has not revoked.

(2) Appeal Tribunal procedure rules may, as respects proceedings to which this section applies, include provision for—

    a) enabling the Appeal Tribunal, on the application of the complainant or of its own motion, to make a restricted reporting order having effect (if not revoked earlier) until the promulgation of the decision of the Appeal Tribunal, and

    b) where a restricted reporting order is made in relation to an appeal which is being dealt with by the Appeal Tribunal together with any other proceedings, enabling the Appeal Tribunal to direct that the order is to apply also in relation to those other proceedings or such part of them as the Appeal Tribunal may direct.

(3) If any identifying matter is published or included in a relevant programme in contravention of a restricted reporting order—

    a) in the case of publication in a newspaper or periodical, any proprietor, any editor and any publisher of the newspaper or periodical,

    b) in the case of publication in any other form, the person publishing the matter, and

    c) in the case of matter included in a relevant programme—

        i) any body corporate engaged in providing the service in which the programme is included, and

        ii) any person having functions in relation to the programme corresponding to those of an editor of a newspaper,

shall be guilty of an offence and liable on summary conviction to a fine not exceeding level 5 on the standard scale.

(4) Where a person is charged with an offence under subsection (3), it is a defence to prove that at the time of the alleged offence he was not aware, and neither suspected nor had reason to suspect, that the publication or programme in question was of, or included, the matter in question.

(5) Where an offence under subsection (3) committed by a body corporate is proved to have been committed with the consent or connivance of, or to be attributable to any neglect on the part of—

a) a director, manager, secretary or other similar officer of the body corporate, or

b) a person purporting to act in any such capacity,

he as well as the body corporate is guilty of the offence and liable to be proceeded against and punished accordingly.

(6) In relation to a body corporate whose affairs are managed by its members "director", in subsection (5), means a member of the body corporate.

(7) "Restricted reporting order" means—

a) in subsection (1), an order which is a restricted reporting order for the purposes of section 12, and

b) in subsections (2) and (3), an order—

    i) made in exercise of a power conferred by rules made by virtue of this section, and

    ii) prohibiting the publication in Great Britain of identifying matter in a written publication available to the public or its inclusion in a relevant programme for reception in Great Britain.

(8) In this section—

"complainant" means the person who made the complaint to which the proceedings before the Appeal Tribunal relate,

"identifying matter" means any matter likely to lead members of the public to identify the complainant or such others persons (if any) as may be named in the order,

"promulgation" has such meaning as may be prescribed by rules made by virtue of this section,

"relevant programme" means a programme included in a programme service, within the meaning of the Broadcasting Act 1990, and

"written publication" includes a film, a sound track and any other record in permanent form but does not include an indictment or other document prepared for use in particular legal proceedings.

Restriction of vexatious proceedings

33.—(1) If, on an application made by the Attorney General or the Lord Advocate under this section, the Appeal Tribunal is satisfied that a person has habitually and persistently and without any reasonable ground—

a) instituted vexatious proceedings, whether in an industrial tribunal or before the Appeal Tribunal, and whether against the same person or against different persons, or

b) made vexatious applications in any proceedings, whether in an industrial tribunal or before the Appeal Tribunal,

the Appeal Tribunal may, after hearing the person or giving him an opportunity of being heard, make a restriction of proceedings order.

(2) A "restriction of proceedings order" is an order that—

a) no proceedings shall without the leave of the Appeal Tribunal be instituted in any industrial tribunal or before the Appeal Tribunal by the person against whom the order is made,

b) any proceedings instituted by him in any industrial tribunal or before the Appeal Tribunal before the making of the order shall not be continued by him without the leave of the Appeal Tribunal, and

c) no application (other than one for leave under this section) is to be made by him in any proceedings in any industrial tribunal or before the Appeal Tribunal without the leave of the Appeal Tribunal.

(3) A restriction of proceedings order may provide that it is to cease to have effect at the end of a specified period, but otherwise it remains in force indefinitely.

(4) Leave for the institution or continuance of, or for the making of an application in, any proceedings in an industrial tribunal or before the Appeal Tribunal by a person who is the subject of a restriction of proceedings order shall not be given unless the Appeal Tribunal is satisfied—

a) that the proceedings or application are not an abuse of the process of the tribunal in question, and

b) that there are reasonable grounds for the proceedings or application.

(5) A copy of a restriction of proceedings order shall be published in the London Gazette and the Edinburgh Gazette.

Costs and expenses

34.—(1) Appeal Tribunal procedure rules may include provision empowering the Appeal Tribunal to order a party to any proceedings before the Appeal Tribunal to pay to any other party to the proceedings the whole or part of the costs or expenses incurred by the other party in connection with the proceedings where in the opinion of the Appeal Tribunal—

a) the proceedings were unnecessary, improper or vexatious, or

b) there has been unreasonable delay or other unreasonable conduct in bringing or conducting the proceedings.

(2) Except as provided by subsection (1), Appeal Tribunal procedure rules shall not enable the Appeal Tribunal to order the payment of costs or expenses by any party to proceedings before the Appeal Tribunal.

Decisions and further appeals

Powers of Appeal Tribunal

35.—(1) For the purpose of disposing of an appeal, the Appeal Tribunal may—

a) exercise any of the powers of the body or officer from whom the appeal was brought, or

b) remit the case to that body or officer.

(2) Any decision or award of the Appeal Tribunal on an appeal has the same effect, and may be enforced in the same manner, as a decision or award of the body or officer from whom the appeal was brought.

Enforcement of decisions etc.

36.—(1) Any sum payable in England and Wales in pursuance of an award of the Appeal Tribunal—

a) made under section 67 or 176 of the Trade Union and Labour Relations (Consolidation) Act 1992, and

b) registered in accordance with Appeal Tribunal procedure rules,

is, if a county court so orders, recoverable by execution issued from the county court or otherwise as if it were payable under an order of that court.

(2) Any order by the Appeal Tribunal for the payment in Scotland of any sum in pursuance of such an award (or any copy of such an order certified by the Secretary of the Tribunals) may be enforced as if it were an extract registered decree arbitral bearing a warrant for execution issued by the sheriff court of any sheriffdom in Scotland.

(3) Any sum payable in pursuance of an award of the Appeal Tribunal under section 67 or 176 of the Trade Union and Labour Relations (Consolidation) Act 1992 shall be treated as if it were a sum payable in pursuance of a decision of an industrial tribunal for the purposes of section 14 of this Act.

(4) No person shall be punished for contempt of the Appeal Tribunal except by, or with the consent of, a judge.

(5) A magistrates' court shall not remit the whole or part of a fine imposed by the Appeal Tribunal unless it has the consent of a judge who is a member of the Appeal Tribunal.

Appeals from Appeal Tribunal

37.—(1) Subject to subsection (3), an appeal on any question of law lies from any decision or order of the Appeal Tribunal to the relevant appeal court with the leave of the Appeal Tribunal or of the relevant appeal court.

(2) In subsection (1) the "relevant appeal court" means—

    a) in the case of proceedings in England and Wales, the Court of Appeal, and

    b) in the case of proceedings in Scotland, the Court of Session.

(3) No appeal lies from a decision of the Appeal Tribunal refusing leave for the institution or continuance of, or for the making of an application in, proceedings by a person who is the subject of a restriction of proceedings order made under section 33.

(4) This section is without prejudice to section 13 of the Administration of Justice Act 1960 (appeal in case of contempt of court).

Part III—Supplementary

Crown employment and Parliamentary staff

Crown employment

38.—(1) This Act has effect in relation to Crown employment and persons in Crown employment as it has effect in relation to other employment and other employees.

(2) In this Act "Crown employment" means employment under or for the purposes of a government department or any officer or body exercising on behalf of the Crown functions conferred by a statutory provision.

(3) For the purposes of the application of this Act in relation to Crown employment in accordance with subsection (1)—

    a) references to an employee shall be construed as references to a person in Crown employment, and

    b) references to a contract of employment shall be construed as references to the terms of employment of a person in Crown employment.

(4) Subsection (1) applies to—

    a) service as a member of the naval, military or air forces of the Crown, and

b) employment by an association established for the purposes of Part XI of the Reserve Forces Act 1996;

but Her Majesty may by Order in Council make any provision of this Act apply to service as a member of the naval, military or air forces of the Crown subject to such exceptions and modifications as may be specified in the Order in Council.

Parliamentary staff

39.—(1) This Act has effect in relation to employment as a relevant member of the House of Lords staff or a relevant member of the House of Commons staff as it has effect in relation to other employment.

(2) Nothing in any rule of law or the law or practice of Parliament prevents a relevant member of the House of Lords staff or a relevant member of the House of Commons staff from bringing before an industrial tribunal proceedings of any description which could be brought before such a tribunal by a person who is not a relevant member of the House of Lords staff or a relevant member of the House of Commons staff.

(3) For the purposes of the application of this Act in relation to a relevant member of the House of Commons staff—

a) references to an employee shall be construed as references to a relevant member of the House of Commons staff, and

b) references to a contract of employment shall be construed as including references to the terms of employment of a relevant member of the House of Commons staff.

(4) In this Act "relevant member of the House of Lords staff" means any person who is employed under a contract of employment with the Corporate Officer of the House of Lords.

(5) In this Act "relevant member of the House of Commons staff" has the same meaning as in section 195 of the Employment Rights Act 1996; and (subject to an Order in Council under subsection (12) of that section)—

a) subsections (6) and (7) of that section have effect for determining who is the employer of a relevant member of the House of Commons staff for the purposes of this Act, and

b) subsection (8) of that section applies in relation to proceedings brought by virtue of this section.

General

Power to amend Act

40.—(1) The Secretary of State may by order—

a) provide that any provision of this Act to which this section applies and which is specified in the order shall not apply to persons, or to employments, of such classes as may be prescribed in the order, or

b) provide that any provision of this Act to which this section applies shall apply to persons or employments of such classes as may be prescribed in the order subject to such exceptions and modifications as may be so prescribed.

(2) This section applies to sections 3, 8, 16 and 17 and to section 18 so far as deriving from section 133 of the Employment Protection (Consolidation) Act 1978.

Orders, regulations and rules

41.—(1) Any power conferred by this Act on a Minister of the Crown to make an order, and any power conferred by this Act to make regulations or rules, is exercisable by statutory instrument.

(2) No recommendation shall be made to Her Majesty to make an Order in Council under section 38(4), and no order shall be made under section 3, 4(4) or 40, unless a draft of the Order in Council or order has been laid before Parliament and approved by a resolution of each House of Parliament.

(3) A statutory instrument containing—

a) an order made by a Minister of the Crown under any other provision of this Act, except Part II of Schedule 2, or

b) regulations or rules made under this Act,

is subject to annulment in pursuance of a resolution of either House of Parliament.

(4) Any power conferred by this Act which is exercisable by statutory instrument includes power to make such incidental, supplementary or transitional provision as appears to the Minister exercising the power to be necessary or expedient.

Interpretation

42.—(1) In this Act—

"the Appeal Tribunal" means the Employment Appeal Tribunal,

"Appeal Tribunal procedure rules" shall be construed in accordance with section 30(1),

"appointed member" shall be construed in accordance with section 22(1)(c),

"conciliation officer" means an officer designated by the Advisory, Conciliation and Arbitration Service under section 211 of the Trade Union and Labour Relations (Consolidation) Act 1992,

"contract of employment" means a contract of service or apprenticeship, whether express or implied, and (if it is express) whether oral or in writing,

"employee" means an individual who has entered into or works under (or, where the employment has ceased, worked under) a contract of employment,

"employer", in relation to an employee, means the person by whom the employee is (or, where the employment has ceased, was) employed,

"employers' association" has the same meaning as in the Trade Union and Labour Relations (Consolidation) Act 1992,

"employment" means employment under a contract of employment and "employed" shall be construed accordingly,

"industrial tribunal procedure regulations" shall be construed in accordance with section 7(1), "statutory provision" means a provision, whether or a general or a special nature, contained in, or in any document made or issued under, any Act, whether of a general or special nature,

"successor", in relation to the employer of an employee, means (subject to subsection (2)) a person who in consequence of a change occurring (whether by virtue of a sale or other disposition or by operation of law) in the ownership of the undertaking, or of the part of the undertaking, for the purposes of which the employee was employed, has become the owner of the undertaking or part, and

"trade union" has the meaning given by section 1 of the Trade Union and Labour Relations (Consolidation) Act 1992.

(2) The definition of "successor" in subsection (1) has effect (subject to the necessary modifications) in relation to a case where—

a) the person by whom an undertaking or part of an undertaking is owned immediately before a change is one of the persons by whom (whether as partners, trustees or otherwise) it is owned immediately after the change, or

b) the persons by whom an undertaking or part of an undertaking is owned immediately before a change (whether as partners, trustees or otherwise) include the persons by whom, or include one or more of the persons by whom, it is owned immediately after the change,

as it has effect where the previous owner and the new owner are wholly different persons.

(3) For the purposes of this Act any two employers shall be treated as associated if—

a) one is a company of which the other (directly or indirectly) has control, or

b) both are companies of which a third person (directly or indirectly) has control;

and "associated employer" shall be construed accordingly.

Final provisions

Consequential amendments

43.—Schedule 1 (consequential amendments) shall have effect.

Transitionals, savings and transitory provisions

44.—Schedule 2 (transitional provisions, savings and transitory provisions) shall have effect.

Repeals and revocations

45.—The enactments specified in Part I of Schedule 3 are repealed, and the instruments specified in Part II of that Schedule are revoked, to the extent specified in the third column of that Schedule.

Commencement

46.—This Act shall come into force at the end of the period of three months beginning with the day on which it is passed.*

*The Act received Royal Assent on 22 May 1996 and comes into force on 22 August 1996.

Extent

47.—This Act does not extend to Northern Ireland.

Short title

48.—This Act may be cited as the Industrial Tribunals Act 1996.

TABLE OF DERIVATIONS

Notes:

1. This Table shows the derivation of the provisions of the consolidation.

2. The following abbreviations are used in the Table—

EP(C)A	= Employment Protection (Consolidation) Act 1978 (c. 44)
TULR(C)A	= Trade Union and Labour Relations (Consolidation) Act 1992 (c.52)
TURERA	= Trade Union Reform and Employment Rights Act 1993 (c. 19)

Provision	Derivation
1(1)	EP(C)A s.128(1).
(2)	—
2	EP(C)A s.128(1).
3(1)	EP(C)A s.131(1); TURERA s.38(a).
(2)	EP(C)A s.131(2).
(3)	EP(C)A s.131(3); TURERA s.38(b).
(4)	EP(C)A s.131(6).
(5)	EP(C)A s.131(7); TURERA s.38(e).
(6)	EP(C)A s.131(7).
4(1), (2)	EP(C)A s.128(2A), (2B); TURERA s.36(2).
(3)	EP(C)A s. 128(2C); TURERA s.36(2); Pension Schemes Act 1993 (c.48) Sch. 8 para.11(2).
(4)	EP(C)A s.128(2D); TURERA s.36(2).
(5)	EP(C)A s.128(2F); TURERA s.36(2).
(6), (7)	EP(C)A s.128(5), (6); TURERA s.36(3).
5(1)	EP(C)A Sch.9 para.9; Transfer of Functions (Minister for the Civil Service and Treasury) Order 1981 (S.I.1981/1670).
(2)	EP(C)A Sch.9 para.10; Transfer of Functions (Minister for the Civil Service and Treasury) Order 1981 (S.I. 1981/1670); Equal Pay (Amendment) Regulations 1983 (S.I.1983/1794) Reg.3(4).
(3)	EP(C)A Sch.9 para.10; Transfer of Functions (Minister for the Civil Service and Treasury) Order 1981 (S.I.1981/1670).
6(1)	EP(C)A Sch.9 para.6.
(2)	EP(C)A Sch.9 para.4.
7(1)	EP(C)A Sch.9 para.1(1).
(2)	EP(C)A s.128(4); Employment Act 1980 (c.42) Sch.1 para.16.
(3)	EP(C)A Sch.9 para.1(2)(a) to (ga), (j); Employment Act 1980 (c.42) Sch.1 para.26; Equal Pay (Amendment) Regulations 1983 (S.I.1983/1794) Reg.3(3); Employment Act 1989 (c.38) Sch.6 para.26.
(4)	EP(C)A Sch.9 para.1(7); Criminal Justice Act 1982 (c.48) ss.38, 46; Equal Pay (Amendment) Regulations 1983 (S.I.1983/1794) Reg.3(3) Criminal Procedure (Consequential Provisions) (Scotland) Act 1995 (c.40) Sch.1.
(5)	EP(C)A Sch.9 para.1(6); TURERA s.40(3).

Provision	Derivation
(6)	EP(C)A Sch.9 para.5.
8(1)	EP(C)A s.131(4).
(2)	EP(C)A s.131(4A); TURERA s.38(c).
(3)	EP(C)A s.131(5).
(4)	EP(C)A s.131(5A); TURERA s.38(d).
9(1)	EP(C)A Sch.9 para.1A(1); Employment Act 1989 (c.38) s.20; TURERA Sch.8 para.28(b).
(2), (3)	EP(C)A Sch.9 para. 1A(2), (3); Employment Act 1989 (c.38) s.20.
(4)	EP(C)A Sch.9 para.1B; TURERA Sch.8 para.28(c).
10(1)	EP(C)A Sch.9 para.1(4A); TURERA Sch.7 para.6(a).
(2)	EP(C)A Sch.9 para.1(5); TULR(C)A Sch.3 para.1(4).
(3)	EP(C)A ss.138(7)(e), 139(1)(d), 139A(3)(a); TURERA Sch.7 para.11.
(4)	EP(C)A Sch.9 para.2(1); TULR(C)A Sch.2 para.24(1), (2).
(5)	EP(C)A Sch.9 para.2(2); TURERA Sch.7 para.6(b); Collective Redundancies and Transfer of Undertakings (Protection of Employment) (Amendment) Regulations (S.I. 1995/2587) Reg.14(4).
(6)	EP(C)A ss.138(7)(c), 139(1)(c).
11(1)	EP(C)A Sch.9 para.1(5A); TURERA s.40(2).
(2) to (5)	EP(C)A Sch.9 para.1(8) to (11); TURERA s.40(4).
(6)	EP(C)A Sch.9 para.1(5A), (8); TURERA s.40(2), (4); Criminal Procedure (Consequential Provisions) (Scotland) Act 1995 (c.40) s.2(4).
12	Disability Discrimination Act 1995 (c.50) s.62.
13(1)	EP(C)A Sch.9 para.1(2)(h), (i).
(2)	EP(C)A Sch.9 para. 1(4); TURERA Sch.8 para.28(a).
14	EP(C)A Sch.9 para.6A; Employment Act 1982 (c.46) Sch.3 Pt.I para.7.
15(1)	EP(C)A Sch.9 para.7(1).
(2)	EP(C)A Sch.9 para.7(2); Employment Act 1980 (c.42) Sch.1 para.27.
(3)	EP(C)A Sch.9 para.7(3).
16(1)	Betting, Gaming and Lotteries Act 1963 (c.2) Sch.5A para.16; EP(C)A s.132(1); TULR(C)A Sch.2 para.19; TURERA Sch.8 para.19; Sunday Trading Act 1994 (c.20) Sch.4 para.16; Deregulation and Contracting Out Act 1994 (c.40) Sch.8.
(2)	EP(C)A s.132(2).
(3)	EP(C)A s.132(2); Social Security Act 1986 (c.50) Sch.10 Pt.II para.50(a); Jobseekers Act 1995 (c.18) Sch.2 para.2(2).
(4)	EP(C)A s.132(3)(a); Social Security Act 1986 (c.50) Sch.10 Pt.II para.50(b)(i); Jobseekers Act 1995 (c.18) Sch.2 para.2(2).
(5)	EP(C)A s.132(3)(b) to (f); Social Security Act 1980 (c.30) Sch.4 para.13; Health and Social Services and Social Security

Provision	Derivation
(5) cont.	Adjudications Act 1983 (c.41) Sch.8 Pt.I para.1; Social Security Act 1986 (c.50) Sch.10 Pt.II para.50(b); Jobseekers Act 1995 (c.18) Sch.2 para.2(2), (3).
(6)	EP(C)A s.132(3)(g).
17(1)	EP(C)A s.132(4); Social Security Act 1986 (c.50) Sch.10 Pt.II para.50(c); Social Security (Consequential Provisions) Act 1992 (c.6) Sch.2 para.50(1); Jobseekers Act 1995 (c.18) Sch.2 para.2(2), (4).
(2)	EP(C)A s.132(5); Jobseekers Act 1995 (c.18) Sch.2 para.2(2).
(3)	EP(C)A s.132(6).
(4)	EP(C)A s.132(6); Jobseekers Act 1995 (c.18) Sch.2 para.2(5).
18(1)	Betting, Gaming and Lotteries Act 1963 (c.2) Sch.5A para.21; Sex Discrimination Act 1975 (c.65) s.64(1); Race Relations Act 1976 (c.74) s.55(1); EP(C)A ss.133(1), 134(1); Employment Act 1980 (c.42) Sch.1 para.17; Wages Act 1986 (c.48) Sch.4 para.9; TULR(C)A s.290; TURERA Sch.8 paras.20, 86; Sunday Trading Act 1994 (c.20) Sch.4 para.21; Deregulation and Contracting Out Act 1994 (c.40) Sch.8; Pensions Act 1995 (c.26) Sch.3 para.8; Disability Discrimination Act 1995 (c.50) Sch.3 para.1; Collective Redundancies and Transfer of Undertakings (Protection of Employment) (Amendment) Regulations (S.I. 1995/2587) Regs. 12(3), 13(3).
(2)	Sex Discrimination Act 1975 (c.65) s.64(1); Race Relations Act 1976 (c.74) s.55(1); EP(C)A ss.133(2), (4), 134(1); Disability Discrimination Act 1995 (c.50) Sch.3 para.1(1).
(3)	Sex Discrimination Act 1975 (c.65) s.64(2); Race Relations Act 1976 (c.74) s.55(2); EP(C)A ss.133(3), (4), 134(3); Employment Act 1980 (c.42) Sch.1 para.18; Disability Discrimination Act 1995 (c.50) Sch.3 para.1(2).
(4)	EP(C)A s.134(2).
(5)	EP(C)A s.134(3); Employment Act 1980 (c.42) Sch.1 para.18.
(6)	Sex Discrimination Act 1975 (c.65) s.64(3); Race Relations Act 1976 (c.74) s.55(3); EP(C)A ss.133(5), 134(4); Disability Discrimination Act 1995 (c.50) Sch.3 para.1(3).
(7)	Sex Discrimination Act 1975 (c.65) s.64(4); Race Relations Act 1976 (c.74) s.55(4); EP(C)A ss.133(6), 134(5); Disability Discrimination Act 1995 (c.50) Sch.3 para.1(4).
(8)	EP(C)A s.133(7).
19	EP(C)A Sch.9 para.1(3).
20(1)	EP(C)A s.135(1).
(2)	EP(C)A Sch.11 paras.13, 14.
(3)	EP(C)A Sch.11 para.12.
21(1)	Betting, Gaming and Lotteries Act 1963 (c.2) Sch.5A para.16; EP(C) s.136(1); Wages Act 1986 (c.48) Sch.4 para.10; TULR(C)A s291(2); Sunday Trading Act 1994 (c.20) Sch.4 para.16; Deregulation and Contracting Out Act 1994 (c.40) Sch.8; Pensions Act 1995 (c.26) Sch.3 para.9; Disability Discrimination Act 1995 (c.50) Sch.6 para.2.

Provision	Derivation
(2)	EP(C)A s.136(5); TULR(C)A s.291(3).
(3)	—
22(1)	EP(C)A s.135(2).
(2)	EP(C)A s.135(3); TULR(C)A Sch.2 para.20.
(3), (4)	EP(C)A s.135(4), (5).
23(1)	EP(C)A Sch.11 para.4.
(2)	EP(C)A Sch.11 paras.5, 6.
(3)	EP(C)A Sch.11 para.7.
(4)	EP(C)A Sch.11 para.9.
(5)	EP(C)A Sch.11 para.11.
24(1)	EP(C)A Sch.11 para.8(1).
(2)	EP(C)A Sch.11 para.8(2); Supreme Court Act 1981 (c.54) Sch.5, entry relating to EP(C)A.
(3)	EP(C)A Sch.11 para.10.
24(1)	EP(C)A Sch.11 para.1.
(2), (3)	EP(C)A Sch.11 para.2; Judicial Pensions and Retirement Act 1993 (c.8) Sch.6 para.30.
(4)	EP(C)A Sch.11 para.3.
26	EP(C)A Sch.11 para.24; Transfer of Functions (Treasury and Minister for the Civil Service) Order 1995 (S.I.1995/269).
27(1)	EP(C)A Sch.11 para.25; Transfer of Functions (Minister for the Civil Service and Treasury) Order 1981 (S.I.1981/1670); Transfer of Functions (Treasury and Minister for the Civil Service) Order 1995 (S.I.1995/269).
(2) to (4)	EP(C)A Sch.11 paras.26 to 28; Transfer of Functions (Minister for the Civil Service and Treasury) Order 1981 (S.I.1981/1670).
28(1)	EP(C)A Sch.11 para.15.
(2) to (5)	EP(C)A Sch.11 para.16; TURERA s.37.
29(1)	EP(C)A Sch.11 para.20.
(2)	EP(C)A Sch.11 para.22(1).
30(1)	EP(C)A Sch.11 para.17(1).
(2)	EP(C)A Sch.11 para.18; Employment Act 1980 (c.42) Sch.1 para.28; Employment Act 1982 (c.46) Sch.3 Pt.I para.8(1); TULR(C)A Sch.2 para.25(a); TURERA Sch.7 para.7, Sch.8 paras.29, 30.
(3)	EP(C)A Sch.11 para.17(2).
31(1) to (6)	EP(C)A Sch.11 para.18A; TURERA s.41.
(7)	EP(C)A Sch.11 para.18A(7); TURERA s.41.
(8)	EP(C)A Sch.11 para.18A(7); TURERA s.41; Criminal Procedure (Consequential Provisions) (Scotland) Act 1995 (c.40) s.2(4).
32(1), (2)	Disability Discrimination Act 1995 (c.50) s.63(1), (2).
(3) to (6)	Disability Discrimination Act 1995 (c.50) ss.62(3) to (6), 63(3).

Provision	Derivation
(7)	Disability Discrimination Act 1995 (c.50) s.63(4), (5).
(8)	Disability Discrimination Act 1995 (c.50) ss.62(7), 63(6).
33(1) to (4)	EP(C)A s.136A(1) to (4); TURERA s.42.
(5)	EP(C)A s.136A(6); TURERA s.42.
34	EP(C)A Sch.11 para.19.
35	EP(C)A Sch.11 para.21.
36(1)	EP(C)A Sch.11 para.21A(1); Employment Act 1980 (c.42) Sch.1 para.29; TULR(C)A Sch. 2 para.25(b).
(2)	EP(C)A Sch.11 para.21A(2); Employment Act 1980 (c.42) Sch.1 para.29.
(3)	EP(C)A Sch.11 para.21A(3); Employment Act 1982 (c.46) Sch.3 Pt.I para.9; TULR(C)A Sch.2 para.25(b).
(4)	EP(C)A Sch.11 para.22(2).
(5)	EP(C)A Sch.11 para.23(2).
37(1), (2)	EP(C)A s.136(4).
(3)	EP(C)A s136A(5); TURERA s.42.
(4)	EP(C)A s.136(4).
38(1), (2)	EP(C)A s.138(1), (2).
(3)	EP(C)A s.138(7)(a), (b).
(4)	EP(C)A ss.138(3), 138A(2)(b); TURERA s.31; Reserve Forces Act 1996 (c.14) Sch.10 para.17.
39(1)	EP(C)A ss.139(1), 139A(1); TURERA Sch.7 para.11.
(2)	EP(C)A ss.139(2), 139A(2); TURERA Sch.7 para.11.
(3)	EP(C)A s.139(1)(a), (b).
(4)	EP(C)A s.139A(5); TURERA Sch.7 para.11.
(5)	EP(C)A s.139(3) to (9).
40(1)	EP(C)A s.149(1).
(2)	EP(C)A s.149(2).
41(1)	EP(C)A ss.154(1).
(2)	EP(C)A ss.128(2E), 131(8), 138A(6), 149(4); TURERA ss.31(2), 36(2).
(3), (4)	EP(C)A s.154(2), (3).
42(1)	
"Appeal Tribunal"	—
"Appeal Tribunal procedure rules"	—
"appointed member"	—
"conciliation officer"	—

Provision	Derivation
"contract of employment", employee", "employer"	EP(C)A s.153(1).
"employers' association"	EP(C)A s.153(1); TULR(C)A Sch.2 para.21(2)(a).
"employment", "employed", "statutory provision"	EP(C)A s.153(1).
"industrial tribunal procedure rules"	—
"successor"	EP(C)A s.153(1); TULR(C)A Sch.2 para.21(2)(d).
"trade union"	EP(C)A s.153(1); TULR(C)A Sch.2 para.21(2)(f).
(2)	EP(C)A s.153(4A); TULR(C)A Sch.2 para.21(3).
(3)	EP(C)A s.153(4).
43	—
44	—
45	—
46	—
47	—
48	—
Sch. 1	—
Sch. 2	—
Sch. 3	—

3.2 The Industrial Tribunals Extension of Jurisdiction (England and Wales) Order 1994 SI No 1623

1.—Citation, commencement and interpretation

(1) This Order may be cited as the Industrial Tribunals Extension of Jurisdiction (England and Wales) Order 1994 and comes into force on the first day after it is made [ie, 12 July 1994].

(2) In this order—

'contract claim' means a claim in respect of which proceedings may be brought before an industrial tribunal by virtue of article 3 or 4; and

'the 1978 Act' means the Employment Protection (Consolidation) Act 1978.

2.—Transitional provision

This Order does not enable proceedings in respect of a contract claim to be brought before an industrial tribunal unless—

a) the effective date of termination (as defined in section 55(4) of the 1978 Act) in respect of the contract giving rise to the claim, or

b) where there is no effective date of termination, the last day upon which the employee works in the employment which has terminated,

occurs on or after the day on which the Order comes into force.

3.—Extension of jurisdiction

Proceedings may be brought before an industrial tribunal in respect of a claim of an employee for the recovery of damages or any other sum (other than a claim for damages, or for a sum due, in respect of personal injuries) if—

a) the claim is one to which section 131(2) of the 1978 Act applies and which a court in England and Wales would under the law for the time being in force have jurisdiction to hear and determine;

b) the claim is not one to which article 5 applies; and

c) the claim arises or is outstanding on the termination of the employee's employment.

4.—Proceedings may be brought before an industrial tribunal in respect of a claim of an employer for the recovery of damages or any other sum (other than a claim for damages, or for a sum due, in respect of personal injuries) if—

a) the claim is one to which section 131(2) of the 1978 Act applies and which a court in England and Wales would under the law for the time being in force have jurisdiction to hear and determine;

b) the claim is not one to which article 5 applies;

c) the claim arises or is outstanding on the termination of the employment of the employee against whom it is made; and

d) proceedings in respect of a claim of that employee have been brought before an industrial tribunal by virtue of this Order.

5.—This article applies to a claim for breach of a contractual term of any of the following descriptions—

a) a term requiring the employer to provide living accommodation for the employee;

b) a term imposing an obligation on the employer or the employee in connection with the provision of living accommodation;

c) a term relating to intellectual property;

d) a term imposing an obligation of confidence;

e) a term which is a covenant in restraint of trade.

In this article, 'intellectual property' includes copyright, rights in performances, moral rights, design right, registered designs, patents and trade marks.

6.—Manner in which proceedings may be brought

Proceedings on a contract claim may be brought before an industrial tribunal by presenting a complaint to an industrial tribunal.

7.—Time within which proceedings may be brought

An industrial tribunal shall not entertain a complaint in respect of an employee's contract claim unless it is presented—

a) within the period of three months beginning with the effective date of termination of the contract giving rise to the claim, or

b) where there is no effective date of termination, within the period of three months beginning with the last day upon which the employee worked in the employment which has terminated, or

c) where the tribunal is satisfied that it was not reasonably practicable for the complaint to be presented within whichever of those periods is applicable, within such further period as the tribunal considers reasonable.

8.—An industrial tribunal shall not entertain a complaint in respect of an employer's contract claim unless—

a) it is presented at a time when there is before the tribunal a complaint in respect of a contract claim of a particular employee which has not been settled or withdrawn;

b) it arises out of a contract with that employee; and

c) it is presented—

i) within the period of six weeks beginning with the day, or if more than one the last of the days, on which the employer (or other person who is the respondent party to the employee's contract claim) received from the tribunal a copy of an originating application in respect of a contract claim of that employee; or

ii) where the tribunal is satisfied that it was not reasonably practicable for the complaint to be presented within that period, within such further period as the tribunal considers reasonable.

9.—Death and bankruptcy

(1) Where proceedings in respect of a contract claim have been brought before an industrial tribunal and an employee or employer party to them dies before their conclusion, the proceedings shall not abate by reason of the death and the tribunal may, if it thinks it necessary in order to ensure that all matters in dispute may be effectively and completely determined and adjudicated upon, order the personal representatives of the deceased party, or other persons whom the tribunal considers appropriate, to be made parties and the proceedings to be carried on as if they had been substituted for the deceased party.

(2) Where proceedings in respect of a contract claim have been brought before an industrial tribunal and the employee or employer who is the applicant party to them becomes bankrupt before their conclusion, the proceedings shall not abate by reason of the bankruptcy and the tribunal may, if it thinks it necessary in order to ensure that all matters in dispute may be effectually and completely adjudicated upon, order the person in whom the interest of the bankrupt party has vested to be made a party and the proceedings to be carried on as if he had been substituted for the bankrupt party.

10.—Limit on payment to be ordered

An industrial tribunal shall not in proceedings in respect of a contract claim, or in respect of a number of contract claims relating to the same contract, order the payment of an amount exceeding £25,000.

3.3 The Industrial Tribunals Extension of Jurisdiction (Scotland) Order 1994 SI No 1624

1.—Citation, commencement and interpretation

(1) This Order may be cited as the Industrial Tribunals Extension of Jurisdiction (Scotland) Order 1994 and comes into force on the first day after it is made [ie, 12 July 1994].

(2) In this Order—

'contract claim' means a claim in respect of which proceedings may be brought before an industrial tribunal by virtue of article 3 or 4; and

'the 1978 Act' means the Employment Protection (Consolidation) Act 1978.

2.—Transitional provision

This Order does not enable proceedings in respect of a contract claim to be brought before an industrial tribunal unless—

a) the effective date of termination (as defined in section 55(4) of the 1978 Act) in respect of the contract giving rise to the claim, or

b) where there is no effective date of termination, the last day upon which the employee works in the employment which has terminated,

occurs on or after the day on which the Order comes into force.

3.—Extension of jurisdiction

Proceedings may be brought before an industrial tribunal in respect of a claim of an employee for the recovery of damages or any other sum (other than a claim for damages, or for a sum due, in respect of personal injuries) if—

a) the claim is one to which section 131(2) of the 1978 Act applies and which a court in Scotland would under the law for the time being in force have jurisdiction to hear and determine;

b) the claim is not one to which article 5 applies; and

c) the claim arises or is outstanding on the termination of the employee's employment.

4.—Proceedings may be brought before an industrial tribunal in respect of a claim of an employer for the recovery of damages or any other sum (other than a claim for damages, or for a sum due, in respect of personal injuries) if—

a) the claim is one to which section 131(2) of the 1978 Act applies and which a court in Scotland would under the law for the time being in force have jurisdiction to hear and determine;

b) the claim is not one to which article 5 applies;

c) the claim arises or is outstanding on the termination of the employment of the employee against whom it is made; and

d) proceedings in respect of a claim of that employee have been brought before an industrial tribunal by virtue of this Order.

5.—This article applies to a claim for breach of a contractual term of any of the following descriptions—

a) a term requiring the employer to provide living accommodation for the employee;

b) a term imposing an obligation on the employer or the employee in connection with the provision of living accommodation;

c) a term relating to intellectual property;

d) a term imposing an obligation of confidence;

e) a term which is a covenant in restraint of trade.

In this article, 'intellectual property' includes copyright, rights in performances, moral rights, design right, registered designs, patents and trade marks.

6.—Manner in which proceedings may be brought

Proceedings on a contract claim may be brought before an industrial tribunal by presenting a complaint to an industrial tribunal.

7.—Time within which proceedings may be brought

An industrial tribunal shall not entertain a complaint in respect of an employee's contract claim unless it is presented—

a) within the period of three months beginning with the effective date of termination of the contract giving rise to the claim, or

b) where the is no effective date of termination, within the period of three months beginning with the last day upon which the employee worked in the employment which has terminated, or

c) where the tribunal is satisfied that it was not reasonably practicable for the complaint to be presented within whichever of those periods is applicable, within such further period as the tribunal considers reasonable.

8.—An industrial tribunal shall not entertain a complaint in respect of an employer's contract claim unless—

a) it is presented at a time when there is before the tribunal a complaint in respect of a contract claim of a particular employee which has not been settled or withdrawn;

b) it arises out of a contract with that employee; and

c) it is presented—

i) within the period of six weeks beginning with the day, or if more than one the last of the days, on which the employer (or other person who is the respondent party to the employee's contract claim) received from the tribunal a copy of an originating application in respect of a contract claim of that employee; or

ii) where the tribunal is satisfied that it was not reasonably practicable for the complaint to be presented within that period, within such further periods as the tribunal considers reasonable.

9.—Death and legal incapacity

Where proceedings in respect of a contract claim have been brought before an industrial tribunal and an employee or employer party to them dies or comes under legal incapacity before the conclusion of the proceedings, the tribunal may order any person who represents that party or his estate to be made a party to the proceedings in place of the party who has died or come under legal incapacity and the proceedings to be carried on accordingly.

10.—Limit on payment to be ordered

An industrial tribunal shall not in proceedings in respect of a contract claim, or in respect of a number of contract claims relating to the same contract, order the payment of an amount exceeding £25,000.

3.4 The Industrial Tribunals (Constitution and Rules of Procedure) Regulations 1993 SI No 2687 *

Citation, commencement and revocation

1.—(1) These Regulations may be cited as the Industrial Tribunals (Constitution and Procedure) Regulations 1993 and the Rules of Procedure contained in Schedules 1, 2, 3, 4 and 5 to these Regulations may be referred to, respectively, as—
   a) the Industrial Tribunals Rules of Procedure 1993;
   b) the Industrial Tribunals Complementary Rules of Procedure 1993;
   c) the Industrial Tribunals (Levy Appeals) Rules of Procedure 1993;
   d) the Industrial Tribunals (Improvement and Prohibition Notice Appeals) Rules of Procedure 1993; and
   e) the Industrial Tribunals (Non-Discrimination Notices Appeals) Rules of Procedure 1993.

(2) These Regulations shall come into force on 16th December 1993.

(3) The following Regulations are hereby revoked—
The Industrial Tribunals (England and Wales) Regulations 1965
The Industrial Tribunals (England and Wales) (Amendment) Regulations 1967
The Industrial Tribunals (England and Wales) (Amendment) Regulations 1970
The Industrial Tribunals (Improvement and Prohibition Notices Appeals) Regulations 1974
The Industrial Tribunals (Amendment) Regulations 1977
The Industrial Tribunals (Non-Discrimination Notices Appeals) Regulations 1977
The Industrial Tribunals (Rules of Procedure) Regulations 1985.

---

*As amended by 1996 SI No 1757, in force 31 July 1996.

Interpretation

2.—(1) In these Regulations and in Schedules 1, 2, 3, 4, and 5, unless the context otherwise requires—

"the 1978 Act" means the Employment Protection (Consolidation) Act 1978;

"the 1992 Act" means the Trade Union and Labour Relations (Consolidation) Act 1992;

"chairman" means the President or a member of the panel of chairmen selected in accordance with regulation 7(1), or the President where a Minister of the Crown so directs in accordance with section 128(6) of the 1978 Act;

"the clerk" means the person appointed as clerk to the tribunal by the Secretary of the Tribunals or a Regional Secretary to act in that capacity at one or more hearings;

"hearing" means a sitting of a tribunal duly constituted for the purpose of receiving evidence, hearing addresses and witnesses or doing anything lawfully requisite to enable the tribunal to reach a decision on any question;

"the Office of the Tribunals" means the Central Office of the Industrial Tribunals (England and Wales);

"panel of chairmen" means the panel appointed under regulation 5(1)(a);

"the President" means the President of the Industrial Tribunals (England and Wales) or the person nominated by the Lord Chancellor to discharge for the time being the functions of the President;

"Regional Chairman" means a member of the panel of chairmen who has been appointed to the position of Regional Chairman in accordance with regulation 6(1) or who has been nominated to discharge the functions of a Regional Chairman in accordance with regulation 6(2);

"Regional Office of the Industrial Tribunals" means a regional office which has been established under the Office of the Tribunals for an area specified by the President [or an office established for an area within such an area];

"Regional Secretary" means the person for the time being acting as the secretary of a Regional Office of the Industrial Tribunals;

"Register" means the Register of applications, appeals and decisions kept in pursuance of regulation 9;

"the Secretary" means the person for the time being appointed to act as the Secretary of the Office of the Tribunals;

"tribunal" means an industrial tribunal (England and Wales) established in pursuance of regulation 4 and in relation to any proceedings means the tribunal to which the proceedings have been referred by the President or a Regional Chairman.

(2) In these Regulations, in so far as they relate to the rules in Schedules 1 and 2, and in those Schedules, unless the context otherwise requires—

"the 1970 Act" means the Equal Pay Act 1970

"the 1975 Act" means the Sex Discrimination Act 1975

"the 1976 Act" means the Race Relations Act 1976

"the 1986 Act" means the Sex Discrimination Act 1986;

"decision" in relation to a tribunal includes—

a declaration,

an order, including an order striking out any originating application or notice of appearance made under rule 4(7) or 13(2),

a recommendation or an award of the tribunal, and

a determination under rule 6,

but does not include any other interlocutory order or any other decision on an interlocutory matter;

"equal value claim" means a claim by an applicant which rests upon entitlement to the benefit of an equality clause by virtue of the operation section 1(2)(c) of the Equal Pay Act;

"expert" means a member of the panel of independent experts within the meaning of section 2A(4) of the Equal Pay Act;

"report" means a report required by a tribunal to be prepared by an expert, pursuant to section 2A(1)(b) of the Equal Pay Act;

"respondent" means a party to the proceedings before a tribunal other than the applicant.

(3) In these Regulations, in so far as they relate to the rules in Schedule 3, and in that Schedule, unless the context otherwise requires—

"the 1982 Act" means the Industrial Training Act 1982;

"the Board" means in relation to an appeal the respondent industrial training board;

"levy" means a levy imposed under section 11 of the 1982 Act.

(4) In these Regulations, in so far as they relate to the rules in Schedule 4, and in that Schedule, unless the context otherwise requires—

"the 1974 Act" means the Health and Safety at Work etc. Act 1974;

"decision" in relation to a tribunal includes a direction under rule 4 and any order which is not an interlocutory order;

"improvement notice" means a notice under section 21 of the 1974 Act;

"inspector" means a person appointed under section 19(1) of the 1974 Act;

"prohibition notice" means a notice under section 22 of the 1974 Act;

"respondent" means the inspector who issued the improvement notice or prohibition notice which is the subject of the appeal.

(5) In these Regulations, in so far as they relate to the rules in Schedule 5, and in that Schedule, unless the context otherwise requires—

"the 1975 Act" means the Sex Discrimination Act 1975;

"the 1976 Act" means the Race Relations Act 1976;

"decision" in relation to a tribunal includes the direction under section 68(3) of the 1975 Act or, as the case may be, under section 59(3) of the 1976 Act and any other order which is not an interlocutory order;

"non-discrimination notice" means a notice under section 67 of the 1975 Act or, as the case may be, under section 58 of the 1976 Act;

"respondent" means the Equal Opportunities Commission established under section 53 of the 1975 Act or, as the case may be, the Commission for Racial Equality established under section 43 of the 1976 Act.

President of Industrial Tribunals

3.—(1) There shall be a President of the Industrial Tribunals (England and Wales) who shall be appointed by the Lord Chancellor and shall be a person having a seven year general qualification within the meaning of section 71 of the Courts and Legal Services Act 1990.

(2) The President may resign his office by notice in writing to the Lord Chancellor.

(3) The President shall vacate his office at the end of the completed year of service in the course of which he attains the age of 72 years.

(4) If the Lord Chancellor is satisfied that the President is incapacitated by infirmity of mind or body from discharging the duties of his office, or the President is adjudged to be bankrupt or makes a composition or arrangement with his creditors, the Lord Chancellor may revoke his appointment.

(5) The functions of President under these Regulations may, if he is for any reason unable to act or during any vacancy in his office, be discharged by a person nominated for that purpose by the Lord Chancellor.

Establishment of industrial tribunals

4.—(1) The President shall from time to time determine the number of tribunals to be established in England and Wales for the purposes of determining proceedings.

(2) The President or, in relation to the area specified in relation to him, a Regional Chairman shall determine at what times and in what places in England and Wales tribunals shall sit.

Panels of members of tribunals

5.—(1) There shall be three panels of members of the Industrial Tribunals (England and Wales), namely—

a) a panel of persons, having a seven year general qualification within the meaning of the Courts and Legal Services Act 1990, appointed by the Lord Chancellor;

b) a panel of persons appointed by the Secretary of State after consultation with such organisations or associations of organisations representative of employees as he sees fit; and

c) a panel of persons appointed by the Secretary of State after consultation with such organisations or associations of organisations representative of employers as he sees fit.

(2) Members of the panels constituted under these Regulations shall hold and vacate office under the terms of the instrument under which they are appointed but may resign their office by notice in writing, in the case of a member of the panel of chairmen, to the Lord Chancellor and, in any other case, to the Secretary of State; and any such member who ceases to hold office shall be eligible for reappointment.

Regional Chairmen

6.—(1) The [Lord Chancellor] may from time to time appoint Regional Chairmen from the panel of chairmen and each Regional Chairman shall be responsible for the administration of justice by tribunals in the area specified by the President in relation to him.

(2) The President or the Regional Chairman for an area may from time to time nominate a member of the panel of chairmen to discharge for the time being the functions of the Regional Chairman for that area.

Composition of tribunals

7.—(1) For each hearing of any matter before a tribunal the President or the Regional Chairman shall, subject to paragraph 5, select a chairman, who shall be the President or a member of the panel of chairmen, and the President or the Regional Chairman may select himself.

(2) In any proceedings which are to be determined by a tribunal comprising a chairman (selected in accordance with paragraph (1) above) and two other members, those other members shall be selected by the President or by the Regional Chairman, as to one member from the panel of persons appointed by the Secretary of State under regulation 5(1)(b) and as to the other from the panel of persons appointed under regulation 5(1)(c).

(3) In any proceedings which are to be determined by a tribunal whose composition is described in paragraph (2), those proceedings may, with the consent of the parties, be heard and determined in the absence of any one member other than the chairman, and in that event the tribunal shall be properly constituted.

(4) The President or the Regional Chairman may at any time select from the appropriate panel another person in substitution for the chairman or other member of the tribunal previously selected to hear any proceedings before a tribunal.

(5) Paragraph (1) does not apply where a Minister of the Crown has issued a direction in accordance with section 128(6) of the 1978 Act (direction on grounds of national security that proceedings be heard and determined by the President).

Proceedings of tribunals

8.—(1) Subject to paragraphs (2), (3) and (4), the rules in Schedule 1 shall apply in relation to all proceedings before a tribunal except where separate rules of procedure made under the provisions of any enactment are applicable.

(2) In proceedings to which the rules in Schedule 1 apply and which involve an equal value claim, the rules in Schedule 2 (including rule 8A) shall apply in place of rules 4, 9, 10, 12, 13 and 20 in Schedule 1.

(3) The rules contained in Schedules 1 and 2 shall apply in proceedings to which they relate where—

a) the respondent or one of the respondents resides or carries on business in England and Wales; or

b) had the remedy been by way of action in the county court, the cause of action would have arisen wholly or in part in England and Wales; or

c) the proceedings are to determine a question which has been referred to the tribunal by a court in England or Wales.

(4) The rules in Schedules 3, 4 and 5 shall apply in relation to proceedings before a tribunal which relate to matters arising in England and Wales and consist, respectively, in—

a) an appeal by a person assessed to levy imposed under a levy order made under section 12 of the 1982 Act;

b) an appeal against an improvement or prohibition notice under section 23 of the 1974 Act; and

c) an appeal against a non-discrimination notice under section 68 of the 1975 Act or section 59 of the 1976 Act.

Register

9.—(1) The Secretary shall maintain a Register of applications, appeals and decisions [at the Office of the Tribunals] which shall be open to the inspection of any person without charge at all reasonable hours.

[(2) The Register, or any part of it, may be kept by means of a computer.]

Proof of decisions of tribunals

10.—The production in any proceedings in any court of a document purporting to be certified by the Secretary to be a true copy of an entry of a decision in the Register shall, unless the contrary is proved, be sufficient evidence of the document and of the facts stated therein.

Transitional provisions relating to rules of procedure

11.—(1) The rules in Schedules 1, 2, 3, 4 and 5 (in this regulation referred to as "the new rules") shall apply in all proceedings to which they relate, irrespective of when those proceedings were commenced, as from 16th December 1993, and the rules of procedure in—

a) Schedule 2 to the Industrial Tribunals (England and Wales) Regulations 1965;

b) the Schedule to the Industrial Tribunals (Improvement and Prohibition Notices Appeal) Regulations 1974;

c) the Schedule to the Industrial Tribunals (Non-Discrimination Notices Appeals) Regulations 1977;

d) the Industrial Tribunals Rules of Procedure 1985 ("the 1985 rules"); and

e) the Industrial Tribunals Complementary Rules of Procedure 1985,

(in this regulation together referred to as "the old rules") shall cease to have effect in relation to proceedings on that date.

(2) Anything done validly under or pursuant to the old rules before 16th December 1993 shall be treated as having been done validly for the purposes of these Regulations and the new rules, whether or not what was done could have been done under or pursuant to these Regulations and the new rules.

(3) Notwithstanding paragraph (1), in any proceedings in which a pre-hearing assessment (under Rule 6 of the 1985 rules) has taken place or commenced before 16th December 1993, Rule 6 of those rules shall continue to have effect in relation to those proceedings and no pre-hearing review (under rule 7 in Schedule 1) may take place.

(4) Where the first fixing of the date of a pre-hearing assessment occurs before 16th December 1993 but paragraph (3) does not apply, the hearing shall be refixed as a pre-hearing review (under rule 7 in Schedule 1).

Transitional provisions relating to composition of tribunals

12.—(1) Except as mentioned in paragraph (2), a tribunal hearing an originating application on or after 16th December 1993 shall be composed of a chairman and two other members (or, with the consent of the parties, a chairman and one other member) where the first fixing of a date for the hearing of the originating application occurred before 30th November 1993.

(2) A tribunal hearing such an originating application on or after 16th December 1993 may be composed of a chairman alone for either of the following purposes—

a) making an order dismissing the proceedings where the appellant or applicant has given written notice of the abandonment of the proceedings; and

b) deciding an application in accordance with the written agreement of the parties.

3.5 Industrial Tribunal Rules 1993 (Schs 1 and 2 to foregoing)

SCHEDULE 1

[Regulation 8(1)]

RULES OF PROCEDURE

Originating application

1.—(1) Where proceedings are brought by an applicant, they shall be instituted by the applicant presenting to the Secretary an originating application, which shall be in writing and shall set out—

    a) the name and address of the applicant and, if different, an address within the United Kingdom to which he requires notices and documents relating to the proceedings to be sent;

    b) the names and addresses of the person or persons against whom relief is sought; and

    c) the grounds, with particulars thereof, on which relief is sought.

(2) Where the Secretary is of the opinion that the originating application does not seek or on the facts stated therein cannot entitle the applicant to a relief which a tribunal has power to give, he may give notice to that effect to the applicant stating the reasons for his opinion and informing him that the application will not be registered unless he states in writing that he wishes to proceed with it.

(3) An application in respect of which such a notice has been given shall not be treated as having been received for the purpose of rule 2 unless the applicant intimates in writing to the Secretary that he wishes to proceed with it; and upon receipt of such an intimation the Secretary shall proceed in accordance with that rule.

(4) In the case of an originating application in respect of a complaint under section 6(4A) of the 1986 Act relating to a term of a collective agreement, the following persons, whether or not identified in the originating application, shall be regarded as the persons against whom relief is sought and shall be treated as respondents for the purposes of these rules, that is to say—

    a) the applicant's employer (or prospective employer), and

    b) every organisation of employers and organisation of workers, and every association of or representative of such organisations, which, if the term were to be varied voluntarily, would be likely, in the opinion of the tribunal, to negotiate the variation;

provided that such an organisation or association shall not be treated as a respondent if the tribunal, having made such enquiries of the applicant and such other enquiries as it thinks fit, is of the opinion that it is not reasonably practicable to identify the organisation or association.

(5) Where proceedings are referred to a tribunal by a court, these rules shall be applied to them, except where the rules are inappropriate, as if the proceedings had been instituted by the presentation of an originating application.

[(5A) Paragraph (1)(b) does not apply to an originating application in respect of an application under section 3C of the Employment Agencies Act 1973 for the variation or revocation of a prohibition order, but on any such application the Secretary of State shall be treated as the respondent for the purpose of these rules.]

Action upon receipt of originating application

2.—(1) Upon receiving an originating application the Secretary shall—
   a) send a copy of it to the respondent;
   b) give every party notice in writing of the case number of the application (which shall constitute the title of the proceedings) and of the address to which notices and other communications to the Secretary shall be sent; and
   c) send to the respondent a notice in writing which includes information, as appropriate to the case, about the means and time for entering an appearance, the consequences of failure to do so, and the right to receive a copy of the decision.

(2) The Secretary shall, subject to rule 13(6), enter particulars of an originating application in the Register either within 28 days of receiving it or, if that is not practicable, as soon as reasonably practicable thereafter.

(3) The Secretary shall also, in all cases, notify the parties that in every case where an enactment provides for conciliation, the services of a conciliation officer are available to them.

Appearance by respondent

3.—(1) A respondent shall, within [21] days of receiving the copy of the originating application, enter an appearance to the proceedings by presenting to the Secretary a written notice of appearance—
   a) setting out his full name and address and, if different, an address within the United Kingdom to which he requires notices and documents relating to the proceedings to be sent;
   b) stating whether or not he intends to resist the application; and
   c) if he does intend to resist it, setting out sufficient particulars to show on what grounds.
   Upon receipt of a notice of appearance the Secretary shall send a copy of it to each other party.

(2) A respondent who has not entered an appearance shall not be entitled to take any part in the proceedings except—
   a) to apply under rule 15 for an extension of the time appointed by this rule for entering an appearance;
   b) to make an application under rule 4(1)(a);
   c) to make an application under rule 11(4) in respect of rule 11(1)(b);
   d) to be called as a witness by another person;
   e) to be sent a copy of a document or corrected entry in pursuance of rule 10(5), 10(10) or 10(11);
   and in the rules which follow, the word "party" only includes such a respondent in relation to his entitlement to take such a part in the proceedings, and in relation to any such part which he takes.

(3) A notice of appearance which—
   a) is presented to the Secretary after the time appointed by this rule for entering appearances, and

b) sets out the reasons why the notice has been presented after that time shall be deemed to include an application under rule 15 for an extension of the time so appointed on the grounds disclosed by those reasons.

(4) Where a chairman grants an application under rule 15 for an extension of the time so appointed (including an application deemed to be made by virtue of paragraph (3)) he shall determine whether, having regard to the grounds of the application, it would have been reasonably practicable for the respondent to present his notice of appearance within the time so appointed. If the chairman determines that it would have been so practicable, the respondent shall be treated as having acted unreasonably for the purposes of rule 12(1) and the chairman shall make an order under that rule if he considers it appropriate.]

Power to require further particulars and attendance of witnesses and to grant discovery

4.—(1) A tribunal may, on the application of a party made either by notice to the Secretary or at the hearing of the originating application, or of its own motion—

a) require a party to furnish in writing to the person specified by the tribunal further particulars of the grounds on which that party relies and of any facts and contentions relevant thereto,

b) [grant to a party] such discovery or inspection (including the taking of copies) of documents as might be granted by a county court.

and may appoint the time at or within which and the place at which any act required in pursuance of this rule is to be done.

(2) A tribunal may, on the application of a party made either by notice to the Secretary or at the hearing of the originating application, or of its own motion—

a) require the attendance of any person, including a party, as a witness, wherever such person may be within Great Britain, and

b) if it does so require the attendance of a person, require him to produce any document relating to the matter to be determined,

and may appoint the time and place at which the person is to attend and, where appropriate, the time at or within which and the place at which any such document is to be produced.

(3) A tribunal may, on the application of a party made by notice to the Secretary or of its own motion, require a party in writing to furnish to the tribunal a written answer to any question if it considers—

a) that the answer of the party to that question may help to clarify any issue likely to arise for determination in the proceedings, and

b) that it would be likely to assist the progress of the proceedings for that answer to be available to the tribunal before the hearing,

and may appoint the time within which the written answer is to be furnished. Upon the imposition of such a requirement, the Secretary shall send a copy of the requirement to each other party; and he shall send a copy of the answer to each other party.

(4) The tribunal shall take account of a witten answer furnished pursuant to paragraph (3) in the same way as it takes account of representations in writing presented by a party pursuant to rule 8(5).

(5) Where a requirement has been imposed under paragraph (1), (2) or (3)—
   a) on a party in his absence; or
   b) on a person other than a party,
   that party or person may make an application to the tribunal to vary or set aside the requirement by notice to the Secretary given before the time at which or, as the case may be, the expiration of the time within which the requirement is to be complied with; and the Secretary shall give notice of the application to each party or, where applicable, to each party other than the party making the application.

(6) Every document containing a requirement imposed under paragraph (1)(b) or (2) shall contain a reference to the fact that, under paragraph 1(7) of Schedule 9 to the 1978 Act, any person who without reasonable excuse fails to comply with any such requirement shall be liable on summary conviction to a fine, and the document shall state the amount of the current maximum fine.

(7) If a requirement under paragraph (1) or (3) is not complied with, a tribunal, before or at the hearing, may strike out the whole or part of the originating application, or, as the case may be, of the notice of appearance, and, where appropriate, direct that a respondent shall be debarred from defending altogether: but a tribunal shall not so strike out or direct unless it has sent notice to the paraty who has not complied with the requirement giving him an opportunity to show cause why the tribunal should not do so.

Time and place of hearing

5.—(1) The President or a Regional Chairman shall fix the date, time and place of the hearing of the originating application and the Secretary shall send to each party a notice of hearing together with information and guidance as to attendance at the hearing, witnesses and the bringing of documents, representation by another person and the making of written representations.

(2) The Secretary shall send the notice of hearing to every party not less than 14 days before the date fixed for the hearing except—
   a) where the Secretary has agreed a shorter time with the parties; or
   b) on an application for interim relief made under section 77 of the 1978 Act or section 161 of the 1992 Act.

Entitlement to bring or contest the proceedings

6.—(1) A tribunal may at any time before the hearing of an originating application, on the application of a party made by notice to the Secretary or of its own motion, [hear and] determine any issue relating to the entitlement of any party to bring or contest the proceedings to which the originating application relates.

(2) A tribunal shall not determine such an issue unless the Secretary has sent notice to each of the parties giving them an opportunity to submit representations in writing and to advance oral argument before the tribunal.

Pre-hearing review

7.—(1) A tribunal may at any time before the hearing of an originating application, on the application of a party made by notice to the Secretary or of its own motion, conduct a pre-hearing review, consisting of a consideration of—

a) the contents of the originating application and notice of appearance;

b) any representations in writing; and

c) any oral arugment advanced by or on behalf of a party.

(2) If a party applies for a pre-hearing review and the tribunal determines that there shall be no review, the Secretary shall send notice of the determination to that party.

(3) A pre-hearing review shall not take place unless the Secretary has sent notice to the parties giving them an opportunity to submit representations in writing and to advance oral argument at the review if they so wish.

(4) If upon a pre-hearing review the tribunal considers that the contentions put forward by any party in relation to a matter required to be determined by a tribunal have no reasonable prospect of success, the tribunal may make an order against that party requiring the party to pay a deposit of an amount not exceeding £150 as a condition of being permitted to continue to take part in the proceedings relating to that matter.

(5) No order shall be made under this rule unless the tribunal has taken reasonable steps to ascertain the ability of the party against whom it is proposed to make the order to comply with such an order, and has taken account of any information so ascertained in determining the amount of the deposit.

(6) An order made under this rule, and the tribunal's reasons for considering that the contentions in question have no reasonable prospect of success, shall be recorded in summary form in a document signed by the chairman. A copy of that document shall be sent to each of the parties and shall be accompanied by a note explaining that if the party against whom the order is made persists in participating in proceedings relating to the matter to which the order relates, he may have an award of costs made against him and could lose his deposit.

(7) If a party against whom an order has been made does not [pay] the amount specified in the order to the Secretary either—

a) within the period of 21 days beginning with the day on which the document recording the making of the order is sent to him, or

b) within such further period, not exceeding 14 days, as the tribunal may allow in the light of representations made by that party within the said period of 21 days,

the tribunal shall strike out the originating application or notice of appearance of that party or, as the case may be, the part of it to which the order relates.

(8) The deposit paid by a party under an order made under this rule shall be refunded to him in full except where [rule 12(8) applies].

(9) No member of a tribunal which has conducted a pre-hearing review shall be a member of the tribunal at the hearing of the originating application.

(10) Paragraph (9) does not apply where, acting pursuant to a direction issued by a Minister of the Crown in accordance with section 128(6) of the 1978 Act, the President has conducted a pre-hearing review alone.

The hearing

8.—(1) Any hearing of an originating application shall be heard by a tribunal composed in accordance with section 128(2A), (2B) and (2C), or section 128(6), of the 1978 Act.

(2) Any hearing of or in connection with an originating application shall take place in public except where a Minister of the Crown has directed a tribunal to sit in private on grounds of national security in accordance with paragraph 1(4A) of Schedule 9 to the 1978 Act.

(3) Notwithstanding paragraph (2), a tribunal may sit in private for the purpose of—

a) hearing evidence which in the opinion of the tribunal relates to matters of such a nature that it would be against the interests of national security to allow the evidence to be given in public; or

b) hearing evidence from any person which in the opinion of the tribunal is likely to consist of—

  i) information which he could not disclose without contravening a prohibition imposed by or under any enactment, or

  ii) any information which has been communicated to him in confidence, or which he has otherwise obtained in consequence of the confidence reposed in him by another person, or

  iii) information the disclosure of which would cause substantial injury to any undertaking of his or any undertaking in which he works for reasons other than its effect on negotiations with respect to any of the matters mentioned in section 244(1) of the 1992 Act.

(4) A member of the Council on Tribunals shall be entitled to attend any hearing taking place in private in his capacity as a member.

(5) If a party wishes to submit representations in writing for consideration by a tribunal at the hearing of the originating application he shall present his representations to the Secretary not less than 7 days before the hearing and shall at the same time send a copy to each other party.

(6) The Secretary of State if he so elects shall be entitled to appear as if he were a party and be heard at any hearing of or in connection with an originating application in proceedings which may involve a payment out of the National Insurance Fund, and in that event he shall be treated for the purposes of these rules as if he were a party.

Procedure at hearing

9.—(1) The tribunal shall, so far as it appears to it appropriate, seek to avoid formality in its proceedings and shall not be bound by any enactment or rule of law relating to the admissibility of evidence in proceedings before the courts of law. The tribunal shall make such enquiries of persons appearing before it and witnesses as it considers appropriate and shall otherwise conduct the hearing in such manner as it considers most appropriate for the clarification of the issues before it and generally to the just handling of the proceedings.

(2) Subject to paragraph (1), at the hearing of the originating application a party shall be entitled to give evidence, to call witnesses, to question any witnesses and to address the tribunal.

(3) If a party fails to attend or to be represented at the time and place fixed for the hearing, the tribunal may, if that party is an applicant, dismiss or, in any case, dispose of the application in the absence of that party or may adjourn the hearing to a later date: provided that before dismissing or disposing of any application in the absence of a party the tribunal shall consider his originating application or notice of appearance, any representations in writing presented by him in pursuance of rule 8(5) and any written answer furnished to the tribunal pursuant to rule 4(3).

(4) A tribunal may require any witness to give evidence on oath or affirmation and for that purpose there may be administered an oath or affirmation in due form.

Decision of tribunal

10.—(1) Where a tribunal is composed of three members its decision may be taken by a majority; and if a tribunal is composed of two members only, the chairman shall have a second or casting vote.

(2) The decision of a tribunal, which may be given orally at the end of a hearing or reserved, shall be recorded in a document signed by the chairman.

(3) The tribunal shall give reasons for its decision in a document signed by the chairman. That document shall contain a statement as to whether the reasons are given in summary or extended form and where the tribunal—

a) makes an award of compensation, or

b) comes to any other determination by virtue of which one party is required to pay a sum to another (excluding an award of costs or allowances),

the document shall also contain a statement of the amount of compensation awarded, or of the sum required to be paid, followed either by a table showing how the amount or sum has been calculated or by a description of the manner in which it has been calculated.

(4) The reasons for the decision of the tribunal shall be given in summary form except where—

a) the proceedings involved the determination of an issue arising under or relating to the 1970 Act, the 1975 Act, the 1986 Act, the 1976 Act [or the Disability Discrimination Act 1995];

b) a request that the reasons be given in extended form is made orally at the hearing by a party;

c) such a request is made in writing by a party after the hearing either—

i) before any document recording the reasons in summary form is sent to the parties, or

ii) within 21 days of the date on which that document was sent to the parties; or

d) the tribunal considers that reasons given in summary form would not sufficiently explain the grounds for its decision;

and in those circumstances the reasons shall be given in extended form.

(5) The clerk shall transmit the documents referred to in paragraphs (2) and (3) to the Secretary who shall enter them in the Register and shall send a copy of the entry to each of the parties and where the proceedings were referred to the tribunal by a court, to that court.

(6) The document referred to in paragraph (3) shall be omitted from the Register in any case in which—

    a) a Minister of the Crown has directed the tribunal, in accordance with paragraph 1(4A) of Schedule 9 to the 1978 Act, to sit in private on grounds of national security, or

    b) evidence has been heard in private and the tribunal so directs.

In such a case the Secretary shall send that document to each of the parties; and where there are proceedings before a superior court relating to the decision in question, he shall send the document to that court, together with a copy of the entry in the Register of the document referred to in paragraph (2).

(7) In any case appearing to involve allegations of a sexual offence, the document referred to in paragraph (3) shall be entered on the Register with such deletions or amendments as have been made in accordance with rule 13(6).

(8) [. . .]

(9) Clerical mistakes in the documents referred to in paragraphs (2) and (3), or errors arising in those documents from an accidental slip or omission, may at any time be corrected by the chairman by certificate under his hand.

(10) If a document is corrected by certificate under paragraph (9), or if a decision is—

    a) [revoked or varied under the Chairman's hand] under rule 11, or

    b) altered in any way by order of a superior court,

the Secretary shall alter any entry in the Register which is affected to conform with the certificate or order and send a copy of any entry so altered to each of the parties and, where the proceedings were referred to the tribunal by a court, to that court.

(11) Where a document omitted from the Register pursuant to paragraph (6) is corrected by certificate under paragraph (9), the Secretary shall send a copy of the corrected document to each of the parties; and where there are proceedings before any superior court relating to the decision in question, he shall send a copy to that court together with a copy of the entry in the Register of the document referred to in paragraph (2), if it has been altered under paragraph (10).

(12) Where this rule requires a document to be signed by the chairman of a tribunal composed of three or two persons, but by reason of death or incapacity the chairman is unable to sign it, the document shall be signed by the other members or member of the tribunal, who shall certify that the chairman is unable to sign.

Review of tribunal's decision

11.—(1) Subject to the provisions of this rule, a tribunal shall have power, on the application of a party or of its own motion, to review any decision on the grounds that—

    a) the decision was wrongly made as a result of an error on the part of the tribunal staff;

    b) a party did not receive notice of the proceedings leading to the decision;

    c) the decision was made in the absence of a party;

    d) new evidence has become available since the conclusion of the hearing to which the decision relates, provided that its existence could not have been reasonably known of or foreseen at the time of the hearing; or

    e) the interests of justice require such a review.

(2) A tribunal may not review a decision of its own motion unless it is the tribunal which issued the decision.

(3) A tribunal may only review a decision of its own motion if, within the period beginning with the date of the hearing and ending with the fourteenth day after the date on which the decision was sent to the parties, it has sent notice to each of the parties explaining in summary form the ground upon which and reasons why it is proposed to review the decision and giving them an opportunity to show cause why there should be no review.

(4) An application for the purposes of paragraph (1) may be made at the hearing. If no application is made at the hearing, an application may be made to the Secretary at any time from the date of the hearing until 14 days after the date on which the decision was sent to the parties and must be in writing stating the grounds in full.

(5) An application for the purposes of paragraph (1) may be refused by the President or by the chairman of the tribunal which decided the case or by a Regional Chairman if in his opinion it has no reasonable prospect of success.

(6) If such an application is not refused under paragraph (5) it shall be heard by the tribunal which decided the case, or—

    a) where it is not practicable for it to be heard by that tribunal, or

    b) where the decision was made by a chairman acting alone under rule 13(8),

    by a tribunal appointed by either the President or a Regional Chairman.

(7) On reviewing its decision a tribunal may confirm the decision, or vary or revoke the decision under the chairman's hand; and if it revokes the decision, the tribunal shall order a re-hearing before either the same or a differently constituted tribunal.

Costs

12.—(1) Where, in the opinion of the tribunal, a party has in bringing or conducting the proceedings acted frivolously, vexatiously, abusively, disruptively or otherwise unreasonably, the tribunal may make—

    a) an order containing an award against that party in respect of the costs incurred by another party;

    b) an order that that party shall pay to the Secretary of State the whole, or any part, of any allowances (other than allowances paid to members of tribunals) paid to the Secretary of State under paragraph 10 of Schedule 9 to the 1978 Act to any person for the purposes of, or in connection with, his attendance at the tribunal.

(2) Paragraph (1) applies to a respondent who has not entered an appearance in relation to the conduct of any part in the proceedings which he has taken.

(3) An order containing an award against a party ("the first party") in respect of the costs incurred by another party ("the second party") shall be—

    a) where the tribunal thinks fit, an order that the first party pay to the second party a specified sum not exceeding £500;

    b) where those parties agree on a sum to be paid by the first party to the second party in respect of those costs, an order that the first party pay to the second party a specified sum, being the sum so agreed; or

    c) in any other case, an order that the first party pay to the second party the whole or a specified part of the costs incurred by the second party as taxed (if not otherwise agreed).

(4) Where the tribunal has on the application of a party postponed the day or time fixed for or adjourned the hearing, the tribunal may make orders, of the kinds mentioned in paragraphs (1)(a) and (1)(b), against or, as the case may require, in favour of that party as respects any costs incurred or any allowances paid as a result of the postponement or adjourment.

(5) A tribunal shall make orders against a respondent of the kinds mentioned in paragraphs 1(a) and 1(b) as respects any costs or any allowances paid as a result of the postponement or adjournment of a hearing where, on a complaint of unfair dismissal—

    a) the applicant has expressed a wish to be reinstated or re-engaged which has been communicated to the respondent at least 7 days before the hearing of the complaint, or

    b) the proceedings arise out of the respondent's failure to permit the applicant to return to work after an absence due to pregnancy or confinement,

and the postponement or adjournment has been caused by the respondent's failure, without a special reason, to adduce reasonable evidence as to the availability of the job from which the applicant was dismissed, or, as the case may be, which she held before her absence, or of comparable or suitable employment.

(6) Any costs required by an order under this rule to be taxed may be taxed in the county court according to such of the scales prescribed by the county court rules for proceedings in the county court as shall be directed by the order.

(7) Where—

    a) a party has been ordered under rule 7 to pay a deposit as a condition of being permitted to continue to participate in proceedings relating to a matter,

    b) in respect of that matter, the tribunal has found against that party in its decision, and

    c) there has been no award of costs made against that party arising out of the proceedings on the matter,

the tribunal shall consider whether to award costs against that party on the ground that he conducted the proceedings relating to the matter unreasonably in persisting in having the matter determined by a tribunal; but the tribunal shall not make an award of costs on that ground unless it has considered the document recording the order under rule 7 and is of the opinion that the reasons which caused the tribunal to find against the party in its decision were substantially the same as the reasons recorded in that document for considering that the contentions of the party had no reasonable prospect of success.

(8) Where an award of costs is made against a party who has had an order under rule 7 made against him (whether the award arises out of the proceedings relating to the matter in respect of which the order was made or out of proceedings relating to any other matter considered with that matter), his deposit shall be paid in part or full settlement of the award—

   a) where an award is made in favour of one party, to that party, and

   b) where awards are made in favour of more than one party, to all of them or any one or more of them as the tribunal thinks fit, and if to all or more than one, in such proportions as the tribunal considers appropriate,

and if the amount of the deposit exceeds the amount of the award of costs, the balance shall be refunded to the party who paid it.

Miscellaneous powers

13.—(1) Subject to the provisions of these rules, a tribunal may regulate its own procedure.

   (2) A tribunal may—

   a) if the applicant at any time gives notice of the withdrawal of his originating application, dismiss the proceedings;

   b) if both or all the parties agree in writing upon the terms of a decision to be made by the tribunal, decide accordingly;

   c) consider representations in writing which have been submitted by a party to the Secretary (pursuant to rule 8(5)) less than 7 days before the hearing;

   d) subject to paragraph (3), at any stage of the proceedings, order to be struck out or amended any originating application of appearance, or anything in such application or notice of appearance, on the grounds that it is scandalous, frivolous or vexatious;

   e) subject to paragraph (3), at any stage of the proceedings, order to be struck out any originating application or notice of appearance on the grounds that the manner in which the proceedings have been conducted by or on behalf of the applicant or, as the case may be, respondent has been scandalous, frivolous or vexatious; and

   f) subject to paragraph (3), on the application of the respondent, or of its own motion, order an originating application to be struck out for want of prosecution.

   (3) Before making an order under sub-paragraph (d), (e) or (f) of paragraph (2) the tribunal shall send notice to the party against whom it is proposed that the order should be made giving him an opportunity to show cause why the order should not be made; but this paragraph shall not be taken to require the tribunal to send such notice to that party if the party has been given an opportunity to show cause orally why the order should not be made.

   (4) Where a notice required by paragraph (3) is sent in relation to an order to strike out an originating application for want of prosecution, service of the notice shall be treated as having been effected if it has been sent by post or delivered in accordance with rule 20(3) and the tribunal may

strike out the originating application (notwithstanding that there has been no direction for substituted service in accordance with rule 20(6)) if the party does not avail himself of the opportunity given by the notice.

(5) A tribunal may, before determining an application under rule 4 or rule 17, require the party making the application to give notice of it to every other party. The notice shall give particulars of the application and indicate the address to which and the time within which any objection to the application shall be made, being an address and time specified for the purposes of the application by the tribunal.

(6) In any case appearing to involve allegations of the commission of a sexual offence, the tribunal or the Secretary shall omit from the Register, or delete from the Register or any decision, document or record of the proceedings, which is available to the public, any identifying matter which is likely to lead members of the public to identify any person affected by or making such an allegation.

(7) A chairman may postpone the day or time fixed for, or adjourn, any hearing (particularly where an enactment provides for conciliation in relation to the case, for the purpose of giving an opportunity for the case to be settled by way of conciliation and withdrawn) and vary any such postponement or adjournment.

(8) Any act required or authorised by these rules to be done by a tribunal may be done by a chairman except—

a) the hearing of an originating application under rule 8;

b) an act required or authorised to be so done by rule 9 or 10 which the rule implies is to be done by the tribunal which is hearing or heard the originating application;

c) the review of a decision under rule 11(1), and the confirmation, variation or revocation of a decision, and ordering of a re-hearing, under rule 11(7).

(9) Any act required or authorised by rules 3(4), 13(7) and 5 to be done by a chairman may be done by a tribunal or on the direction of a chairman.

(10) Any function of the Secretary may be performed by a Regional Secretary or by a person acting with the authority of the Secretary or of a Regional Secretary.

Restricted reporting orders

14.—(1) In any case which involves allegations of sexual misconduct the tribunal may at any time before promulgation of its decision in respect of an originating application, either on the application of a party made by notice to the Secretary or of its own motion, make a restricted reporting order.

[(1A) In proceedings on a complaint under section 8 of the Disability Discrimination Act 1995 in which evidence of a personal nature is likely to be heard by the tribunal, it may at any time before promulgation of its decision in respect of an originating application, either on the application of the complainant made by notice to the Secretary or of its own motion, make a restricted reporting order.

(1B) Where the tribunal makes a restricted reporting order under paragraph (1A) and that complaint is being dealt with together with any other proceedings, the tribunal may direct that the order applies also in relation to those other proceedings or such part of them as the tribunal may direct.]

(2) The tribunal shall not make a restricted reporting order unless it has given each party an opportunity to advance oral argument at a hearing, if they so wish.

(3) Where a tribunal makes a restricted reporting order—

a) it shall specify in the order the persons who may not be identified;

b) the order shall remain in force until the promulgation of the decision of the tribunal on the originating application to which it relates unless revoked earlier; and

c) the Regional Secretary shall ensure that a notice of the fact is displayed on the notice board of the tribunal with any list of the proceedings taking place before the industrial tribunal, and on the door of the room in which the proceedings affected by the order are taking place.

(4) A tribunal may revoke a restricted reporting order at any time if it thinks fit.

(5) For the purposes of this rule "promulgation" occurs on the date recorded as being the date on which the document recording the determination of the originating application was sent to the parties.

Extension of time

15.—(1) A chairman may on the application of a party or of his own motion extend the time for doing any act appointed by or under these rules (including this rule) and may do so whether or not the time so appointed has expired.

(2) An application under paragraph (1) shall be made by presenting to the Secretary a notice of application, which shall state the title of the proceedings and shall set out the grounds of the application.

(3) The Secretary shall give notice to each of the parties of any extension of time granted under this rule.

Directions

16.—(1) A tribunal may at any time, on the application of a party or of its own motion, give directions on any matter arising in connection with the proceedings.

(2) An application under paragraph (1) shall be made by presenting to the Secretary a notice of application, which shall state the title of the proceedings and set out the grounds of the application.

Joinder and representative respondents

17.—(1) A tribunal may at any time, on the application of any person made by notice to the Secretary or of its own motion, direct any person against whom any relief is sought to be joined as a party, and give such consequential directions as it considers necessary.

(2) A tribunal may likewise, on such application or of its own motion, order that any respondent named in the originating application or subsequently added, who appears to the tribunal not to have been, or to have ceased to

be, directly interested in the subject of the originating application, be dismissed from the proceedings.

(3) Where a number of persons [have] the same interest in an originating application, one or more of them may be cited as the person or persons against whom relief is sought, or may be authorised by the tribunal, before or at the hearing, to defend on behalf of all the persons so interested.

Combined proceedings

18.—(1) Where, in relation to two or more originating applications pending before the industrial tribunals, it appears to an industrial tribunal, on the application of a party made by notice to the Secretary or of its own motion, that—

a) a common question of law or fact arises in some or all the originating applications, or

b) the relief claimed in some or all of those originating applications is in respect of or arises out of the same set of facts, or

c) for any other reason it is desirable to make an order under this rule,

the tribunal may order that some (as specified in the order) or all of the originating applications in respect of which it so appears to the tribunal shall be considered together, and may give such consequential directions as may be necessary.

(2) The tribunal shall only make an order under this rule if—

a) each of the parties concerned has been given an opportunity at a hearing to show cause why such an order should not be made; or

b) it has sent notice to all the parties concerned giving them an opportunity to show such cause.

(3) The tribunal may, on the application of a party made by notice to the Secretary or of its own motion, vary or set aside an order made under this rule but shall not do so unless it has given each party an opportunity to make either oral or written representations before the order is varied or set aside.

Transfer of proceedings

19.—(1) On the application of a party made by notice to the Secretary or of his own motion, the President or a Regional Chairman may at any time, with the consent of the President of the Industrial Tribunals (Scotland), direct any proceedings to be transferred to the Office of the Industrial Tribunals (Scotland) if it appears to him that the proceedings could be, and would more conveniently be, determined in an industrial tribunal (Scotland) established in pursuance of the Industrial Tribunals (Constitution and Procedure) (Scotland) Regulations 1993; but no such direction shall be made unless notice has been sent to all parties concerned giving them an opportunity to show cause why a direction should not be made.

(2) Where proceedings have been transferred to the Office of the Industrial Tribunals (England and Wales) under rule 19(1) of the Industrial Tribunals Rules of Procedure (Scotland) 1993 they shall be treated as if in all respects they had been commenced by an originating application pursuant to rule 1.

[References to the European Court of Justice

19A.— Where a tribunal makes an order referring a question to the European Court of Justice for a preliminary ruling under Article 177 of the Treaty establishing the European Community, the Secretary shall send a copy of the order to the Registrar of that Court but shall not do so until the time for appealing against the order has expired or, if an appeal is made within that time, until the appeal has been determined or otherwise disposed of.]

Notices, etc.

20.—(1) Any notice given under these rules shall be in writing.

(2) All notices and documents required by these rules to be presented to the Secretary [other than an originating application] may be presented at the Office of the Tribunals or such other office as may be notified by the Secretary to the parties.

[(2A) An originating application may be presented at the Office of the tribunals or at any Regional Office of the Industrial Tribunals.]

(3) All notices and documents required or authorised by these rules to be sent or given to any person hereinafter mentioned may be sent by post (subject to paragraph (5)) or delivered to or at—

a) in the case of a notice or document directed to the Secretary of State in proceedings to which he is not a party (or in respect of which he is treated as a party for the purposes of these rules by virtue of rule 8(6)), the offices of the Department of [Trade and Industry (Industrial Relations Directorate 2) at 1 Victoria Street, London SW1H 0ET], or such other office as may be notified by the Secretary of State;

b) in the case of a notice or document directed to a court, the office of the clerk of the court;

c) in the case of a notice or document directed to a party—

   i) the address specified in his originating application or notice of appearance to which notices and documents are to be sent, or in a notice under paragraph (4), or

   ii) if no such address has been specified, or if a notice sent to such an address has been returned, to any other known address or place of business in the United Kingdom or, if the party is a corporate body, the body's registered or principal office in the United Kingdom, or, in any case, such address or place outside the United Kingdom as the President or a Regional Chairman may allow:

d) in the case of a notice or document directed to any person (other than a person specified in the foregoing provisions of this paragraph), his address or place of business in the United Kingdom or, if the person is a corporate body, the body's registered or principal office in the United Kingdom;

and a notice or document sent or given to the authorised representative of a party shall be deemed to have been sent or given to that party.

(4) A party may at any time by notice to the Secretary and to the other party or parties (and, where appropriate, to the appropriate conciliation officer) change the address to which notices and documents are to be sent.

(5) The recorded delivery service shall be used instead of the ordinary post—

    a) when a second set of notices or documents is sent to a respondent who has not entered an appearance under rule 3(1); and

    b) for service of an order made under rule 4(2).

(6) The President or a Regional Chairman may direct that there shall be substituted service in such manner as he may deem fit in any case he considers appropriate.

(7) In proceedings brought under the provisions of any enactment providing for conciliation the Secretary shall send copies of all documents and notices to a conciliation officer who in the opinion of the Secretary is an appropriate officer to receive them.

[(7A) Paragraph (7) does not apply in relation to documents or notices falling within a description of documents or notices in respect of which the Secretary and the Advisory, Conciliation and Arbitration Service have agreed that copies need not be sent.]

(8) In proceedings which may involve a payment out of the National Insurance Fund, the Secretary shall, where appropriate, send copies of all documents and notices to the Secretary of State whether or not he is a party.

(9) In proceedings under the 1970 Act, the 1975 Act or the 1986 Act, or the 1976 Act, the Secretary shall send to the Equal Opportunities Commission or, as the case may be, the Commission for Racial Equality copies of every document and copy entry sent to the parties under rules 10(5) and 10(10).

SCHEDULE 2   [Regulation 8(2)]
COMPLEMENTARY RULES OF PROCEDURE

For use only in proceedings involving an equal value claim

Power to require further particulars and attendance of witnesses and to grant discovery

4.—(1) A tribunal may, on the application of a party made either by notice to the Secretary or at the hearing of the originating application, or of its own motion—

    a) require a party to furnish in writing to the person specified by the tribunal further particulars of the grounds on which that party relies and of any facts and contentions relevant thereto,

    b) require one party to grant to another such discovery or inspection (including the taking of copies) of documents as might be granted by a county court,

and may appoint the time at or within which and the place at which any act required in pursuance of this rule is to be done.

(2) A tribunal may, on the application of a party made either by notice to the Secretary or at the hearing of the originating application, or of its own motion—

    a) require the attendance of any person, including a party, as a witness, wherever such person may be within Great Britain, and

    b) if it does so require the attendance of a person, require him to produce any document relating to the matter to be determined, and may appoint the time and place at which the person is to attend and, where appropriate, the time at or within which and the place at which any such document is to be produced.

(2A) Subject to paragraph (2B), a tribunal may, on the application of an expert who has been required by the tribunal to prepare a report—

a) require any person who the tribunal is satisfied may have information which may be relevant to the question or matter on which the expert is required to report to furnish, in writing, such information as the tribunal may require;

b) require any person to produce any documents which are in the possession, custody or power of that person and which the tribunal is satisfied may contain matter relevant to the question on which the expert is required to report;

and any information so required to be furnished or document so required to be produced shall be furnished or produced, at or within such time as the tribunal may appoint, to the Secretary who shall send the information or document to the expert.

(2B) A tribunal shall not make a requirement under paragraph (2A)—

a) of a conciliation officer who has acted in connection with the complaint under section 64 of the 1975 Act, or

b) if it is satisfied that the person so required would have good grounds for refusing to comply with the requirement if it were a requirement made in connection with a hearing before the tribunal.

(3) A tribunal may, on the application of a party made by notice to the Secretary or of its own motion, require a party in writing to furnish to the tribunal a written answer to any question if it considers—

a) that the answer of the party to that question may help to clarify any issue likely to arise for determination in the proceedings, and

b) that it would be likely to assist the progress of the proceedings for that answer to be available to the tribunal before the hearing,

and may appoint the time within which the written answer is to be furnished. Upon the imposition of such a requirement, the Secretary shall send a copy of the requirement to each other party; and he shall send a copy of the answer to each other party.

(4) The tribunal shall take account of a written answer furnished pursuant to paragraph (3) in the same way as it takes account of representations in writing presented by a party pursuant to rule 8(5).

(5) Where a requirement has been imposed under paragraph (1), (2) or (3)—

a) on party in his absence; or

b) on a person other than a party,

that party or person may make an application to the tribunal to vary or set aside the requirement by notice to the Secretary given before the time at which or, as the case may be, the expiration of the time within which the requuirement is to be complied with; and the Secretary shall give notice of the application to each party or, where applicable, to each party other than the party making the application.

(5A) A person, whether or not a party, upon whom a requirement has been made under paragraph (2A), may apply to the tribunal by notice to the Secretary before the appointed time at or within which the requirement is to be complied with to vary or set aside the requirement. Notice of such application shall be given to the parties and to the expert upon whose application the requirement was made.

(6) Every document containing a requirement imposed under paragraph (1)(b), (2) or (2A) shall contain a reference to the fact that, under paragraph 1(7) of Schedule 9 to the 1978 Act, any person who without reasonable excuse fails to comply with any such requirement shall be liable on summary conviction to a fine, and the document shall state the amount of the current maximum fine.

(7) If a requirement under paragraph (1) or (3) is not complied with, a tribunal, before or at the hearing, may strike out the whole or part of the originating application, or, as the case may be, of the notice of appearance, and, where appropriate, direct that a respondent shall be debarred from defending altogether: but a tribunal shall not so strike out or direct unless it has sent notice to the party who has not complied with the requirement giving him an opportunity to show cause why the tribunal should not do so.

Procedure relating to expert's report

8A.—(1) In any case involving an equal value claim where a dispute arises as to whether work is of equal value to other work in terms of the demands made on the person employed on the work (for instance under such headings as effort, skill and decision) (in this rule, hereinafter referred to as "the question"), the tribunal shall, except in cases where it is satisfied that there are no reasonable grounds for determining the question in the affirmative, determine whether to require an expert to prepare a report with respect to the question.

(2) Before determining under paragraph (1) whether to require an expert to prepare a report the tribunal shall give the parties an opportunity to make representation so the tribunal as to whether an expert should be so required.

(3) Where the tribunal has determined not to require an expert to prepare a report it may nevertheless, at any time during its consideration of the question, require an expert to prepare a report, but shall not do so unless it has given the parties a further opportunity to make representations to the tribunal as to whether an expert should be so required.

(4) Any requirement to prepare a report shall be made in writing and shall set out—

a) the name and address of each of the parties;

b) the address of the establishment at which the applicant is (or, as the case may be, was) employed;

c) the question;

d) the identity of the person with reference to whose work the question arises;

e) the date by which the expert is required to send his report to the tribunal; and

f) the length of the intervals, during the currency of the requirement to prepare the report, before the expiration of which the expert must send progress reports pursuant to paragraph (8).

The Secretary shall send a copy of the requirement to each of the parties together with a notice informing them that a party who unreasonably delays the preparation of the expert's report may have an award of costs made against him, which may include an award in respect of the expert's fees, or have his originating application or notice of appearance struck out.

(5) The requirement shall stipulate that the expert shall—

    a) take account of all such information supplied and all such representations made to him as have a bearing on the question;

    b) before drawing up his report, produce and send to the parties a written summary of the said information and representations and invite the representations of the parties upon the material contained therein;

    c) make his report to the tribunal in a document which shall reproduce the summary and contain a brief account of any representations received from the parties upon it, any conclusion he may have reached upon the question and the reasons for that conclusion or, as the case may be, for his failure to reach such a conclusion;

    d) take no account of the difference of sex and at all times act fairly.

(6) Where a tribunal requires an expert to prepare a report, it shall adjourn the hearing.

(7) In paragraphs (8), (9), (10A) and (10B), 'the required date' means the most recent date specified as the date by which the expert must send his report to the tribunal either in the requirement made upon him under paragraph (4) or in a notice given to him under paragraph (10A).

(8) Before the expiration of each interval specified in the requirement given to the expert under paragraph (4), the expert shall send a progress report to the tribunal—

    a) stating whether he considers that he will be able to send his report to the tribunal by the required date; and

    b) if he considers that he will be unable to do so, giving the reasons for the delay and the date by which he now expects to send his report to the tribunal.

Where a progress report states that the expert considers that he will be unable to send his report to the tribunal by the required date the Secretary shall send a copy to each party.

(9) If at any time when a progress report under paragraph (8) is not imminent, the expert comes to the view that he will be unable to send his report to the tribunal by the required date, he shall give notice in writing to the tribunal—

    a) stating that fact; and

    b) giving the reasons for the delay and the date by which he now expects to send his report to the tribunal.

The Secretary shall send a copy of any such notice to each party.

(10) In giving the reasons for any delay, pursuant to paragraph (8) or (9), the expert shall, in particular, state whether he considers that any action (including an omission) by a party has contributed to the delay and, if he so considers—

    i) identify the party,

    ii) give particulars of the action,

    iii) describe how it has contributed to the delay, and

iv) give an assessment of the extent to which the delay is attributable to it.

(10A) On receiving a progress report under paragraph (8) or a notice under paragraph (9) stating that the expert considers that he will be unable to send his report to the tribunal by the required date, the tribunal shall do one of the following—

a) give written notice to the expert that he is still required to send the report by the required date;

b) give written notice to the expert substituting a later date as the required date; or

c) if, but only if, it considers that it would be in the interests of justice to replace the expert, revoke, by notice in writing to the expert, the requirement to prepare a report;

but shall not do so before it has informed the parties of the action it proposes to take and given each party the opportunity to make representations.

(10B) Paragraph (10A) shall also apply where the expert does not send his report to the tribunal by the requred date but as if sub-paragraph (a) were excluded.

(10C) Where, acting under paragraph (10A), a tribunal has revoked the requirement made upon an expert to prepare a report it shall require another expert to prepare a report, and the rule shall apply accordingly.

(10D) Where in giving the reasons for any delay pursuant to paragraph (8) or (9), the expert has, in accordance with paragraph (10), stated that an action by a party has contributed to the delay, the tribunal shall consider whether the party has unreasonably delayed the preparation of the expert's report and, if it so considers, shall either—

a) make an order under and in accordance with rule 12, or

b) strike out the whole or part of the originating application, or, as the case may be, of the notice of appearance and, where appropriate, direct that a respondent shall be debarred from defending altogether;

(10E) Notwithstanding rule 12(1)(b), the tribunal may, in making an order under rule 12 in pursuance of paragraph (10D), order that the party shall pay to the Secretary of State the whole, or any part, of any fees and allowances paid or payable to the expert in respect of the time so far spent by him in carrying out work pursuant to the requirement to prepare a report.]

(11) Where a tribunal has received the report of an expert, it shall send a copy of the report to each party and fix a date for the hearing of the case to be resumed; and the date so fixed shall be the earliest reasonably practicable date after the expiration of 14 days from the date on which the report is sent to the parties.

(12) Upon the resumption of the hearing of the case in accordance with paragraph (11) the report shall be admitted as evidence in the case unless the tribunal has exercised its power under paragraph (13) not to admit the report.

(13) Where the tribunal, on the application of one or more of the parties or otherwise, forms the view—

a) that the expert has not complied with a stipulation in paragraph (5), or

b) that the conclusion contained in the report is one which, taking due account of the information supplied and representations made to the expert, could not reasonably have been reached, or

c) that for some other material reason (other than disagreement with the conclusion that the applicant's work is or is not of equal value or with the reasoning leading to that conclusion) the report is unsatisfactory,

the tribunal may if it thinks fit, determine not to admit the report, and in such a case [the tribunal shall proceed under this rule as if it had just determined to require an expert to prepare a report, and the rule shall apply accordingly.]

(14) In forming its view on the matters contained in paragraph (13)(a), (b) and (c) the tribunal shall take account of any representations of the parties thereon and may in that connection, subject to rule 9(2A) and (2B), permit any party to give evidence upon, to call witnesses and to question any witness upon any matter relevant thereto.

(15) The tribunal may, at any time after it has received the report of an expert, require that expert (or, if that is impracticable, another expert) to explain any matter contained in that report or, having regard to such matters as may be set out in the requirement, to give further consideration to the question.

(16) A requirement under paragraph (15) [. . .] shall stipulate that the expert shall make his reply in writing to the tribunal, giving his explanation or, as the case may be, setting down any conclusion which may result from his further consideration and his reasons for that conclusion.

[(16A) Paragraphs (4), (7) to (10B), (10D) and (10E) shall apply in relation to a requirement under paragraph (15) as if that requirement was a requirement to prepare a report except that—

a) the duty on the Secretary under paragraph (4) to send a notice concerning unreasonable delay by the parties of the preparation of the expert's report shall not apply;

b) for the purpose of such application the following sub-paragraphs shall be substituted for the sub-paragraphs of paragraph (10A)—

'(a) give written notice to the expert that he is still required to send the reply by the required date;

(b) give written notice to the expert substituting a later date as the required date;

(c) notify the expert in writing that the requirement is cancelled without requiring another expert to fulfil it; or

(d) so notify the expert and require another expert to fulfil the requirement in accordance with paragraph (15);'

and;

c) the tribunal may decide not to require the expert to send progress reports to the tribunal if it considers the requirement to be inappropriate in the circumstances and in that event—

(i) paragraphs (4)(f) and (8) shall not apply; and

(ii) paragraph (9) shall apply if the expert at any time comes to the view that he will be unable to send his reply to the tribunal by the required date.]

(17) Where the tribunal has received a reply from the expert under paragraph (16), it shall send a copy of the reply to each of the parties and shall allow the parties to make representations thereon, and the reply shall be treated as information furnished to the tribunal and be given such weight as the tribunal thinks fit.

(18) Where a tribunal has determined not to admit a report under paragraph (13), that report shall be treated for all purposes (other than the award of costs or allowances under rule 12) connected with the proceedings as if it had not been received by the tribunal and no further account shall be taken of it, and the requirement on the expert to prepare a report shall lapse.

Procedure at hearing

9.—(1) The tribunal shall, so far as it appears to it appropriate, seek to avoid formality in its proceedings and shall not be bound by any enactment or rule of law relating to the admissibility of evidence in proceedings before the courts of law. The tribunal shall make such enquiries of persons appearing before it and witnesses as it considers appropriate and, subject to paragraphs (2A), (2B), (2C), (2D) and (2E), shall otherwise conduct the hearing in such manner as it considers most suitable to the clarification of the issues before it and generally to the just handling of the proceedings.

(2) Subject to paragraphs (1), (2A), (2B), (2C) and (2D), at the hearing of the originating application a party shall be entitled to give evidence, to call witnesses, to question any witnesses and to address the tribunal.

(2A) The tribunal may, and shall upon the application of a party, require the attendance of an expert who has prepared a report in connection with an equal value claim in any hearing relating to that claim. Where an expert attends in compliance with such requirement any party may, subject to paragraph (1), cross-examine the expert on his report and on any other matter pertaining to the question on which the expert was required to report.

(2B) At any time after the tribunal has received the report of the expert, any party may, on giving reasonable notice of his intention to do so to the tribunal and to any other party to the claim, call one witness to give expert evidence on the question on which the tribunal has required the expert to prepare a report; and where such evidence is given, any other party may cross-examine the person giving that evidence upon it.

(2C) Except as provided in rule 8A(14) or by paragraph (2D), no party may give evidence upon, or question any witness upon, any matter of fact upon which a conclusion in the report of the expert is based.

(2D) Subject to paragraphs (2A) and (2B), a tribunal may, notwithstanding paragraph (2C), permit a party to give evidence upon, to call witnesses and to question any witness upon any such matters of fact as are referred to in paragraph (2C) if either—

a) the matter of fact is relevant to and is raised in connection with the issue contained in subsection (3) of section 1 of the Equal Pay Act (defence of genuine material factor) upon which the derermination of the tribunal is being sought; or

b) the report of the expert contains no conclusion on the question of whether the applicant's work and the work of the person identified in the requirement of the tribunal under rule 8A(4) are of equal value and the tribunal is satisfied that the absence of that conclusion is wholly or mainly due to the refusal or deliberate omission of a person required by the tribunal under rule 4(2A) to furnish information or to produce documents to comply with that requirement.

(2E) A tribunal may, on the application of a party, if in the circumstances of the case, having regard to the considerations expressed in paragraph (1), it considers that it is appropriate so to proceed, hear evidence upon and permit the parties to address it upon the issue contained in subsection (3) of section 1 of the Equal Pay Act (defence of genuine material factor) before [determining whether to require] an expert to prepare a report under rule 8A.

(3) If a party fails to attend or to be represented at the time and place fixed for the hearing, the tribunal may, if that party is an applicant, dismiss or, in any case, dispose of the application in the absence of that party or may adjourn the hearing to a later date: provided that before dismissing or disposing of any application in the absence of a party the tribunal shall consider his originating application or notice of appearance, any representations in writing presented by him in pursuance of rule 8(5) and any written answer furnished to the tribunal pursuant to rule 4(3).

(4) A tribunal may require any witness to give evidence on oath or affirmation and for that purpose there may be administered an oath or affirmation in due form.

Decison of tribunal

10.—(1) Where a tribunal is composed of three members its decision may be taken by a majority; and if a tribunal is composed of two members only, the chairman shall have a second or casting vote.

(2) The decision of a tribunal, which may be given orally at the end of a hearing or reserved, shall be recorded in a document signed by the chairman.

(3) The tribunal shall give reasons for its decision in extended form in a document signed by the chairman; and where the tribunal—
   a) makes an award of compenstion, or
   b) comes to any other determination by virtue of which one party is required to pay a sum to another (excluding an award of costs or allowances),
   the document shall also contain a statement of the amount of compensation awarded, or of the sum required to be paid, followed either by a table showing how the amount or sum has been calculated or by a description of the manner in which it has been calculated.

   [paragraph (4) is omitted because it has no relevance in proceedings involving an equal value claim]

(4A) There shall be appended to the document referred to in paragraph (3) a copy of the report (if any) of an expert received by the tribunal in the course of the proceedings.

(5) The clerk shall transmit the documents referred to in paragraphs (2) and (3) and the copy of the report referred to in paragraph (4A), if any, to the Secretary who shall enter them in the Register and shall send a copy of the entry to each of the parties and where the proceedings were referred to the tribunal by a court, to that court.

(6) The document referred to in paragraph (3) and the copy of the report referred to in paragraph (4A), if any, shall be omitted from the Register in any case in which—

    a) a Minister of the Crown has directed the tribunal, in accordance with paragraph 1(4A) of Schedule 9 to the 1978 Act, to sit in private on grounds of national security, or

    b) evidence had been heard in private and the tribunal so directs.

In such a case the Secretary shall send that document to each of the parties; and where there are proceedings before a superior court relating to the decision in question, he shall send the document to that court, together with a copy of the entry in the Register of the document referred to in paragraph (2).

(7) In any case appearing to involve allegations of a sexual offence, the document referred to in paragraph (3) shall be entered on the Register with such deletions or amendments as have been made in accordance with rule 13(6).

(8) The Register shall be kept at the Office of the Tribunals and shall be open to the inspection of any person without charge at all reasonable hours.

(9) Clerical mistakes in the documents referred to in paragraphs (2) and (3), or errors arising in those documents from an accidental slip or omission, may at any time be corrected by the chairman by certificate under his hand.

(10) If a document is corrected by certificate under paragraph (9), or if a decision is—

    a) revoked or varied [under the chairman's hand] under rule 11, or

    b) altered in any way by order of a superior court,

the Secretary shall alter any entry in the Register which is affected to conform with the certificate or order and send a copy of any entry so altered to each of the parties and, where the proceedings were referred to the tribunal by a court, to that court.

(11) Where a document omitted from the Register pursuant to paragraph (6) is corrected by certificate under paragraph (9), the Secretary shall send a copy of the corrected document to each of the parties; and where there are proceedings before any superior court relating to the decision in question, he shall send a copy to that court together with a copy of the entry in the Register of the document referred to in paragraph (2), if it has been altered under paragraph (10).

(12) Where this rule requires a document to be signed by the chairman of a tribunal composed of three or two persons, but by reason of death or incapacity the chairman is unable to sign it, the document shall be signed by the other members or member of the tribunal, who shall certify that the chairman is unable to sign.

Costs

12.—(1) Where, in the opinion of the tribunal, a party has in bringing or conducting the proceedings acted frivolously, vexatiously, abusively, disruptively or otherwise unreasonably, the tribunal may make—

    a) an order containing an award against that party in respect of the costs incurred by another party;

    b) an order that that party shall pay to the Secretary of State the whole, or any part, of any allowances (other than allowances paid to members of tribunals) paid by the Secretary of State under paragraph 10 of

Schedule 9 to the 1978 Act to any person for the purposes of, or in connection with, his attendance at the tribunal.

(2) Paragraph (1) applies to a respondent who has not entered an appearance in relation to the conduct of any part in the proceedings which he has taken.

(2A) For the purposes of paragraph (1)(a), the costs in respect of which a tribunal may make an order include costs incurred by the party in whose favour the order is to be made in or in connection with [any] investigations carried out by [an] expert in preparing his report.

(3) An order containing an award against a party ("the first party") in respect of the costs incurred by another party ("the second party") shall be—

   a) where the tribunal thinks fit, an order that the first party pay to the second party a specified sum not exceeding £500;

   b) where those parties agree on a sum to be paid by the first party to the second party in respect of those costs, an order that the first party pay to the second party a specified sum, being the sum so agreed; or

   c) in any other case, an order that the first party pay to the second party the whole or a specified part of the costs incurred by the second party as taxed (if not otherwise agreed).

(4) Where the tribunal has on the application of a party postponed the day or time fixed for or adjourned the hearing, the tribunal may make orders, of the kinds mentioned in paragraphs (1)(a) and (1)(b), against or, as the case may require, in favour of that party as respects any costs incurred or any allowances paid as a result of the postponement or adjournment.

(5) A tribunal shall make orders against a respondent of the kinds mentioned in paragraphs 1(a) and 1(b) as respects any costs or any allowances paid as a result of the postponement or adjournment of a hearing where, on a complaint of unfair dismissal—

   a) the applicant has expressed a wish to be reinstated or re-engaged which has been communicated to the respondent at least 7 days before the hearing of the complaint, or

   b) the proceedings arise out of the respondent's failure to permit the applicant to return to work after an absence due to pregnancy or confinement,

   and the postponement or adjournment has been caused by the respondent's failure, without a special reason, to adduce reasonable evidence as to the availability of the job from which the applicant was dismissed, or, as the case may be, which she held before her absence, or of comparable or suitable employment.

(6) Any costs required by an order under this rule to be taxed may be taxed in the county court according to such of the scales prescribed by the county court rules for proceedings in the county court as shall be directed by the order.

(7) Where—

   a) a party has been ordered under rule 7 to pay a deposit as a condition of being permitted to continue to participate in proceedings relating to a matter,

   b) in respect of that matter, the tribunal has found against that paraty in its decision, and

c) there has been no award of costs made against that party arising out of the proceedings on the matter,

the tribunal shall consider whether to award costs against that party on the ground that he conducted the proceedings relating to the matter unreasonably in persisting in having the matter determined by a tribunal; but the tribunal shall not make an award of costs on that ground unless it has considered the document recording the order under rule 7 and is of the opinion that the reasons which caused the tribunal to find against the party in its decision were substantially the same as the reasons recorded in that document for considering that the contentions of the party had no reasonable prospect of success.

(8) Where an award of costs is made against a party who had had an order under rule 7 made against him (whether the award arises out of the proceedings relating to the matter in respect of which the order was made or out of proceedings relating to any other matter considered with that matter), his deposit shall be paid in part or full settlement of the award—

a) where an award is made in favour of one party, to that party, and

b) where awards are made in favour of more than one party, to all of them or any one or more of them as the tribunal thinks fit, and if to all or more than one, in such proportions as the tribunal considers appropriate,

and if the amount of the deposit exceeds the amount of the award of costs, the balance shall be refunded to the party who paid it.

Miscellaneous powers

13.—(1) Subject to the provisions of these rules, a tribunal may regulate its own procedure.

(2) A tribunal may—

a) if the applicant at any time gives notice of the withdrawal of his originating application, dismiss the proceedings;

b) if both or all the parties agree in writing upon the terms of a decision to be made by the tribunal, decide accordingly;

c) consider representations in writing which have been submitted by a party to the Secretary (pursuant to rule 8(5)) less than 7 days before the hearing;

d) subject to paragraph (3), at any stage of the proceedings, order to be struck out or amended any originating application or notice of appearance, or anything in such application or notice of appearance, on the grounds that it is scandalous, frivolous or vexatious;

e) subject to paragraph (3), at any stage of the proceedings, order to be struck out any originating application or notice of appearance on the grounds that the manner in which the proceedings have been conducted by or on behalf of the applicant or, as the case may be, respondent has been scandalous, frivolous or vexatious; and

f) subject to paragraph (3), on the application of the respondent, or of its own motion, order an originating application to be struck out for want of prosecution.

(3) Before making an order under sub-paragraph (d), (e) or (f) of paragraph (2) the tribunal shall send notice to the party against whom it is proposed that the order should be made giving him an opportunity to show cause

why the order should not be made; but this paragraph shall not be taken to require the tribunal to send such notice to that party if the party has been given an opportunity to show cause orally why the order should not be made.

(4) Where a notice required by paragraph (3) is sent in relation to an order to strike out an originating application for want of prosecution, service of the notice shall be treated as having been effected if it has been sent by post or delivered in accordance with rule 20(3) and the tribunal may strike out the originating application (notwithstanding that there has been no direction for substituted service in accordance with rule 20(6)) if the party does not avail himself of the opportunity given by the notice.

(5) A tribunal may, before determining an application under rule 4 or rule 17, require the party making the application or, in the case of an application under rule 4(2A), the expert, to give notice of it to every other party (or, in the case of an application by the expert, to the parties and any other person on whom the tribunal is asked, in the application, to impose a requirement). The notice shall give particulars of the application and indicate the address to which and the time within which any objection to the application shall be made, being an address and time specified for the purposes of the application by the tribunal.

(6) In any case appearing to involve allegations of the commission of a sexual offence, the tribunal or the Secretary shall omit from the Register, or delete from the Register or any decision, document or record of the proceedings, which is available to the public, any identifying matter which is likely to lead members of the public to identify any person affected by or making such an allegation.

(6A) without prejudice to paragraph (7), the tribunal shall, before proceeding to hear the parties on an equal value claim, invite them to apply for an adjournment for the purpose of seeking to reach a settlement of the claim and shall, if both or all the parties agree to such a course, grant an adjournment for that purpose.

(6B) If, after the tribunal has adjourned the hearing under rule 8A(6) but before the tribunal has received the report of the expert, the applicant gives notice under paragraph (2)(a), the tribunal shall notify the expert that the requirement to prepare a report has ceased. The notice shall be without prejudice to the operation of rule 12(2A).

(7) A chairman may postpone the day or time fixed for, or adjourn, any hearing (particularly where an enactment provides for conciliation in relation to the case, for the purpose of giving an opportunity for the case to be settled by way of conciliation and withdrawn) and vary any such postponement or adjournment.

(8) Any act required or authorised by these rules to be done by a tribunal may be done by a chairman except—
   a) the hearing of an originating application under rule 8;
   b) an act required or authorised to be so done by rule 9 or 10 which the rule implies is to be done by the tribunal which is hearing or heard the originating application;
   c) the review of a decision under rule 11(1), and the confirmation, variation or revocation of a decision, and ordering of a re-hearing, under rule 11(7).

(9) Any act required or authorised by rules 3(4), 13(7) and 15 to be done

by a chairman may be done by a tribunal or on the direction of a chairman.

(10) Any function of the Secretary may be performed by a Regional Secretary or by a person acting with the authority of the Secretary or of a Regional Secretary.

Notices, etc.

20.—(1) Any notice given under these rules shall be in writing.

(2) All notices and documents required by these rules to be presented to the Secretary [other than an originating application] may be presented at the Office of the Tribunals or such other office as may be notified by the Secretary to the parties.

[(2A) An originating application may be presented at the Office of the Tribunals or at any Regional Office of the Industrial Tribunals.]

(3) All notices and documents required or authorised by these rules to be sent or given to any person hereinafter mentioned may be sent by post (subject to paragraph (5)) or delivered to or at—

   a) in the case of a notice or document directed to the Secretary of State in proceedings to which he is not a party (or in respect of which he is treated as a party for the purposes of these rules by virtue of rule 8(6)), the offices of the Department of [Trade and Industry (Industrial Relations Directorate 2) at 1 Victoria Street, London SW1H 0ET], or such other office as may be notified by the Secretary of State;

   b) in the case of a notice or document directed to a court, the office of the clerk of the court;

   c) in the case of a notice or document directed to a party—

      i) the address specified in his originating application or notice of appearance to which notices and documents are to be sent, or in a notice under paragraph (4), or

      ii) if no such address has been specified, or if a notice sent to such an address has been returned, to any other known address or place of business in the United Kingdom or, if the party is a corporate body, the body's registered or principal office in the United Kingdom, or, in any case, such address or place outside the United Kingdom as the President or a Regional Chairman may allow;

   d) in the case of a notice or document directed to any person (other than a person specified in the foregoing provisions of this paragraph), his address or place of business in the United Kingdom or, if the person is a corporate body, the body's registered or principal office in the United Kingdom;

   and a notice or document sent or given to the authorised representative of a party shall be deemed to have been sent or given to that party.

(4) A party may at any time by notice to the Secretary and to the other party or parties (and, where appropriate, to the appropriate conciliation officer) change the address to which notices and documents are to be sent.

(5) The recorded delivery service shall be used instead of the ordinary post—

   a) when a second set of notices or documents is sent to a respondent who has not entered an appearance under rule 3(1); and

   b) for service of an order made under rule 4(2) or (2A).

(6) The President or a Regional Chairman may direct that there shall be

substituted service in such manner as he may deem fit in any case he considers appropriate.

(7) In proceedings brought under the provisions of any enactment providing for conciliation the Secretary shall send copies of all documents and notices to a conciliation officer who in the opinion of the Secretary is an appropriate officer to receive them.

(7A) Paragraph (7) does not apply in relation to documents and notices falling within a description of documents or notices in respect of which the Secretary and the Advisory, Conciliation and Arbitration Service have agreed that copies need not be sent.

(8) In proceedings which may involve a payment out of the National Insurance Fund, the Secretary shall, where appropriate, send copies of all documents and notices to the Secretary of State whether or not he is a party.

(9) In proceedings under the 1970 Act, the 1975 Act or the 1986 Act, or the 1976 Act, the Secretary shall send to the Equal Opportunities Commission or, as the case may be, the Commission for Racial Equality copies of every document and copy entry sent to parties under rules 10(5) and 10(10).

3.6 Industrial Tribunals (Constitution and Rules of Procedure) (Scotland) Regulations 1993 SI No 2688 *

These are basically the same as the English Regulations but adjusted for differences between the Scottish and English legal systems.

1 'Assistant Secretary' is substituted for 'Regional Secretary' throughout.

2 The President (reg 3) and chairmen of tribunals (reg 5) must be advocates or solicitors of at least seven years' standing and are appointed by the Lord President (not the Lord Chancellor).

3 The rules in Schs 1 and 2 are stated to apply to Scotland (reg 8(3)) and to proceedings which 'relate to a contract of employment the place of execution or performance of which is in Scotland' (reg 8(3)(b)).

4 In the Scottish rules (Sch 1) and Complementary Rules of Procedure for equal pay claims (Sch 2), costs under r12 are taxed 'according to such part of the table of fees prescribed for proceedings in the sheriff court as shall be directed by the order, and thereafter the tribunal may issue an order for payment of the amount as taxed.'

5 In relation to striking out, r13(2) and (4) refers to 'excessive delay in proceeding' rather than 'want of prosecution' of claims.

3.7 Industrial Tribunals (Constitution and Rules of Procedure) Regulations (Northern Ireland) 1996 SR No 173

These are basically the same as the English Regulations but adjusted to take account of differences between the two legal systems and the different administrative arrangements.

*As amended by 1996 SI No 1758, in force 31 July 1996.

The Fair Employment Tribunals, set up to combat sectarian discrimination (see p10), are outside the scope of these Regulations, although in practice they share staff and premises with ITs.

There is at present no equivalent of the British RRA in Northern Ireland. The Labour Relations Agency performs the functions of ACAS. There is a panel of chairmen for Northern Ireland tribunals. Lay members are appointed by the Department of Economic Development.

Differences

1 There are no regional chairmen: instead, the rules refer to the President or Vice-President.

2 There is no equivalent of the English r1(2) allowing the Secretary to express the opinion that an application should not be registered.

3 Rule 20 is modified for local differences (eg, no CRE).

4 There is no equivalent of r19 (transfer of proceedings).

3.8 The Employment Appeal Tribunal Rules 1993 SI No 2854

Citation and commencement

1.—(1) These Rules may be cited as the Employment Appeal Tribunal Rules 1993 and shall come into force on 16th December 1993.

(2) As from that date the Employment Appeal Tribunal Rules 1980, the Employment Appeal Tribunal (Amendment) Rules 1985 and the Employment Appeal Tribunal (Amendment) Rules 1988 shall be revoked.

Interpretation

2.—In these Rules, unless the context otherwise requires—

"the 1978 Act" means the Employment Protection (Consolidation) Act 1978 and a section or Schedule referred to by number means the section or Schedule so numbered in the 1978 Act;

"the 1992 Act" means the Trade Union and Labour Relations (Consolidation) Act 1992;

"the Appeal Tribunal" means the Appeal Tribunal established under section 87 of the Employment Protection Act 1975 and continued in existence under section 135 of the 1978 Act and includes the President, a judge, a member or the Registrar acting on behalf of the Tribunal;

"the Certification Officer" means the person appointed to be the Certification Officer under section 7(1) of the Employment Protection Act 1975 or section 254(2) of the 1992 Act, as the case may be;

"judge" means a judge of the Appeal Tribunal nominated under section 135(2)(a) or (b) and includes a judge nominated under paragraph 5 or 6 and a judge appointed under paragraph 8 of Schedule 11 to act temporarily in the place of a judge of the Tribunal;

"member" means a member of the Appeal Tribunal appointed under section 135(2)(c) and includes a member appointed under paragraph 7 of Schedule 11 to act temporarily in the place of a member appointed under that section;

"the President" means the judge appointed under section 135(4) to be President of the Appeal Tribunal and includes a judge nominated under paragraph 4 of Schedule 11 to act temporarily in his place;

"the Registrar" means the person appointed to be Registrar of the Appeal Tribunal and includes any officer of the Tribunal authorised by the President to act on behalf of the Registrar;

"the Secretary of Industrial Tribunals" means the person acting for the time being as the Secretary of the Central Office of the Industrial Tribunals (England and Wales) or, as may be appropriate, of the Central Office of the Industrial Tribunals (Scotland);

"taxing officer" means any officer of the Appeal Tribunal authorised by the President to assess costs or expenses.

Institution of appeal

3.—(1) Every appeal to the Appeal Tribunal shall be instituted by serving on the Tribunal the following documents—
- a) a notice of appeal in, or substantially in, accordance with Form 1 or 2 in the Schedule to these Rules;
- b) a copy of the decision or order of an industrial tribunal or of the Certification Officer which is the subject of the appeal;
- c) in the case of an appeal from an industrial tribunal, a copy of the extended written reasons for the decision or order of that tribunal.

(2) The period within which an appeal to the Appeal Tribunal may be instituted is 42 days from the date on which extended written reasons for the decision or order of the industrial tribunal were sent to the appellant, or, in the case of an appeal from a decision of the Certification Officer, 42 days from the date on which the written record of that decision was so sent.

(3) Where it appears to the Registrar that the grounds of appeal stated in the notice of appeal do not give the Appeal Tribunal jurisdiction to entertain the appeal, he shall notify the appellant accordingly informing him of the reasons for the opinion and, subject to paragraphs (4) and (6) of this rule, no further action shall be taken on the appeal.

(4) Where notification has been given under paragraph (3) of this rule, the appellant may serve a fresh notice of appeal within the time remaining under paragraph (2) or within 28 days from the date on which the Registrar's notification was sent to him, whichever is the longer period.

(5) Where the appellant serves a fresh notice of appeal under paragraph (4) of this rule the Registrar shall consider such fresh notice of appeal with regard to jurisdiction as though it were an original notice of appeal lodged pursuant to paragraphs (1) and (2) of this rule.

(6) Where an appellant expresses dissatisfaction in writing with the reasons given by the Registrar, under paragraph (3) of this rule, for his opinion that the grounds of appeal stated in a notice do not give the Appeal Tribunal jurisdiction to entertain the appeal, the Registrar shall place the papers before the President or a judge for his direction as to whether any further action should be taken on the appeal.

Service of notice of appeal

4.—On Receipt of notice under rule 3, the Registrar shall seal the notice with the

Appeal Tribunal's seal and shall serve a sealed copy on the appellant and on—

    a) every person who, in accordance with rule 5, is a respondent to the appeal; and

    b) The Secretary of Industrial Tribunals in the case of an appeal from an industrial tribunal; or

    c) the Certification Officer in the case of an appeal from any of his decisions; or

    d) the Secretary of State in the case of an appeal under Part VI of the 1978 Act or Chapter II of Part IV of the 1992 Act to which he is not a respondent.

Respondents to appeals

5.—The respondents to an appeal shall be—

    a) in the case of an appeal from an industrial tribunal or of an appeal made pursuant to section 95 or 104 of the 1992 Act from a decision of the Certification Officer, the parties (other than the appellant) to the proceedings before the industrial tribunal or the Certification Officer;

    b) in the case of an appeal made pursuant to section 9 of the 1992 Act from a decision of the Certification Officer, that Officer.

Respondent's answer and notice of cross-appeal

6.—(1) The Registrar shall, as soon as practicable, notify every respondent of the date appointed by the Appeal Tribunal by which any answer under this rule must be delivered.

(2) A respondent who wishes to resist an appeal shall, within the time appointed under paragraph (1) of this rule, deliver to the Appeal Tribunal an answer in writing in, or substantially in, accordance with Form 3 in the Schedule to these Rules, setting out the grounds on which he relies, so, however, that it shall be sufficient for a respondent to an appeal referred to in rule 5(a) who wishes to rely on any ground which is the same as a ground relied on by the industrial tribunal or the Certification Officer for making the decision or order appealed from to state that fact in his answer.

(3) A respondent who wishes to cross-appeal may do so by including in his answer a statement of the grounds of his cross-appeal, and in that event an appellant who wishes to resist the cross-appeal shall, within a time to be appointed by the Appeal Tribunal, deliver to the Tribunal a reply in writing setting out the grounds on which he relies.

(4) The Registrar shall serve a copy of every answer and reply to a cross-appeal on every party other than the party by whom it was delivered.

(5) Where the respondent does not wish to resist an appeal, the parties may deliver to the Appeal Tribunal an agreed draft of an order allowing the appeal and the Tribunal may, if it thinks it right to do so, make an order allowing the appeal in the terms agreed.

Disposal of appeal

7.—(1) The Registrar shall, as soon as practicable, give notice of the arrangements made by the Appeal Tribunal for hearing the appeal to—

a) every party to the proceedings; and

b) the Secretary of Industrial Tribunals in the case of an appeal from an industrial tribunal; or

c) the Certification Officer in the case of an appeal from one of his decisions; or

d) the Secretary of State in the case of an appeal under Part VI of the 1978 Act or Chapter II of Part IV of the 1992 Act to which he is not a respondent.

(2) Any such notice shall state the date appointed by the Appeal Tribunal by which any interlocutory application must be made.

Application in respect of exclusion or expulsion from, or unjustifiable discipline by, a trade union

8.—Every application under section 67 or 176 of the 1992 Act to the Appeal Tribunal for:

a) an award of compensation for exclusion or expulsion from a trade union; or

b) one or both of the following, that is to say—

  i) an award of compensation for unjustifiable discipline;

  ii) an order that the union pay to the applicant an amount equal to any sum which he has paid in pursuance of any such determination as is mentioned in section 64(2)(b) of the 1992 Act;

shall be made in writing in, or substantially in, accordance with Form 4 in the Schedule to these Rules and shall be served on the Appeal Tribunal together with a copy of the decision or order declaring that the applicant's complaint against the trade union was well-founded.

9.—If on receipt of an application under rule 8(a) it becomes clear that at the time the application was made the applicant had been admitted or re-admitted to membership of the union against which the complaint was made, the Registrar shall forward the application to the Central Office of Industrial Tribunals.

Service of application under rule 8

10.—On receipt of an application under rule 8, the Registrar shall seal it with the Appeal Tribunal's seal and shall serve a sealed copy on the applicant and on the respondent trade union and the Secretary of Industrial Tribunals.

Appearance by respondent trade union

11.—(1) Subject to paragraph (2) of this rule, a respondent trade union wishing to resist an application under rule 8 shall within 14 days of receiving the sealed copy of the application enter an appearance in, or substantially in, accordance with Form 5 in the Schedule to these Rules and setting out the grounds on which the union relies.

(2) Paragraph (1) above shall not require a respondent trade union to enter an appearance where the application is before the Appeal Tribunal by virtue of having been transferred there by an industrial tribunal and, prior to that transfer, the respondent had entered an appearance to the proceedings before the industrial tribunal.

12.—On receipt of the notice of appearance under rule 11 the Registrar shall serve a copy of it on the applicant.

Application for restriction of proceedings order

13.—Every application to the Appeal Tribunal by the Attorney General or the Lord Advocate under section 136A for a restriction of proceedings order shall be made in writing in, or substantially in, accordance with Form 6 in the Schedule to these Rules, accompanied by an affidavit in support, and shall be served on the Tribunal.

Service of application under rule 13

14.—On receipt of an application under rule 13, the Registrar shall seal it with the Appeal Tribunal's seal and shall serve a sealed copy on the Attorney General or the Lord Advocate, as the case may be, on the Secretary of Industrial Tribunals and on the person named in the application.

Appearance by person named in application under rule 13

15.—A person named in an application under rule 13 who wishes to resist the application shall within 14 days of receiving the sealed copy of the application enter an appearance in, or substantially in, accordance with Form 7 in the Schedule to these Rules, accompanied by an affidavit in support.

16.—On receipt of the notice of appearance under rule 15 the Registrar shall serve a copy of it on the Attorney General or the Lord Advocate, as the case may be.

Disposal of application

17.—(1) The Registrar shall, as soon as practicable, give notice to the parties to an application under rule 8 or rule 13 of the arrangements made by the Appeal Tribunal for hearing the application.

(2) Any such notice shall state the date appointed by the Appeal Tribunal by which any interlocutory application must be made.

Joinder of parties

18.—The Appeal Tribunal may, on the application of any person or of its own motion, direct that any person not already a party to the proceedings be added as a party, or that any party to proceedings shall cease to be a party, and in either case may give such consequential directions as it considers necessary.

Interlocutory applications

19.—(1) An interlocutory application may be made to the Appeal Tribunal by giving notice in writing specifying the direction or order sought.

(2) On receipt of a notice under paragraph (1) of this rule, the Registrar shall serve a copy on every other party to the proceedings who appears to him

to be concerned in the matter to which the notice relates and shall notify the applicant and every such party of the arrangements made by the Appeal Tribunal for disposing of the application.

Disposal of interlocutory applications

20.—(1) Every interlocutory application made to the Appeal Tribunal shall be considerd in the first place by the Registrar who will have regard to the just and economical disposal of the application, to the expense which may be incurred by the parties in attending an oral hearing and, where applicable, to rule 23(5).

(2) Every interlocutory application other than an application for a restricted reporting order shall be disposed of by the Registrar except that any matter which he thinks should properly be decided by the President or a judge shall be referred by him to the President or a judge, who may dispose of it himself or refer it in whole or in part to the Appeal Tribunal as required to be constituted by paragraph 16(1) and (2) of Schedule 11 or refer it back to the Registrar with such directions as he thinks fit.

(3) Every interlocutory application for a restricted reporting order shall be disposed of by the President or a judge or, if he so directs, the application shall be referred to the Appeal Tribunal as required to be constituted by paragraph 16(1) and (2) of Schedule 11 who shall dispose of it.

(4) Paragraphs (2) and (3) of this rule are subject to rule 22(2).

Appeals from Registrar

21.—(1) Where an application is disposed of by the Registrar in pursuance of rule 20(2) any party aggrieved by his decision may appeal to a judge and in that case (subject to rule 22(2)) the judge may determine the appeal himself or refer it in whole or in part to the Appeal Tribunal as required to be constituted by paragraph 16(1) and (2) of Schedule 11.

(2) Notice of appeal under paragraph (1) of this rule may be given to the Appeal Tribunal, either orally or in writing, within five days of the decision appealed from and the Registrar shall notify every other party who appears to him to be concerned in the appeal and shall inform every such party and the appellant of the arrangements made by the Tribunal for disposing of the appeal.

Hearing of interlocutory applications

22.—(1) The Appeal Tribunal may, subject to rule 30 and, where applicable, to rule 23(6), sit either in private or in public for the hearing of any interlocutory application.

(2) Where a Minister of the Crown has given such a direction as is referred to in paragraph 16(4) of Schedule 11, any hearing of an interlocutory application shall be by the Appeal Tribunal comprised of the President alone.

Cases involving allegations of sexual misconduct or the commission of sexual offences

23.—(1) This rule applies to any proceedings to which paragraph 18A of Schedule 11 applies.

(2) In any such proceedings where the appeal appears to involve allegations of the commission of a sexual offence, the Registrar shall omit from any register kept by the Appeal Tribunal, which is available to the public, or delete from any order, judgment or other document, which is available to the public, any identifying matter which is likely to lead members of the public to identify any person affected by or making such an allegation.

(3) In any proceedings to which this rule applies where the appeal involves allegations of sexual misconduct the Appeal Tribunal may at any time before promulgation of its decision either on the application of a party or of its own motion make a restricted reporting order having effect, if not revoked earlier by the Appeal Tribunal, until the promulgation of its decision.

(4) A restricted reporting order shall specify the persons who may not be identified.

(5) The Appeal Tribunal shall not make a restricted reporting order unless it has given each party to the proceedings an opportunity to advance oral argument at a hearing, if they so wish.

(6) Any such hearing shall, subject to rule 30 or unless the Appeal Tribunal decides for any of the reasons mentioned in rule 29(2) to sit in private to hear evidence, be held in public.

(7) The Appeal Tribunal may revoke a restricted reporting order at any time where it thinks fit.

(8) Where the Appeal Tribunal makes a restricted reporting order, the Registrar shall ensure that a notice of the fact is displayed on the notice board of the Appeal Tribunal at the office in which the proceedings in question are being dealt with, on the door of the room in which those proceedings are taking place and with any list of the proceedings taking place before the Appeal Tribunal.

(9) In this rule, "promulgation of its decision" means the date recorded as being the date on which the Appeal Tribunal's order finally disposing of the appeal is sent to the parties.

Appointment for direction

24.—(1) Where it appears to the Appeal Tribunal that the future conduct of any proceedings would thereby be facilitated, the Tribunal may (either of its own motion or on application) at any stage in the proceedings appoint a date for a meeting for directions as to their future conduct and thereupon the following provisions of this rule shall apply.

(2) The Registrar shall give to every party in the proceedings notice of the date appointed under paragraph (1) of this rule and any party applying for directions shall, if practicable, before that date give to the Appeal Tribunal particulars of any direction for which he asks.

(3) The Registrar shall take such steps as may be practicable to inform every party of any directions applied for by any other party.

(4) On the date appointed under paragraph (1) of this rule, the Appeal Tribunal shall consider every application for directions made by any party and any written representations relating to the application submitted to the Tribunal and shall give such directions as it thinks fit for the purpose of securing the just, expeditious and economical disposal of the proceedings, including, where appropriate, directions in pursuance of rule 36, for the purpose of ensuring that the parties are enabled to avail themselves of opportunities for conciliation.

(5) Without prejudice to the generality of paragraph (4) of this rule, the Appeal Tribunal may give such directions as it thinks fit as to—
   a) the amendment of any notice, answer or other document,
   b) the admission of any facts or documents;
   c) the admission in evidence of any documents;
   d) the mode in which evidence is to be given at the hearing;
   e) the consolidation of the proceedings with any other proceedings pending before the Tribunal;
   f) the place and date of the hearing.

(6) An application for further directions or for the variation of any directions already given may be made in accordance with rule 19.

Appeal Tribunal's power to give directions

25.—The Appeal Tribunal may either of its own motion or on application, at any stage of the proceedings, give any party directions as to any steps to be taken by him in relation to the proceedings.

Default by parties

26.—If a respondent to any proceedings fails to deliver an answer or, in the case of an application made under section 67 or 176 of the 1992 Act or section 136A, a notice of appearance within the time appointed under these Rules, or if any party fails to comply with an order or direction of the Appeal Tribunal, the Tribunal may order that he be debarred from taking any further part in the proceedings, or may make such other order as it thinks just.

Attendance of witnesses and production of documents

27.—(1) The Appeal Tribunal may, on the application of any party, order any person to attend before the Tribunal as a witness or to produce any document.

(2) No person to whom an order is directed under paragraph (1) of this rule shall be treated as having failed to obey that order unless at the time at which the order was served on him there was tendered to him a sufficient sum of money to cover his costs of attending before the Appeal Tribunal.

Oaths

28.—The Appeal Tribunal may, either of its own motion or on application, require any evidence to be given on oath.

Oral hearings

29.—(1) Subject to paragraph (2) of this rule and to rule 30, an oral hearing at which any proceedings before the Appeal Tribunal are finally disposed of shall take place in public before, where applicable, such members of the Tribunal as (subject to paragraph 16 of Schedule 11) the President may nominate for the purpose.

(2) The Appeal Tribunal may sit in private for the purpose of—

a) hearing evidence which in the opinion of the Tribunal relates to matters of such a nature that it would be against the interests of national security to allow the evidence to be given in public; or

b) hearing evidence from any person which in the opinion of the Tribunal is likely to consist of—

   i) information which he could not disclose without contravening a prohibition imposed by or under any enactment; or

   ii) any information which has been communicated to him in confidence, or which he has otherwise obtained in consequence of the confidence reposed in him by another person; or;

   iii) information the disclosure of which would cause substantial injury to any undertaking of his or any undertaking in which he works for reasons other than its effect on negotiations with respect to any of the matters mentioned in section 244(1) of the 1992 Act.

Proceedings to be conducted in private on grounds of national security

30.—The Appeal Tribunal shall sit in private in circumstances in which an industrial tribunal has been required to sit in private by virtue of paragraph 1 of Schedule 9.

Drawing up, reasons for, and enforcement of orders

31.—(1) Every order of the Appeal Tribunal shall be drawn up by the Registrar and a copy, sealed with the seal of the Tribunal, shall be served by the Registrar on every party to the proceedings to which it relates and—

a) in the case of an order disposing of an appeal from an industrial tribunal or of an order under section 136A, on the Secretary of the Industrial Tribunals; or

b) in the case of an order disposing of an appeal from the Certification Officer, on that Officer.

(2) The Appeal Tribunal shall, on the application of any party made within 14 days after the making of an order finally disposing of any proceedings, give its reasons in writing for the order unless it was made after the delivery of a reasoned judgment.

(3) Subject to any order made by the Court of Appeal or Court of Session and to any directions given by the Appeal Tribunal, an appeal from the Tribunal shall not suspend the enforcement of any order made by it.

Registration and proof of awards in respect of exclusion or expulsions from, or unjustifiable discipline by, a trade union

32.—(1) This rule applies where an application has been made to the Appeal Tribunal under section 67 or 176 of the 1992 Act.

(2) Without prejudice to rule 31, where the Appeal Tribunal makes an order in respect of an application to which this rule applies, and that order—

a) makes an award of compensation, or

b) is or includes an order of the kind referred to in rule 8(b)(ii),

or both, the Registrar shall as soon as may be enter a copy of the order, sealed with the seal of the Tribunal, into a register kept by the Tribunal (in this rule referred to as "the Register").

(3) The production in any proceedings in any court of a document, purporting to be certified by the Registrar to be a true copy of an entry in the Register of an order to which this rule applies shall, unless the contrary is proved, be sufficient evidence of the document and of the facts stated therein.

Review of decisions and correction of errors

33.—(1) The Appeal Tribunal may, either of its own motion or on application, review any order made by it and may, on such review, revoke or vary that order on the grounds that—

a) the order was wrongly made as the result of an error on the part of the Tribunal or its staff;

b) a party did not receive proper notice of the proceedings leading to the order; or

c) the interests of justice require such review.

(2) An application under paragraph (1) above shall be made within 14 days of the date of the order.

(3) A clerical mistake in any order arising from an accidental slip or omission may at any time be corrected by, or on the authority of, a judge or member.

Costs or expenses

34.—(1) Where it appears to the Appeal Tribunal that any proceedings were unnecessary, improper or vexatious or that there has been unreasonable delay or other unreasonable conduct in bringing or conducting the proceedings the Tribunal may order the party at fault to pay any other party the whole or such part as it thinks fit of the costs or expenses incurred by that other party in connection with the proceedings.

(2) Where an order is made under paragraph (1) of this rule, the Appeal Tribunal may assess the sum to be paid or may direct that it be assessed by the taxing officer, from whose decision an appeal shall lie to a judge.

(3) Rules 21 and 22 shall apply to an appeal under paragraph (2) of this rule as they apply to an appeal from the Registrar.

(4) The costs of an assisted person shall be taxed or assessed in accordance with regulation 149(7) of the Civil Legal Aid (General) Regulations 1989.

Service of documents

35.—(1) Any notice or other document required or authorised by these Rules to be served on, or delivered to, any person may be sent to him by post to his address for service or, where no address for service has been given, to his registered office, principal place of business, head or main office or last known address, as the case may be, and any notice or other document required or authorised to be served on, or delivered to, the Appeal Tribunal may be sent by post or delivered to the Registrar—

a) in the case of a notice instituting proceedings, at the central office or any other office of the Tribunal; or

b) in any other case, at the office of the Tribunal in which the proceedings in question are being dealt with in accordance with rule 38(2).

(2) Any notice or other document required or authorised to be served on, or delivered to, an unincorporated body may be sent to its secretary, manager or other similar officer.

(3) Every document served by post shall be assumed, in the absence of evidence to the contrary, to have been delivered in the normal course of post.

(4) The Appeal Tribunal may inform itself in such manner as it thinks fit of the posting of any document by an officer of the Tribunal.

(5) The Appeal Tribunal may direct that service of any document be dispensed with or be effected otherwise than in the manner prescribed by these Rules.

Conciliation

36.—Where at any stage of any proceedings it appears to the Appeal Tribunal that there is a reasonable prospect of agreement being reached between the parties, the Tribunal may take such steps as it thinks fit to enable the parties to avail themselves of any opportunities for conciliation, whether by adjourning any proceedings or otherwise.

Time

37.—(1) The time prescribed by these Rules or by order of the Appeal Tribunal for doing any act may be extended (whether it has already expired or not) or abridged, and the date appointed for any purpose may be altered, by order of the Tribunal.

(2) Where the last day for the doing of any act falls on a day on which the appropriate office of the Tribunal is closed and by reason thereof the act cannot be done on that day, it may be done on the next day on which that office is open.

(3) An application for an extension of the time prescribed for the doing of an act, including the institution of an appeal under rule 3, shall be heard and determined as an interlocutory application under rule 20.

Tribunal offices and allocation of business

38.—(1) The central office and any other office of the Appeal Tribunal shall be open at such times as the President may direct.

(2) Any proceedings before the Tribunal may be dealt with at the central office or at such other office as the President may direct.

Non-compliance with, and waiver of, rules

39.—(1) Failure to comply with any requirements of these Rules shall not invalidate any proceedings unless the Appeal Tribunal otherwise directs.

(2) The Tribunal may, if it considers that to do so would lead to the more expeditious or economical disposal of any proceedings or would otherwise be desirable in the interests of justice, dispense with the taking of any step required or authorised by these Rules, or may direct that any such steps be taken in some manner other than that prescribed by these Rules.

(3) The powers of the Tribunal under paragraph (2) extend to authorising the Institution of an appeal notwithstanding that the period prescribed in rule 3(2) may not have commenced.

Transitional provisions

40.—(1) Where, prior to 16th December 1993, an industrial tribunal has given full written reasons for its decision or order, those reasons shall be treated as extended written reasons for the purposes of rule 3(1)(c) and rule 3(2) and for the purposes of Form 1 in the Schedule to these Rules.

(2) Anything validly done under or pursuant to the Employment Appeal Tribunals Rules 1980 shall be treated as having been done validly for the purposes of these Rules, whether or not what was done could have been done under or pursuant to these Rules.

SCHEDULE

Rule 3

FORM 1

Notice of Appeal from Decision of Industrial Tribunal

1. The appellant is (*name and address of appellant*).
2. Any communication relating to this appeal may be sent to the appellant at (*appellant's address for service, including telephone number if any*).
3. The appellant appeals from (*here give particulars of the decision of the industrial tribunal from which the appeal is brought including the date*).
4. The parties to the proceedings before the industrial tribunal, other than the appellant, were (*names and addresses of other parties to the proceedings in decision appealed from*).
5. A copy of the industrial tribunal's decision or order and of the extended written reasons for that decision or order are attached to this notice.

6. The grounds upon which this appeal is brought are that the industrial tribunal erred in law in that (*here set out in paragraphs the various grounds of appeal*).

Date

Signed

FORM 2   Rule 3
Notice of Appeal from Decision of Certification Officer

1. The appellant is (*name and address of appellant*).
2. Any communication relating to this appeal may be sent to the appellant at (*appellant's address for service, including telephone number if any*).
3. The appellant appeals from (*here give particulars of the order or decision of the Certification Officer from which the appeal is brought*).
4. The appellant's grounds of appeal are (*here state the grounds of appeal*).
5. A copy of the Certification Officer's decision is attached to this notice.

Date

Signed

FORM 3   Rule 6
Respondent's Answer

1. The respondent is (*name and address of respondent*).
2. Any communication relating to this appeal may be sent to the respondent at (*respondent's address for service; including telehone number if any*).
3. The respondent intends to resist the appeal of (*here give the name of appellant*). The grounds on which the respondent will rely are [the grounds relied upon by the industrial tribunal/Certification Officer for making the decision or order appealed from] [and] [the following grounds]: (*here set out any grounds which differ from those relied upon by the industrial tribunal or Certification Officer, as the case may be*).
4. The respondent cross-appeals from (*here give particulars of the decision appealed from*).
5. The respondent's grounds of appeal are: (*here state the grounds of appeal*).

Date

Signed

FORM 4   Rule 8
Application to the Employment Appeal Tribunal for Compensation for Exclusion or Expulsion from a Trade Union or for Compensation or an Order in respect of Unjustifiable Discipline

1. My name is
   My address is
2. Any communication relating to this application may be sent to me at (*state address for service, including telephone number, if any*).
3. My complaint against (*state the name and address of the trade union*) was

declared to be well-founded by (*state tribunal*) on (*give date of decision or order*).

4. (*Where the application relates to exclusion or expulsion from a trade union*) I have not been admitted/re-admitted* to membership of the above-named trade union and hereby apply for compensation on the following grounds.

(*Where the application relates to unjustifiable discipline*) The determination infringing my right not to be unjustifiably disciplined has not been revoked./The trade union has failed to take all the steps necessary for securing the reversal of things done for the purpose of giving effect to the determination.*

(*Delete as appropriate)

Date

Signed

NB.—A copy of the decision or order declaring the complaint against the trade union to be well-founded must be enclosed with this application.

FORM 5

Notice of appearance to Application to Employment Appeal Tribunal for Compensation for Exclusion or Expulsion from a Trade Union or for Compensation or an Order in respect of Unjustifiable Discipline

1. The respondent trade union is (*name and address of union*).
2. Any communication relating to this application may be sent to the respondent at (*respondent's address for service, including telephone number, if any*).
3. The respondent intends to resist the application of (*here give name of the applicant*). The grounds on which the respondent will rely are as follows:
4. (*Where the application relates to exclusion or expulsion from the trade union, state whether or not the applicant had been admitted or re-admitted to membership on or before the date of application.*)
   (*Where the application relates to unjustifiable discipline, state whether*—
   a) *the determination infringing the applicant's right not to be unjustifiably disciplined has been revoked; and*
   b) *the trade union has taken all the steps necessary for securing the reversal of anything done for the purpose of giving effect to the determination.*)

Date

Signed

Position in union

FORM 6   Rule 13

Application to the Employment Appeal Tribunal Under Section 136A of the Employment Protection (Consolidation) Act 1978 for a Restriction of Proceedings Order

1. The applicant is (*the Attorney General/Lord Advocate*).
2. Any communication relating to this application may be sent to the applicant at (*state address for service, including telephone number*).
3. The application is for a restriction of proceedings order to be made against

(*state the name and address of the person against whom the order is sought*).
4. An affidavit in support of the application is attached.

Date

Signed

FORM 7   Rule 15
*Notice of appearance to Application to the Employment Appeal Tribunal under
section 136A of the Employment Protection (Consolidation) Act 1978 for a
Restriction of Proceedings Order*

1. The respondent is (*state name and address of respondent*).
2. Any communication relating to this application may be sent to the respondent
   at (*respondent's address for service, including telephone number, if any*).
3. The respondent intends to resist the application. An affidavit in support is
   attached to this notice.

Date

Signed

3.9 Industrial Tribunals Practice Direction Number 1

Guidance on judicial procedure for the industrial tribunals in England and Wales – November 1994

1 *Chairmen sitting alone*
  i) *On cases heard under s128 of the 1978 Act and s36 of TURERA*
     — where there is discretion to decide that a full tribunal should hear a case,
       Parties' views should not be solicited.*
     — where sitting alone is normally compulsory, the normal notice of hearing
       should be used without any statement as to whether the tribunal will
       include lay members.
     — cases listed as floaters should be taken by the first available tribunal on the
       day, irrespective of whether it includes lay members or not.
     Nothing in this guidance detracts from Chairmen's obligation to consider the
     views expressed (if any) by parties as to whether a case should be heard by a
     Chairman sitting alone.
       The key point is that the system, as it appears to parties, is the same in all regions.
  ii) *On pre-hearing reviews*
     In general, these will be held by a Chairman sitting alone. However in a three
     person tribunal is available and the start of their full hearing has otherwise
     been delayed, they may take a pre-hearing review in the meantime.
  iii) *Rule 6 determinations*
     This guidance is subject to subsequent appellate clarification though, in a
     recent case, the Employment Appeal Tribunal did not question the legality of a
     Chairman sitting alone for a rule 6 determination.

*Most cases involve disputes of fact. Where there are particularly unusual features, they may
suggest that a three person tribunal should hear the case.

— All preliminary issues may be dealt with under Rule 6. A preliminary issue, for this purpose, is defined as anything that may dispose of the case other than a consideration of the merits.
— Preliminary issues should be heard as quickly as possible since this often expedites final disposal of the case.
— At the conclusion of a Rule 6 hearing, consider whether a Directions hearing is appropriate (see 3 below).

iv) *Interim relief cases*
These should be dealt with under the criteria described at 1(i) above.

2 *Notices of appearance*

The overall premise is that it is the respondent's responsibility to keep the tribunal informed of their correct address for service.

The tribunal, having served the application on the respondent's address, does not have any obligation to issue reminders. There is no obligation to make enquiry calls if the respondent or the applicant fails to appear on the day of hearing.

Normal practice therefore should be that
— no reminders are issued or phone calls made. Instead tribunals will be more generous in allowing late entries of appearance where a request to do so is made.
— 'appearance not entered' cases should be listed for hearing promptly.
— where applicants cannot be traced, the power to strike out the case should be used after the necessary warnings have been issued.

3 *Directions hearings*

Use of these may vary according to office size and caseload but in general directions hearings should
— fix the date of the full hearing so that further listing correspondence is not needed.
— NOT be held as a matter of course or for particular jurisdictions. They should only be used where necessary for the effective handling of an individual case.
— ideally be considered by the Chairman who will preside over the full hearing.
— be confined to lengthy or very complex cases.
— where there is a rule 6 determination or pre-hearing review, a directions hearing should, if required, follow on immediately. This will save listing time and expenses.

4 *Listing*

i) *Overall guideline*
Parties should not normally be consulted about dates in advance, save in specific cases where it would be appropriate for the parties to be canvassed. Examples are cases where the hearing is likely to be particularly prolonged or where the number of parties is unusually large. Such cases may have been covered in 3 above.

Regions should
— use the notice of hearing laid out in the attached example (Appendix 1) which includes guidance notes for parties and their representatives and witnesses.
— where consultation on dates is unavoidable, the letter attached to this note should be used (Appendix 2).
— where parties indicate within the fourteen days allowed that they have good

reason why the date should be changed, regions will make reasonable efforts to meet their wishes. Postponements in other circumstances should be exceptional.
— not enter into any special arrangements for frequent users (e.g. trade unions or firms of solicitors or trade associations) except on a strictly case by case basis. Current arrangements of this sort should be discontinued immediately.
— relist part heard cases as a priority with dates for reconvened hearings *agreed before parties leave* when the case is adjourned. Counsel and solicitors should not be allowed any leeway simply to allow them to accept a new brief; only if they are part heard in another court with a reconvened hearing arranged should this be taken into account.

It is accepted that prelisting is more likely to be helpful for infrequently used hearing centres.

ii) *Postponements*

The guideline is that, apart from the period of 14 days after the first notice of hearing is despatched (assuming no prior consultation), postponements will be allowed in exceptional circumstances only. In particular they will not normally be granted because a lawyer is unavailable.

5 *Section 131 [breach of contract claims]*

The aim is to handle these cases as simply as possible, consistent with legal requirements. In particular the following principles should apply
— respondents in cases coded as breach of contract jurisdiction will not be encouraged to submit counterclaims by the provision of special forms. (The code is TUR38).
— employers' claims will not be notified to ITCO [i.e. COIT] as soon as they are received in regions. [Instead extra boxes will be incorporated in the statistical form completed at the end of each case, asking whether an employers' claim had been received, what the outcome was and what amount of damages (if any) had been awarded.]
— Chairmen are advised to be alert for the possibility that a TUR38 claim may be present in documents supplied by a respondent, irrespective of the jurisdiction coding applied by ITCO.
— ITCO will code cases as Wages Act or TUR38 only if the application specified one or the other, otherwise they should apply both codes to cases concerning wage payments.

Administrative staff are being instructed accordingly.

6 *Witnesses reading prepared statements in hearings*

The guidelines to be followed on this are:
— Chairmen should be aware that they can allow the reading of written statements.
— If a Chairman does not permit reading written statements in a case, he should be prepared to give reasons if asked by a party.
— Guidance to parties should be on the following lines.
    'The length of this hearing and the consequent expense may be reduced if you are able to prepare written statements for yourself and each of your witnesses. In addition, such statements may help you and your witnesses to include all the matters that you consider important. You can then apply at the hearing for the evidence you wish your witness to give, to be read by him from the statement. It will be for the Tribunal to decide whether you

can do so, after hearing what you and the other party have to say about it. If the written statement is read, the witness may be questioned by the other party, and the Tribunal. You should bring five copies of the statement to the hearing in addition to your own copy.'
— Statements may be exchanged between parties prior to the hearing. It is one of the matters that might be canvassed under 3 above.

7 *Rules 13(6) and 14*

Where both these rules apply to a case, the notices posted in tribunal premises to alert those attending the hearing to the existence of a Restricted Reporting Order, should simply state in large bold type
'A REPORTING RESTRICTION ORDER APPLIES TO THIS CASE UNDER THE PROVISIONS OF RULE 14. FOR DETAILS OF THE RESTRICTIONS IMPOSED, PLEASE CONSULT THE REGIONAL SECRETARY OR THE TRIBUNAL CLERK.'
CASE NUMBER XXXXXXXX

Practice Direction Number 1 Appendix 1

Phoenix House, 1–3 Newhall Street, Birmingham, B3 3NH

Telephone 0121-236-6051
FAX 0121-236-6029

THE INDUSTRIAL TRIBUNALS—NOTICE OF HEARING

Case No

The application/case of
against
will be heard at the Industrial Tribunals, Birmingham on
or as soon thereafter as the Tribunal can hear it.

1 You are responsible to ensure that all the witnesses you may wish to call, can attend on the hearing date.
2 UNLESS THERE ARE WHOLLY EXCEPTIONAL CIRCUMSTANCES, NO APPLICATION FOR POSTPONEMENT DUE TO NON-AVAILABILITY OF WITNESSES OR FOR OTHER REASONS, WILL BE ENTERTAINED IF IT IS RECEIVED MORE THAN 14 DAYS AFTER THE DATE OF THIS NOTICE. ANY SUCH APPLICATION MUST BE IN WRITING AND STATE THE FULL GROUNDS AND ANY OTHER AVAILABLE DATES IN THE SIX WEEKS FOLLOWING THE ABOVE HEARING DATE.
3 If you consider that the hearing is likely to last more than one day, you must inform the tribunal office within 14 days after the date of this notice.
4 All representatives must inform those they represent of the date, time and place of the hearing.

Signed
For Regional Secretary of the Tribunals

Date

Form IT4 – 11/94

Notes to accompany notices of hearing

1 The hearing list

The hearing of this case will take place at the time stated in the Notice of Hearing or as soon thereafter as the Tribunal can hear it.

Most cases are heard on time but the daily caseload varies to such an extent that it is sometimes difficult to match it to our available resources. Exceptionally it may become necessary to withdraw your case from the list at short notice, usually on the day before the hearing. In that event your case would be given priority on re-listing.

You may find, on arrival on the day of the hearing, that you are asked to wait until the Tribunal completes other hearings. If it should become clear that there is no reasonable prospect of your case being taken on the day of the hearing, you will be offered a new hearing date before you leave which will be given priority.

We do our best to avoid these difficulties and to minimise the inconvenience to parties.

2 Attendance

A map showing where you should attend is enclosed. This may show public car parks. There is no car parking for the public at the tribunal.

In order that the case can proceed without delay, please ensure that you attend with your witnesses and arrive at least 30 minutes before the hearing is due to start to enable details to be obtained of those attending and to give you any necessary information before the start of the hearing. Parties can present their cases themselves or can be represented, if they wish, by anyone of their choice.

You may decide not to attend, but to make representations in writing instead. However, if you do that and if the facts of your case are in dispute, the Tribunal may find it difficult to decide what is the truth without hearing witnesses from both sides. If you make representations in writing, you can still attend the hearing to put your case and give evidence. If you do decide to make any written representations, you must send a copy to the Tribunal, and a copy to the other party, 7 days or more before the hearing.

A respondent who has not entered a Notice of Appearance will not be entitled to take part in the hearing.

If an applicant (or somebody else acting for the applicant) is due to attend a hearing but fails to appear, the Tribunal may dismiss or hear and dispose of the application in his or her absence; similarly the Tribunal may make an award against a respondent in his or her absence.

3 Note for representatives

It is up to you to inform the person you represent of the date, time and place of the hearing. If you are a professional adviser, would you please prepare a bundle containing all the papers you intend to rely on at the hearing, arranged in the right order and numbered consecutively. If possible, there should be an agreed bundle with the pages numbered consecutively. Six copies of any agreed bundle will be needed including your own.

4 Witnesses and written statements

If you have any witnesses you should arrange for them to attend to give evidence. It is not usually satisfactory to rely solely upon the production of signed statements from witnesses. If a witness, who can give relevant evidence, will not attend voluntarily you may apply to the Tribunal for a witness order compelling attendance.

The length of the hearing and the consequent expense may be reduced if you prepare written statements for yourself and your witnesses. Such statements may help you and your witnesses to include all the matters that you consider important. You may then apply at the hearing for the evidence you wish your witness to give to be read by him or her from the statement. It will be for the Tribunal to decide whether the witness can do so after hearing what you and the other party have to say about it. If the written statement is read, the witness may be questioned by the other party, and the Tribunal. You should bring 5 copies of any statement to the hearing in addition to your own copy.

5 Papers

If you intend to refer to any papers in support of your case at the hearing, it would help if you would send a list of those papers to the other party well in advance of the hearing. The other party may then ask to see or have a copy of any such papers. Please try to co-operate with each other on this. It can help us all by avoiding delays at the hearing.

It is very important that both parties bring to the hearing any papers that may be relevant—for example, letter of appointment, contract or written terms of employment, working rule agreement, letter of dismissal, minutes of meetings, disciplinary warnings, pay slips, income tax forms, wages book. Copies of relevant documents will be needed and it will help if you bring to the hearing:

— your own set of papers
— one copy for the use of witnesses (not a copy for each);
— a copy for the other party (unless you have already sent it);
— three copies for the members of the Tribunal.

If your claim could result in compensation being awarded for loss of wages or salary, you will need to produce all papers which show the extent of your loss, including any letters you may have about jobs you have applied for and wage slips for any new job, whether permanent or temporary.

6 Postponements

Late postponement of a hearing is rarely granted.

We will normally only postpone the hearing if something serious happens to prevent the attendance of someone whose absence would put either side at a serious or unfair disadvantage. Non-availability of a particular counsel, solicitor or paid representative is not normally a sufficient reason for postponing a hearing.

Postponement requests must be in writing and include full reasons.

7 Note to employers—Reinstatement

If the applicant succeeds in a complaint of unfair dismissal (or failing to permit a woman to return to work after pregnancy), the tribunal may consider ordering reinstatement or re-engagement. You should, therefore, be prepared to give evidence at the hearing as to:

— the availability of the job which the applicant held or of similar jobs;
— whether you would take the applicant back either in the old job, or in a similar one.

8 *Settlements*

If your case settles prior to the date of hearing, notify the tribunal at once: everyone is likely to be saved time and money.

9 *Public telephone*

Usually, the tribunal has a British Telecom Cardphone or cash call box available for public use.

10 *Expenses*

No professional representative is entitled to claim expenses for attendance at an Industrial Tribunal unless they are on the staff of Citizens' Advice Bureaux, or a Free Representation Unit.

This is because Treasury authority allows payment of travel and subsistence costs to representatives drawn from voluntary organisations such as these. However all Free Representation Unit claimants must make a declaration on the claim form that they have received no fee.

Examples of professional representatives *not entitled to claim* include

— barristers
— solicitors
— accountants
— consultants
— full time officials of workers or employers organisations

Examples of unpaid representatives who *are entitled to claim* include:

— spouse or friend
— volunteer workers from Citizens Advice Bureaux and similar agencies
— volunteer trade union officials such as a shop steward

11 *Disability*

If you, or anyone attending with you, is a person with a disability and you are concerned about the accessibility of the tribunal and necessary facilities, please contact the tribunal to discuss the matter.

12 *Smoking policy*

All parties are advised that the Industrial Tribunal has a *no smoking* policy. Smoking is therefore not permitted on the premises.

Practice Direction Number 1 Appendix 2

3rd Floor, Dukes Keep, Marsh Lane, Southampton SO14 3EX

Telephone 01703 639555
Fax 01703 635506

Case Number

THE INDUSTRIAL TRIBUNALS
Applicant   Respondent
....   *v.*   ....

This case will be listed during ....
(IF YOU HAVE A REPRESENTATIVE, PASS THIS FORM TO THEM)
If I do not hear from you by ...., a date for hearing will be fixed
and you will be informed of the time and place. Once a date has been fixed, a
postponement will be allowed *only in exceptional circumstances* and requests must
be made in writing, stating the full grounds.

....
for Regional Secretary to the Tribunals
Date ....
(PLEASE TICK RELEVANT BOX)   Applicant ☐   Respondent ☐
Delete those dates on which you CANNOT attend

1	2	3	4	5	6	7	8	9	10	11	12
13	14	15	16	17	18	19	20	21	22	23	24
25	26	27	28	29	30	31					

The case will be listed for one day unless there are circumstances which make you
think that this case will take longer. If so, please indicate your estimate of the
number of days required and give your reasons, so that appropriate arrangements
can be made.

HOW MANY WITNESSES DO YOU EXPECT TO CALL? ....
(Witnesses: see Booklet ITL1)

DATE .... NAME IN BLOCK CAPITALS ....
Form IT4D1 11/94

3.10 Employment Appeal Tribunal Practice Direction: Procedure

(April 1996)

1 INTRODUCTION

(1) This Practice Direction suspersedes the Practice Directions issued on 17
February 1981 and 15 July 1985.
(2) The Employment Appeal Tribunal Rules 1993 (SI 1993 No.2854) (the Rules)
came into operation on 16 December 1993.

(3) By virtue of paragraph 17(2) of Schedule 11 to the Employment Protection (Consolidation) Act 1978 (the 1978 Act) the Employment Appeal Tribunal (the EAT) has power, subject to the Rules, to regulate its own procedure.

(4) Where the Rules do not otherwise provide, the following procedure will apply to all appeals to the EAT.

(5) The provisions of this Practice Direction are subject to any specific directions which the EAT may make in any individual case: but, subject to that, the directions set out below must be complied with in all cases.

(6) The Practice Direction comes into force on 15 April 1996.

2 INSTITUTION OF APPEAL

(1) The Notice of Appeal must be in, or substantially in, accordance with forms 1 or 2 of the Schedule to the Rules and, in the case of an appeal from an Industrial Tribunal, a copy of the extended written reasons for the decision or order of that tribunal must also be served on the EAT.

(2) Where a request for extended written reasons has been refused by the Industrial Tribunal, an Appellant may appeal against that refusal and may also apply to the EAT to exercise its discretion to hear the appeal on summary reasons only.

(3) The Notice of Appeal must clearly identify the point of law which forms the ground of appeal from the decision of the Industrial Tribunal to the EAT. It may also state the Order which the Appellant will ask the EAT to make at the hearing.

(4) Subject to Rule 3(3) of the Rules, if it appears to the Registrar that a Notice of Appeal or an application gives insufficient particulars of, or lacks clarity in identifying, a point of law, the Registrar may postpose the decision under Rule 3(3) pending amplification or clarification of the Notice of Appeal by the intending Appellant or Applicant.

(5) It is not acceptable for an Appellant to state as a ground of appeal simply that "the decision was contrary to the evidence" or that "there was no evidence to support the decision" or that "the decision was one that no reasonable Tribunal could have reached and was perverse" or similar general grounds, unless the Notice of Appeal also sets out full and sufficient particulars of the matters relied on in support of those general grounds.

(6) It is not permissible for the parties (either the Appellant in his Notice of Appeal or the Respondent in the Respondent's Answer) to reserve a right to amend, alter or add to any pleading. No such right exists in the Rules. Amendment can only be made pursuant to an order on an interlocutory application and that should be made as soon as the need for amendment is known.

(7) The processing of the appeal will be accelerated if the Appellant also serves on the EAT, with the Notice of Appeal, a copy of the Originating Application (IT1) and of the Notice of Appearance (IT3).

(8) A Respondent who wishes to resist the appeal and/or to cross appeal, but has not delivered a Respondent's Answer as directed by the Registrar, may, unless leave is granted to serve an Answer out of time, be precluded from taking part in the Appeal.

3 APPEALS OUT OF TIME

(1) By virtue of Rule 3(2) of the Rules every appeal under Section 136 of the 1978 Act, or Section 4 of the Employment Act 1980, to the EAT shall be instituted by serving on the EAT, within 42 days from the date on which extended written reasons for the decision or order of the Industrial Tribunal were sent to the Appellant, a Notice of Appeal. Time runs even though the question of remedy and assessment of compensation by the Industrial Tribunal has been adjourned and even though an application has been made to the Industrial Tribunal for a review.

(2) Every Notice of Appeal served after the expiration of the prescribed period of 42 days must be accompanied by a written application for an extension of time, explaining clearly and concisely the reasons for delay in serving the Notice of Appeal.

(3) Applications for an extension of time for appealing cannot be considered until a Notice of Appeal in the prescribed form has been served.

(4) Unless otherwise ordered, the application for extension of time will be considered and determined as though it were an Interlocutory Application to the Registrar, who will normally determine the application in the first instance after inviting and considering written representations from each side. An Interlocutory Appeal lies from the Registrar's decision to a Judge. Such an appeal must be notified within 5 days of the decision of the Registrar.

(5) In determining whether to extend the time for appealing particular attention will be paid to whether any good excuse for the delay has been shown and to the guidance contained in the decisions of the EAT, as recently summarised in the case of *United Arab Emirates v Abdelghafar* [1995] I.C.R 65.

(6) It is not usually a good reason for late service of a Notice of Appeal that an application for legal aid has been made, but not yet determined, or that support is being sought from, but has not yet been provided by, some other body, such as a Trade Union or the Equal Opportunities Commission or the Commission for Racial Equality.

(7) In any case of doubt or difficulty, a Notice of Appeal should be served in time and an application made to the Registrar for directions.

4 INTERLOCUTORY APPLICATIONS

(1) On receipt of an Interlocutory Application the Registrar will send a copy of the application to the other side and will indicate that, if it is not intended to oppose the application, it may be unnecessary for the parties to be heard and that the appropriate order may be made without an oral hearing.

(2) Where the application is opposed the Registrar will usually determine the application on the basis of written submissions.

(3) Save where the President or a Judge otherwise directs, every Interlocutory Application to strike out an appeal or pleading or to debar a party from taking any further part in the proceedings pursuant to the Rules will be heard on the day appointed for the hearing of the appeal immediately preceding the hearing of the appeal.

5 MEETING FOR DIRECTIONS

(1) In some cases the Registrar may, where necessary, appoint a day when the parties should attend on an appointment for directions after the service of the Respondent's Answer or of a reply to a cross appeal.

(2) The Registrar will normally give written directions, including fixing a date for the hearing of the appeal.

6 EXHIBITS AND DOCUMENTS FOR USE AT THE HEARING

(1) The EAT will prepare copies of all documents for use by members of the EAT at the hearing, in addition to those which the Registrar is required to serve on the parties under the Rules.

(2) It is the responsibility of the parties to ensure that all documents submitted for consideration at the hearing are capable of being legibly photocopied.

(3) It is the duty of the parties or their advisers to ensure that only those documents are included which are (a) relevant to the point of law raised in the appeal *and* (b) likely to be referrred to at the hearing. The relevant contract of employment should usually be included.

(4) It is the responsibility of the parties or their advisers to ensure that all exhibits and documents used before the Industrial Tribunal which are considered to be necessary for use at the hearing of the appeal are sent to the EAT as soon as possible after the service of the Notice of Appeal and at least 6 weeks before the date fixed for the hearing of the appeal. This will enable the EAT staff to prepare in advance of the hearing sufficient copies, to number pages and to compile an index for the use of the members of the EAT at the hearing.

(5) At least 4 weeks before a full hearing a copy of the index will be sent by the EAT to the parties or their advisers so that they may prepare their bundles of documents in the same order.

7 CHAIRMAN'S NOTES OF EVIDENCE

(*This part of the Practice Direction does not apply to appeals heard in Scotland*)

(1) An Appellant who considers that a point of law raised in the Notice of Appeal cannot be argued without access to copies of the Chairman's notes of evidence should submit with the Notice of Appeal an application for production of the Chairman's notes or should make an application in writing as soon as possible after service of the Notice of Appeal.

(2) Any other party seeking production of Chairman's notes of evidence should make a written application for them to the EAT (*not* to the Industrial Tribunal) as soon as possible after the service of the Notice of Appeal and, in the case of a Respondent, the application should accompany the Respondent's Answer.

(3) The application must in either case explain why it is considered necessary to refer to the Chairman's notes in order to argue the point of law raised in the Notice of Appeal or Respondent's Answer. The application must identify

    a) the issues in the Notice of Appeal or Respondent's Answer to which the notes of evidence are relevant; and

    b) the names of the witnesses whose evidence is considered relevant; and

    c) the parts of their evidence alleged to be relevant.

(4) The application will be considered in the first instance by the Registrar who may determine the application on written representations.

(5) A party dissatisfied with the Registrar's decision on the application may request that the matter be referred to the President or to a Judge of the EAT who may direct an oral hearing of the application.

(6) The EAT will only order production of the Chairman's notes and the supply of copies to the parties if satisfied that all or parts of such notes are *necessary* for the purpose of arguing the point of law on the appeal.

(7) Notes of evidence are *not* ordered to be produced and supplied to the parties to enable them to check or double check the reasoning or findings in the decision against evidence given to or submissions made at the hearing or to enable the parties to embark on a "fishing expedition" to establish grounds of appeal or additional grounds of appeal.

8 SKELETON ARGUMENTS

(*This part of the Practice Direction does not apply to appeals heard in Scotland unless otherwise directed by the EAT Office in Edinburgh*)

(1) Skeleton Arguments should be provided by all parties in the case of all appeals, unless the EAT otherwise directs in individual cases. It is the practice of the EAT for all the members to read the papers in advance. A well structured Skeleton Argument helps the members and the parties to focus on the point of law raised by the appeal and thereby makes the oral hearing more effective.

(2) A Skeleton Argument should be concise and should identify and summarise the points of law, the steps or stages in the legal argument and the statutory provisions and authorities to be relied upon, identifying them by name, page and paragraph and stating the legal proposition sought to be derived from them. It is not, however, the purpose of a Skeleton Argument to argue the case on paper in detail.

(3) The Skeleton Argument should state the form of order which the party will ask the EAT to make on the appeal: for example, in the case of the Appellant, whether the EAT will be asked to remit the whole or part of the case to the same Industrial Tribunal or to a different Industrial Tribunal or whether the EAT will be asked to substitute a different decision for that of the Industrial Tribunal.

(4) The Appellant's Skeleton Argument should be accompanied by a written chronology of events relevant to the appeal which, if possible, should be agreed by the parties. That will normally be taken as an uncontroversial document, unless corrected by the Respondent or the EAT.

(5) A Skeleton Argument may be served by the Appellant with the Notice of Appeal or by the Respondent with the Respondent's Answer or Cross Appeal.

(6) Skeleton Arguments should be exchanged by the parties and copies should be served on the EAT not less than 2 weeks before the date fixed for the hearing of the full appeal. In the case of preliminary hearings, the Skeleton Argument should be served by the Appellant on the EAT at least seven days before the hearing or, if the preliminary hearing is fixed at less than seven days' notice, as soon as possible after the hearing date has been notified.

(7) In a case where the Chairman's notes of evidence have been produced the Skeleton Argument should identify the part of the notes to which that party

wishes to refer. The Skeleton Argument should cross refer to the particular passages in the notes relied on. Where practicable the Skeleton Argument should be prepared using the pagination in the index to the Appeal Bundle.

(8) The fact that settlement negotiations are in progress in relation to the appeal does not excuse delay in lodging and exchanging Skeleton Arguments.

(9) Where a party is represented it is the duty of the representative to obtain the instructions necessary to enable him or her to comply with this procedure within the time limits.

(10) Failure to follow this procedure may lead to an adjournment of an appeal or even to dismissal for non-compliance with the Practice Direction.

9   COMPLAINTS ABOUT THE CONDUCT OF THE HEARING BY THE INDUSTRIAL TRIBUNAL

(1) A party who intends to complain about the conduct of the Industrial Tribunal (for example, bias or improper conduct by the Chairman or lay members or procedural irregularities at the hearing) must include in the Notice of Appeal full and sufficient particulars of the complaint.

(2) In any such case the Registrar may inquire of the party making the complaint whether it is intended to proceed with it. If so, the Registrar will give appropriate directions for the hearing.

(3) Such directions will normally include the swearing and filing of affidavits by the complainant or his or her advisers or other witnesses or by the Respondent or his or her advisers or any others who can give relevant evidence as to the facts which form the basis of the complaint and the provision of further particulars of the matters relied on.

(4) When the direction has been complied with the Registrar will notify the Chairman of the Industrial Tribunal and provide copies of the Notice of Appeal, the affidavits and other relevant documents to the Chairman so that he has and, if appropriate, the lay members of the Industrial Tribunal have, an opportunity to comment on them. Those comments will be supplied by the EAT to the parties.

(5) A copy of any affidavit or of directions for further particulars will be supplied to the other side.

(6) The EAT will not permit complaints of the kind mentioned above to be raised or developed at the hearing of the appeal unless this procedure is developed.

10   ADMISSIBILITY OF DOCUMENTS

(1) Where an application is made by a party to an appeal to put in, at the hearing of the appeal, any agreed document which was not before the Industrial Tribunal, the application should be submitted in writing as soon as practicable after the service of the Respondent's Answer along with copies of the documents sought to be admitted at the hearing. Such documents may include a note of evidence given to the Industrial Tribunal *only* if that note is agreed by both parties.

(2) The Registrar shall forthwith communicate the nature of the application and of the documents sought to be admitted to the other party and, where appropriate, to the Chairman of the Industrial Tribunal for comments by him and, if appropriate, by the lay members.

(3) A copy of the comments will be forwarded to the party making the application by the Registrar, who will either dispose of it in accordance with the Rules or refer it for a ruling at the hearing. A copy of the comments received from the Chairman and lay members of the Tribunal will be sent to both parties.

11 THE RIGHT TO INSPECT THE REGISTER AND CERTAIN DOCUMENTS AND TO TAKE COPIES

(1) Any document lodged in the Central Office of the EAT in London or in the office of the EAT in Edinburgh in any proceedings before the EAT shall be sealed with the seal of the EAT showing the date and time on which the document was lodged.

(2) Particulars of the time of delivery at the Central Office of the EAT or in the office of the EAT in Edinburgh of any document for filing or lodgment, the date of the document and the title of the appeal of which the document forms part of the record shall be entered in the Register of Cases kept in the Central Office and in Edinburgh or in the file which forms part of the Register of Cases.

(3) Any person shall be entitled during office hours to inspect and request a copy of any of the following documents filed or lodged in the Central Office or the office in Edinburgh, namely
   a) any Notice of Appeal or any copy thereof;
   b) any judgment or order given or made in court or any copy of such judgment or order; and
   c) with the leave of the EAT, which may be granted on any application made *ex parte*, any other document.

(4) A copying charge per page will be payable for those documents mentioned in (3) above.

(5) Nothing in this provision shall be taken as preventing any party to an appeal inspecting and requesting a copy of any document filed or lodged in the Central Office or the office in Edinburgh before the commencement of the appeal, but made with a view to its commencement.

12 LISTING OF APPEALS

(1) *Fast Track Appeals*
   Full appeals are normally heard in the order in which they are received. However, there are times when it is deemed expedient to hear an appeal as soon as it can be fitted into the list. Appeals are placed in this category at the discretion of the President or the Registrar and will normally fall into the following categories:
   a) appeals involving new legislation or changes to Industrial Tribunal procedures;
   b) appeals involving reinstatement, re-engagement or interim relief;
   c) appeals on the outcome of which other applications to the Industrial Tribunal depend;
   d) appeals which are likely to go forward to the Court of Appeal or to the European Court of Justice;
   e) appeals (including appeals on time limits) against decisions of an Industrial Tribunal as to a party's entitlement to bring or contest proceedings;

f) appeals concerning Trade Union rights (*Trade Union & Labour Relations (Consolidation) Act 1992 S67(2)*);

g) appeals against interlocutory orders and directions of an Industrial Tribunal (for example, adjournments, particulars, amendments, discovery and witness orders);

h) appeals where the parties have made a reasoned case on the merits for an expedited hearing.

(2) *Estimate of Length of Hearing*
The lay members of the EAT are part-time members. They attend when available on pre-arranged dates. They do not sit for continuous periods. Consequently any appeals which run beyond their estimated length invariably have to be adjourned part-heard (often with substantial delay) until a day on which both the lay members are available so that the same Tribunal may be reconvened. To avoid inconvenience to the parties and to the EAT, and to avoid additional delay and costs suffered as a result of adjournment of part heard appeals, both parties are required to ensure that the estimates of length of hearing are accurate when first given and that any change in the estimate is notified immediately to the Listing Office, even if it is made as late as the day of the hearing. If the Tribunal concludes that the hearing is likely to exceed the estimate, it may seek to avoid such adjournment by placing each side under appropriate time limits in order to complete the presentation of the submissions within the estimated time.

(3) *Listing Practice in England and Wales*
a) When all the appeal documents have been received an an index compiled, the parties will be contacted to agree a hearing date. Once the agreed date is fixed the appeal will be set down in the list. In addition to this fixed date procedure a list (called an "undated warned list") is drawn up at the beginning of each calender month. Parties or their representatives will be notified that their case has been included in this list and preferred dates will be sought. When "fixed date" cases are settled or withdrawn, cases from the "undated warned list" will be substituted and parties notified as soon as possible of the hearing date. If a case in that list has been "warned" but not reached, the parties may apply for a fixed date for hearing.

b) A party finding that the date which has been agreed causes serious difficulties may apply to the Listing Office before the 15th of the month in which the case first appears on the list. No change will be made to the listing, unless the listing officer agrees, but reasonable efforts will be made to accommodate parties in serious difficulties. Changes after the 15th of the month in which the list appears can only be made on application to the President or Registrar of the EAT. Arrangements for the making of such an application should be through the Listing Office.

c) Other cases may be put in the list by the listing officer with the consent of the parties at shorter notice: for example, where other cases have been settled or withdrawn or where it appears that they will take less time than originally estimated. Parties who wish their cases to be taken as soon as possible and at short notice should notify the listing officer.

d) Each week an up-to-date list for the following week will be prepared, including any changes which have been made, in particular specifying cases which by then have been given fixed dates.

(4) *Scotland*

When the Respondent's Answer has been received and a copy served on the Appellant, both parties will be notified in writing that the appeal must be ready for hearing in approximately 6 weeks. The proposed date of hearing will be notified to the parties three or four weeks ahead. Any party who wishes to apply for a different date must do so within seven days of the receipt of such notification. Thereafter a formal notice of the date fixed for the hearing will be issued not less than 14 days in advance. This will be a peremptory direction. It will not be discharged, except by the Judge on cause shown.

13 DISPOSAL OF APPEALS BY CONSENT

(1) An Appellant who wishes to abandon or withdraw an appeal should notify the Respondent and the EAT immediately. If a settlement is reached the parties should inform the EAT as soon as possible.

(2) The Appellant should submit to the EAT a letter signed by the Appellant or on the Appellant's behalf and signed also by, or on behalf of, the Respondent, asking the EAT for leave to withdraw the appeal and to make a consent order in the form of an attached draft signed by both parties dismissing the appeal, together with any other agreed order.

(3) If the Respondent does not agree to the proposed order (where for example, the Respondent wishes to apply for an order for costs against the Appellant) the EAT should be informed. In such cases it will be necessary to fix an oral hearing to determine the outstanding matters in dispute between the parties.

(4) If the parties reach an agreement that the appeal should be *allowed* by consent and that an order made by the Industrial Tribunal should be reversed or varied or the matter remitted to the Industrial Tribunal on the ground that the decision contains an error of law, it is usually necessary for the matter to be heard by the EAT to determine whether there is a good reason for making the order which both parties agree should be made. In order to save costs, it may be appropriate for the Appellant or a representative only to attend to argue the case for allowing the appeal and making the order that the parties wish the EAT to make.

(5) If the application for leave to withdraw an appeal is made close to the hearing date the EAT may require the attendance of the Appellant and/or a representative to explain the reasons for delay in making a decision not to pursue the appeal.

14 PRELIMINARY HEARING

(*This part of the Practice Direction does not apply to appeals heard in Scotland*)

(1) At the discretion of the EAT appeals may be listed as ex parte preliminary hearings to determine whether the grounds in the Notice of Appeal raise a reasonably arguable point of law so as to give the EAT jurisdiction to entertain and determine it at a full hearing.

(2) Both parties will be notified of the decision to list the appeal as a preliminary hearing, but only the Appellant and/or a representative should attend to make submissions to the EAT on the issue whether the Notice of Appeal raises a reasonably arguable point of law. The Respondent is not required to attend the hearing and is not usually permitted to take part in it. If the

Appellant does not attend, the appeal may nevertheless be dealt with on written submissions and dismissed.

(3)   The hearing will normally last no more than one hour.

(4)   If satisfied that a reasonably arguable point of law is established, the EAT will give appropriate directions (for example, a time estimate, leave to amend the Notice of Appeal, or the production of Chairman's notes, the exchange and lodging of Skeleton Arguments) to enable the appeal to proceed to a full hearing without unnecessary delay, on all or only some of the grounds of appeal.

(5)   If not satisfied that a reasonably arguable point of law is raised by the appeal, the EAT will give a judgment explaining why the appeal is dismissed at that stage.

(6)   Some preliminary hearings will be listed to be heard in the list of the President of the EAT and will not be assigned for hearing by a particular Tribunal until the day of the hearing. The Appellant and/or his representative will be notified on their arrival at the EAT of the arrangements for the hearing of the appeal.

(7)   It is open to any Respondent to an appeal to make a written application to the EAT on the service of the Respondent's Answer for the appeal to be listed as a preliminary hearing to determine whether it shall proceed further.

(8)   The Preliminary Hearing Procedure may be applied to cross appeals as well as appeals.

15   CITATION OF AUTHORITIES

(1)   Lists of authorities, limited to those necessary for arguing the point of law on the appeal, should be sent to the Librarian of the EAT using the form provided or by fax not less than 24 hours before the appeal is due to be heard.

(2)   It is undesirable for parties to cite the same case from different sets of reports. The parties should, if practicable, agree upon which report will be used at the hearing.

(3)   If an unreported case is to be cited by a party, it is the responsibility of the party citing such a case to provide photocopies for the use of each member of the Tribunal and to the other party to the hearing. The same applies to cases not reported in the principal series of law reports, to foreign cases and to extracts from text books and periodicals.

(4)   Parties are advised not to cite an unnecessary number of authorities either in Skeleton Arguments or in oral argument at the hearing. It is rarely necessary to cite more than one case for a legal proposition. It is a waste of the parties' time and of the EAT's time for parties or representatives to cite cases unnecessarily. It is of assistance to the EAT if parties attach photocopies of the most important authorities to the Skeleton Arguments submitted by them and highlight the passages relied on by them.

(5)   Only in exceptional circumstances will it be necessary to cite any authority at a preliminary hearing.

(6)   In the case of reports of decisions of the European Court of Justice, the official report should be used where possible, though it is appreciated that there is a long time lag in the reporting of cases in the official series.

(7)   It is often unnecessary for a party citing a case in oral argument to read it in full to the EAT. Whenever a case is cited in a Skeleton Argument or in an

oral argument the legal proposition for which it is cited should be stated. References need only be made to the relevant passages in the report. If the formulation of the legal proposition based on the authority cited is not in dispute, further examination of the authority will often be unnecessary.

16 FAILURE TO GIVE NOTICE OF APPEARANCE

(1) If the Appellant in a case has not entered a Notice of Appearance before the Industrial Tribunal and has not applied to the Industrial Tribunal for an extension of time for doing so or has applied for such an extension and been refused it, the Notice of Appeal will be immediately set down to be heard as a preliminary hearing.

(2) The Appellant will not be permitted to pursue the appeal unless the EAT is satisfied at the preliminary hearing that:
1) there is a good excuse for failing to enter a Notice of Appearance and (if that be the case) for failing to apply for such an extension of time; and
2) there is a reasonably arguable defence to the claim in the Originating Application.

(3) In order to satisfy the EAT on these matters, the Appellant must swear and lodge with the EAT an affidavit explaining in detail the circumstances in which there has been a failure to serve a Notice of Appearance in time or apply for such an extension of time, the reason for that failure to do so and the facts and matters relied upon for contesting the claim on the merits. There should be exhibited to the affidavit all relevant documents and a completed draft Notice of Appearance (IT3).

(4) The Respondent to the appeal may swear and lodge with the EAT an affidavit in reply to the Appellant's affidavit.

17 HANDING DOWN JUDGMENTS

(1) When the Tribunal reserves judgment, the parties will be notified of the date when it is ready to be handed down.

(2) Copies of the judgment may be made available to the parties or their representatives on the morning of the day on which it is handed down or if so directed by the President or a Judge of the EAT, on the previous day on request by representatives of both parties to the Clerk to the President or a Judge of the EAT, subject to terms as to confidentiality. Copies will be made available to recognised law reporters.

(3) The judgment will be pronounced without being read aloud.

(4) Applications for leave to appeal to the Court of Appeal and other applications (for example, costs) may be made either when the judgment is handed down or by written application soon after.

Addresses

Tribunals: England and Wales

Central Office of the Industrial Tribunals, 100 Southgate Street, Bury St Edmunds, Suffolk IP33 2AQ
Tel: 01284 762 300 Fax: 01284 766 334

ROITs and OITs

London North ROIT, 19/29 Woburn Place, London WC1H 0LU
Tel: 0171 273 8602/3/4 Fax: 0171 278 5068

Stratford East OIT, 44 The Broadway, London E15 1XH
Tel: 0181 221 0914 Fax 0181 221 0398

London South ROIT, Montague Court, 101 London Road, Croydon CR0 2RF
Tel: 0181 667 9131 Fax: 0181 649 9470

Ashford OIT, Tufton House, Tufton Street, Ashford, Kent TN23 1RJ
Tel: 01233 621346 Fax: 01233 624423

Bedford ROIT, 8/10 Howard Street, Bedford MK40 3HS
Tel: 01234 351306 Fax: 01234 352315

Birmingham ROIT, Phoenix House, 1/3 Newhall Street, Birmingham B3 3NH
Tel: 0121 236 6051 Fax: 0121 236 6029

Bristol ROIT, 1st Floor, The Crescent Centre, Temple Back, Bristol BS1 6EZ
Tel: 0117 929 8261 Fax: 0117 925 3452

Exeter OIT, Renslade House, Bonhay Road, Exeter EX4 3BX
Tel: 01392 79665 Fax: 01392 430063

Cardiff ROIT, Caradog House, 1-6 Andrews Place, Cardiff CF1 3BE
Tel: 01222 372693 Fax: 01222 225906

Shrewsbury OIT, Prospect House, Belle Vue Road, Shrewsbury SY3 7NR
Tel: 01743 358341 Fax: 01743 244186

Leeds ROIT, 3rd Floor, 11 Albion Street, Leeds LS1 5ES
Tel: 0113 245 9741 Fax: 0113 242 8843

Sheffield OIT, 14 East Parade, Sheffield S1 2ET
Tel: 0114 276 0348 Fax: 0114 276 2521

Manchester ROIT, Alexandra House, 14–22 The Parsonage, Manchester M3 2JA
Tel: 0161 833 0581 Fax: 0161 832 0249

Liverpool OIT, 1 Union Court, Cook Street, Liverpool L2 4UJ
Tel: 0151 236 9397 Fax: 0151 231 1484

Newcastle ROIT, Quayside House, 110 Quayside, Newcastle-upon-Tyne NE1 3DX
Tel: 0191 232 8865 Fax: 0191 222 1680

Nottingham ROIT, 3rd Floor, Byron House, 2A Maid Marion Way, Nottingham
NG1 6HS
Tel: 0115 947 5701 Fax: 0115 950 7612

Leicester OIT, 5A New Walk, Leicester LE1 6TE
Tel: 0116 253 0119 Fax: 0116 251 7602

Southampton ROIT, 3rd Floor, Dukes Keep, Marsh Lane, Southampton SO14 3EX
Tel: 01703 639 555 Fax: 01703 635 506

Brighton OIT, St James House, 51 New England Street, Brighton BN1 4GQ
Tel: 01273 571 488 Fax: 01273 623 645

Reading OIT, 30-31 Friar Street, Reading RG1 1DY
Tel: 01734 594 917 Fax: 01734 568066

Tribunals: Scotland

Central Office of the Industrial Tribunals, Eagle Building, 215 Bothwell Street,
Glasgow G2 2TS
Tel: 0141 204 0730 Fax: 0141 204 0732

Aberdeen OIT, 2nd Floor, Inverlain House, 84 West North Street, Aberdeen AB9
1AL
Tel: 01224 643307 Fax: 01224 631551

Dundee OIT, 2nd Floor, 13 Albert Square, Dundee DD1 1DD
Tel: 01382 21578 Fax: 01382 27136

Edinburgh OIT, 124–125 Princes Street, Edinburgh EH2 4AD
Tel: 0131 226 5584 Fax: 0131 220 6847

Tribunals: Northern Ireland

Office of the Industrial Tribunals and the Fair Employment Tribunal, Long Bridge
House, 20–24 Waring Street, Belfast BT1 2EB
Tel: 01232 327666 Fax: 01232 230184

ACAS Regional Offices

Northern Region
Westgate House
Westgate Road
Newcastle-upon-Tyne NE1 1TJ
Tel: 0191 261 2191

Yorkshire and Humberside Region
Commerce House
St Alban's Place
Leeds LS2 8HH
Tel: 0113 243 1371

South East Region
Westminster House
125 Fleet Road
Fleet
Aldershot
Hants GU13 8PD
Tel: 01252 811 868

South West Region
Regent House
27A Regent Street
Clifton
Bristol BS8 4HR
Tel: 0117 974 4066

Midlands Region
Leonard House
319/323 Bradford Street
Birmingham B5 6ET
Tel: 0121 622 5050

London Region
Clifton House
83 Euston Road
London NW1 2RB
Tel: 0171 396 5100

North West Region
Boulton House
17 Chorlton Street
Manchester M1 3HY
Tel: 0161 237 1790

Scotland
Franbrough House
123 Bothwell Street
Glasgow G2 7JR
Tel: 0141 248 1400

Wales
Phase 1
Ty Glas Road
Llanishen
Cardiff CF4 5PH
Tel: 01222 762636

Other addresses

Free Representation Unit
Room 140
1st Floor
49-51 Bedford Row
London WC1R 4LR
Tel: 0171 831 0692
Fax: 0171 831 2398

Law Centres Federation
Duchess House
18-19 Warren Street
London WC1P 5DP
Tel: 0171 387 8570
Fax: 0171 387 8368

**National Association of Citizens
Advice Bureaux** (NACAB)
Myddleton House
115-123 Pentonville Road
London N1 9LZ
Tel: 0171 833 2181
Fax: 0171 833 4371

Trade Union Congress
Congress House
Great Russell Street
London WC1 3LW
Tel: 0171 636 4030
Fax: 0171 636 0632

Equal Opportunities Commission
Overseas House
Quay Street
Manchester M3 3HN
Tel: 0161 833 9244
Fax: 0161 835 1657

Commission for Racial Equality
Elliott House
10–12 Allington Street
London SW1E 5EH
Tel: 0171 828 7022
Fax: 0171 630 7605

Disability Law Service
Room 241
49–51 Bedford Row
London WC1R 4LR
Tel: 0171 831 8031
Fax: 0171 831 5582

Commissioner for the Rights of Trade Union Members/Commissioner for Protection Against Unlawful Action
First Floor
Bank Chambers
2A Rylands Street
Warrington WA1 1EN
Tel: 01925 415 771
Fax: 01925 415 772

Index

Absence of party, 204
Abusive conduct
  costs, award of, 178
Academic appeal, 222
Acknowledgment of originating
  application (IT5), 238
Address
  modes of, 1–2
Addresses
  ACAS regional offices, 382
  England and Wales, 380–381
  Northern Ireland, 381
  Scotland, 381
Adjournment and postponement
  appeal, 126
  costs, 126–127
  criminal proceedings, 125–126
  factors relevant to decision, 123–126
  foreign proceedings, 125
  general powers, 122
  High Court proceedings, 124–125
  ill-health of parties and witnesses,
    123
  internal procedures, 126
  position of party making application,
    123
  proceedings in other cases, 124
  representation at tribunal, 154
  unavailability of parties and
    witnesses, 123
Administration
  arrangements at tribunal, 147–148
  authorities to be referred to, 149
  documents, 148

Administration – cont
  generally, 3–4
  listing, 148
Administrator
  pre-action considerations, 19
Admissibility of evidence, 161–163, 167
Advisers
  wrong advice or delay, effect on time
    limits, 40
Advisory, Conciliation and Arbitration
  Service (ACAS)
  agreement through, effect of, 134–
    135
  conciliation officers, communications
    with, 90
  establishment of, 132
  primary function of, 132
  regional offices, 382
  role in tribunal claims, 132–134
Affirmation
  evidence given on, 2
Agreed facts, 144
Allegations
  new, 156
  sexual misconduct, of, 152–153
  sexual offence, of, 152–153
Allowances
  parties, to, 184
  witnesses, to, 184
Amendment
  generally, 67
  late, 156
  notice of appearance, of, 69
  originating application, of, 67–68

Appeal
  academic, 222
  adjournment pending, 126
  bias, 222
  constitution, 218–220
  costs, 228
  directions,
    chairmen's notes, 224–225
    restriction order, 225
  error of law, 220
  evidence,
    absence of, 221
    new, 227
  generally, 218
  hearing, 225–226
  interlocutory application, 223
  internal, delay caused by, 41–42
  judgment, 227–228
  jurisdiction, lack of, 224
  new evidence, 227
  no arguable point of law, 224
  no evidence, 221
  order, 228–229
  perversity, based on, 220–221
  points of law,
    new, 226–227
    no arguable, 224
  precedents, 277–280
  preliminary matters,
    directions, 224–225
    interlocutory application, 223
    lack of jurisdiction, 224
    no arguable point of law, 224
    witnesses, 225
  questions of law,
    bias, 222
    error of law, 220
    generally, 220
    no evidence, 221
    perversity, 220–221
    wrongful exercise of discretion,
      221
  review and, 211–213, 229
  settlement, 229
  time limits, 222–223
  witnesses, 225
  wrongful exercise of discretion, 221
Appearance, notice of. *See* Notice of
    appearance
Arrangements at tribunal, 147–148

Audience
  rights of, 1
Authorities to be referred to, 145, 149
Award
  enforcement of,
    death, rights after, 217
    insolvent employer, 217
    interest, 216–217
    monetary award, 215–216
    non-monetary award, 215
  monetary, 215–216
  non-monetary, 215

Bias
  appeal relating to, 222
Burden of proof
  like work claim, 187–188

Central Office of Industrial Tribunals
    (COIT)
  addresses, 380, 381
  Form IT1, 45–46
  location, 3, 4
Chairman
  full tribunal or chairman alone,
      preference for,
    notice of appearance, 63
    originating application, 53
  notes of, 224–225
  role of, 4–5
  sitting alone, 5–7, 143, 149
Checklist
  discovery, 97–98
  interlocutory stages, 114
  pre-action considerations, 23
  review of decisions, 213–214
  settlement and conciliation, 140–
    141
Clerical mistakes
  review, power of, 202
Clerk
  appointment of, 8
Closing speeches, 170–171
Combined proceedings
  interlocutory stages, 105–107
Commencement of proceedings
  time limits, effect on, 34–35
Complaint
  originating application, contents of,
    50, 53–54

Composition of tribunal
  chairman, 4–7
  challenge to, 149–151
  equal pay claim, 8
  lay members, 7
  race discrimination claim, 8
  sex discrimination claim, 8
  tribunal clerks, 8
Compromise agreements and contracts
  effective, requirements of, 136–137
  generally, 135–136
  meaning, 135–136
Compromising statutory rights, 130–
    131
Computer disks
  discovery and inspection, 84
Conciliation. *See* Settlement and
    conciliation
Conduct of hearing
  admissibility of evidence,
    estoppel, 161
    hearsay, 161–162
    material before and after relevant
      event, 162
  closing speeches, 170–171
  credibility and collateral matters,
    162–163
  formality, 160–161
  generally, 159
  natural justice, 159–160
  notes of evidence, 164
  recall of witnesses, 169–170
  sequence of evidence,
    admissibility of evidence, 167
    cross-examination, 165–166
    evidence-in-chief, 165
    half-time submission of no case to
      answer, 167–168
    questions by tribunal, 166
    re-examination, 166
    rulings during course of hearing,
      166–169
    unfairness during hearing, 168–
      169
  sworn evidence, 163–164
  without prejudice communications,
    162
  witness,
    recall of, 169–170
    statements, 164–165

Confidentiality
  general guidelines as to, 85–87
Consent
  decisions by, 137–139
Constitution
  administration of tribunal, 3–4
  appeal, 218–220
  composition of tribunals,
    chairman, 4–7
    equal pay claim, 8
    lay members, 7
    race discrimination claim, 8
    sex discrimination claim, 8
    tribunal clerks, 8
  contempt, 3
  generally, 1–2
  legal system, position of industrial
    tribunals in, 2–3
  location of tribunal, 3–4
  tribunal consultative groups, 8–9
Consultative groups
  role of, 8–9
Contempt
  punishment of, 3
Contents of originating application,
    50–54
Contingency fees, 181
Correct respondent, 17–19
Costs
  adjournment, on, 126–127
  allowances, 184
  amounts to be awarded, 183–184
  appeal, 228
  application for, 176, 182–183
  contingency fees, 181
  deposit order, at main hearing after,
    117
  equal value claims, 181
  generally, 176
  in-house lawyers, 180
  other representatives, 180
  pre-action considerations, 21–22
  relevant considerations for order,
    contingency fees, 181
    equal value claims, 181
    generally, 180
    in-house lawyers, 180
    other representatives, 180
    volunteer representatives, 181
    wasted costs, 181

Costs – *cont*
  respondents, against, 178–179
  taxation, 184
  volunteer representatives, 181
  wasted, 181
  when awarded,
    generally, 177
    pregnancy, 179
    re-engagement, 179
    reinstatement, 179
    right to return to work, 179
    unreasonable conduct, 177–179
Credibility and collateral matters, 162–163
Criminal proceedings
  adjournment, 125–126
  postponement, 125–126
  time limits, extension of, 42
Cross-examination
  sequence of evidence, 165–166

Dates
  action complained of (other than
    dismissal), of, 52–53
  employment, of,
    notice of appearance, 61–62
    originating application, 52
  hearing, suggested dates for (IT4D2)
    242
Deadline. *See* Time limits
Death
  rights after, enforcement and, 217
Decision
  appeal against. *See* Appeal
  clerical mistakes, correction of,
    174
  consent, by, 137–139
  formal characteristics, 172
  meaning, 208
  notes on (IT9), 253–256
  post-decision,
    appeal. *See* Appeal
    review. *See* Review
  reasons for, 172–175
  registration of, 172, 174
  review of. *See* Review
  signature of chairman, 172, 175
Defence
  job evaluation study, based on, 189–190

Defining issues
  further particulars,
    equal pay case, 77
    failure to comply with order, 76–77
    power to order, 76–77
    questionnaire, of, 77
    request for, 74–75
    setting aside order, 76
    varying order, 76
  generally, 70
  questionnaire,
    responding to, 72
    scope, 70–71
    time limits on, 72–73
    use of procedure, 71–72
  written answers,
    failure to comply with order, 78–79
    generally, 77–78
    power to order, 78–79
    setting aside order to provide, 78
    varying order to provide, 78
Delay
  adviser, position of, 40
  internal appeal, caused by, 41–42
Deposit
  order to pay, 116–117
Diplomatic privilege, 88
Directions
  chairmen's notes, 224–225
  hearings, 113–114
  restriction orders, 225
Disclosure
  discovery. *See* Discovery
  late, 156
Discovery
  checklist, 97–98
  confidentiality, 85–87
  diplomatic privilege, 88
  discrimination cases, 95–96
  documents,
    meaning, 84
    no duty to create, 83–84
    relevance, 84–85
    voluntary disclosure, 81
  equal pay cases, 95–96
  failure to comply with order, 83–84
  general principles, 80–82
  generally, 80
  inspection, and,

Discovery – *cont*
  documents, 84
  relevance, 84–85
  legal privilege,
    ACAS conciliation officers,
      communications with, 90
    legal advice privilege, 89
    legal adviser, meaning, 89
    legal proceedings privilege, 89
    without prejudice communications,
      89–90
  medical reports, 90–91
  mistaken disclosure, 92
  national security, 88
  oppressive requests, 94–95
  partly privileged documents, 92–93
  power to order, 82–84
  privilege,
    confidentiality, 85–87
    diplomatic, 88
    legal, 89–90
    meaning, 85
    medical reports, 90–91
    mistaken disclosure, 92
    national security, 88
    partly privileged documents, 92–
      93
    public interest immunity, 87–88
    third parties, documents from, 93–
      94
    waiver of, 91–92
  public interest immunity, 87–88
  relevance of documents, 84–85
  third parties, documents from, 93–94
  waiver of privilege, 91–92
Discrimination
  contractual term unlawful by way of,
    32
  discovery, 95–96
  race. *See* Race discrimination case
  sex. *See* Sex discrimination case
  time limits, 31–33
Dismissal
  health and safety reasons, for, 99–
    100
  trade union reasons, for, 99–100
  unfair. *See* Unfair dismissal claim
Disruptive conduct
  costs, award of, 178
  disclosure of. *See* Discovery

Documents – *cont*
  meaning, 84
  partly privileged, 92–93
  preparing for hearing, 145
  relevance, 84–85

Earnings
  average take home, meaning, 62
  basic wage/salary, meaning, 62
  notice of appearance, contents of,
    62–63
  originating application, contents of,
    52
Effective date of termination (EDT)
  meaning, 29
Employment
  dates of,
    notice of appearance, 61–62
    originating application, 52
  death, rights after, 217
  employer's claim in contract,
    acknowledgment of, 250
    notice of, 251
    notice of appearance by applicant
      to, 252
    respondent employer, 249
  insolvent employer,
    enforcement, 217
    pre-action considerations, 19
  protection of, time limits for claim,
    34
Employment appeal tribunal (EAT)
  appeal from, 2–3
  appeal to, 2
  divisions of, 2
Enforcement of award
  death, rights after, 217
  insolvent employer, 217
  interest, 216–217
  monetary award, 215–216
  non-monetary award, 215
Equal pay claim
  composition of tribunal, 8
  costs, 181
  discovery, 95–96
  Equal Pay Act, procedures under,
    burden of proof, 187–188
    comparable male worker, 186–187
    like work claim, 186
    procedure, 188

Equal pay claim – *cont*
  equal value claim,
    completion of IT1/IT3, 191
    costs, 181
    generally, 190–191
    independent expert, commissioning
      report from, 194–197
    initial hearing, 193–194
    interlocutory stages, 192–193
    invitation to adjourn, 193
    procedural steps, 191–199
    receipt of report, 197
    resumed hearing, 197–199
  European law, 185–186
  further particulars, 77
  grounds for, 185
  job evaluation study, claim based on,
    applicant's claim for equal pay,
      188–189
    generally, 188
    respondent's defence, 189–190
  like work claim,
    burden of proof, 187–188
    comparable male worker, 186–187
    generally, 186
    procedure, 188
  pre-action questionnaire, 21
  tactical advice for applicants, 199–
    200
  time limits, 30–31
Equal value claim. *See* Equal pay claim
Errors and mistakes
  clerical, 202
  error of law, appeal relating to, 220
  respondent, incorrect identification
    of, 64–65
  staff, by, 202–203
Escape clauses
  time limits on, 27–28, 42–43
Estoppel
  admissibility of evidence, 161
European Court of Justice
  reference of preliminary point to,
    120–121
European Union
  equal pay claims, 185–186
  tribunal required to give effect to law
    of, 1
Evidence
  absence of, appeal relating to, 221

Evidence – *cont*
  admissibility of,
    estoppel, 161
    hearsay, 161–162
    material before and after relevant
      event, 162
    sequence of evidence, 167
  affirmation, on, 2
  cross-examination, 165–166
  estoppel, 161
  evidence-in-chief, 165
  half-time submission of no case to
    answer, 167–168
  hearsay, 161–162
  material before and after relevant
    event, 162
  new,
    appeal on ground of, 227
    review, application for, 204–206
  no case to answer, half-time
    submission of, 167–168
  notes of, 164
  oath, on, 2
  questions by tribunal, 166
  re-examination, 166
  rulings during course of hearing,
    166–169
  sequence of,
    admissibility of evidence, 167
    cross-examination, 165–166
    evidence-in-chief, 165
    half-time submission of no case to
      answer, 167–168
    questions by tribunal, 166
    re-examination, 166
    rulings during course of hearing,
      166–169
    unfairness during hearing, 168–169
  sworn, 163–164
  unfairness during hearing, 168–169
Expert evidence
  equal value claim, 194–197, 198–199
Extending deadline. *See* Time limits

Failure to meet deadline. *See* Time
    limits
Fees
  contingency, 181
Finance
  pre-action considerations, 21–22

Foreign proceedings
postponement, 125
Formality
conduct of hearing, 160–161
Forms
acknowledgment of originating
application (IT5), 238
employer's claim in contract,
acknowledgment of, 250
notice of, 251
notice of appearance by applicant
to, 252
respondent employer, 249
notes of tribunal decisions (IT9),
253–256
notice of appearance (IT3), 55–57,
240–241
notice of hearing,
entitlement to bring or contest
proceedings, 245
form IT4, 243–244
preliminary hearing, 246
notice of originating application
(IT2), 239
originating application (IT1), 45–46,
234–237
pre-hearing review, notice of, 247,
248
suggested dates for hearing (IT4D2),
242
Free Representation Unit (FRU)
referral agency to, 22
Frivolous application
costs, award of, 177–178
striking out, 69, 110–112
Further particulars
equal pay case, 77
failure to comply with order, 76–
77
power to order, 76–77
questionnaire, of, 77
request for, 74–75
setting aside order, 76
varying order, 76

Half-time submission of no case to
answer, 167–168
Health and safety
dismissal relating to, 99–100
interim relief, claim for, 31

Hearing
adjournment. *See* Adjournment and
postponement
administration,
arrangements at tribunal, 147–148
authorities to be referred to, 149
documents, 148
listing, 148
admissibility of evidence,
estoppel, 161
hearsay, 161–162
material before and after relevant
event, 162
sequence of evidence, 167
allegations,
new, 156
sexual offences and sexual
misconduct, of, 152–153
appeal, 225–226
authorities to be referred to, 145, 149
chairman, 149
closing speeches, 170–171
conduct of,
admissibility of evidence, 161–163
closing speeches, 170–171
credibility and collateral matters,
162–163
formality, 160–161
generally, 159
natural justice, 159–160
recall of witnesses, 169–170
sequence of evidence, 165–166
sworn evidence, 163–164
without prejudice communications,
162
witness statements, 164–165
credibility and collateral matters,
162–163
cross-examination, 165–166
directions, 113–114
equal value claim, 193–194, 197–
199
evidence,
admissibility of, 161–163, 167
cross-examination, 165–166
evidence-in-chief, 165
half-time submission of no case to
answer, 167–168
questions by tribunal, 166
re-examination, 166

Hearing – *cont*
  rulings during course of hearing,
    166–169
  sequence of, 165–166
  sworn, 163–164
  unfairness during hearing, 168–169
  formality, 160–161
  half-time submission of no case to
    answer, 167–168
  interim relief, 101
  issues to be determined, 154–156
  late amendment, 156
  late disclosure, 156
  members,
    absence of, 151
    challenge to composition of
      tribunal, 149–151
  natural justice, 159–160
  new allegations, 156
  notice of, 142
  opening speech, 158–159
  postponement. *See* Adjournment and
    postponement
  pre-hearing review,
    deposit, order to pay, 116–117
    procedure, 115–116
    purpose, 115
  preparing for,
    agreed facts, 144
    authorities to be referred to, 145,
      149
    chairman alone, 143
    documents, 145
    listing, 142, 148
    notice of hearing, 142
    preliminary points of law, 143
    public, hearing in, 143
    skeleton arguments, 143
    warning witnesses to attend, 145–
      146
    witness statements, 144
    written representations, 143
  principal features, 147–171
  procedure, 149
  public, in, 143, 151–153
  questions by tribunal, 166
  re-examination, 166
  recall of witnesses, 169–170
  representation at tribunal, 153–154
  review, application for, 210–211

Hearing – *cont*
  rulings during course of, 166–169
  sequence of evidence,
    admissibility of evidence, 167
    cross-examination, 165–166
    evidence-in-chief, 165
    half-time submission of no case to
      answer, 167–168
    questions by tribunal, 166
    re-examination, 166
    rulings during course of hearing,
      166–169
    unfairness during hearing, 168–169
  sexual offences and sexual
    misconduct, allegations of, 152–
    153
  speeches,
    closing, 170–171
    opening, 158–159
  suggested dates for (IT4D2), 242
  sworn evidence, 163–164
  unfairness during, 168–169
  who goes first, 156–159
  without prejudice communications,
    162
  witnesses,
    recall of, 169–170
    statements, 164–165
    written representations, 154
Hearsay evidence, 161–162
High Court proceedings
  adjournment, 124–125
  postponement, 124–125

Ignorance of rights
  time limits, extension of, 38–40
Ill-health
  parties, of, 123
  witnesses, of, 123
In-house lawyers
  costs, 180
Independent expert
  commissioning report from, 194–197
Industrial pressure from third parties,
  104
Industrial tribunals
  aim, 1
  audience, rights of, 1
  constitution. *See* Constitution
  establishment of, 1

Industrial tribunals – *cont*
  litigants in person, 2
  modes of address, 1–2
  role of, 1
Insolvent employer
  enforcement, 217
  pre-action considerations, 19
Inspection
  discovery and. *See* Discovery
Interest
  enforcement of award, 216–217
Interests of justice
  procedural mishaps, 207
  review, application for, 206–208
  subsequent events, 207–208
Interim relief
  generally, 99
  health and safety reasons, dismissal
    for, 99–100
  hearing, 101
  procedural steps, 100
  remedies, 101–102
  time limits, 31
  trade union reasons, dismissal for,
    99–100
Interlocutory application, 223
Interlocutory stages
  checklist, 114
  combined proceedings, 105–107
  directions hearings, 113–114
  equal value claim, 192–193
  joinder,
    generally, 103–104
    National Insurance Fund, 105
    race discrimination case, 105
    sex discrimination case, 105
    third parties, industrial pressure
      from, 104
  precedents, 270–273
  striking out,
    frivolous application, 110–112
    scandalous application, 110–
      112
    vexatious application, 110–112
    want of prosecution, 112–113
  test cases, 107–108
  witness orders, 108–110
Internal appeal
  delay caused by, effect on time limits,
    41–42

Internal procedures
  adjournment, 126
  postponement, 126
Interrogatories
  written answers compared with, 77–
    78
Invitation to adjourn
  equal value claim, 193
Issue to be determined, 154–156

Job evaluation study
  claim based on, 188–190
  equal pay, applicant's claim for, 188–
    189
  respondent's defence based on, 189–
    190
Joinder of parties
  correct respondent, 17–18
  generally, 103–104
  National Insurance Fund, 105
  race discrimination case, 105
  sex discrimination case, 105
  third parties, industrial pressure
    from, 104
Judgment
  appeal, 227–228
Jurisdiction
  general, 10
  lack of, appeal relating to, 224
  Northern Ireland, 10, 11
  notice of appearance, 65–66
  preliminary hearing on, 118–120
  Scotland, 10, 11
  territorial, 11
  time limits, 12–16, 28–29

Late amendment, 156
Late disclosure, 156
Lay members
  appointment of, 7
Legal adviser
  meaning, 89
Legal aid
  availability of, 21
Legal privilege
  ACAS conciliation officers,
    communications with, 90
  legal advice privilege, 89
  legal adviser, meaning, 89
  legal proceedings privilege, 89

Legal privilege – *cont*
  without prejudice communications,
    89–90, 162
Legal system
  position of industrial tribunals in, 2–
    3
Letter before action, 20–21
Like work claim
  basis of, 186
  burden of proof, 187–188
  comparable male worker, 186–187
  procedure, 188
Listing, 142, 148
Litigants in person
  generally, 2
Location of tribunals, 3–4, 393–394

Material before and after relevant
    event, 162
Maternity rights case
  costs, award of, 179
  notice of appearance, contents of,
    63
Medical reports
  disclosure of, 90–91
Members of tribunal
  absence of member, 151
  composition of tribunal. *See*
    Composition of tribunal
Mental impediment
  time limits, extension of, 38–40
Microfilms
  discovery and inspection, 84
Mistaken disclosure, 92
Mistakes. *See* Errors and mistakes
Modes of address, 1
Monetary award
  enforcement of, 215–216

National Insurance Fund
  joinder of parties, 105
National security, 88
Natural justice
  conduct of hearing, 159–160
New allegations, 156
New evidence
  review, application for, 204–206
No case to answer
  half-time submission of, 167–168
No notice of proceedings, 203

Non-monetary award
  enforcement of, 215
Normal working hours
  originating application, contents of,
    51–52
Northern Ireland
  administration of tribunals, 4
  appeal from tribunal sitting in, 3
  Form IT1, 45
  jurisdiction, 10, 11
  public, hearing in, 152
Notes
  chairman, of, 224–225
  evidence, of, 164
Notice of appearance
  action on receipt of, 58–59
  amendment of, 69
  applicant, of, 66
  consequences of not entering, 58–59
  contents of,
    dates of applicant's employment,
      61–62
    details of respondent's
      representative, 62
    earnings of applicant, details of,
      62–63
    generally, 59
    grounds of resistance, details of,
      63–64
    maternity rights cases, details
      relating to, 63
    preference for chairman alone or
      full tribunal, 63
    reason for dismissal, 60–61
    respondent's details, 59
    whether application is resisted, 59
    whether dismissal is admitted, 60–
      61
  Form IT3, 55–57, 240–241
  generally, 55
  incorrect identification of respondent,
    64–65
  jurisdictional points, 65–66
  lack of, application for review, 203
  minimum requirements, 55–57
  nature of, 55
  respondent,
    details of, 59
    incorrect identification of, 64–65
    representative of, details of, 62

Notice of appearance – *cont*
  striking out, 69
  time limits, 57–58
Notice of hearing
  entitlement to bring or contest
    proceedings (IT4), 245
  Form IT4, 243–244
  generally, 142
  lack of, application for review, 203
  preliminary hearing (IT4), 246
Number of applications, 209

Oath
  evidence given on, 2
Offices of Industrial Tribunals (OIT)
  addresses, 393–394
  administration, 3, 4
  originating application, presentation
    of, 48
Onus of proof
  time limits, extension of, 36
Opening speech, 158–159
Oppressive requests for discovery, 94–
  95
Orders
  appeal, relating to, 228–229
  costs order, relevant considerations
    for, 180
  restriction, 225
  witness, 108–110
Originating application
  acknowledgment of (IT5), 238
  action on receipt of,
    generally, 48
    informing others, 49
    initial vetting procedure, 48–49
    register, 49
  amendment of, 67–68
  contents of,
    applicant's details, 50
    connection with respondent, 51
    date of action complained of other
      than dismissal, 52–53
    dates of employment, 52
    details of applicant's
      representative, 51
    details of complaint, 53–54
    earnings, details of, 52
    generally, 50
    normal working hours, 51–52

Originating application – *cont*
    preference for chairman alone or
      full tribunal, 53
    respondent's details, 51
    type of complaint, 50
    unfair dismissal case, remedy
      sought in, 53
  Form IT1, 45–46, 234–239
  generally, 45
  informing others of, 49
  initial vetting procedure, 48–49
  minimum requirements, 45–46
  notice of (IT2), 241
  pleadings distinguished from, 47
  precedents, 265–277
  presentation of, 48
  register, 49
  stages before,
    checklist, 23
    correct respondent, 17–19
    costs implications, 21–22
    financing case, 21–22
    insolvent employer, 19
    letter before action, 20–21
    questionnaires, 21
Own motion of tribunal, 209

Parties
  absence of, 204
  allowances, 184
  ill-health of, 123
  joinder. *See* Joinder of parties
  review, application for, 210
  third. *See* Third parties
  unavailability of, 123
Partly privileged documents, 92–93
Perversity
  appeal relating to, 220–221
Photographs
  discovery and inspection, 84
Physical inability
  time limits, extension of, 36–37
Pleadings
  originating application distinguished
    from, 47
Points of law
  new, 226–227
  no arguable, 224
Post-decision
  appeal. *See* Appeal

Post-decision – *cont*
  review. *See* Review
Postal delays
  time limits, extension of, 37–38
Postponement. *See* Adjournment and
    postponement
Pre-action
  checklist, 23
  correct respondent, 17–19
  costs implications, 21–22
  financing case, 21–22
  insolvent employer, 19
  letter before action, 20–21
  questionnaires, 21, 70–73
Pre-hearing review
  deposit, order to pay, 116–117
  notice of, 247, 248
  procedure, 115–116
  purpose, 115
Precedents
  interlocutory requests and responses,
    278–281
  originating application, 265–277
  post-decision: reviews and appeals,
    285–288
  settlement and conciliation, 282–284
Pregnancy
  costs, award of, 179
Preliminary hearing
  European Court, reference to, 120–
    121
  generally, 118
  jurisdiction, on, 118–120
  preliminary point of law, 120
Preliminary points of law, 120, 143
Preparing for hearing, 142–146
President of Industrial Tribunals
  general qualification, 3–4
Privilege
  confidentiality, 85–87
  diplomatic, 88
  legal,
    ACAS conciliation officers,
      communications with, 90
    legal advice privilege, 89
    legal adviser, meaning, 89
    legal proceedings privilege, 89
    without prejudice communications,
      89–90, 162
  medical reports, 90–91

Privilege – *cont*
  mistaken disclosure, 92
  national security, 88
  nature of, 85
  partly privileged documents, 92–93
  public interest immunity, 87–88
  third parties, documents from, 93–94
  waiver of, 91–92
Procedural mishaps, 207
Proof. *See* Burden of proof
Prosecution
  striking out for want of, 112–113
Public
  hearing in, 143, 151–153
Public interest immunity
  class immunity, 87–88
  when arising, 87

Questionnaire
  pre-action, 21, 70–73
  procedure, use of, 71–72
  responding to, 72
  scope, 70–71
Questions by tribunal, 166
Questions of law
  appeal relating to, 220–222

Race discrimination case
  composition of tribunal, 8
  discovery, 95–96
  joinder of parties, 105
  pre-action questionnaire, 21
  time limits, 31–33, 43
Re-engagement
  costs, award of, 179
Re-examination
  sequence of evidence, 166
Recall of witnesses, 169–170
Redundancy pay claim
  relevant date, meaning, 30
  time limits, 30, 44
Regional Offices of Industrial Tribunals
    (ROITs)
  addresses, 380–381
  administration, 3, 4
  consultative groups, 8–9
  originating application, presentation
    of, 48
Reinstatement
  costs, award of, 179

Remedies
  interim relief, 101–102
  unfair dismissal case, 53
Representation at tribunal
  adjournment, 154
  generally, 153–154
  postponement, 154
  written representations, 154
Representatives
  costs, 180, 181
  volunteer, 181
Respondent
  correct, 17–19
  costs against, 178–179
  incorrect identification of, 64–65
  job evaluation study, defence based
    on, 189–190
  joining party to proceedings as, 17–
    18
  notice of appearance, 59, 64–65
  notice of originating application sent
    to (IT2), 239
  originating application, contents of, 51
  unincorporated association, position
    of, 18–19
Responding to questionnaire, 72
Restriction order, 225
Return to work
  costs, award of, 179
Review
  absence of party, 204
  appeal and, 211–213, 229
  checklist, 213–214
  clerical mistakes, 202
  decision,
    generally, 208–209
    meaning, 208
    revocation of, 213
    variation of, 213
  error by staff, 202–203
  hearing application, 210–211
  interests of justice,
    generally, 206–207
    procedural mishaps, 207
    subsequent events, 207–208
  new evidence, 204–206
  no notice of proceedings, 203
  number of applications, 209
  original decision, revocation or
    variation of, 213

Review – *cont*
  party,
    absence of, 204
    application of, 210
  power to review,
    absence of party, 204
    decision, 208–209
    error by staff, 202–203
    generally, 202
    hearing application, 210–211
    interests of justice, 206–208
    new evidence, 204–206
    no notice of proceedings, 203
    number of applications, 209
    party, application of, 209, 210
    tribunal's own motion, on, 209
  precedents, 277–280
  revocation of original decision, 213
  scope, 201
  staff, error by, 202–203
  tribunal's own motion, application
    of, 209
  variation of original decision, 213
Revocation of original decision, 213
Rulings during course of hearing, 166–
  169

Scandalous application
  striking out, 69, 110–112
Scope of questionnaire, 70–71
Scotland
  administration of tribunals, 4
  criminal proceedings, 126
  employment appeal tribunal cases, 2
  Form IT1, 45
  hearing in public, 152
  insolvent employer, position of, 19
  jurisdiction, 10, 11
  recovery in, 80
Secretary of Tribunals
  originating application, presentation
    of, 48
Sequence of evidence, 165–169
Settlement and conciliation
  ACAS,
    agreement through, effect of, 134–
      135
    establishment of, 132
    primary function, 132
    role in tribunal claim, 132–134

Settlement and conciliation – *cont*
  appeal, 229
  checklist, 140–141
  compromise agreements and
      contracts,
    effective, requirements of, 136–137
    generally, 135–136
  compromising statutory rights, 130–
      131
  decisions by consent, 137–139
  general considerations, 128–129
  precedents, 273–277
Sex discrimination case
  composition of tribunal, 8
  discovery, 95–96
  joinder of parties, 105
  pre-action questionnaire, 21
  time limits, 31–33, 43
Sexual misconduct
  allegations of, 152–153
Sexual offence
  allegation of, 152–153
Skeleton arguments, 143
Speech
  closing, 170–171
  opening, 158–159
Staff
  error by, review of, 202–203
Statements
  witness, 144, 164–165
Statutes, regulations and directions,
      281–379
Striking out
  frivolous application, 69, 110–112
  notice of appearance, 69
  scandalous application, 69, 110–
      112
  vexatious application, 69, 110–112
Suggested dates for hearing (IT4D2),
      242
Sunday trading
  time limits for claim, 33
Sworn evidence, 163–164

Tape recordings
  discovery and inspection, 84
Taxation of costs, 184
Territorial jurisdiction, 11
Test cases
  interlocutory stages, 107–108

Third parties
  documents from, 93–94
  industrial pressure from, 104
Time limits
  appeal, 222–223
  commencement of proceedings, 34–35
  counting of time,
    discrimination, 31–33
    equal pay, 30–31
    interim relief, 31
    redundancy pay, 30
    rules on, 33–34
    Sunday trading case, 33
    unfair dismissal, 29–30
    wages protection, 33
    when starting to run, 29–33
    written particulars, 31
  escape clause, on, 27–28, 42–43
  extending deadline,
    advisers, 40
    criminal proceedings, 42
    failure to meet, 36–44
    generally, 35–36
    ignorance of rights, 38–40
    internal appeal, delay caused by,
        41–42
    onus of proof, 36
    other proceedings, 42
    physical inability, 36–37
    postal delays, 37–38
    race discrimination case, 43
    redundancy pay, 44
    sex discrimination case, 43
  failure to meet deadline,
    escape clause, 42–43
    just and equitable, 43
    not reasonably practicable, 36–42
  general principles, 24–29
  in general, 24–27
  jurisdiction and, 12–16, 28–29
  notice of appearance, 57–58
  race discrimination claim, 31–33, 43
  redundancy pay claim, 30, 44
  sex discrimination claim, 31–33, 43
  statutory rights subject to, 24–27
  unfair dismissal claim, 29–30
Trade union activity
  dismissal relating to, 99–100
  industrial pressure from third parties,
      104

Trade union activity – *cont*
  interim relief, claim for, 31
Trustee in bankruptcy
  pre-action considerations, 19

Unavailability of parties and witnesses,
  123
Unfair dismissal claim
  costs, award of, 179
  effective date of termination,
    meaning, 29
  remedy sought in, 53
  time limits, 29–30
Unfairness during hearing, 168–169
Unincorporated association
  respondent, as, 18–19
Unreasonable conduct
  abusively, disruptively, meaning, 178
  costs, award of, 177–179
  frivolously, meaning, 177–178
  vexatiously, meaning, 178

Variation of original decision, 213
Vexatious application
  costs, award of, 178
  striking out, 69, 110–112
  vexatious litigant, 112
Videotapes
  discovery and inspection, 84
Volunteer representative
  costs, 181

Wages protection
  time limits for claim, 33
Waiver of privilege, 91–92
Want of prosecution
  striking out, 112–113
Wasted costs, 181
Without prejudice communications,
  89–90, 162
Witness
  allowances, 184
  appeal, 225
  ill-health of, 123
  orders, 108–110
  recall of, 169–170
  statements, 144, 164–165
  unavailability of, 123
  warning to attend, 145–146
Written answers
  failure to comply with order, 78–
    79
  generally, 77–78
  interrogatories compared with, 77–
    78
  power to order, 78–79
  setting aside order to provide, 78
  varying order to provide, 78
Written particulars
  time limits for claim, 31
Written representations, 143
Wrongful exercise of discretion,
  221